1999

THE ZONDERVAN

PASTOR'S
ANNUAL

An Idea and Resource Book

T. T. Crabtree

ZondervanPublishingHouse
Grand Rapids, Michigan

A Division of HarperCollinsPublishers

THE ZONDERVAN 1999 PASTOR'S ANNUAL
Copyright © 1978, 1998 by The Zondervan Corporation
Grand Rapids, Michigan 49530

Requests for information should be addressed to:

ZondervanPublishingHouse
Grand Rapids, Michigan 49530

Much of the contents of this book was previously published in *Pastor's Annual 1979*.

ISBN 0–310–22215–X

Interior design by Sue Vandenberg Koppenol

Printed in the United States of America

99 00 01 02 03 04 /❖ DC/ 10 9 8 7 6 5 4 3

CONTENTS

MISCELLANEOUS HELPS

Messages on the Lord's Supper

Messages for Children and Young People

Funeral Meditations

Weddings

Sentence Sermonettes

Indexes

ACKNOWLEDGMENTS

All Scripture quotations, unless otherwise noted, are taken from the *King James Version*. Additional translations used are the following:

The Amplified Bible, copyright © 1965 by Zondervan Publishing House.

The Bible: An American Translation by Smith and Goodspeed. Copyright © 1931 by the University of Chicago Press.

The HOLY BIBLE, NEW INTERNATIONAL VERSION®. NIV®. Copyright © 1973, 1978, 1984 by International Bible Society.

The Living Bible. Copyright © 1971 by Tyndale House Publishers, Wheaton, Illinois.

The New American Standard Bible. Copyright © the Lockman Foundation 1960, 1962, 1963, 1968, 1971, 1972, 1973, 1975, 1977.

The New English Bible: New Testament, copyright © 1961 by The Delegates of the Oxford University Press and The Syndics of the Cambridge University Press.

The New Testament in Modern English by J. B. Phillips, copyright © 1958, 1959, 1960 by J. B. Phillips.

The New Testament in Today's English Version. Copyright © 1966 by the American Bible Society.

Revised Standard Version, copyright © 1946, 1952, 1956, 1971, and 1973 by the Division of Christian Education of the National Council of the Churches of Christ in the United States of America.

PREFACE

Favorable comments from ministers who serve in many different types of churches suggest that the *Pastor's Annual* provides valuable assistance to many busy pastors as they seek to improve the quality, freshness, and variety of their pulpit ministry. To be of service to a fellow pastor in his or her continuing quest to obey our Lord's command to Peter, "Feed my sheep," is a calling to which I respond with gratitude.

I pray that this issue of the *Pastor's Annual* will be blessed by our Lord in helping each pastor to plan and produce a preaching program that will better meet the spiritual needs of his or her congregation.

This issue contains series of sermons by several contributing authors who have been effective contemporary preachers and successful pastors. Each author is listed with his sermons by date in the section titled "Contributing Authors." I accept responsibility for those sermons not listed there.

This issue of the *Pastor's Annual* is dedicated to the Lord with a prayer that he will bless these efforts to let the Holy Spirit lead us in preparing a planned preaching program for the year.

T. T. CRABTREE
Springfield, Missouri

CONTRIBUTING AUTHORS

Morris Ashcraft . . . . A.M. October 3, 10, 17, 24, 31
Tom S. Brandon . . . . P.M. April 4, 11, 18, 25
                                                  May 2, 9, 16, 23, 30
Harold T. Bryson . . . . P.M. January 3, 10, 17, 24, 31
                                                  February 7, 14, 21, 28
                                                  March 7, 14, 21, 28
Edgar H. Burks . . . . P.M. November 28
                                                  December 5, 12, 19, 26
Hiram Campbell . . . . .A.M. March 28
                                                  April 4, 11, 18, 25
James E. Carter . . . . P.M. January 6, 13, 20, 27
                                                  February 3, 10, 17, 24
                                                  March 3, 10, 17, 24, 31
                                                  April 7, 14, 21, 28
T. T. Crabtree . . . . All messages other than those
                                                  attributed to others
David R. Grant . . . . A.M. May 9, 16, 23, 30
                                                  June 6, 20
James F. Heaton . . . . A.M. June 27
                                                  July 4, 11, 18, 25
                                                  August 1, 8, 15, 22, 29
David L. Jenkins . . . . P.M. June 6, 13, 20, 27
                                                  July 11, 18, 25
                                                  August 1, 8, 15, 22, 29
Howard S. Kolb . . . . A.M. February 28
                                                  March 7, 14, 21
                                                  November 28
                                          P.M. July 7, 14, 21, 28
Gerold McBride . . . . Miscellaneous Section
Lowell D. Milburn . . . . P.M September 5, 12, 19, 26
                                                  October 3, 10, 17, 24, 31
                                                  November 7, 14, 21
Leonard Sanderson . . . . P.M. August 4, 11, 18, 25
                                                  September 1, 8, 15, 22, 29
                                                  October 6, 13, 20, 27
                                                November 3, 10, 17, 24
                                                  December 1, 8, 15, 22, 29

JANUARY

■ **Sunday Mornings**

Let us rejoice at the privilege of being alive in this new year with the opportunity and responsibility of opening up God's Word and speaking his message to his people.

In recent years the church has been under severe attack from enemies without and from critics within. One of the great needs of each Christian is to have a better understanding of our Lord's plan and purpose for his church. The suggested theme for the morning messages is "Being the Church Today."

■ **Sunday Evenings**

"Great Truths About Christ That Make a Real Difference" is the theme for a series of messages focusing on the life and ministry of our Lord.

■ **Wednesday Evenings**

Begin a series of expository and inspirational messages based on the letter to the Philippians. The suggested theme is "A Pathway Through Philippians."

SUNDAY MORNING, JANUARY 3

Title: The Church Jesus Is Building

Text: "I will build my church, and the powers of death shall not prevail against it" (**Matt. 16:18** RSV).

Scripture Reading: Colossians 1:24–29

Hymns: "God, Our Father, We Adore Thee," Frazer
"I Love Thy Kingdom, Lord," Dwight
"The Church's One Foundation," Stone

Offertory Prayer: Gracious and loving Father, we come on this first Lord's Day of the new year to thank you for the many blessings bestowed on us during the past year. We thank you for the privilege of being alive and able to worship and witness and give to your kingdom's work. We come bringing ourselves afresh, dedicating ourselves to the work of your kingdom and to the glory of your name. We also bring our tithes and offerings as symbols of our desire to be completely committed to that which will advance your spiritual kingdom and bring your blessings into the hearts and lives of people in this community and to the ends of the earth. Bless these offerings we pray. In Jesus' name. Amen.

Introduction

Jesus spent his early years as a carpenter building furniture and homes. By engaging in this type of work, he affirmed the divine approval of everything that contributes to wholesome personal and family living.

Toward the end of his earthly ministry of seeking to bring the will of God into people's lives, Jesus verbalized his determination to build his church. The word he used for the church is the same word used for the people of God throughout the Old Testament.

On the Day of Pentecost he came in the person of the Holy Spirit to administer the work of his church. He continues to abide within the hearts of believers, and it is through them that he accomplishes the redemptive work of God in the world.

Across the centuries the divine carpenter has continued to build his church in quality and size. Jesus did not think of his church as a building in the sense of its being a physical structure at a particular address. He thought of his church as people. The structures that often are identified as churches today are but the meeting places for the church.

Jesus thought of his church as a body of born-again, baptized believers. He began the construction of this beautiful temple, this body of believers, from the beginning of his ministry. John's gospel records how "Jesus was making and baptizing more disciples than John" (4:1). The coming of the Holy Spirit upon these disciples on the Day of Pentecost was the divine way of authenticating them as the church that Jesus was building and through which he would carry on his redemptive work.

Our text records Jesus' desire, decision, and dedication.

I. Jesus builds his church through the evangelistic activity of his disciples.

The Great Commission has a universal application to each of Jesus' disciples. We must guard against interpreting it as applying only to clergy or only to foreign missions. It is as each disciple of the Lord shares a testimony concerning God's gracious work within his or her life that the gift of faith is imparted to unbelievers. As each of us shares the good news of God's love, Jesus is at work in us building his church.

II. Jesus builds his church through the missionary activity of congregations.

Every congregation should have a heart big enough to hold the whole world and should be contributing to foreign missions. But giving an offering for foreign missions does not exempt us from being responsible for our local community. Likewise, having concern for the local community does not exempt us from responsibility toward those who live on the other side of the globe. It is a both/and proposition rather than either/or.

III. Jesus builds up his church from within.

Our Lord is concerned not only about the exterior extension of his kingdom, which can be measured by the increase of churches and believers, but also about building up his church from within that it might become the true family of God, the household of faith.

In writing about the gifts of the Holy Spirit, Paul urges the disciples in Corinth to "strive to excel in building up the church" (1 Cor. 14:12 RSV). In Paul's epistle to the Ephesians he speaks about the gifts of the Holy Spirit that have been bestowed upon the church for the equipping of "the saints for the work of ministry, for building up the body of Christ, until we all attain to the unity of the faith and of the knowledge of the Son of God, to mature manhood, to the measure of the stature of the fullness of Christ; so that we may no longer be children, tossed to and fro and carried about with every wind of doctrine, by the cunning of men, by their craftiness in deceitful wiles" (Eph. 4:12–14 RSV).

A. *Jesus wants his church to be a school in Christian discipleship.*

The so-called Sermon on the Mount was in reality a lecture on the plain from our Lord to his disciples. They sat before him and he taught them rather than preaching to them. The word *disciple* itself means learner, follower. The new birth, as essential and wonderful as it is, is but the beginning of our Lord's plan for us, not the crowning climax. To grow in Christ we must follow the example of the early church, who "devoted themselves to the apostles' teaching and fellowship, to the breaking of bread and the prayers" (Acts 2:42 RSV). Jesus builds his church when we meet together to study his Word and when we put his teachings into practice.

B. *Jesus wants his church to be a fellowship of spiritual brothers and sisters.*

Through the miracle of the new birth we become children of God through faith in Christ Jesus. We become brothers and sisters. Paul speaks of the church as "the household of faith." The fellowship of the early disciples was a source of great enrichment of their spiritual well-being. They were not isolated, solitary believers. They were a real family in which love and compassion and unselfishness were the rule of the day.

C. *Jesus wants his church to be reverent and worshipful.* "Fear came upon every soul" (Acts 2:43). We come together as a crowd of people, but reverence for the presence of Christ causes a crowd to become a congregation of worshipers.

Christ comes to church every time his disciples come together in his name (Matt. 18:20). We need more of the reverence that filled the heart of Simon Peter when he fell down at Jesus' knee saying, "Depart from me, for I am a sinful man, O Lord" (Luke 5:8). Peter had a feeling of unworthiness for close contact with Jesus. Recognition of our sinfulness along with a response to the holiness of God would cause us to be more reverent and worshipful when we come together in the name of our precious Lord.

D. *Jesus builds his church when the members give themselves devotedly to prayer (Acts 1:14; 12:5).*

E. *Jesus builds his church when the disciples recognize and respond to the Holy Spirit's leadership (Acts 4:31; 13:1–3).*

The Holy Spirit came to indwell the church on the Day of Pentecost. He will remain in the church until the Lord returns to claim his own. The Holy Spirit has come to be our divine teacher, leader, and helper. When believers neglect or refuse to recognize the Holy Spirit's loving leadership, the work of Christ and the growth of the church are brought to a standstill.

Conclusion

Jesus, the divine carpenter, is at work in our midst. He comes to meet with us, speak to us, correct us, commission us, and encourage us.

If you are not yet one of his disciples, open the door and let him begin his good work in you today. Let him have command over your life. Let him become your teacher, guide, and helper beginning today.

SUNDAY EVENING, JANUARY 3

Title: A Unique Birth Certificate

Text: "Behold, a virgin shall be with child, and shall bring forth a son, and they shall call his name Emmanuel, which being interpreted is, God with us" (**Matt. 1:23**).

Scripture Reading: Matthew 1:18–25

Introduction

One of my favorite hobbies is to visit old houses and rummage through their contents. Of special interest to me are literary works and documents. I am intrigued by old newspaper headlines, magazine advertisements, and skilled handwriting on official documents.

Suppose that archaeologists had a dig in Nazareth. What if during the process of their excavation they discovered the birth certificate of Jesus of Nazareth. We do not know if such documents existed in those days, but if a document similar to a modern birth certificate existed, it would be quite interesting. Jesus' birth certificate would be unusual in many ways. The space for the father of the child would be blank. Civil authorities would probably declare a mistake. But Mary conceived of the Holy Spirit. She had no sexual relations before Jesus was born. What a strange birth certificate!

What interesting facts could we learn from Jesus' birth certificate?

I. We could learn the reality of his life.

A birth certificate proves the reality of life. One does not need such a document to prove the reality of Jesus' life, for historians have recorded his existence and numerous people throughout history have experienced his reality.

A. *Strangely enough, some people have tried to minimize the reality of Jesus.* Historians have sought to prove that he was an illegitimate child of a Roman soldier. Philosophers have tried to minimize his teachings. Millions have merely ignored him.

B. *Nevertheless, Jesus is real.* The Bible records the birth experience in simple, straightforward narration: "Then Joseph being raised from sleep did as the angel of the Lord had bidden him, and took unto him his wife: and knew her not till she had brought forth her firstborn son: and he called his name JESUS" (Matt. 1:24–52). Matthew did not go into elaborate details to prove Jesus' reality. He knew the Lord's reality because he had encountered and followed the Master.

A birth certificate might be nice. It would substantiate what millions already know. Jesus is a real person!

II. We could learn the characteristics of his life.

Birth certificates describe pertinent facts and characteristics of a person's life. If such a document were found, we could verify many characteristics that we already know about the Lord.

A. *The human nature of Jesus is evident.* Looking at the birth certificate would give the conclusion that Jesus is a part of history. He was born by the natural processes of childbearing.

The other thirty-three years confirm Jesus' humanity. He had the limitations of humanity and experienced such things as growing tired and being tempted.

B. *The divine nature of Jesus is also evident.* The absence of the name of Jesus' father would suggest something unique—that he had no human father. His mother conceived by the Holy Spirit.

Jesus was fully human and fully God. No one can explain this great mystery. Yet Jesus can explain God to us, and he can give us insight on how to be successful humans.

III. We could learn his family associations.

A birth certificate has a place for the number of other children born to the family as well as blanks for the names of the father and mother. Jesus' birth certificate would record relevant family matters.

A. *Jesus obeyed the will of the heavenly Father.* The birth certificate might record the name of Jesus' father as the Lord God Almighty, but it could not disclose to us how Jesus obeyed the Father's will.

B. *Jesus acknowledged a family of brothers and sisters.* Jesus had half-brothers and sisters, but he also had a spiritual family. There would not be room on a birth certificate for the names of all Jesus' spiritual brothers and sisters. "For whosoever shall do the will of my Father which is in heaven, the same is my brother, and sister, and mother" (Matt. 12:50).

Jesus had a unique family in that he had no earthly father and was born of a virgin. His real family are those who respond to him in faith.

Conclusion

You can be included in the family of God by becoming his child through faith in Jesus Christ.

WEDNESDAY EVENING, JANUARY 6

Title: How to Be a Saint

Text: "Paul and Timotheus, the servants of Jesus Christ, to all the saints in Christ Jesus which are at Philippi, with the bishops and deacons..." **(Phil. 1:1).**

Scripture Reading: Philippians 1:1–11

Introduction

What is a saint? Some may think of saints only as those who have been declared to be saints by the Roman Catholic Church for some outstanding accomplishment or virtuous lifestyle. They have been deceased for centuries and are recognized on church calendars. Others may think of saints as pious but not very nice persons. Still others use the word *saint* as a loose term of respect applied to a particularly good person.

When you read Paul's letter to the Philippians, you know that Paul had still another meaning. *Saint* is the translation of a word that means "holy," to be separated to God. So saints are not people who are dead so much as they are people who are different. The first-century Christians were different because they were committed to Christ.

The Philippian letter was written to people Paul called saints. They were the Christians in the church.

I. As saints Christians are called to be something.

There is a distinction between being and doing. Many of us are very willing to be doing—doing good deeds, doing programs and activities, doing ministry. But we are soon made aware that before we can *do* for Christ we must *be*. To Nicodemus, the Jewish ruler who visited Jesus at night, the Savior said, "Ye must be born again" (John 3:7). Even he would have to do something before he could become a citizen of the heavenly commonwealth.

Christianity is more than an ethic to follow, a philosophy by which to live, or a theology to believe. It is a person to follow. We are to follow Jesus Christ and give our lives to him in faith.

By following Jesus we can understand what kind of person we ought to be. He is always our guide and example. Leonard Griffith, in his book *This Is Living*, pointed out that great Christians have always taken Jesus as a pattern. The selfless Francis of Assisi prayed that he might be as selfless as Christ; Brother Lawrence, performing the lowliest tasks in the monastery kitchen, prayed that he might be as humble as Christ; the virtuous Catherine of Sienna prayed that she might be as pure as Christ; David Livingstone, in the perils of darkest Africa, prayed that he might be as adventurous as Christ.

II. As saints Christians are called to be something different.

There are many differences between Christians and non-Christians. One obvious distinction is the commitment of their lives. Christians have made a commitment in faith to Jesus Christ. Their lives are centered in him. Therefore, they have a distinctive lifestyle. In Jesus' Sermon on the Mount, he proclaimed to his followers, those who were people of the kingdom, what kind of character they should have if they followed him. The lives of saints are marked by grace, peace, strength of character and purpose, and love. Remember, the word *saint* comes from the root for "holy," which means separate. Christians are to be distinct from the world.

III. As saints Christians are called to be something different for a purpose.

Saints of God are not different just for the sake of being different. Different does not have to mean odd. Christians are to exemplify the life of Christ and thus point others to him. William Barclay tells of a little girl who went with her mother to church one day. She asked her mother about the figures in the stained-glass windows. Her mother replied that they were saints. Then later in the week she visited an older woman with her mother. As they left the house, the mother said, "You have seen a saint today." Trying to put the two together, she finally said, "Oh, I know what a saint is. A saint is someone who lets the light shine through."

Conclusion

You, too, can be a saint by following Christ.

SUNDAY MORNING, JANUARY 10

Title: The Church: The People of God

Text: "But you are a chosen race, a royal priesthood, a holy nation, God's own people, that you may declare the wonderful deeds of him who called you out of darkness into his marvelous light" **(1 Peter 2:9 RSV).**

Scripture Reading: 1 Peter 2:9–12

Hymns: "Onward, Christian Soldiers," Baring-Gould
"I Love Thy Kingdom," Dwight
"The Church's One Foundation," Stone

Offertory Prayer: Holy and loving heavenly Father, we thank you for the steadfastness of your love. We rejoice in the truth that there is nothing in the past, present, or future, nothing in the heights above or in the depths beneath, that can separate us from your love. We rejoice in the blessed privilege of being members of your family. Help us to respond not only to the privileges but also to the responsibilities of this relationship.

Father, today we come bringing tithes and offerings indicating our love for you and our desire to further your kingdom and to minister to those who stand in need of help. Accept these gifts and bless them in a way that will bring glory to your name and help to others. Through Jesus Christ our Lord we pray. Amen.

Introduction

Our Savior, who was also a master carpenter, continues the process of building his church. The church is not a building—a structure made of brick, steel, stone, wood, or glass. The church is not a place—a location, site, or address. The church that Jesus Christ is building is composed of people, living stones who are established in a spiritual temple so they can offer up spiritual sacrifices acceptable to God. These people are born-again believers who have received Jesus Christ as Lord and Savior, who have been baptized and have publicly proclaimed their faith in him as the One who died for their sins and conquered death and the grave. These people are learning, study-ing, listening people who are seeking to be his true disciples. They are wor-shiping people who bow before God in recognition of his supreme worth and their dependence on him for life and all things pertaining to their exis-tence. The church Jesus is building is made of praying people who not only talk to God but who also listen when God speaks to them. They are a sharing people who give because they have received from God's gracious hand. They are also a serving people who follow the example of the ultimate Servant.

What does it mean to really be the church today? What is Jesus Christ trying to do in the world through the church that he organized and has per-petuated to this day?

We must understand who we are if we are to be all that God intends for us to be and to accomplish all that he has planned for us. The biblical writ-ers spoke of the church in a variety of ways. In fact, the New Testament con-tains at least eighty different images to describe the nature, function, and ministry of the church. If we survey these many varied images and functions of the church, we will be greatly aided in understanding what our Lord wants us to be.

One of the dominant New Testament figures of the church is "the people of God." Peter used this term to instruct and encourage the Lord's disciples, who had been scattered abroad as a result of persecution and other factors. This morning we will look at his description of the church as the new Israel. Peter speaks to the church as God spoke through Moses to the people of Israel when the covenant was established with them at the foot of Mount Sinai (Ex. 19:1–6).

I. "You are a chosen race."

This is not a mere compliment. It is a divine commission.

On the Day of Pentecost God identified the 120 disciples who were gathered together in an upper room as the new Israel, the people through whom he would work to carry on his redemptive ministry in the world.

The sound of a rushing, mighty wind that came from heaven pro-claimed the breath and life of God as abiding within this body of believers. As God had taken the dust of the earth and breathed into man's nostrils the breath of life and he became a living soul, so God was breathing his Spirit into these new disciples that they might become the living body of Christ.

The tongues of fire that lighted upon the heads of the members of this infant church were the Shechinah of the Old Testament, the glory of God's presence upon them.

In these miraculous events God was announcing to the Jewish nation and to the Jewish exiles who had returned for the Feast of Pentecost that Jesus of Nazareth was indeed the Messiah, the Son of God, and that his dis-ciples now constituted the new Israel, the new people of God, the new chosen people through whom God would do his work. God never limited his blessings to those who were Abraham's successors by biological descent. Through believing in Jesus, even Gentiles could be God's chosen people.

Jesus said to his disciples on one occasion, "You did not choose me, but I chose you and appointed you that you should go and bear fruit and that your fruit should abide; so that whatever you ask the father in my name, he may give it to you" (John 15:16 RSV). Jesus had already declared, "By this my father is glorified, that you bear much fruit, and so prove to be my disciples" (v. 8 RSV). God had called Abraham and later the nation of Israel to be his chosen people in order that they might be a fruitful missionary force in the world. The nation of Israel failed to bring forth the fruit that our Lord desired, so he extended his call to all people. At this point in history the church is his chosen people.

One becomes a member of the family of God not by biological descent but by a spiritual birth into the family of God through faith in Jesus Christ (Mark 3:34; 1 Peter 1:23).

II. You are "a royal priesthood."

This is not a mere compliment. It is a divine commission. Through Moses God had told the people of Israel, "You shall be to me a kingdom of priests" (Ex. 19:6 RSV).

A. *A priest is a go-between.*
B. *A priest is a meeting place.*
C. *A priest is a bridge builder.*

This passage does not teach an exclusive priestly clergy. Instead, it proclaims the priesthood of every believer and the responsibility of every believer to help unbelievers come to know God as they have come to know him in and through Jesus Christ. As the people of God, we are to perform the function of a holy priesthood. We are to be the instrument for bringing the message of God's grace and love to a needy world. We are to be the kind of people through whom an unsaved world will be drawn to the Lord Jesus Christ because of the Holy Spirit's ministry in our midst and through our efforts. We have a responsibility to God and to the unbelieving world to be the meeting place where God can come into contact with them and where they can get acquainted with God.

III. You are "a holy nation."

This is not a mere compliment. It is a divine commission.

To Israel God had said, "For I am the LORD who brought you up out of the land of Egypt, to be your God; you shall therefore be holy, for I am holy" (Lev. 11:45 RSV).

Paul wrote to the church at Ephesus declaring the divine choice of the church as the people of God: "He chose us in him before the foundation of the world, that we should be holy and blameless before him" (Eph. 1:4 RSV).

The word *holy* is not a familiar word in the vocabulary of modern people. To the Hebrews it meant to be separate, distinct. It was used in reference to that which belonged to Deity and to denote something different from the common and profane. By his holiness, God is proclaiming his difference from humanity. This can be illustrated by the fact that God's house is different from other houses, that God's day is different from other days, that God's ways are different from human ways. In calling us to a life of holiness and proclaiming us to be a holy nation, God is calling us to be different from ordinary people. We are not to be secular or materialistic.

The members of the church are called to a holy life, to a life different from that of the world, because they have voluntarily chosen to make Jesus Christ the Lord of their lives and to live by the law of love. We are to be different in the way we live, speak, labor, study, and serve. Because of the presence of the living Lord in our lives, all Christians—salespersons, doctors, mechanics, athletes, students, spouses, and others—should be different from non-Christians.

To the degree that we are truly a holy people, we will find ourselves to be "blameless" before God (Eph. 1:4). To be holy does not mean that we will be cantankerous or peculiar or self-righteous. Instead, it means just the opposite: We will be so filled with love, grace, and the wisdom of God that we could not conceal our presence even if we tried.

IV. You are "God's own people."

This is not a mere compliment. It is a divine fact and a divine commission. For Christians to claim that they are God's people is something infinitely more than an egotistical boast. Falsely proclaiming to be God's people is blasphemy. To be God's people is to be totally his possession.

A. *The church is God's personal possession.* That means that he is God, Lord, and owner. His authority is recognized and his will is respected and appreciated. We can measure the degree to which we are indeed his people by the degree to which we dedicate ourselves to the doing of his will and to the obedience of his commandments.

B. *The church is God's purchased possession (1 Cor. 6:20; 1 Peter 1:18–19).* Paul declares in Ephesians that "Christ loved the church and gave himself up for her, that he might sanctify her, having cleansed her by the washing of water with the word, that he might present the church to himself in splendor, without spot or wrinkle or any such thing, that she might be holy and without blemish" (5:26–27 RSV). The church has been purchased by a loving God at a great cost. This indicates the degree and permanency of his love for his people.

C. *The church is God's precious possession (John 3:16).* This tremendous verse that proclaims the greatness of God's love for a lost world reveals to us how extensive God's love is for those who respond to his grace and mercy. Paul rejoiced in this love and tried to describe it in his epistle to the Romans (8:31–32).

Conclusion

God calls us to be a royal priesthood so that we "may declare the wonderful deeds of him who called [us] out of darkness into his marvelous light" (1 Peter 2:9 RSV). On the Day of Pentecost the infant church proclaimed in a powerful and gracious manner "the mighty works of God" (Acts 2:11). These mighty acts of God were manifest in the coming of Jesus Christ to earth, his sacrificial death on the cross, his victory over death and the grave, his triumphant ascension back to the Father, and his gracious generosity in the gift of the Holy Spirit on the Day of Pentecost.

God has called us to be a chosen race, a royal priesthood, a holy nation, his own special people in order that those who are "without mercy" may now "receive mercy," that all "outsiders" might become "insiders." If you are among the outsiders, please realize that the great God of heaven is like the energy that flows through electric wires. Faith on your part will throw the switch that makes it possible for the very life and love and grace of God to come into your life.

To use another metaphor, if your life is desolate and unfruitful, then God is like the stream that flows through an irrigation ditch. Faith opens the gate to let the life-giving water flow out onto the dry soil to produce life and growth and beauty and fruitfulness.

Respond to Jesus Christ with faith that says, "Yes, I will receive you, trust you, follow you, obey you, depend on you." Do it now.

SUNDAY EVENING, JANUARY 10

Title: An Unusual Baptismal Service

Text: "And it came to pass in those days, that Jesus came from Nazareth of Galilee, and was baptized of John in Jordan. And straightway coming up out of the water, he saw the heavens opened, and the Spirit like a dove descending upon him" **(Mark 1:9–10).**

Scripture Reading: Mark 1:1–10

Introduction

A baptismal service is an interesting experience. During my nineteen years as a pastor, I have witnessed many baptismal services. Memory brings to mind a family of four who were baptized together. Several times I had the unique pleasure of baptizing a father and child or a husband and wife. Once a paralyzed man was helped into the baptistery by two deacons. Another time a minister friend of mine baptized his own daughter. That was quite a baptism.

But perhaps the most unusual baptismal service of all time was one in the Jordan River in the Judean wilderness nearly two thousand years ago. Jesus of Nazareth came to John the Baptist and requested baptism. John backed away from the request, but Jesus persuaded John to baptize him. In a simple setting void of ornamentation and convenience, this was the most significant baptism ever to occur. It was unusual in the sense that the Son of God asked John, an ordinary man, to baptize him. It was unique because the voice of God was heard saying, "This is my beloved Son, in whom I am well pleased" (Matt. 3:17). Then the heavens opened and Jesus saw the Spirit of God descending upon him like a dove.

The gospel writers included Jesus' baptism in the record because of its great importance. We can apply practical lessons from our Lord's baptism to our lives.

I. The first lesson is unhesitating obedience.

We are told little of what happened to Jesus during the eighteen years between his visit to the temple and his baptismal service. When Jesus went to John, he ended the period of silence and emerged in his formal ministry.

A. *The response of Jesus to baptism showed an unhesitating obedience to the Father's will.* Often we hear, "Was Jesus not different from the others whom John baptized? They needed to confess their sins, and their baptism signified their repentance. But why would Jesus need to be baptized?"

Jesus submitted to baptism as a sign of obedience. He dedicated himself openly to God's will and purpose for his life.

B. *The response of our baptism.* Behind every baptismal service is a person who submits to the will and purpose of God for his or her life. Our baptism shows a willingness to obey God's will. Baptism marked a significant commitment in our Lord's life in his unhesitating obedience to God's will. For us to be baptized for any other reason would be a mockery. Baptism sets believers apart from the world as a sign that they are willing to obey God.

II. The second lesson is an intimate identity.

When Jesus requested baptism, John hesitated. He said, "I have need to be baptized of thee, and comest thou to me?" (Matt. 3:14). Jesus replied, "Suffer it to be so now: for thus it becometh us to fulfil all righteousness" (v. 15).

A. *Jesus came to identify with people's needs.* He did not come merely to meet the righteousness requirements of the law; he came to fulfill all righteousness. Because the demands of righteousness could not be fulfilled by human beings, Jesus came to identify with people and to help them fulfill righteousness.

B. *Believers submit to baptism as a symbol of identification.* We die to our selfish life, we are buried with Christ, and we are raised with him in newness of life. Our baptism says that we have identified with a new lifestyle—life in Christ.

III. The third lesson is a divine anointing.

What followed Jesus' baptism shows the interest that God took in the event—the opened heavens, the descending dove, and the voice of approval. One could discover many figurative meanings of these events, yet one truth prevails over all the others: God anointed Jesus for a special ministry.

A. *Jesus received an anointing from the Father.* The testimony of sight and sound from the Father revealed that he was anointing Jesus for a most unusual ministry. Reading about Jesus' ministry yields the conclusion that God had a special anointing for him.

B. *Each baptized believer receives an anointing from God.* God pledges us his presence. We undertake service for the Master in the power of the Spirit of God (read 2 Cor. 1:21–22).

Just as baptism marked the time when God anointed Jesus in a unique manner, so our baptism marks the time when we are anointed to serve in the Lord's church.

Conclusion

Jesus was the Son of God in a way all his own. His baptism rises above and beyond every other baptism. But it is true that everyone who opens his or her life to Christ becomes a child of God. When we trust the Lord, we submit to an unusual experience—namely, baptism. By this we demonstrate our relationship with and affection for Jesus Christ.

WEDNESDAY EVENING, JANUARY 13

Title: My Prayer for You

Text: "I thank my God upon every remembrance of you, always in every prayer of mine for you all making request with joy. . . .And this I pray, that your love may abound yet more and more in knowledge and in all judgment" (**Phil 1:3–4, 9**).

Scripture Reading: Philippians 1:3–11

Introduction

Intercessory prayer for another is one of the highest Christian services possible. First Samuel 12 records the farewell speech of the old prophet Samuel to the people of Israel, in which he said, "God forbid that I should sin against the LORD in ceasing to pray for you" (v. 23). He had been both a prophet and a judge, but the people had now chosen a king. As Samuel was stepping down, he showed his continued concern for them.

The apostle Paul showed this to be his heart also in his letter to the Philippians. He opens his letter with a prayer that begins with gratitude and then moves to petition. His prayer is the prayer of a pastor. The pastoral heart is displayed when a pastor prays for his or her people.

I. My prayer for you is for an abundance of love.

In verse 9 Paul prays that the Philippians' love "may abound yet more and more in knowledge and in all judgment." It is a picture of the tides of the sea that just keep rolling in, or of a cup that is poured full and yet the pouring doesn't cease. It is much like the old French woman who had spent her life in the slums of Paris. When she went to the seashore for the first time in her life and saw the waves rolling in one after another without end, she ran down to the beach and fell to her knees, scooping up the water and exclaiming, "Thank God for something of which there is enough."

There is enough love; we just need to develop it. Love ought never to be limited in scope, amount, or direction. Notice the kind of love Paul was writing about.

A. *Love with knowledge.* Love without knowledge can be dangerous. My father was a feed merchant. In past years at Eastertime, seed and feed stores sold colored baby chicks. One year my father gave each of my two boys a brightly colored Easter chick. They loved those little chicks. In fact, one son loved his chick, petted it, and squeezed it so much that by evening the chick had died. That was love without knowledge. The love for which we pray is with knowledge.

B. *Love with discernment.* Love must use good judgment.

II. My prayer for you is for growth in character.

A. *Growth in character includes the ability to tell right from wrong.* Paul continues by adding, "that ye may approve things that are excellent; that ye may be sincere and without offence till the day of Christ." The word "approve" here is from the Greek word that is used of testing metals to see if they are pure. Growth in character calls for a sense of ethical sensitivity.

B. *Growth in character will also include purity of heart.* There is definitely a place in today's world for the person who is pure in heart and life and character. "Sincere" actually means "tested by the sun." And the English word comes from the French through Latin. It means *sans cere*, without wax, and came from the practice of Roman sculptors and art dealers of filling in bad places in the art with wax. When the artwork was set out in the courtyards of noble Roman homes, the sun would cause the wax to melt and run. Thus, people requested that their sculpture be sold *sans cere*, without wax. That is what God demands of us. Growth in character includes a blameless life.

III. My prayer for you is for development in grace.

The way to development is given: "being filled with the fruits of righteousness, which are by Jesus Christ" (v. 11). This is the only way we can develop in grace, for the fruit of righteousness comes only through Jesus Christ.

The goal of development is given: "unto the glory and praise of God." The Westminster Catechism says that the chief end of man is to glorify God and to enjoy his presence forever. How far that is from the goal that we often set for ourselves! But how essential it is.

There is a story of an Indian sage who had identical pictures at each end of the hall. At least that is the way it looked. Upon closer inspection, it could be seen that on one end was the picture, on the other end was a mirror that accurately reflected the other. Reflecting the life of Christ should be the goal for Christians.

Conclusion

My prayer for you is for an abundance of love, for growth of character, and for development in grace. How are you doing in these essential things?

SUNDAY MORNING, JANUARY 17

Title: The Church: The Body of Christ

Text: "Now you are the body of Christ and individually members of it" (**1 Cor. 12:27** RSV).

Scripture Reading: Romans 12:4–5; 1 Corinthians 12:12–14.

Hymns: "Blessed Be the Name," Wesley
           "Jesus, the Very Thought of Thee," Bernard of Clairvaux
           "He Lifted Me, " Gabriel

Offertory Prayer: Gracious and loving Father, we thank you for the beauty of this day and for your goodness to us. We rejoice in the awareness of your abiding presence. We respond positively to your purpose for each of us. As we come bringing tithes and offerings, we pray that you will help us to love you with every part of our being and to use the time that you have allotted to us in a manner that will be beneficial to your kingdom's work and to all with whom we associate. Help us to be channels through which your blessings can flow into the lives of others. Because you have been so gracious and generous to us, we give ourselves afresh to you and to your work in the world. Through Jesus Christ our Lord. Amen.

Introduction

The Holy Spirit inspired the scriptural writers to use many different images, metaphors, and figures of speech to communicate divine truths to readers' hearts and minds. One of the most variegated figures of speech used to describe the nature and function of the church is the body of Christ. In this figure of speech, the inspired writer is declaring that the church is a living organism in which Jesus Christ lives and through which he continues his ministry.

The church of the New Testament is not a building made of brick, steel, stone, wood, or glass. The church of the New Testament is not a place or a street address. By using the figure "the body of Christ," the inspired writer is declaring that the church is more than an organization made up of people. It is a living organism that was brought into existence by Jesus Christ, and it continues to be such because of his power and his purpose.

In Paul's epistle to the Ephesians, he declares that God "has put all things under his feet and has made him the head over all things for the church, which is his body, the fulness of him who fills all in all" (Eph. 1:22–23 RSV). It is comforting and challenging to recognize that Christ as the head of the church relates himself to and acts in a variety of ways toward the church.

I. Christ is Lord of the church.

Christ exercises lordship and authority over the church (Eph. 5:23). Some churches have a democratic form of church government. Because of this, some think of the church as a democracy. It is not. We would be closer to the Scriptures if we thought of the church as a Christocracy in which Christ rules and his will is followed.

II. Christ loves the church.

Christ loves the church and gives himself for it (Eph. 5:25). Christ not only loved the church and gave himself for it by dying on the cross, but he continues to love the church and gives himself to it and for it day by day.

III. Christ cleanses the church.

Christ sanctifies and washes the church so that it may become glorious and holy (Eph. 5:26). Christ continually works to bring about the full dedication of his people to the purposes of God so they can display the beauty of holiness in their lives and in the ministries they render.

IV. Christ nourishes the church.

Christ nourishes and cherishes the church (Eph. 5:29). Our Lord did all that he could to build up and nourish the infant church made up first of the apostles and later increased to more than three thousand on the Day of Pentecost. He continues this ministry of nourishing and cherishing his body, which is in reality the people of God.

V. Christ and the church are inseparable.

Christ as the head of the church is incomplete and unproductive without the body. I say this reverently and without any desire at all to take away from the importance of the head. This image, the body of Christ, shows the absolute necessity of the body functioning if the work of the head of the church is to proceed according to the divine plan. The poet has put it appropriately:

> *Christ has no hands but our hands*
> *To do His work today;*
> *He has no feet but our feet*
> *To lead men in His way;*
> *He has no tongue but our tongue*
> *To tell men how He died;*
> *He has no help but our help*
> *To bring them to His side.*
>
> Annie Johnson Flint

Conclusion

The good news of God's Word is that the Christ who came to communicate God's love has conquered death and the grave and, as the living Lord, wants to come and take up residency in your heart. To let Jesus come into your life is to experience the forgiveness of sin. It is to receive the gift of new life that God has for you. You can become a part of the body of Christ.

SUNDAY EVENING, JANUARY 17

Title: The World's Strongest Person

Text: "Then the devil leaveth him, and, behold, angels came and ministered unto him" (**Matt. 4:11**).

Scripture Reading: Matthew 4:1–11

Introduction

My two sons, like most adolescent boys, are impressed with strength. They marvel at the muscles of large linemen on football teams. They also stand in awe of weight lifters. They once brought me the *Book of World Records* and showed me the picture of Paul Anderson of Toccoa, Georgia. He weighed 365 pounds and raised the greatest weight ever lifted by a human— 6,270 pounds. He claimed to be the world's strongest man.

History records many fascinating men of strength, yet no man has ever excelled the strength of Jesus of Nazareth. The Bible gives us no record of Jesus' size. We do not know his height or weight, the size of his biceps, or how much he could lift. But the Bible does leave us with the record of Jesus as the world's strongest person.

Jesus' strength can be seen in his experience with the devil immediately after his baptism. At his baptism Jesus received an anointing from God. Afterward he was assaulted by the devil. He triumphed over all of the devil's tempting solicitations, ultimately living a sinless life. That is something no other human has ever done, so Jesus must be the world's strongest person.

The powerful force of evil strives against God's work in people. We cannot emerge victorious in our own strength, but we can depend on the Lord, for he will give sufficient strength over satanic attacks. Let's look at the ways that Satan attacks.

I. Satan tempts us to give precedence of the physical over the spiritual.

According to Matthew and Luke, Jesus was led of the Spirit into the wilderness. During this time Jesus became extremely hungry, and the devil took advantage of his need by tempting him to turn stones into bread.

A. *Jesus was tempted to use divine power to satisfy physical need.* The devil sought to persuade the Lord to abandon his position of dependence on God and to use divine power for selfish ends. Satan took advantage of Jesus' low resistance. To be sure, it was tempting for Jesus to use his power to satisfy his need.

But Jesus defeated the devil. He repulsed Satan's attack by quoting Deuteronomy 8:3 from a portion of Scripture that tells how God provided for the sustenance of the children of Israel and describes their dependence on God.

B. *Every person is tempted to give greater concern to the physical than the spiritual.* Satan seeks to destroy people's dependence on God by getting them to trust the temporal. He tries to convince people that their physical drives are far more important than their spiritual needs. To be delivered from this temptation we need the strength of Jesus Christ. The world's strongest person can cause us to give greater priority to the spiritual. This temptation teaches us our need for dependence on God's strength. Invitations to abuse God-given physical desires come to us, but we can be sustained during the assault and led on to victory.

II. Satan tempts us to exploit the providence of God.

Jesus' second temptation came immediately after the first one. Satan blatantly misused Scripture, asking the Lord to jump from the highest part of the temple and misquoting Psalm 91:11–12 as a promise of Jesus' protection.

A. *Jesus was tempted to do something spectacular.* The devil provided the Lord with an opportunity to demonstrate his trust in God in a spectacular way. Jesus emerged victorious in the first temptation when he declared that he would trust God. Now the devil wanted Jesus to show his trust by presuming on God for personal advantage. Jesus repelled the attack with a quotation from Deuteronomy 6:16 that deals with the providence of God. God provided for the Israelites, but Moses cautioned them not to exploit God's provisions.

B. *Every believer is tempted to exploit God's providence.* Often we are tempted to take unnecessary risks and then expect God to protect us. God promises his protection, but he does not promise his providence in our selfish choosing. He provides for us and protects us when we tread the pathway of his will. We must never be guilty of presuming upon God for our personal advantage.

III. Satan tempts us to use any means to get what we want.

Finally, Satan departed from his clever subtlety and candidly stated his real objective. He took Jesus to a high mountain and showed him all the kingdoms of the world, saying, "All these things will I give thee, if thou wilt fall down and worship me" (Matt. 4:9). This strongest attack, his most attractive offer, would result in domination over others.

A. *Jesus was tempted to look past the means to the ends.* Satan offered Jesus the kingdoms of the world, with one condition: "If thou wilt fall down and worship me" (Matt. 4:9). The devil reasoned that the good that would come would be sufficient reason for the method. His suggestion belittled the way of self-sacrifice. Jesus again turned to Scripture to defeat the devil. He quoted Deuteronomy 6:13, in which Moses prescribed that to be a great nation, Israel must worship the one true God.

B. *Every believer is tempted to use wrong means for a right purpose.* There must be no alliance or compromise with evil. In our service for the Lord, we must do God's work in God's way. Often we are tempted to depart from God's way of self-denial and to compromise with the world. Yet even the slightest compromise gives the devil an advantage.

Conclusion

Every day Satan attacks us. He tempts us to gratify our selfish physical desires and urges us to exploit God's divine providence for our self-advancement. He presents us with a plausible means for our selfish interest. Only one person has ever fought and won. Jesus is the champion over temptation. Victory comes not through the avoidance of the assault but through the abundant resources of the world's strongest person.

WEDNESDAY EVENING, JANUARY 20

Title: Getting Good Out of Bad

Text: "But I would ye should understand, brethren, that the things which happened unto me have fallen out rather unto the furtherance of the gospel; so that my bonds in Christ are manifest in all the palace, and in all other places; and many of the brethren in the Lord, waxing confident by my bonds, are much more bold to speak the word without fear" **(Phil 1:12–14).**

Scripture Reading: Philippians 1:12–20

Introduction

One of the main challenges of life is turning things that seem to be bad for us into good. Sometimes it is difficult to see the hand of God when things go against us, for example, plans that do not materialize, schemes that fail, dreams that burst, opportunities that never come, sickness, transfers in jobs, or death. Although these things present a problem for us, they also present a tremendous opportunity.

Paul experienced this. He had longed to go to Rome to preach the gospel. He was in Rome at this time, but he was there as a prisoner. What would that do to him? Paul Rees asks, "When you physically fetter a spirit as daring and venturesome as Paul's, what happens?" (Paul S. Rees, *The Adequate Man* [Westwood, N.J.: Revell, 1959], 24).

What happens, indeed? To set at ease the minds of his friends at Philippi, Paul asserted that the things that had happened to him resulted in the furtherance of the gospel. It seemed that Paul was in an impossible situation. Nevertheless, he was able to get good from bad; and in so doing, he served as a shining example and source of inspiration for Christians ever since.

I. The method for getting good out of bad is shown.

In verses 12–18 Paul showed the method used to get good out of bad. He rejoiced that Christ was preached and the gospel was furthered. This was accomplished by his sharing the gospel with his Roman guards and by the preaching of Christ by others. Some of the others preached Christ sincerely while others preached out of a partisan spirit, but all in all Christ was preached.

What had happened to Paul had become an opportunity to witness for Christ. And we, too, can use our negative experiences as an opportunity to witness to others.

We can be witnesses to Christ as our personal Savior. When Pope Gregory sent Augustine to England to preach, Augustine discovered that a pure form of Christianity already existed there. In the Synod of Whitby (664) the Roman type of Christianity prevailed. What was the source of this earlier type of Christianity in England? It could have come from the members of the Praetorian Guard who were transferred to England after Paul witnessed to them in Rome from his prison cell.

We can witness by our Christian character. A missionary couple had gone to India. After a short while the husband became ill. In a period of depression his wife expressed that she did not understand what was happening; she felt that God had sent them there to witness. Her husband replied that perhaps God wanted them to show how Christians handled suffering.

II. Two means of getting good out of bad are expressed.

In verse 19 Paul expressed two means for getting good out of bad. One of the means is intercessory prayer of other Christians. Paul's friends prayed for him when he was imprisoned. Through their prayers he was strengthened and encouraged for his witnessing ministry.

Another means is the power of the Holy Spirit. The one greatest resource Christians have for accomplishing anything is the power of the Holy Spirit at work in their lives.

III. The motive for getting good out of bad is stated.

The motive as Paul expressed it in verse 20 was that Christ might be magnified through the life of the Christian. Whether it occurred by Paul's death or through his life, the one thing Paul desired was that Christ would be magnified.

Some Christians witness by their death. Stephen is an example. His death contributed to Paul's conversion. Others witness through their lives. Many people have been drawn to Christ by the witness of a devoted Christian's life.

Conclusion

It is possible: Good can come out of bad. When we look at the cross and at Paul's imprisonment, we know it can.

SUNDAY MORNING, JANUARY 24

Title: Being the Body of Christ Today

Text: "Now you are the body of Christ and individually members of it" (**1 Cor. 12:27** RSV).

Scripture Reading: 1 Corinthians 12:12–14

Hymns: "When Morning Gilds the Skies," Caswall

"Blessed Redeemer," Christiansen

"Let Others See Jesus in You," McKinney

Offertory Prayer: Heavenly Father, we thank you today for your blessings to us through your people who make up the body of Christ. We thank you for your people of the past and for your people of the present. We rejoice in the privilege of being a part of the body of Christ. Today we bring offerings and give them into your service that others might come to know Jesus Christ as Lord and Savior and receive ministries of mercy in his name. Amen.

Introduction

It is one thing to know what the Scriptures teach concerning the past, yet it is something else to put the great truths of Scripture into practice in the present. The picture of the church contained in the New Testament is different from the image that comes to mind when one speaks about the church of today.

We need to study afresh what the New Testament has to say about the church and then put forth a sincere effort to be the church in the present. The church is more than an organization. It is an organism.

1. *Christ is the source of the life of the church that is his body.* He came to earth and died on a cross that we might receive the gift of eternal life. Eternal life should be thought of as qualitative rather than merely quantitative.
2. *Christ is the sustainer of the life of the body.* In his initial announcement to his apostles concerning the church, he promised to perpetuate this institution through which he works to accomplish his redemptive purpose (Matt. 16:18).
3. *Christ is sovereign over his body.* The pastor is to be the bishop, the overseer, the manager, but Jesus Christ is to be the Lord. Deacons have an important ministry to render, but it is not that of "running the church." The only "boss" the church needs has already been appointed, and his name is Jesus Christ.

To be the Lord, the head of the church, means that God has appointed him to a position of authority. As the head of the church, Christ has been given the right to make requests, to issue orders, and to make requisitions.

If we want to experience a rich and abundant life, we must recognize that we belong to him and act like it.

The New Testament views the church as the body of Christ, which has been constituted through the work of the Holy Spirit in all who have submitted to the lordship of Jesus Christ.

I. Unity in the body.

The body needs unity (1 Cor. 12:12). The church at Corinth was divided and torn asunder by a party spirit and much rivalry. Paul wrote his epistle to try to solve some of the problems that divided them.

II. Diversity in the body.

The great diversity in the church body is illustrated by the various organs that make up the human body. As the different organs of the human body have their unique function, even so different members in the church have been given unique ministries to render by the one Holy Spirit (1 Cor. 12:4–11).

III. Harmony in the body.

There must be harmony in the body of Christ.

A. *No members are to look down upon themselves because they do not have the gift that other members have (1 Cor. 12:15–20).*

B. *No individual member of the church is to be considered as of little value or as being unneeded (1 Cor. 12:21).*

C. *No individual member is to act superior to the other members of the body.*

D. *No member is to be treated as inferior to the other members.* For a football team to be a winner, all players must play their own positions. A team does not need eleven quarterbacks. In addition to a quarterback, the team needs guards, tackles, blocks, backs, and a center. All players must play their own positions. So should it be in the church.

IV. The solidarity of the body (1 Cor. 12:12–13, 24–26).

A. *If one member suffers, all of the members should suffer together with that member (v. 26).*

B. *If one member is honored, all of the members should rejoice together with that member (v. 26).*

C. *The members of the body are to have the same care one for another as they have for themselves (v. 25).*

V. Being the body of Christ today.

If the church is the living organism through which the living Christ carries out his purpose and performs his work in the present, there are some great truths that we need to accept and practice. In the conversion experience, Christ came to live within each believer (Rev. 3:20; cf. Gal. 2:20).

A. *Christ came in to make our body a dwelling place for the Holy Spirit.*
B. *Christ came in to see with our eyes the needs of others and opportunities for ministry and service.*
C. *Christ came in to hear with our ears the cries of distress as well as the voice of God calling us to serve.*
D. *Christ came in to think with our mind and to fill it with the very thoughts of God. Only when we come to think as Jesus thinks can we truly become like Jesus in our life.*
E. *Christ came in to live so that he might work with our hands in rendering ministries of mercy and helpfulness in the world today.*
F. *Christ came in that he might walk through the world with our feet carrying the gospel to one and all.*

Conclusion

If you have not yet let Jesus Christ come into your life to be Savior, you would be wise to do so now. He stands at your heart's door to bring you the gifts of forgiveness and new life if you will but trust him as Lord and Savior, teacher and friend. Let him become the Lord of your life.

Perhaps there are those today whom the living Lord is inviting to become members of this local expression of his body in the world. Today if you hear his voice, do not harden your heart, but respond to him with faith and love and joy.

SUNDAY EVENING, JANUARY 24

Title: The Great Physician

Text: "I say unto thee, Arise, and take up thy bed, and go thy way into thine house" (**Mark 2:11**).

Scripture Reading: Mark 2:1–12

Introduction

Much of Jesus' ministry was spent alleviating people's suffering. The Gospels are full of healing accounts. Mark opens the story of Jesus with the concept of Jesus as "the Great Physician." Chapter 1 of Mark alone has six references to Jesus' healing.

In chapter 2, Mark continues his portrayal of Jesus as healer by giving an expanded account of the healing of a palsied man. Jesus was in Capernaum teaching in a house. Crowds gathered to the extent that no one else could get inside. Four people brought a paralyzed man to the house, and seeing that they could not get through the crowd, they went up the outside stairs to the rooftop. Then they uncovered the roof and lowered the man into Jesus' presence. Jesus must have been surprised to see this patient, but he healed him. This incident furnishes us insights into the techniques of Jesus in dealing with a paralyzed man.

I. The Great Physician considered the patient to be important.

Jesus greeted the paralyzed man with an interesting word: "Son." On the surface that may not be significant, but a closer look into the word "son" helps us to see how Jesus regarded this man as an important person.

A. *The assessment of society.* In Jesus' day people looked upon the handicapped, sick, and diseased as property. They felt that something caused them to be less than persons. Consequently, the paralyzed man felt alienated from society. He lived in his own lonely world of physical and mental suffering.

Often society assesses people by who they are, what family they were born into, or what they have done. People are judged in worth by possessions they have or by the social accomplishments they attain. Various societies have their "nobodies" and their "somebodies."

B. *The assessment of Jesus.* When Jesus spoke the first word to the paralyzed man, it was a healing word—"son." Irrespective of this man's position in society, Jesus regarded this patient as a person of immense importance. The word translated "son" here is the Greek word that describes a child in a family. Jesus regarded this poor, paralyzed man as a person.

Irrespective of who you are or where you were born, Jesus regards you as important. Whether you have made a million dollars or are a person of meager means, you are important. Jesus regards every person of utmost value.

II. The Great Physician cured the patient.

The test of a good physician is whether he or she can diagnose and treat problems so that patients can get better. Jesus was the greatest physician, for he recognized a problem that no one else had diagnosed. Other physicians said, "You are paralyzed." Jesus said, "You are paralyzed, but your sins are also a problem." Jesus cured the patient both physically and spiritually.

A. *The problem of sin.* In Jesus' day the prevailing theology was that people suffered because of their sin. People would look at the paralyzed man and diagnose his case with a theological passage: "That person must be a great sinner." The paralytic himself was deeply troubled over his sin. Jesus dealt with the man's sin before he healed him of his paralysis. Many people suffer from guilt and the consequences of sin.

B. *The solution to sin.* Jesus spoke these meaningful words to the man: "Your sins are forgiven." Only Jesus can speak those words and grant forgiveness. To be forgiven means to have the sin debt canceled, to have the penalty of sin removed, and to have sin covered. Only Jesus has the solution to humanity's deepest guilt—divine, unmerited forgiveness.

III. The Great Physician gave some orders.

A doctor's capability is also measured by helping patients to live better lives after they are treated. No one would want to go to a physician for long if he or she continued to be sick after the visit. When Jesus, the Great Physician, confronted the paralytic, he gave some orders that would change his life: "Arise, and take up thy bed, and walk."

A. *An old life.* The paralytic lived a miserable life. His days consisted of begging for bread, and he had to seek others' help to get inside when the weather was inclement. Frustration, misery, disappointment, and numerous other negative feelings filled his life.

One does not have to be paralyzed to live a miserable life. Many able-bodied people live empty lives and need the Great Physician.

B. *The new life.* Think of the new kind of life Jesus gave this man. He told him to pick up his pallet and walk. For years that pallet had carried him; now he was to carry the pallet. Life would now take on a new dimension.

Jesus gives new life. One who had received orders from the Great Physician testified, "If any man be in Christ, he is a new creature: old things are passed away, behold, all things are become new" (2 Cor. 5:17).

Conclusion

Let me recommend my Physician to you. He healed me when I was sick with self-will, self-trust, and self-assertion. The Lord encountered me, and I yielded my life to him. He made me whole, and he can also cure you.

WEDNESDAY EVENING, JANUARY 27

Title: This Is Living!

Text: "For me to live is Christ, and to die is gain" **(Phil. 1:21).**

Scripture Reading: Philippians 1:12–22

Introduction

There is the story about a Texas oil millionaire who specified in his will that he wanted to be buried in his Cadillac. So when the man died, a firm of undertakers prepared to carry out his instructions. They dug an enormous grave, placed the Cadillac on a huge lowering device, dressed the corpse in his sports jacket, put a cigar in his mouth, seated him at the steering wheel, and set the speedometer at sixty miles per hour. The mourners gathered around the grave. As the strange coffin slowly sank into the ground, to the appropriate words of committal, another millionaire, looking at his dead friend with a tear in his eye, said, "Man, that's living!" (Leonard Griffith, *This is Living* [Nashville: Abingdon Press, 1966], 42).

Of course, it was not living but dying; nothing could have been more dead. But we know what he meant. Whenever you do something that gives you pleasure, you express your enjoyment by saying, "This is living!" What makes you say it?

Paul said it in prison. He believed in Jesus Christ and had committed his life to him. "To me," he said, "to live is Christ." For Christians this is living.

I. This is living: Life begins with Christ.

"Life begins at forty" is an oft-spoke expression. The truth is, however, that life begins at whatever age one finds Christ as personal Savior. When we are born again we find real life, new life in Christ.

Paul discovered this truth when he met Christ on the Damascus Road. Augustine was born again when he heard the voice of Christ in a quiet garden. Francis of Assisi started a new life on the day he heard Christ's voice in a broken-down church. John Wesley found new life on an evening when Christ spoke to him in a Moravian chapel. Truly we begin living with Christ.

II. This is living: Life is lived in Christ.

Dr. Harry P. Stagg retired after many years as the executive secretary of the New Mexico Baptist Convention. He had returned to his native Louisiana after service in World War I, during which he suffered lung damage due to poisonous gas. It looked as though he would surely die. But he went to New Mexico, and not only did he live, but he had a long and distinguished ministry there. He found a climate in which he could live.

Christ provides the climate in which Christians live. A daily devotional life and fellowship with other Christians in the church help to provide this environment. A coal cannot remain live and burning alone. Neither can Christians remain alive and growing outside the church.

III. This is living: Life is loved for Christ.

What is the purpose of your life? Paul could affirm that his purpose was to live for Christ. Too many people drift along without purpose for existence. Life needs some meaning, some goal. Those who aim at nothing usually attain it. Living for Christ makes life worth living.

IV. This is living: Eternal life is found through Christ.

Leonard Griffith tells of a young man who came to William Gladstone when he was prime minister of England and said, "Mr. Gladstone, I should appreciate your giving me a few minutes in which I might lay before you the plans for my future. I should like to study law."

"Yes," said the great statesman, "and what then?"

"Then sir, I should like to gain entrance to the Bar of England."

"Yes, young man, what then?" asked Gladstone.

"Then, sir, I hope to have a place in Parliament, in the House of Lords."

"Yes, young man, what then?" asked Gladstone.

"Then I hope to do great things for Britain."

"Yes, young man, and what then?"

"Then, sir, I hope to retire and take life easy."

"Yes, young man, and what then?" he tenaciously asked.

"Well, then, Mr. Gladstone, I suppose I will die."

"Yes, young man, and what then?"

The young man hesitated and said, "I never thought any further than that, sir."

Gladstone looked at the young man sternly and steadily and said, "Young man, you are a fool. Go home and think life through."

— This Is Living, 48–49

Paul had thought life through. To die would put him in the presence of Christ.

Conclusion

This is living! All of life is found in Christ and centers in him.

SUNDAY MORNING, JANUARY 31

Title: The Church: The Flock of God

Text: "Tend the flock of God that is your charge, not by constraint but willingly, not for shameful gain but eagerly, not as domineering over those in your charge but being examples to the flock" (**1 Peter 5:2 RSV**).

Scripture Reading: Acts 20:28–32

Hymns: "The Church's One Foundation," Stone
"All the Way My Savior Leads Me," Crosby
"Where He Leads Me," Blandy

Offertory Prayer: Holy and loving Father, we thank you for your great love for us revealed in the life and death of Jesus Christ, your Son and our Savior. We thank you for the visible continuing expression of your family in the church, the household of faith. We thank you for all of your blessings to us in and through the church. We come praying now for the growth of your church, both quantitatively and qualitatively. Help us to experience inward growth in the realm of the Spirit as we seek to grow numerically. We come bringing our tithes and offerings for the advancement of your work in the world. Bless these gifts to that end we pray in Jesus' name. Amen.

Introduction

In the Old Testament one of the favorite images used to describe the relationship of God to his people is that of the shepherd and the flock. The psalmist declared, "Know that the LORD is God! It is he that made us, and we are his; we are his people, and the sheep of his pasture" (Ps. 100:3 RSV).

Concerning the Messiah, Isaiah declared, "He will feed his flock like a shepherd, he will gather the lambs in his arms, he will carry them in his bosom, and gently lead those that are with young" (Isa. 40:11 RSV).

One of the most beautiful pictures of Jesus found in the New Testament is in John 10, in which he describes himself as the Good Shepherd: "I am the good shepherd. The good shepherd lays down his life for the sheep. . . .I am the good shepherd; I know my own and my own know me, as the Father knows me and I know the Father; and I lay down my life for the sheep. And I have other sheep, that are not of this fold; I must bring them in also, and they will heed my voice. So there shall be one flock, one shepherd" (vv. 11, 14–16).

In the Old Testament faithful priests and prophets were often referred to as the shepherds of Israel. When Paul spoke to the leaders of the church at Ephesus, he made reference to the relationship between the leaders of God's people and those for whom they care in terms of the shepherd and the flock. Peter, as he approached the end of his life, also used these terms to describe the relationship of spiritual leaders to the church membership. It is no accident that in the New Testament the church is spoken of as the flock of God, and the pastors are referred to as the shepherds, or undershepherds, over the flock of God.

I. The flock is the possession of God (Ps. 100:3).

Jesus called his followers a little flock (Luke 12:32). He registered with them the firm faith that the Father God was going to be generous to them. Later he affirmed that there were other sheep that he would bring into this one fold.

In his closing comments to Peter following his resurrection, Jesus gave to him a threefold commission with reference to the flock of God. He said, "Feed my lambs," "Tend my sheep," and "Feed my sheep" (John 21:15–17 RSV).

Jesus laid down his life on the cross for the sheep of God's flock. He purchased the sheep with his own precious blood. Therefore, we should always see the church as God's property rather than as an organization that belongs to people. The church is not a building. It is made up of people who have been born again and who have been baptized as followers of the Lord Jesus Christ. The church is the flock of God.

God as a shepherd serves as a *watchman* over the flock. With eyes wide open, he is vigilant and alert. He is also the flock's *guard*, their *protector* and *defender* who provides security. He is their *guide*, a much-needed leader. Further, God as the shepherd is the *physician* for the flock. He wants to heal their hurts. Psalm 23:2 says that he is also the *feeder* of the flock. And most important, he is the *Savior* of the flock. It is he who seeks and rescues and restores the wayward.

II. Undershepherds have been provided for the flock of God.

A. *The work of the pastor is that of being a shepherd.*
B. *The Good Shepherd is to be the pattern for each undershepherd.* The Good Shepherd:
    1. Loves the flock.
    2. Knows the flock.
    3. Leads the flock.
    4. Feeds the flock.
    5. Guards the flock.
    6. Increases the flock.
    7. Rescues the sheep from their enemies.

III. In God's flock every shepherd is a sheep and every sheep is a shepherd.

A. *The pastor, as the shepherd of the flock, is responsible for caring for and overseeing the whole flock.*
B. *Elected leaders in the church are to serve as shepherds.*
    1. Deacons are to serve as shepherds.
    2. Bible school officers and teachers are to serve as shepherds.
C. *Every individual member of the church is to be a shepherd to those in the sphere of his or her influence.*
D. *Individuals are to serve as shepherds to individuals.*
E. *There is a shepherding responsibility in the home.*

Conclusion

Peter promised those who are faithful and devoted in their service as shepherds, "When the Chief Shepherd appears, you will receive the crown of glory that will never fade away" (1 Peter 5:4 NIV).

Jesus is the door into the sheepfold. He is the door out, the door through, and the door up. Let Jesus Christ be your Good Shepherd today. Respond to him in such a manner that you can truly say, "The Lord is *my shepherd!*"

SUNDAY EVENING, JANUARY 31

Title: The Communication Expert
Text: "He who has ears, let him hear" (**Matt. 13:9** NIV).
Scripture Reading: Matthew 13:1–9, 18–23

Introduction

Three factors are necessary for communication. First, there must be a person who sends a message. The sender brings his or her cultural and personal factors to the message. Second, the medium is important. Technology is continually providing new mediums for communication. The third factor in the communication process is the receiver. The omission of any one of these three factors hinders communication.

A look at the ministry of Jesus reveals that he was a master of communication. He had both divine and human personality factors that influenced his message. Because he knew people's hearts, he could focus his message to meet their needs. He used illustrations with which the people could readily identify. No greater communicator has emerged than Jesus Christ.

Using a simple story of a sower scattering seed, Jesus illustrated the lives of his hearers. He said that the abundance of the harvest in their lives depended on the receptivity of the soil, their hearts. Let's notice how people respond to the gospel of Jesus Christ.

I. Some have a closed response.

Jesus called attention to a sower sowing in a field. He said, "Some [seeds] fell along the parth" (Matt. 13:4 NIV). Because the path was hardened from traffic, the seeds found no lodgment. Birds came and ate them. This is the way some people respond to Jesus Christ.

A. *The refusal to think about the gospel.* There are times when the gospel of Christ is presented to a person, and he or she refuses to even let it enter. When such people close their minds, the gospel cannot penetrate.

B. *The failure to comprehend the gospel.* Jesus said, "When anyone hears the message about the kingdom and does not understand it, the evil one comes and snatches away what was sown in his heart" (Matt. 13:19 NIV). Such persons may be able to grasp the meaning of the gospel intellectually yet fail to see the importance of applying it to their own lives.

II. Some have an impulsive response.

Jesus said, "Some fell on rocky places" (Matt 13:5 NIV). This was thin topsoil on top of rock. The seed would grow quickly, but when the plant could find no more nutrition, moisture, or room for the roots to grow, it would wither.

A. *The response from fascination.* Many people followed Jesus out of fascination. They enjoyed watching his miracles. Yet they had no concept of what following Jesus as a disciple meant. They were enthusiastic about his ministry but not serious about following him when times got tough.

B. *A premature pledge.* Once when Jesus and his disciples were walking along the road, a man came up to him and said, "I will follow you wherever you go." Jesus replied, "Foxes have holes and birds of the air have nests, but the Son of Man has no place to lay his head" (Luke 9:57–58 NIV). Jesus quenched this man's sudden enthusiasm, insisting that people consider the cost before deciding to follow him. He wanted people to see that discipleship means a revolutionary change of life. People often express a premature promise but fail to follow Jesus "wherever" he leads.

III. Some have a divided response.

Jesus further said, "Other seed fell among thorns" (Matt 13:7 NIV). This ground was either already covered with thorns or filled with latent weed seeds that would spring up and choke out the crop.

A. *The impossibility of divided loyalty.* Jesus taught that two crops cannot grow at the same time. On another occasion he said, "Ye cannot serve God and mammon" (Matt. 6:24). No one can serve Jesus Christ and the world at the same time. These are irreconcilable loyalties.

B. *The peril of duplicity.* The main problem of the weeds amid the good seed was one of crop production. The weeds prevented good fruit. "The worries of this life and the deceitfulness of wealth choke it, making it unfruitful" (Matt. 13:22 NIV). Daily cares prohibit the harvest of the Spirit in a Christian's life.

IV. Some have an open response.

Jesus analyzed the best response of his hearers with the example of the good ground. "Still other seed fell on good soil" (Matt. 13:8 NIV). This soil received the seed and brought a healthy harvest.

A. *A harvest depends on an open reception.* Jesus compared the person who opens his or her life to his message with good soil. This is the person who hears the message of Jesus Christ, comprehends its importance, and opens his or her life to him.

B. *An abundant harvest depends on a continued reception.* One becomes a Christian in the miracle of a moment. It takes a lifetime of openness to the Lord to produce an abundant harvest.

Conclusion

Jesus cautioned, "Take heed therefore how ye hear." Hearing is important. The adequacy of the sower of the seed or the quality of the seed are not in question. We can make the toil of Jesus a success when we open to him.

FEBRUARY

■ **Sunday Mornings**

Complete the series "Being the Church Today." On the last Sunday of the month begin a series called "The Miracle Working Power of Our Lord," lessons based on four of our Lord's miracles.

■ **Sunday Evenings**

Continue the series "Great Truths About Christ That Make a Real Difference."

■ **Wednesday Evenings**

Continue the series "A Pathway Through Philippians."

WEDNESDAY EVENING, FEBRUARY 3

Title: The Great Dilemma

Text: "I am torn between the two: I desire to depart and be with Christ, which is better by far; but it is more necessary for you that I remain in the body" (**Phil. 1:23–24** NIV).

Scripture Reading: Philippians 1:21–26

Introduction

We can live on many different levels. Some live only on the level of pleasure or duty or selfishness or demand. But others live on the level of love. We are often in a dilemma about what we should do with life. When we reduce our predicament to its simplest terms, it is a dilemma between desire and duty.

Remember that in our earlier lessons Paul was in prison and facing trial. He had just told the Philippians that even in jail he was able to get good out of bad, that his imprisonment was resulting in the furtherance of the gospel.-His goal was that Christ be magnified in him whether by life or by death. This brings Paul's statement of identification with Christ: "For me to live is Christ." But there is more to it. For Paul "to die is gain." So his dilemma is life or death, duty or desire.

Paul's great dilemma often becomes our great dilemma. "How will I live my life?" we ask.

44

I. The dilemma: duty or desire.

Most of us are familiar with Hamlet's soliloquy (Act III, Scene 1):

To be, or not to be: that is the question:
Whether 'tis nobler in the mind to suffer
The slings and arrows of outrageous fortune,
Or to take arms against a sea of troubles,
And by opposing end them? To die: to sleep. . . .

Paul was not thinking of ending his life to escape his troubles. Nor was he morbidly preoccupied with death. He was simply making a statement of trust and faith. For him to live meant promoting the gospel of Christ. But death would be gain, for he would immediately be in the presence of Christ his Lord. This is a fine statement of the Christian view of death. We may be in awe of death because of the unknown, but we need not have fear.

II. The reason for the dilemma: self-regarding life or other-regarding life.

Paul stated the reason for his predicament. He would welcome death, but must also think of the Philippians. As we face a similar dilemma, we must ask ourselves: "Will I live solely for myself, or will I live for others?"

All of us face this question in our own way. Teachers must decide whether they are just filling a position or are imparting skills to students. Parents must decide whether they are simply providing the necessities for a child or are nurturing that child in an atmosphere of love and security. Merchants must question whether they are just making money or are providing community members with personal service. And students must ask whether they are merely earning a degree or are preparing themselves for life and service.

III. The resolution of the dilemma: duty.

Paul resolved his dilemma between desire and duty by doing what was best for the people. He would heed the call to duty. Like Paul, we must see our duty in relation to ourselves, to others, and to God.

I once heard Billy Graham tell of a wealthy family from the Shenandoah Valley of Virginia who responded to a call to missions when a missionary visited their church. They sold their estate and went to China. Then they moved to the border of Tibet. Two of their children died with a fever. Then the mother got sick and the parents had to take a three-day journey by raft to another mission station. She died on the morning of the third day. But she had whispered in her husband's ear, "Go back." That is duty.

Conclusion

God's command to us is that we serve him with love and devotion. That duty will take precedence over desire.

SUNDAY MORNING, FEBRUARY 7

Title: The Church: A Fellowship of Believers

Text: "God is faithful, by whom you were called into the fellowship of his Son, Jesus Christ our Lord" **(1 Cor. 1:9 RSV).**

Scripture Reading: 1 Corinthians 1:1–9

Hymns: "Holy, Holy, Holy," Heber
"I Stand Amazed in the Presence," Gabriel
"Come, Thou Almighty King," Anonymous

Offertory Prayer: Holy and loving Father, we approach your throne of grace with reverence and joy. Thank you for the glad consciousness of forgiven sin. Thank you for the gift of eternal life as a present possession. Thank you for membership in your family. And thank you for calling us into the fellowship of your dear Son, Jesus Christ, that we might share with him in communicating the good news of your love to a needy and suffering world. Bless these tithes and offerings that we bring on this Lord's Day as tokens of our desire to give ourselves completely into your service. We pray in Jesus' name. Amen.

Introduction

We have discovered that the church is not a building but is a people who belong to God. It is spoken of in terms of a flock of God with Jesus as the Good Shepherd and pastors serving as undershepherds. The church is the body of Christ in which he lives and through which he carries on his redemptive mission in the world.

The church is a fellowship of believers. The Father God has called us out of darkness into light, out of despair into hope, and out of death into life and into the fellowship of his Son. Because of the gracious, loving ministry of the Father God, we share in a partnership of spiritual intimacy. By virtue of the relationship established with him, all believers share in a remarkable unity.

1. Ours is the unity of the new birth experience. If we are children of God through faith in Christ Jesus, we are brothers and sisters in Christ because of a common new birth experience.
2. Ours is the unity of a common faith in the one Lord. Each believer owes to him an undivided loyalty.
3. Ours is the unity of the indwelling Spirit. The Holy Spirit is the gift of God to each believer at the moment of conversion, and those who have not the Holy Spirit do not belong to Jesus Christ.
4. Ours is the unity of one mission as revealed in the Great Commission (Matt. 28:19).

5. Ours is the unity of the same sustaining hope, the glorious promise of the return of Jesus Christ for his own.
6. Ours is the unity of having one great enemy in common in the devil (1 Peter 5:8).
7. Ours is the unity of one day standing before the same Judge and giving an account to him (Rom. 14:12).

I. God calls the church into being as a fellowship by the resurrection of Jesus Christ.

It was the resurrection of Jesus Christ that transformed tragedy into triumph, that transformed a group of defeated disciples into a dynamic force in the world.

A. *During the life of our Lord, Peter confessed that Jesus of Nazareth was the Christ, the Son of the living God (Matt. 16:16).*

B. *It was Jesus' resurrection from the dead that identified and vindicated him to indeed be the Christ of God who had come with great power and authority (Rom. 1:4).* Following his resurrection, Jesus claimed to have all the authority of both heaven and earth (Matt. 28:18–20).

C. *People come into a right relationship with God by a faith response to a risen Christ, confessing him as Lord and Savior (Rom. 10:8–10).*

D. *In baptism we affirm and declare without apology our belief in the Christ who died and rose from the dead.*

It is by the message of the resurrected Christ that God calls the church as a fellowship into being.

II. God calls the church into being as a fellowship by the message of a crucified Christ.

A. *Jesus affirmed, "I, when I am lifted up from the earth, will draw all men to myself" (John 12:32 RSV).*

B. *By dying on the cross for the sins of guilty humanity, Jesus Christ gave proof of God's love for sinners (Rom. 5:8).*

C. *The preaching of a crucified Savior (1 Cor 2:2).* Knowing that God gave his only Son to die on a cross for our sins lets us know that we are of much value to him.

God uses the message of Christ on the cross to melt the cold hearts of sinners and to bring them to salvation.

III. God calls the church into being as a fellowship by means of his gift of the Holy Spirit.

On the Day of Pentecost, God gave to the church the Holy Spirit to be an indwelling administrator, leader, guide, comforter, and helper.

A. *The Holy Spirit brings conviction of sin to the hearts of unbelievers (John 16:7–11).* The Holy Spirit does not come to condemn, but to bring about a conviction of sin that will cause people to turn away from a life of sin to God.

B. *The Holy Spirit brings about the miracle of the new birth within the hearts of believers.* The new birth is a birth from above, the realm of the Spirit, and it is effected by the Holy Spirit of God (John 3:5–7; Titus 3:5).

If you have within your heart today an awareness of guilt and sin against God, it is because the Holy Spirit is seeking to bring you to the joy of forgiveness and into a right relationship with God. God did not send his Son into the world to condemn the world but that the world through him might be saved (John 3:17). God is for you. He will help you when you come to him in repentance and faith.

IV. God calls the church into being as a fellowship by means of the witness of believers.

Jesus commissioned his disciples to act as personal witnesses for him. He was referring to them being more than "eyewitnesses" to the great redemptive acts of his ministry; he further intended that they be speaking witnesses, testators rather than spectators.

The church as a witnessing fellowship of believers is the world's only hope. God needs your personal testimony to call others out of the darkness of death into the beauty of spiritual life. Figuratively speaking, he needs the testimony of every satisfied customer in order that an unbelieving world will be convinced that they should receive this product that Jesus Christ offers.

Conclusion

God calls you today by a resurrected, living Christ, by his precious Holy Spirit, and by the testimony of his children. He calls you today because he needs you to help him reach others. God is honest and faithful. You can show your trust in him by putting your faith in him today.

SUNDAY EVENING, FEBRUARY 7

Title: The Master Economist

Text: "For what is a man profited, if he shall gain the whole world, and lose his own soul? or what shall a man give in exchange for his soul?" **(Matt. 16:26).**

Scripture Reading: Matthew 16:24–28

Introduction

One of the most frequent topics of conversation today is the economy. We talk about the national economy and our personal finances. But have you ever thought of Jesus Christ as an economist? Look through the Gospels and see what Jesus had to say regarding the economy. He talked about true treasures: "Lay not up for yourselves treasures upon earth, where moth and rust doth corrupt, and where thieves break through and steal: But lay up for yourselves treasures in heaven, where neither moth nor rust doth corrupt, and where thieves do not break through nor steal: For where your treasure is, there will your heart be also" (Matt. 6:19–21). He substantiated the Old Testament teaching that man does not live by bread alone. He used parables filled with economic issues. For example, he told of a prosperous farmer who thought much of greater barns and little of the spiritual side of life.

Jesus used many economic words that are recorded in our text—*save, lose, profited, gain,* and *exchange.* These words speak of our individual, spiritual economy. Let's look at Jesus' teachings on spiritual economy.

I. Jesus wants us to speculate.

Jesus presented the disciples with an interesting speculation: "What is a man profited, if he should gain the whole world, and lose his own soul? or what shall a man give in exchange for his soul?" (Matt. 16:26). This is a masterful question. Think of the possibility of gaining the whole world. Then think of the possibility of losing life.

A. *The impossibility of gaining the whole world.* Gaining the whole world is beyond our imagination. Even owning a city is incomprehensible. Some, however, have sought to gain the whole world. Alexander the Great, for example, conquered one country after another. Someone has said that when Alexander reached the banks of the Indian Ocean, he wept because he had no more worlds to conquer. Napoleon, emperor of France, conquered Europe and set his heart on England and Russia. But Napoleon met his Waterloo.

Since no one can gain the whole world, isn't it foolish to lose your life for so little of this world?

B. *The temporary state of the world.* Even if we could gain the world, we could not retain it forever. Both humans and the world are in a temporary state. Even heaven and earth will eventually pass away. Life is short even at its longest. It is like a vapor or puff of smoke.

C. *The world fails to satisfy.* Even if we could gain the world, we still would not have genuine happiness, for the world cannot fully satisfy a person. Solomon was the playboy of the Eastern world, but he considered life as a vanity. Fame, wealth, and power soon pass, so we should not give ourselves to such temporary matters. Since we were made by God, we cannot have true happiness until we have a right relationship with him.

Jesus wants you to speculate. Think about gaining the whole world and losing your soul.

II. Jesus wants us to examine our holdings.

Jesus also wants us to examine our present holdings. We need to examine who we are and what we hold in our personal economy.

A. *The intrinsic worth of a soul.* Every human being has two sides: a dust side and a divine side. The dust side is the physical body. We all have God-given physical desires and drives. But every person also has a divine side. God breathed into the physical body, and man became a living soul.

Jesus taught that one soul was of more worth than all the world. That is hard to imagine. One person, any person living anywhere, has more worth than the entire world system. Because of the intrinsic worth of our lives, we ought to guard our holdings.

B. *The immense capacities of the soul.* God made humankind with enormous capacities, including power to dominate the created order and use it. Furthermore, human beings are the crown of God's creation, capable of fellowship with him. No other part of God's creation has the capacity for this unique communion with God.

C. *The immortality of the soul.* Every person born into the world will live forever. The Bible teaches that every person will live either with God or apart from God, depending on that person's choice. Knowing that we are going to live forever should cause us to closely examine our holdings.

III. Jesus wants us to invest our lives.

After having us speculate about gaining the world and losing our souls, and after having us examine the worth of a soul, Jesus wants us to invest our lives with him.

A. *Think of the loss.* A sensible economist must think of losses. This is true especially in a spiritual economy. If you do not invest your life with the Lord, you need to look from the outset at the losses.

1. You lose your soul. Since you belong to God, to put your life anywhere else is to lose it.

2. The loss of your soul has no compensations. Some people have lost financially or materially, and profits have come from those losses. For example, the great London fire destroyed thirteen thousand buildings, but from the tragic loss a more beautiful and improved city emerged. There are, however, no compensations for the loss of a soul.

3. The loss of your soul is irrevocable. At times one can lose and retrieve the loss. But the loss of the soul is irrevocable.

B. *Think of the gain.* A sensible economist considers the gain of an investment. If you invest your life with the Lord, there are numerous profits.

1. Genuine happiness. Money can buy almost everything but happiness. Jesus gives genuine happiness.

2. Abundant life. You can have a relationship with God that leads to a wholeness of self and better relations with others.
3. Eternal life with God forever. When you open your life to the Lord, you gain a life of unhindered relationship with God beyond the grave.

Conclusion

If you are thinking about investing your life, let me suggest a wise investment that has paid enormous dividends for me and countless others. Invest your life in Jesus Christ and his kingdom.

WEDNESDAY EVENING, FEBRUARY 10

Title: Christian Behavior

Text: "Only let your conversation be as it becometh the gospel of Christ: that whether I come and see you, or else be absent, I may hear of your affairs, that ye stand fast in one spirit, with one mind striving together for the faith of the gospel" **(Phil. 1:27).**

Scripture Reading: Philippians 1:27–30

Introduction

One September morning a father and his son were on their way to Grand Central Station in New York City. The son was taking the train to a college in New England. For a moment the father just stood there, wanting to say so many things but saying only one, though it was quite enough: "Son, never forget who you are." Worth more than a book of rules or a score of lectures on behavior was that one challenge to something deep in a boy's remembrance: "Never forget who you are." The basis of the boy's behavior was his own identity.

That is the basis of the plea that Paul made to the Christians at Philippi and through them to us: "Only let your conversation be as it becometh the gospel of Christ. . . ." Paul was saying, "In the way you act, never forget who you are."

"Conversation" here refers to the whole manner of life. This plea for Christian behavior is based on our identity as citizens of the kingdom of God.

I. Christian behavior should be consistent.

The primary characteristic of Christian behavior is that it is consistent with the gospel of Christ. One's behavior in life should confirm rather than contradict the gospel.

The word translated "conversation" actually meant "citizen life." It would have had special meaning for the Philippians since Philippi was a colony of Rome and was therefore governed exactly as though it were a part of Rome. The people used the Latin language, wore Roman dress, and insisted on being stubbornly Roman. To these people who were conscious and proud of their identity as Romans, Paul appealed to a higher identity, that as Christians.

As Christians we belong to a colony of heaven that is located on earth. Thus, our lives should be consistent with the principles on which the colony was founded—the gospel of Christ.

II. Christian behavior should be constant.

Christian behavior is also to be constant. Paul's admonition is to "stand fast." But how are we to stand fast? How are we to be constant in Christian behavior?

Constancy demands unity—people of one spirit and one mind "striving together for the faith of the gospel." Our word *athlete* is derived from one part of the word translated "striving." The best athletic teams are those with unity, who strive together in teamwork for a common goal.

III. Christian behavior should be courageous.

In verse 28 Paul added courage as a necessary ingredient of Christian behavior: "In nothing [be] terrified by your adversaries." Christians are to show courage in the face of persecution and suffering. The fact that they had adversaries indicated that some kind of persecution was at hand. When Christians show courage, the adversaries of Christ and doubters of Christianity will be confounded.

Conclusion

Paul nowhere intimated that living a Christian life would be easy, but he did believe that the outcome would be grand.

SUNDAY MORNING, FEBRUARY 14

Title: The Church: God's Lampstand

Text: "As for the mystery of the seven stars which you saw in my right hand, and the seven golden lampstands, the seven stars are the angels of the seven churches and the seven lampstands are the seven churches" **(Rev. 1:20 RSV).**

Scripture Reading: Revelation 1:12–20

Hymns: "To God Be the Glory," Crosby
              "I Will Sing the Wondrous Story," Rawley
              "Love Lifted Me," Rowe

Offertory Prayer: Holy Father, we thank you for the light of your love that has shined into our hearts through faith in Jesus Christ. We thank you for the illuminating work of the Holy Spirit as he opens up our understanding to the truth in your Scriptures. We thank you for the opportunity to serve and to minister and to be a blessing to others. We come today bringing tithes and offerings, praying your divine blessings upon them to the end that your name might be exalted and that your kingdom might come and that people might know your love and grace through Jesus Christ our Lord. Amen.

Introduction

We would go far astray in attempting to interpret the book of Revelation if we ignored the fact that the writer uses apocalyptic language to convey the great truths about the Lord Jesus Christ's future work in the world. John uses "sign language" to describe events revealed to him by Christ that were beyond the imagination of the people of his day. Apocalyptic literature was often used by scriptural writers during times of great international stress. This was certainly the case when the Revelation was given to John. The early Christians were under severe persecution, and John was in exile on the isle of Patmos because of his faith. With eager longing he looked across to the mainland, where the churches were experiencing severe attack by the forces of darkness. It is not incidental that his vision of the exalted Christ described in chapter 1 contains the image of the seven churches as seven lampstands with the triumphant Christ walking in the midst of them. The churches are described as precious, beautiful lampstands lifting up the light and dispelling the darkness.

I. The world is filled with darkness.

Darkness is a metaphor for such things as ignorance, failure, confusion, despair, loneliness, fear, disappointment, and death. Even in a world where knowledge is doubling about every five years, people still remain in tragic darkness. They continue to ask, "Where did I come from?" "What is the real purpose for my being?" "What is to be my ultimate destiny?" Apart from divine revelation in the Word, these questions cannot be answered.

II. Jesus Christ came as the light of God into the world to dispel darkness.

The prophet Isaiah had said of the time when the Christ would be born, "The people living in darkness have seen a great light; on those living in the land of the shadow of death a light has dawned" (Matt. 4:16; cf. Isa. 9:2 NIV). And it was by the light of a heavenly star that the wise men found the Christ child (Matt. 2:2). When Jesus was dedicated at the temple, Simeon proclaimed that the Christ had come as "a light for revelation to the Gentiles, and for glory to [God's] people Israel" (Luke 2:32 RSV). John said of

Jesus, "In him was life, and the life was the light of men. The light shines in the darkness, and the darkness has not overcome it" (John 1:4–5 RSV).

It was no accident, with this prophetic background, that Jesus later declared, "I am the light of the world; he who follows me will not walk in darkness, but will have the light of life" (John 8:12 RSV). As God had led the children of Israel through the wilderness by a pillar of fire, so Jesus Christ came to lead people by means of a divine light.

Jesus came to disperse the darkness about God and humanity, life and eternity.

A. *Christ came to cause the darkness that beclouds the souls of people to disappear.* He continues to light the way by providing guidance and answers for people who trust in him.

   1. Christ the light of the world comes silently like the sun each day.
   2. Christ the light of the world shines continuously like the sun century after century.
   3. Christ the light of the world comes in grace rather than on the basis of human merit just as the sun comes up graciously every day.
   4. Christ the light of the world comes powerfully like the sun to bring life, love, hope, and beauty.

B. *Christ came that those who dwell in spiritual death and darkness might have eternal life.* This life is to be found in Jesus Christ and in him alone (1 John 5:11–12).

C. *Christ, as the light of the world, came to reveal the way to abundant life.*

   A full life is not found through going one's own way or pursuing material gain; it is found only through Jesus Christ. People do not find real life by simply eating earthly bread. They find it as they take into their innermost beings the Bread of Life, "every word that proceeds from the mouth of God" (Matt. 4:4). This spiritual nourishment will provide them with all they need for abundant living.

III. Each church, like a beautiful lampstand, is to be a dispenser of the light that gives life to those who will respond to Jesus Christ.

A. *Individual Christians and congregations are reflectors of the divine light.* We are to serve the same function for Jesus as the moon serves as a reflector of sunlight. The sun is a tremendous source of heat and light while the moon is cold and frigid. Nevertheless, the moon does serve as a reflector of the sun's light, providing illumination to those who live on earth's surface.

B. *We are to reflect the glorious light of Jesus Christ as he reveals the way to God and to abundant life.*

C. *We are to reflect the unsetting light of Jesus Christ.* Somewhere on the face of the earth at all times the moon is reflecting the light of the sun.

D. *We are to reflect the all-sufficient light of Jesus Christ, for he is sufficient to meet the deepest needs of all.*

E. *We are to reflect the essential light of Jesus Christ without which people dwell in darkness and death.*

F. *We are to let Christ live in us in such a way as to constantly send forth the light of love, joy, peace, patience, kindness, goodness, faithfulness, gentleness, and self-control (Gal 5:22–23).*

You are the light of the world. Jesus did not say, "You are *a* light of the world." He said, "You are *the* light of the world."

Conclusion

Everywhere we see computerized signs that convey a continuous series of messages. In a sense, this is a picture of what each church should be in its community. The light that shines forth must come from the love of Jesus Christ within us. And our individual lights will blend with the lights of others with whom we worship, work, fellowship, and minister. God wants us to send forth a radiant, cheering, helpful, benevolent, revealing light into the darkness of the world. You are God's lampstand. Let it shine! Let it shine! Let it shine!

SUNDAY EVENING, FEBRUARY 14

Title: The Master Historian

Text: "Let both grow together until the harvest: and in the time of harvest I will say to the reapers, Gather ye together first the tares, and bind them in bundles to burn them: but gather the wheat into my barn" **(Matt. 13:30).**

Scripture Reading: Matthew 13:24–30

Introduction

History was one of my favorite subjects in school. Studying the various civilizations and the directions they have taken through the years intrigued me. Furthermore, learning the actions of previous generations helped me to understand human behavior today. A high school history teacher inspired this interest in history. She taught the subject as if she had lived it. She spoke with such familiarity of Socrates, Plato, and Aristotle that you would have thought they were her relatives.

The study of history continued through my college years. It was a blessing to study under notable scholars who introduced me to Arnold Toynbee, author of *A Study of History,* which is a multivolume set that traces the history of twenty-six civilizations. They also introduced me to Will Durant's multivolume philosophical work, *The Story of Civilization*. Will Durant and Arnold Toynbee became my heroes in history. I consider them to be master historians.

Yet, as I have studied the life and ministry of Jesus Christ, I have discovered that Jesus knows and understands history as no human. In the parable of the wheat and tares, Jesus gives insights into history.

I. Jesus knows the course of history.

A farmer sowed some good wheat seed in a field. While he slept, an enemy sowed tares among the wheat. In this simple story Jesus gives us insight into how he knows the direction of history.

A. *God works.* The parable teaches that God works in history. God has been dealing with humankind since the beginning of creation. God sought Adam after he rebelled against God. He chose Abraham as the father of a chosen nation—Israel—through whom all could be saved. God worked in varied ways throughout the history of Israel.

God worked in a decisive way in history when he sent his Son, Jesus Christ, to earth as a baby at Bethlehem. While Jesus was in the flesh, he taught, preached, and performed miracles. He died on a cross and was triumphant over death. He ascended back to glory, but he did not cease to work in history. Instead, he sent the Holy Spirit. God is at work in the Spirit today.

B. *The enemy works.* Throughout the course of history, while God works, the enemy tries to counter God's works. Jesus does not give us cut-and-dried solutions to the enigma of evil. He simply says, "An enemy hath done this" (Matt. 13:28).

II. Jesus knows the consummation of history.

In Jesus' parable the servants of the farmer were disturbed. "Sir, didst not thou sow good seed in thy field? from whence then hath it tares?" (Matt. 13:27). The servants wanted to go into the field and carefully pick the tares from the wheat. The farmer knew that the servants could not tell the wheat from the tares during their growth, so he said, "Let both grow together until the harvest" (Matt. 13:30). Jesus used the term "harvest" here to describe the consummation of history.

A. *Varied views of history's consummation.* Many serious people have predicted how the world will end. Some think the earth's ecology will be thrown out of balance and destroyed by poor environmental management. Many believe that the world will be destroyed by a nuclear war. Others go to the opposite extreme and say that the world will get better and finally graduate to a utopia. Jesus has a clear view of the consummation of history. He says that history is moving toward a great climax in a great harvest day.

B. *Features of history's consummation.* Jesus taught that good and evil would exist together until the harvest day. This final return of the Lord, commonly known as the second coming of Christ, will terminate history. Let's notice some features of Jesus' return.
   1. It will be sudden. No person can predict the closing of history. Jesus will come as a thief in the night.
   2. It will be victorious. Jesus came the first time as a despised and rejected person. The next time he will come as a ruling, reigning prince. Good will triumph over evil.
   3. It will be a world-shaking event, not an isolated event in one spot on the globe. It will involve every person.

III. Jesus knows the consequences of history.

The farmer allowed the wheat and tares to grow together until the harvest day. When the proper time arrived, he harvested the wheat and put it in barns. He bundled the tares and destroyed them. This gives us insight into what happens as a result of a person's experience.

A. *The fate of the wheat.* Jesus explained the meaning of the wheat: "The field is the world; the good seed are the children of the kingdom" (Matt. 13:38). The person who receives Jesus Christ experiences the abundant blessings of God forever. This is a happy consequence of history.

B. *The fate of the tares.* Jesus explained the meaning of the tares: "The tares are the children of the wicked one. . . .As therefore the tares are gathered and burned in the fire; so shall it be in the end of this world. . . .And shall cast them into the furnace of fire; there shall be wailing and gnashing of teeth" (Matt. 13:38, 40, 42). Because of a person's refusal to open his or her life to the Lord, the Lord grants this continued experience. No more awful consequence could be described than to reject Christ in history and to live apart from him throughout eternity.

Conclusion

You can change the course of your personal history. By opening your life to the master historian, you can experience happy days in history now that will continue forever.

WEDNESDAY EVENING, FEBRUARY 17

Title: A Plea for Unity

Text: "Let nothing be done through strife or vainglory; but in lowliness of mind let each esteem other better than themselves. Look not every man on his own things, but every man also on the things of others" **(Phil. 2:3–4).**

Scripture Reading: Philippians 2:1–4

Introduction

During the Second Continental Congress when it was decided that the thirteen colonies would resist England, Benjamin Franklin said at one point in the discussion, "We must all hang together or assuredly we will all hang separately." The cause for which they had asserted themselves demanded unity. They had to stay together to be successful.

The cause for which we have asserted ourselves—Christ's cause—demands even more harmony. We must present a united front against the presence of evil in this world.

The only flaw in the Philippian church was the threat of disunity. As much joy as they had in Christ, as much love as they showed for Paul, there are indications that there was a tiny threat of disunity before them. Paul made a plea for unity that we would do well to notice.

I. There are some causes for the lack of unity.

As we look at verses 3 and 4 we can detect some of the causes for a lack of unity. They are:

A. *Selfish ambition.* Often believers allow selfish ambition to rule their lives, and this in turn causes disunity in a Christian fellowship.

William Barclay tells of an incident in the life of Ambrose, a bishop and scholar in the early church. Before he became bishop, however, he was governor of the Roman provinces of Liguria and Aemilia. He governed with such loving care that the people regarded him as a father. The bishop of the district died, and the question of his successor arose. In the midst of the discussion suddenly a young child's voice arose: "Ambrose—bishop! Ambrose—bishop!" The whole crowd took up the cry. To Ambrose it was unthinkable. He fled by night to avoid the office. It was only the direct intervention and command of the emperor that made him agree to become bishop of Milan. This is the opposite of selfish ambition.

B. *The desire for personal prestige.* Christians should seek to focus attention on God and not on themselves. Nevertheless, some have such a desire for prestige that they try to "lord" it over others in the church. This, too, causes disunity.

C. *Self-interest.* Jesus showed us how to serve selflessly without striving for personal gain. We must follow his example. To do otherwise is to run the risk of disunity.

II. There are also some cures for the lack of unity.

Philippians 2:1 says, "If you have any encouragement from being united with Christ, if any comfort from his love, if any fellowship with the spirit, if any tenderness and compassion. . ." (NIV). As we analyze the phrases in this verse, the cure for a lack of unity will become apparent.

A. *Encouragement in Christ.* The first cure is the encouragement we receive from Christ himself. As the Good Shepherd and as our constant guide, he gives us an encouragement to unity.

B. *Incentive of love.* As Christians who have been taught to love one another, the incentive of love helps us to overcome disunity. Love stands as the greatest of all incentives for overcoming the small, insignificant things that might divide us.

C. *Fellowship of the Spirit.* We live in fellowship with the Holy Spirit as individuals and with other Spirit-filled believers. If we maintain this kind of fellowship, there cannot be disunity.

D. *Tenderness and compassion.* As we show our love toward one another and seek to bear one another's burdens, any lack of unity is bridged. The relationships we have with one another work against disunity and for unity of faith.

Conclusion

An ox and a colt both appeared at a watering hole at the same time. They fought over who had precedence—until they saw the vultures circling overhead awaiting the outcome of the fight. With so much at stake in Christian witness, we must have unity for Christ's sake.

SUNDAY MORNING, FEBRUARY 21

Title: The Church: You Are the Salt of the Earth

Text: "You are the salt of the earth. But if the salt loses its saltiness, how can it be made salty again?" **(Matt. 5:13 NIV).**

Scripture Reading: Matthew 5:1–13

Hymns: "Crown Him with Many Crowns," Bridges
             "Free from the Law," Bliss
             "Amazing Grace," Newton

Offertory Prayer: Holy Father, you are the giver of every good and perfect gift. Thank you for this beautiful Lord's Day and for all the blessings that come to us in it. Thank you for your holy Word and for its message to our lives. Thank you for the Holy Spirit who helps us in our understanding as well as in our ministries to others. Today we come bringing the gratitude of our heart, the praise of our lips, and the fruit of our labor. Accept these tithes and offerings and add your blessing to them so that others may come to know Jesus Christ. In his name we pray. Amen.

Introduction

The Sermon on the Mount was not given to provide guidelines to an unbelieving world; it was given to provide a description of the character of ideal kingdom citizens. When Jesus said, "You are the salt of the earth," he was speaking specifically to his disciples, those who were characterized by the virtues set forth in the verses we commonly call the Beatitudes (Matt. 5:3–9). The Beatitudes are not beautiful pious platitudes. They constitute a vivid description of the characteristics of ideal citizens of the kingdom of God.

Those who possess these spiritual characteristics will provoke a response from others around them. People who are ill-disposed toward God and his way of life will respond with persecution toward sincere followers of Jesus Christ (Matt. 5:10–11). Ideal kingdom citizens will have a wholesome effect on those who are well-disposed toward God by serving as the salt of the earth and the light of the world (Matt. 5:3–16). In Matthew 5:10–16 our Lord describes the negative and the positive responses of the unbelieving world toward his disciples.

Jesus was a master communicator. He used common experiences and objects to communicate great truths about God, about people, and about various roles and responsibilities. Salt was one common yet very significant metaphor Jesus used to describe the nature and function of his church. People living close to the sea could obtain plenty of salt, but people living inland often had to barter for it. Part of a Roman soldier's pay was given to him in salt, and it was called *salarium*. From this Latin word comes our word *salary*. Hence we can understand why salt was considered valuable.

Jesus expects his church to function as salt in the earth. Are you like salt? Or have you lost your saltiness?

I. As salt the church is very valuable.

The church is valuable to the heart of Father God and to the living Christ for the carrying forward of the work he began during his earthly ministry. As salt the church is also valuable to the community and to the world. Few people would want to live in a community where the influence of the church was not felt. It would be difficult for those of us in the Western world to fully evaluate the value the people of God have brought into our culture, our government, and our total way of life.

II. As salt the church is essential to the world's well-being.

Our Lord used this metaphor to describe the church's simple but essential function in the community. Salt performed a number of unique and significant functions.

A. *Salt was used as a condiment to add zest to food.* When foods, especially vegetables, taste flat and are in need of seasoning, more salt is the remedy. It is also a necessity for the health of the human body.

The ideal Christian and the ideal congregation will bring a beauty, fragrance, and flavor to the life of the community that will be wholesome and helpful.

B. *Salt was used as an antiseptic.* It was a cleansing agent that served the same function that peroxide or alcohol does today.

When the church is functioning as it should, it will perform a cleansing and antiseptic function in the community.

C. *Salt was used primarily as a preserver from decay.* Jesus and his disciples were close to the Sea of Galilee. All about them were the evidences of the fishing industry. When the newly caught fish were not used immediately, the fishermen would salt them or place them in brine to preserve them.

When the church is truly the church it will preserve the moral, spiritual, and cultural life of the community from decline and decay.

D. *Salt was a silent but positive force.* Salt does not make a great outward display and does not blow a trumpet concerning its presence. Salt simply and silently performs its function. It is a decisive and positive force. Jesus would have his church to be just as positive.

III. A warning concerning possible calamity.

Jesus points out the possibility of salt losing its saltiness. When this happens, it is of absolutely no value. It is dumped on the roadway where it cannot harm crops and will be crushed by traffic. Jesus used this powerful illustration to warn his disciples against the peril of losing their Christian witness and their Christian influence.

A. *Salt could lose its saltiness by isolation.* When you separate the crystalline grains of salt from each other, they lose their saltiness. The same is true with disciples of our Lord who separate themselves from the fellowship of believers and walk either in disobedience or in indifference and noninvolvement.

B. *Salt can lose its saltiness by contaminating contact with other substances.* If dirt or sawdust or some other substance is mixed with salt, it will lose its saltiness and will be unable to perform its unique function.

Believers are thus put on guard against letting attitudes and ambitions enter their hearts that would contaminate their lives, destroying their influence and preventing them from being the distinctive followers of Jesus Christ that they were called to be.

C. *If we are to retain our true saltiness and perform our true ministry, we must stay close to the attitudes expressed in the Beatitudes and let Jesus be the Lord of our lives.* We must make a positive response to the cleansing fire of the Holy Spirit so that he can purge out attitudes and actions that would contaminate our lives and ruin our witness.

Conclusion

Putting a lump of salt on your tongue will intensify your thirst for water. Being a genuine follower of Jesus Christ will cause your life to function as the salt that creates thirst for the living water found only in Jesus Christ. Salt performs many functions, but it does not have the power to give new life. Only Jesus Christ can do that. The Holy Spirit will use the witness of those who are the salt of the earth to create a thirst in the hearts of unbelievers to know the Savior. Apart from his church, our Lord has no program by which the service that we are intended to render can be accomplished. "You are the salt of the earth."

SUNDAY EVENING, FEBRUARY 21

Title: The Mountain Mover

Text: "If ye have faith as a grain of mustard seed, ye shall say unto this mountain, Remove hence to yonder place; and it shall remove; and nothing shall be impossible unto you" **(Matt. 17:20).**

Scripture Reading: Matthew 16:14–21

Introduction

A canvas of Raphael depicts a commentary on the scene found in our text. The painter portrayed the glorious Mount of Transfiguration and the frustration of events in the valley below with one picture. Beneath the mountain is a father, his epileptic son, and nine humiliated disciples. The disciples, unable to heal the boy, point upward to the Master.

While three disciples enjoyed the splendor of the transfigured Christ on the mountain, nine others experienced disappointment over their inability to heal a man's epileptic son. The disciples represent how people try to remove difficulties without an openness to God.

Jesus used this episode to teach the disciples an important lesson on the necessity of faith. Jesus talked of removing a "mountain," a word the Jews often used to refer to life's difficulties. Let's look at various aspects of life's difficulties and how we can face them.

I. The malady of mountains.

The man with an epileptic son had a mountain in his life. Caring for the boy daily was difficult, and he desired for someone to remove his mountain. Difficulties are not restricted to a few. They are universal.

A. *Inward difficulties.* Many people have inward difficulties, such as guilt, anxiety, depression, or frustration. They cannot make sense out of life. An emptiness abounds. They want this mountain to be moved.

B. *Outward mountains.* Maladies come from outside sources. Often people have to care for a loved one who has a handicap or illness. Some have difficulties with their family and work relationships. Some are victims of the mistakes, foolishness, or violence of others. Many are hurt by the harsh words or cruel deeds of malicious people. Maybe you have some other mountain that you want to be removed.

II. Mistakes in mountain moving.

The disciples made a mistake in seeking to remove the mountain: They tried to do it with human strength. We, too, make mistakes in moving our mountains.

A. *Escape the mountain.* Some look at the difficulties that face them and try to escape through drugs, alcohol, sex, gambling, or some other avenue.

B. *Magnify the mountain.* Often people look at some personal difficulty and make a mountain out of a hill. Small, petty problems can be blown out of proportion.

C. *Climb the mountain.* We make a mistake when we try to master our difficulties with human strength. We cannot deal with the burdens of life without God's help.

III. Mastery of mountains.

The man mastered his difficulty when he went to Jesus. The Lord healed the boy and then rebuked the disciples for their lack of faith.

A. *A relationship with the Lord.* The mastery of difficulties begins with a relationship with Jesus Christ. To trust the Lord removes life's greatest problem—the sin problem.

B. *A continued expression of faith.* Faith does not always remove the obstacles or difficulties. Whatever situation or difficulty a Christian faces, it can be mastered by an openness to the Lord.

Conclusion

The man with an epileptic son met an unusual person in Jesus Christ— a mountain mover. Whatever your difficulty is, you can relate to the Mountain Mover. Trust in him.

WEDNESDAY EVENING, FEBRUARY 24

Title: The Most Unforgettable Character: Christ

Text: "Being found in fashion as a man, he humbled himself, and became obedient unto death, even the death of the cross" **(Phil. 2:8).**

Scripture Reading: Philippians 2:5–11

Introduction

Reader's Digest used to carry a regular feature entitled "The Most Unforgettable Character I Have Met." Sometimes these characters were world-famous people; other times they were known by few outside their own family. But they all had something in common—for some reason they could not be forgotten.

The testimony of every Christian should be "The most unforgettable character I have ever met is the Lord Jesus Christ." Every salvation experience is the experience of meeting Christ and giving one's life to him. The Christian life itself is a continuous process of trying to mold one's life into the pattern of Christ's. If Jesus is that important to us, we must learn all we can about him. If his life has so radically altered ours, we ought to be intimately familiar with his life.

These verses from Philippians come about as close as any in the Scriptures to a systematic statement about the person of Christ. Interestingly, they were not written as a theological statement but as an illustration. Paul called for unity. For unity to come about, each Christian would have to be as humble as Jesus was willing to be as he assumed human form.

I. Christ is the most unforgettable person because of his preexistence (vv. 5–6).

The preexistence of Christ means that he existed before he was born at Bethlehem. This is a mystery of faith. We cannot explain how Christ existed as God before he was born to a virgin in Bethlehem.

A. *The* fact *of his preexistence.* Consider the butterfly. When you look at its beauty, you can hardly believe that it once existed as a caterpillar. It was just the reverse with Christ; his glory was before and his exaltation will come later.

B. *The* manner *of his preexistence.* He existed in the form of God. He had the essential deity of God and was equal to the Father God. He shared in the glory of God yet was willing to give it up to become a man. He set aside the outward glories without giving up his essential oneness with the Father.

C. *The* attitude *that possessed his mind.* He was willing to renounce his rights, privileges, prerogatives, and claims for our sake that he might bring us salvation.

II. Christ is the most unforgettable person because of his incarnation (vv. 7–8).

A. *The reality of the Incarnation.* Incarnation means being clothed in flesh. Jesus emptied himself of the glories of deity and clothed himself in flesh; he became a man. In relation to God he became a servant. He suffered and was tempted and anguished just like any other human. Yet he was still God.

B. *The aim of the Incarnation.* By becoming a human, Jesus could have a sympathetic heart with people. He could know human problems firsthand. But his aim is seen most completely in the statement of his obedience, an obedience that led even to the cross. We can see the extent of God's love when we see the extent of Christ's obedience. We were in sin, and something had to be done for us. That something was done in Christ's death for us.

If a person jumped in the ocean and swam out to another person when nothing was wrong, it would be folly. But if one were drowning and another jumped in, swam to him, and rescued him, it would be an act of love. That is what Jesus did for us.

III. Christ is the most unforgettable person because of his exaltation (vv. 9–11).

A. *Christ is exalted because of his redemptive deed.*
B. *His exaltation is absolute.* His lordship is universal, and he wants to be Lord in every area of our lives.

Conclusion

The most unforgettable person ever is Jesus Christ. He can be unforgettable to you as you make him Lord of your life.

SUNDAY MORNING, FEBRUARY 28

Title: Water into Wine

Text: "And he saith unto them, Draw some out now, and bear unto the governor of the feast" **(John 2:8).**

Scripture Reading: John 2:1–11

Hymns:　　"To God Be the Glory," Crosby
　　　　　　"I Love to Tell the Story," Hankey
　　　　　　"O, for a Thousand Tongues to Sing," Wesley

Offertory Prayer: Heavenly Father, we thank you for the privilege of being in your house with your people today for worship. We thank you for the new opportunities and responsibilities we will face during this coming week. We bring our tithes and gifts of our love today, offering ourselves afresh to you. Help us day by day to give ourselves in ministries of mercy to others. Accept and bless these gifts for the advancement of your kingdom's work in the world. In Christ's name we pray. Amen.

Introduction

I believe in miracles for at least four reasons: (1) I believe in the theistic view of the world. God is, God made this world, and God sustains this world. (2) I believe in Jesus Christ, the only begotten divine Son of God. Jesus Christ is a supernatural person who does supernatural works. (3) I believe in salvation through faith in Jesus Christ. Salvation from sin by Jesus Christ enables me to believe in miracles. It took a miracle to save me. (4) I believe that the miraculous element is vital to the Gospels; if you remove the miracles, you have very little of value left.

What is a miracle? Someone said, "A miracle is an occurrence in the natural order worked by a supernatural power." Dr. W. T. Conner said, "A miracle is the injection of the will of God into the natural or human order in such a way as to bring about a result which would be impossible without this special injection of the will of God."

Jesus' turning water into wine at a wedding in Cana was his first recorded miracle. "This beginning of miracles did Jesus in Cana of Galilee" (John 2:11). This miracle is recorded by John alone. There is no parallel in the Synoptic Gospels.

Let's note three aspects of our Lord's first recorded miracle.

I. The setting of the turning of the water into wine was a home in Cana of Galilee (John 2:1–5).

Jesus' first miracle took place at a wedding in a home in Cana of Galilee. Cana was five miles northeast of Nazareth. It is mentioned four times in John's gospel (2:1–11; 4:36–54; 2:12) and nowhere else in the Bible. Cana was the home of Nathanael, and it was in Cana that Jesus announced to the nobleman the healing of his dying son.

The home in which Jesus' first miracle took place was a meager home; thus, the wine supply was limited. The wedding was in the home of the bride, but the feast was provided by the bridegroom. The ruler was a guest who had been asked to preside. Mary, Jesus, and his disciples John, Andrew, Simon, Philip, and Nathanael were invited guests.

The miracle took place on the third day of the party (John 2:1) after the calling of Jesus' first disciples. When the wedding party lacked wine, Mary said to Jesus: "They have no wine" (v. 2). Jesus replied, "Woman, what have I to do with thee? Mine hour is not yet come" (v. 4). It is reasonable to believe that Mary expected a miracle. However, it was customary for guests to make contributions to such feasts.

When Jesus said: "Mine hour is not yet come," he was indicating that the time of his manifestation as Messiah had not yet come. Mary said to the servants: "Whatever he saith unto you, do it" (v. 5). She was confident that he would not allow the distress of the situation to go unheeded.

II. The symbolism of the turning of the water into wine (John 2:6–8).

John tells us there were six stone waterpots at the home in Cana of Galilee. Each would hold approximately twenty to twenty-seven gallons of water. The pots were used for the ceremonial cleansing of hands (v. 6; cf. 2 Kings 3:11; Mark 7:3).

Jesus said to the servants, "Fill the waterpots with water." And they filled them up to the brim (v. 7). Then Jesus commanded: "Draw out now, and bear unto the governor of the feast" (v. 8).

What is the meaning of all this? Is there any symbolism involved? Surely Jesus' first miracle means more than that he relieved the host from embarrassment.

The six waterpots for the purifying of the Jews perhaps represent the Jewish legalistic ritual of dealing with the sin problem by endless washings. The number six is one short of seven, the perfect and complete number. Jewish legalism had fallen short. Filling the pots to the brim probably symbolized the fulfillment of the law by Jesus (Matt. 5:17).

The superior wine made by Jesus and served to the ruler teaches us that what Jesus has to offer is superior to all others. He imparts the life of the Spirit. He is superior to the Jewish legalistic system and supplies supernaturally something that supersedes that system.

III. The significance of the turning of the water into wine (John 2:9–11).

The significance of the turning of water into wine is at least fivefold.

A. *The turning of water into wine reveals Christ's creative power (1:3).* We do not know exactly when or how this miracle took place. We do know that Jesus silently put forth his will and the water turned into wine.

B. *The turning of water into wine reveals Christ's purpose to hallow family life.* Jesus performed his first miracle in a home, not in a temple or synagogue. This is the last place one would expect him to perform his first miracle. By performing his first miracle in a home, Jesus hallowed every corner of family life, home life.

C. *The turning of water into wine reveals Christ's glory (2:11).* The disciples saw his glory, his divine person manifested. How? By his command and control of nature; by his impact on the ruler of the feast, the bridegroom, and the bride; and by performing a miracle that would radiate his glory forever.

D. *The turning of water into wine reveals Christ's self-sufficiency.* Jesus has power to meet our needs, our shortages in life. We can come with our cups of need and let him fill them. He can satisfy the hunger and thirst of every soul who longs for him.

E. *The turning of water into wine reveals better things to come (v. 10).* The world gives its best first. Jesus' gifts become sweeter, better with each passing day. The last is better than the first. When we die and go to heaven, we will find it better than words can describe and better than we had ever dreamed it should be. "Thou hast kept the good wine until now" (v. 10).

Conclusion

Jesus is a miracle worker. He can turn water into wine, and he can work a miracle in your life. Let him do it today! He offers you his best!

SUNDAY EVENING, FEBRUARY 28

Title: The Greatest Teacher

Text: "Master, we know that thou art true, and teachest the way of God in truth, neither carest thou for any man: for thou regardest not the person of men" **(Matt. 22:16).**

Scripture Reading: Matthew 22:15–22

Introduction

Even if Jesus had no other claim to fame, he would be regarded as one of the world's greatest teachers. Friends and foes alike called him "Teacher." When some cynics came to Jesus with a testing question, they began by saying, "Master, we know that thou art true, and teachest the way of God in truth" (Matt. 22:16).

In the gospel narratives Jesus is called "teacher" more than fifty times. Jesus devoted large portions of his time and strength to the ministry of teaching. One cannot study the life of Jesus without a consideration of his teaching ministry. Studying the Master's teaching method will open for us a new window on Jesus himself. We will also have an impact on the world if we seriously consider and faithfully practice Jesus' teachings.

Let's take note of the reasons why Jesus is the greatest teacher.

I. He has something valuable to say.

Some teachers use good techniques but say little of value. Jesus, however, had something vital to say.

A. *Universal appeal.* What Jesus taught applied to everyone. One of the most amazing characteristics of Jesus' subject matter was its universal appeal. He spoke with scholars in the temple and synagogue. He rode in boats and conversed with fishermen. He walked the streets and roads teaching people. One of the gospel writers says, "The common people heard him gladly" (Mark 12:37).

B. *Ultimate issues.* Other teachers speak of important issues. We cannot discount the importance of teaching language, science, geography, mathematics, and other subjects. But Jesus taught about vital life issues. Every generation seeks to know Who am I? Why am I here? Where am I going? People related to Jesus because he spoke words they desperately needed to hear.

II. He knows how to say it.

Having something to say and knowing how to say it make a beautiful combination. Jesus had something to say, and he used effective techniques to get his message across.

A. *The figurative element.* Jesus taught in such a way that his message was immediately arresting, readily intelligible, and permanently memorable. To accomplish this, he used the figurative element in his teaching. He used impressionable epigrams, phrases that hit the mind and stick (cf. Matt. 16:26; 23:12; Luke 12:15). He also utilized humor.

One prominent element in Jesus' teaching was the parable. The simple story is one of the most ancient and most useful teaching methods. Jesus' parables had the power to put the deep truths of God in a simple, appealing manner.

B. *The freedom element.* Jesus was an authoritative teacher. He did not depend on tradition. Nor did he have to buttress his teaching with quotes from other teachers. Though Jesus was authoritative, he did not force his teachings on anyone, but allowed others to follow him at will.

III. He embodies what he teaches.

Many teachers can communicate effectively to students in a classroom setting. Few, however, have the ability to combine what they teach with what they do. For example, most coaches I know are good coaches, but they are not outstanding athletes. Jesus embodied what he taught in living.

A. *The example for others.* Jesus lived out his lessons for others. He taught his followers to forgive injuries from others, and he forgave wholeheartedly. He taught the importance of prayer and prayed all night long. He spoke of the necessity for service and self-sacrifice, and he took up a towel and washed his disciples' feet. He made orations about brotherhood and went to the homes of the despised and sat at their tables and called them friends and brothers. Jesus furnishes a live example of his teaching in action.

B. *The energy for ourselves.* Other teachers tell what to do, but they cannot give the energy to do it. Jesus tells us how to live, and he lives within us by his Spirit to provide energy for accomplishing God's will.

Conclusion

You have an opportunity to learn under life's greatest teacher, Jesus Christ. He invites you to enroll in his school. You can enlist today. Open your life to him in faith.

MARCH

■ **Sunday Mornings**

Complete the four-part study "The Miracle Working Power of Our Lord." Then on Palm Sunday begin a series entitled "Our Great Redeemer and Our Great Redemption." The death of Christ and his resurrection should be prominent in our preaching program at all times.

■ **Sunday Evenings**

Continue the series "Great Truths About Christ That Make a Real Difference."

■ **Wednesday Evenings**

Continue the series "A Pathway Through Philippians."

WEDNESDAY EVENING, MARCH 3

Title: Our Responsibility in Obedience

Text: "Wherefore, my beloved, as ye have always obeyed, not as in my presence only, but now much more in my absence, work out your own salvation with fear and trembling" **(Phil. 2:12).**

Scripture Reading: Philippians 2:12–18

Introduction

In one of the many art galleries of Europe there is an old Greek statue of Apollo that is a beautiful figure of physical perfection. Someone visiting the gallery said he did not know which impressed him more, to look at the statue or to watch the crowd as they looked. Invariably, he said, everyone who stood before it, even for a casual glance, began to straighten up, put back his or her shoulders, and stand tall. The statue has the lifting power of loftiness.

This is something of the sensation we have as we read the lofty description of the journey of Christ from glory to the cross and back to glory by way of the cross. Paul gave us this marvelous description of the grace and glory of Christ as an appeal to unity. He wanted us to have the mind of Christ, an attitude of humility and service. For his obedience he received the exaltation of God.

Paul went back to exhortation and appeal in verse 12, picking up from verse 8 as a point of reference. Christ was obedient even to the cross. We are to be obedient also.

I. Our responsibility for obedience shows in the certainty of salvation (vv. 12–13).

Obedience to God is manifested in salvation. When Paul exhorts us, "Work out your own salvation," it sounds strange to our ears, for Paul is the one who insisted that salvation is wholly by grace. Two things must be kept in mind: (1) He said "work *out*" not "work *for*." Salvation is by grace. (2) Paul was referring to the final result of the salvation we enjoy in Christ.

Salvation is wholly accomplished in the work of Jesus Christ. In verse 13 Paul asserted that it is God who works within us. Although salvation is entirely a gift from God, we must cooperate with God in obedience and faith in order to receive it.

How are we to go about working out the salvation that God has given us, bringing to a final conclusion the results of God's grace? A constructive fear of God keeps us from perilous self-confidence. Spurgeon told of a servant girl who gave as the proof of her conversion that now she swept under the mats and behind the door. This is a proper combination of awe and responsibility, fear and trembling.

II. Our responsibility for obedience shows up in the splendor of salvation (vv. 14–15).

Paul's exhortation in verse 14 is, "Do all things without murmurings and disputings." His reason is in verse 15, "that. . .in the midst of a crooked and perverse nation. . .ye shine as lights in the world." That is the splendor of salvation—that Christians shine in a world of darkness and perversity.

Paul has given us three ways in verse 15 that show how we are to shine as lights in the world: We are to be "blameless," "harmless," and "without rebuke." To the world Christians should be blameless. Their lives should be so pure that no one can find blame in them. In themselves Christians should be harmless. Literally the word used here means unmixed or unadulterated. When used of people it implies absolute sincerity. In the sight of God Christians are without rebuke. They should be able to withstand even the scrutiny of God.

III. Our responsibility for obedience shows up in the service of salvation (vv. 16–18).

What is our service? We are to hold forth the word of life by proclaiming God's message of salvation and by demonstrating Christian living. If we do this, our lives will have purpose and will not have been in vain. Paul uses two very vivid pictures to show this. One has to do with athletics and the other with religion. He does not want to train as an athlete and then find that he has run in vain. He does not mind sacrificing his life to serve God.

What is the result of this kind of service in salvation? Joy and rejoicing in life.

Conclusion

We have a responsibility to be obedient to God. And as we are obedient to him, we will have real joy in life.

SUNDAY MORNING, MARCH 7

Title: The Feeding of the Five Thousand

Text: "There is a lad here, who hath five barley loaves and two small fishes. . . .And Jesus took the loaves; and when he had given thanks, he distributed to the disciples, and the disciples to them that were set down; and likewise of the fishes as much as they would. When they were filled, he said unto his disciples, Gather up the fragments that remain, that nothing be lost" **(John 6:9, 11–12).**

Scripture Reading: John 6:1–15

Hymns: "My Faith Looks Up to Thee," Palmer
"Christ Receiveth Sinful Men," Neumeister
"Though Your Sins Be As Scarlet," Crosby

Offertory Prayer: Heavenly Father, you have been so generous in bestowing your good gifts upon us. We thank you for the gift of membership in your family. We thank you for granting to us the forgiveness of our sin. We thank you for the gift of new life. We thank you for sending your Holy Spirit to dwell in our hearts. We come today bringing tithes and offerings as tokens of our desire to give ourselves completely into your service. We pray your blessings upon these gifts to the end that others might come to know your mercy and grace and the redeeming power of the Lord Jesus Christ. It is in his name we pray. Amen.

Introduction

The feeding of the five thousand is the only miracle of Jesus recorded in all four Gospels (Matt. 14:15–21; Mark 6:30–44; Luke 9:10–17; John 6:1–13). It took place one year before Jesus' crucifixion, shortly before the Passover (John 6:4). The Feast of the Passover was celebrated on the first month of the religious year, the fourteenth day of Nisan (April). It commemorated the deliverance of the Jews from Egypt and the establishment of Israel as a nation by God's redemptive act. Let's look at this great miracle.

I. The scene of the feeding of the five thousand.

The feeding of the five thousand took place on a grassy mountainside, in the spring of the year, near Bethsaida, northeast of the Sea of Galilee. Bethsaida is known also as Bethsaida Julius. Matthew said it was a "remote place" (Matt. 14:15 NIV).

Great crowds, including people on their way to Jerusalem to attend the Passover Feast, came to hear Jesus (John 6:4). He was already popular because of his previous miracles (v. 2). When Jesus saw the multitude, "he was moved with compassion toward them, because they were as sheep not having a shepherd" (Mark 6:34).

These excited people greatly needed teaching. The crowds had plenty of official leaders, but their rabbis were spiritually blind leaders of the blind.

II. The shrewdness of the Savior in the feeding of the five thousand.

Jesus said to Philip: "Whence shall we buy bread, that these may eat? And this he said to prove him; for he himself knew what he would do" (John 6:5–6). Philip said: "Two hundred pennyworth [denarii] of bread is not sufficient for them, that every one of them may take a little" (v. 7). One denarius equals sixteen cents, so about thirty-two dollars would not feed the five thousand plus the women and the children. Philip had his eyes fixed on the tangible and lost sight of the intangible of faith.

Andrew said, "There is a lad here, which hath five barley loaves, and two small fishes: but what are they among so many?" (John 6:9). Jesus replied, "Make the men sit down. Now there was much grass in the place. So the men sat down, in number about five thousand" (v. 10).

The disciples were helpless to supply food for the five thousand, but the powerful Savior could multiply the boy's meal to feed five thousand.

III. The supply of the Savior and the satisfaction of the five thousand.

A. *The supply of the Savior.* Jesus did three things:
1. He looked up (Matt. 14:19). Those who have hungry souls to feed will need to look up often. This bread must come down from heaven (Matt. 4:4).
2. He blessed (Matt. 14:19). The disciples could see nothing worthy of special thanks, but Jesus believed that having asked he had received (Mark 11:24).
3. He gave (Matt. 14:19). The one who looks up and blesses will have something to give.

B. *The satisfaction of the multitude.* "They were filled" (John 6:12). "They did all eat, and were filled" (Matt. 14:20). Jesus alone can satisfy the hungry multitudes. Psalm 107:9 says: "For he satisfieth the longing soul, and filleth the hungry soul with goodness." The Lord can and is eager to meet every need of the multitude, every need of the individual.

IV. The significance of the feeding of the five thousand.

A. *Some wanted to make Jesus a king.* "When Jesus therefore perceived that they would come and take him by force, to make him a king, he departed again into a mountain himself alone" (John 6:15). The crowd was looking for the wrong kind of king. They wanted to start a revolution and get rid of Pilate and the Roman yoke. Jesus came to be a Savior, not a political messiah.

B. *Jesus used the miracle to teach that he is the Bread of Life (John 6:25–27, 33, 35).*
C. *Jesus puts problems before us to settle, but we cannot settle them without him.* Jesus is necessary for the solutions to life's problems.
D. *Jesus makes use of little gifts.* He can multiply what we have and use it.
E. *Jesus is sufficient for all emergencies (John 6:11).*

Conclusion

If you are not saved, it is not because Jesus lacks power, nor because there is not enough saving power for all. The twelve baskets left over will be a swift witness against the unbeliever.

Why will you go away without him? He can meet your deepest needs. He can save you from your sins. Let him do it today!

SUNDAY EVENING, MARCH 7

Title: The Cross of Christ

Text: "Carrying his own cross, he went out to the place of the Skull which in Aramaic is called Golgotha. Here they crucified him, and with him two others—one on each side and Jesus in the middle" **(John 19:17–18 NIV).**

Scripture Reading: John 19:13–24

Introduction

In 1960 the motion picture industry benefited Christianity with the epic production of Lew Wallace's novel *Ben Hur.* This story stands in a class by itself. It is a blending of one fictional character named Ben-Hur with the historical character of Jesus Christ. Though many people talk about the chariot race scene in the movie, I continue to marvel over the presentation of Jesus' life. I am especially impressed by the crucifixion scene, which caused me to look at the cross with greater seriousness.

The cross was a profound event in the life and ministry of Jesus Christ. In today's message we will look at some words that describe Jesus' crucifixion.

I. Voluntary.

The cross of Jesus Christ was no accidental occurrence. Nor was it a trap set by treacherous people. He voluntarily laid down his life. The Lord invites people to volunteer for the cross today.

A. *Jesus volunteered for the cross.* The death of Jesus came as no surprise to him. As we look over his ministry, we can see the evidence that he knew about his forthcoming death. His victory over temptation meant that he would be God's kind of Messiah, a suffering servant. He revealed information about his crucifixion and resurrection to his disciples on several occasions.

Luke makes the voluntary nature of the cross explicit. "And it came to pass, when the time was come that he should be received up, he stedfastly set his face to go to Jerusalem" (Luke 9:51). During Jesus' earthly ministry, his enemies made many attempts to kill him, but he avoided them saying, "My hour is not yet come." When Jesus felt the time had arrived, he volunteered for the cross.

B. *Jesus invites people to volunteer.* Whenever Jesus spoke of discipleship, he used a figure of the cross. "If any man will come after me, let him deny himself, and take up his cross, and follow me" (Matt. 16:24). Jesus will not place a cross on anyone. The cross represents death to self-will, self-trust, and self-assertion. One has to volunteer for discipleship.

II. Vicarious.

The cross of Jesus Christ was a vicarious death, a deed done for others. The Lord invites people to involve themselves in a life for him and for others.

A. *Jesus died for others.* Paul wrote, "Christ died for our sins according to the scriptures" (1 Cor. 15:3). It is important to remember what the word "for" means. It does not mean that Christ died in our place. It means "on behalf of," or "for the sake of." Jesus died to do something on behalf of our sins.

The New Testament records four images of what Christ did for our sins. First, he redeemed people from the slavery of sin (cf. Mark 10:45). Second, he defeated the powers of evil (cf. Col. 2:15). Third, he made the final sacrifice for sin (cf. Heb. 2:8–10, 17). Fourth, he reconciled erring humanity to a righteous God (2 Cor. 5:16–21).

B. *Jesus bids people to live for others.* Jesus urges potential disciples that the highest life is one lived for others. "For whosoever will save his life shall lose it: and whosoever will lose his life for my sake shall find it" (Matt. 16:25). Jesus gave his life for others, and he urges his disciples to do the same.

III. Vicious.

The cross of Jesus is one of the most brutal scenes of history. The Son of God suffered enormous pain. The life of a Christian is also one of suffering.

A. *Jesus endured the suffering.* No historian can describe the suffering encountered by dying on a cross. Hours before the pain of the cross, Jesus was scourged. This was a harsh beating from which many people died. Moreover, Jesus suffered mental torture, for his disciples had deserted him at Calvary.

B. *Jesus invites followers to adversity.* When Jesus asks people to follow him, it is not to a life of ease. It is to a cross. This means that when one dares to live for God, suffering will occur.

IV. Victorious.

Contrary to the thinking of the world, the cross of Jesus means victory. Of course the cross was not good news until the Resurrection. The Lord wants people to participate in the victorious life.

A. *Jesus defeated sin and death at Calvary.* The work of Jesus on Calvary dealt a death blow to sin and death. No one can imagine all that Jesus has done to defeat the powers of sin and death. Three days after his death he emerged from the tomb as "victor from the dark domain."

B. *Jesus invites people to share the victory.* Since Jesus Christ conquered sin and death by dying on the cross and rising again to life, we can draw on him for victorious power over sin. His resurrection also assures those who identify with him in faith of victory over the grave.

Conclusion

No movie can give us a sufficient understanding of what it means to have a relationship with Jesus Christ. We must find out for ourselves by asking him to be our Savior and Lord.

WEDNESDAY EVENING, MARCH 10

Title: Adequacy in Christian Service

Text: "But I trust in the Lord Jesus to send Timotheus shortly unto you, that I also may be of good comfort, when I know your state. For I have no man likeminded, who will naturally care for your state. For all seek their own, not the things which are Jesus Christ's" **(Phil. 2:19–21).**

Scripture Reading: Philippians 2:19–30

Introduction

Dr. Daniel Poling was for many years editor of the *Christian Herald* and president of Christian Endeavor International. He had a son who was also a minister. He was one of the four chaplains who went down on the ship *Dorchester* not far from the British coast in the early days of World War II. The four chaplains who went down with the ship gave their lifebelts to others when there were not enough to go around. Before the ship had set sail, he had written a letter to his family in which he said, "I know I shall have your prayers; but please don't pray simply that God will keep me safe. War is dangerous business. Pray that God will make me adequate."

We ought always to pray for adequacy in service to Christ. Paul showed us the meaning of adequacy in Christian service in the way he commended his fellow laborers Timothy and Epaphroditus to the church at Philippi.

I. Adequacy in Christian service demands a sympathetic person.

Notice in verse 20 that Paul gives Timothy a signal commendation. He said that no one else he could send to the church would care for them as he would. Timothy could sympathize with others and have a real concern for them and their problems.

To sympathize means to feel for others in their troubles. A little girl was once late in returning home and her mother began to get concerned about her. When she did come home, her mother asked her what had happened that made her late. She replied that her friend Mary had broken her doll. Then her mother asked why that had caused her to be late. She said that she had stopped to help Mary cry over her broken doll.

II. Adequacy in Christian service demands a selfless person.

The commendation in verse 21 is the highest that can be given to a Christian servant. He or she seeks the things of Christ. Timothy was a man who always looked for the highest good that could come to the Christian cause. Too often the first question people ask is what good something can do for them.

Missionary pioneer Henry Martyn said, "I go to burn out for Christ." Not only does this kind of selfless service place the cause of Christ above personal gain but it also places the cause of Christ above life itself. The reference in verse 30 is to Epaphroditus, who "not regarding his [own] life," supported Paul.

Epaphroditus was sent with a message and a gift from the church at Philippi to Paul in Rome, where Paul was imprisoned. While Epaphroditus was there he got very sick, "nigh unto death." He apparently got homesick, too, but Paul sent him back home with a tremendous testimonial of his worth.

The word translated "not regarding his [own] life" was a gambling term. In the early church there was an association of "gamblers," men and women who visited those who were sick with dangerous and infectious diseases. In A.D. 252 when the plague broke out in Carthage, the heathens threw out the bodies of their dead and fled. Cyprian, the Christian bishop, gathered his congregation and set them to burying the dead and nursing the sick in the plague-ridden city. At the risk of their own lives they saved the city from destruction.

III. Adequacy in Christian service demands a seasoned person.

Seasoning enables us to do our tasks with competence and efficiency. It means that we are responsible for being faithful to the task. It does not, however, mean that we are responsible for the results.

A farmer hired a worker and asked him for his qualifications. The man responded by saying that he could sleep during a storm. Shortly thereafter a storm came. Not sure that the hired hand had done his job, the farmer got up in the stormy night to check the stock, the doors, and the locks. Finding everything secure, he remembered the hired hand's remark that he could sleep in a storm.

Conclusion

Adequacy in Christian service is greatly to be desired. Let's pray that God will make us adequate.

SUNDAY MORNING, MARCH 14

Title: The Paralytic Borne of Four

Text: "When Jesus saw their faith, he said unto the sick of the palsy, Son, thy sins are forgiven thee" **(Mark 2:5).**

Scripture Reading: Mark 2:1–12

Hymns: "Great Redeemer, We Adore Thee," Harris
"Majestic Sweetness Sits Enthroned," Stennett
"I Know That My Redeemer Liveth," Pounds

Offertory Prayer: Holy Father, today we come praying for eyes that can see the bounty of your blessings upon us. We also pray for eyes that can see the world's need of the Savior. Help us day by day to give our testimony to others and to accept a lifestyle that will show them that Jesus Christ makes a difference. Today we bring our tithes and offerings that the gospel might be preached not only here but to the ends of the earth. We pray your blessings on all the institutions, agencies, and people that these offerings help. In Jesus' name we pray. Amen.

Introduction

The miracle of the healing of the man with palsy who was brought by four friends into Jesus' presence is recorded in Matthew 9:1–8, Mark 2:1–12, and Luke 5:17–26. G. Campbell Morgan points out that this is the first occasion on record where Jesus declared a man's sins to be forgiven. Jesus' authority was immediately challenged by the scribes (Mark 2:7).

This paralytic's healing took place in Capernaum, a village Matthew calls Jesus' "own town" (9:1 NIV). Jesus made his headquarters in Capernaum during his ministry in Galilee and performed many miracles there, including the healing of the centurion's palsied servant (Matt. 8:5–13); the healing of the nobleman's son (John 4:46–54); and the healing of the paralytic borne of four (Mark 2:1–12).

Crowds surrounded Jesus while he was preaching in Capernaum (Mark 2:2). The house, the doorways, and the yard were packed. During the course of his preaching an unusual thing took place. Four friends of a paralytic let him down through the roof of the home into Jesus' presence. When Jesus saw their faith, he said: "Son, thy sins be forgiven thee" (Mark 2:5).

Let's examine some great truths that come to us from the paralytic's healing.

I. Sinners are helpless.

Mark describes the man as "one sick of the palsy" (Mark 2:3). He could not walk because of his paralysis, and it had ruined his life. The man's disability was the result of a moral malady. Jesus said, "Son, thy *sins* be forgiven thee" (Mark 2:5). No doubt the man had tried doctors to no avail. Thus, Jesus spoke to him about his sins. Because of his sins, he was wretched, helpless, and hopeless. All sinners are. Sin paralyzes sinners so that they cannot help themselves; only Jesus can set them free.

II. Sinners need those who will bring them to Jesus.

The paralytic had at least four friends. And evidently they were the right kind of friends, for they told him of One who could set him free of his infirmity.

Jesus said three things to the paralytic: "Son, be of good cheer" (Matt. 9:2); "Thy sins be forgiven thee" (v. 2); and "Arise, take up thy bed, and go unto thine house" (v. 6).

Bringing someone to Jesus is the greatest thing a friend can do for another.

III. Hindrances must be overcome for one to come to Jesus.

Hindrances often keep people from coming to Jesus.

A. *People can stand in the way of other people coming to Jesus.* Mark says, "They could not come near him because of the crowd" (2:4 RSV). You would have expected these people to step aside and let this man and his friends into Jesus' presence.

B. *Property can stand in the way of people coming to Jesus.* This home probably belonged to Simon Peter. To get the palsied man to Jesus, the four men had to tear up Peter's roof.

C. *Propriety can stand in the way of people coming to Jesus.* Webster defines propriety as being proper or fitting. The four friends of the paralytic did the improper thing when they tore up the roof to let the man down into Jesus' presence.

D. *Religious leaders can stand in the way of people coming to Jesus.* The Pharisees and scribes did not want this man to be healed or saved. They did not believe that Jesus was God, and they were blinded by their prejudice. They were enemies rather than friends of Jesus.

Well-meaning people are often wrong. They stand in the way of others coming to Jesus. There are still religious leaders today who do not understand Jesus, who witness against him and stand in the way of others coming to him.

Conclusion

Don't be afraid of Jesus. When he spoke to the paralytic, he used the word *teknon,* which means child. Jesus spoke tenderly to the paralytic as he would have spoken to a child. Only Jesus can say to you, "Thy sins be forgiven" (Mark 2:5). Trust him now for salvation, healing, and a victorious life!

SUNDAY EVENING, MARCH 14

Title: The Difference of the Resurrection

Text: "Then the same day at evening, being the first day of the week, when the doors were shut where the disciples were assembled for fear of the Jews, came Jesus and stood in their midst, and saith unto them, Peace be unto you. And when he had so said, he shewed unto them his hands and his side. Then were the disciples glad, when they saw the Lord" **(John 20:19–20)**.

Scripture Reading: John 20:13–23

Introduction

In John Masefield's drama *The Trial of Jesus,* there is a striking passage in which Longinus, the Roman centurion in command of the soldiers of the cross, comes back to Pilate to hand in his report of the day's work. After Longinus gives the report, Procula, Pilate's wife, asks the centurion to tell her how the prisoner died. She asks, "Do you think he is dead?"

"No, lady," answers Longinus, "I don't."

"Then where is he?"

"Let loose in the world, lady, where neither Roman nor Jew can stop his truth."

We have followed Jesus to the cross in our series of messages. We paused under the shadow of the cross but knew that it was not the end. Jesus' resurrection made the difference for his disciples and for us. Conscientious meditation on the resurrection of Jesus Christ can give us new perspectives for living.

I. The Resurrection assures us of a living Christ.

A. *Jesus assured the early disciples of his presence.* Jesus showed himself to the apostles to satisfy them of the reality of his resurrection. Later he appeared to Thomas to convince him.

Scripture records eleven different appearances of Jesus during the forty days between the Resurrection and Ascension. Reading the narratives of the appearances of the risen Christ, we are struck with the fact that the Christ whom people saw was certainly the same person they had known days earlier.

B. *Jesus continues to assure people of his continued presence.* If Christ is risen, people can continue to encounter him. R. W. Dale, a great preacher from Birmingham, England, described how one day, while he was writing an Easter sermon, the fact of the Resurrection broke in upon him as it never had before. The reality of the Resurrection came as a burst of sudden glory. He said, "Christ is alive!" Then he paused—"Alive!" And paused again—"Alive!" This reality made a difference in his life and can also make a difference in our lives today.

II. The risen Christ assigns us a task.

A. *Jesus assigned the disciples a task.* When Jesus Christ appeared to the Eleven, he gave them an assignment: "All power is given unto me in heaven and in earth. Go ye therefore, and teach all nations, baptizing them in the name of the Father, and of the Son, and of the Holy Ghost. Teaching them to observe all things whatsoever I have commanded you: and lo, I am with you alway, even unto the end of the world" (Matt. 28:19–20). Jesus commissioned these men to go out and make the kingdom of the world into the kingdom of God.

B. *The risen Christ assigns us a task.* Modern disciples also have been entrusted with a task: We are to continue Jesus' ministry in the power of his Holy Spirit. The Spirit within us can enable us to be Jesus' witnesses by word and deed. His abiding presence can enable us to awaken people to the depth and urgency of their need. By God's power, we can lead people to Jesus, the one in whom their needs can be met.

III. The risen Christ brings sustenance for life.

A. *The risen Christ helped the disciples in a variety of ways after the tragic event of the cross.* Thomas doubted. Two disciples on the road to Emmaus gave in to depression. Peter and some other disciples thought the cause of Christ was lost, so they returned to fishing. Jesus ministered to their needs during the forty days after the Resurrection, renewing, strengthening, and sustaining them.

B. *The risen Christ sustains us during life's trials.* Those who respond to the Lord in faith find his comforting presence as they pass through times of conflict and suffering.

IV. The risen Christ brings us immortality.

A. *Jesus defeated death.* Throughout his ministry, Jesus affirmed that he ruled over all powers including death itself. He assured his disciples that even if he died he would rise again. "From that time forth began Jesus to shew unto his disciples, how that he must go into Jerusalem, and suffer many things of the elders, and chief priests and scribes, and be killed, and be raised on the third day" (Matt. 16:21).

When Jesus died on the cross, death felt that it held its prey. But when Jesus rose from the grave, he proved that death had been defeated.

B. *The risen Christ gives us victory over death.* Since Christ won the victory over death, his followers share in his victory. "Because I live, ye shall live also" (John 14:19). Easter morning brought immortality to light.

Conclusion

Jesus Christ is alive. Thousands of people have met him since his ascension. Now they can face life victoriously. Because they have experienced the risen Christ, they can walk to death with courage. Have you met him? He stands at your life seeking entrance.

WEDNESDAY EVENING, MARCH 17

Title: Who are the True Believers?

Text: "For we are the circumcision, which worship God in the spirit, and rejoice in Christ Jesus, and have no confidence in the flesh" **(Phil. 3:3).**

Scripture Reading: Philippians 3:1–3

Introduction

There has never been any lack of people who were convinced that they were the true worshipers of God. The Jews today think that they worship God correctly. Muslims are sure that they are the only proper worshipers of God, for they are convinced that Mohammed was the last prophet. Christians, of course, are convinced that they worship God correctly. And among Christians there are many denominations, and each is certain that its approach to God is right.

Nonbelievers must have a difficult time determining whom to follow. Who is right? The ones who worship according to liturgy or according to the movement of the Spirit? The ones who hold out for a strict morality or those who say that one's personal conduct makes little difference? Those who say that the Bible alone tells of salvation and God's standard or those who say the Bible must be supplemented by tradition and interpretation? What is the standard for finding true believers?

The early church had this problem too. In this section of his letter to the Philippians, Paul warned about the Judaizers. Circumcision was a distinguishing mark of the men of Israel. True believers also have a distinguishing mark that makes them the true circumcision, the people of God's covenant community.

I. True believers have a distinctive worship.

Believers "worship God in the Spirit," or through the agency of the Holy Spirit. The Jews had been proud of their rituals, but now this was a spiritual approach to the worship of God.

We can worship God by the Holy Spirit because God is Spirit. Jesus affirmed this in John 4:23–24. Because God is spirit and is not bound, he can be worshiped in truth by the help of the Holy Spirit anywhere anytime in many ways. The Holy Spirit indwells individual lives in the church body and guides us in how to worship.

II. True believers have joy.

The second phrase of this verse mentions those who "rejoice in Christ Jesus." Joy is one of the distinctive marks of the Christian.

A. *We rejoice in Jesus Christ because of the work he has done in us.* Christ has performed a work of grace in our lives that makes us new creatures. There is joy in knowing Christ and the life that we have in him.

Billy Sunday often told of his decision to leave baseball and work for the Lord. After reciting the results of the lives of his fellow baseball players, he would ask, "Who won the game of life?"

B. *We rejoice in Jesus Christ because his presence is with us.* Jesus promised to be with us to the end of the world, and he always makes good on his promises. The sovereign God is our constant companion. How that gives joy!

III. True believers have a definite faith.

Paul spoke of believers as those who "have no confidence in the flesh." "Flesh" here is practically equal to the "self." God's people have a confidence that is not rooted in themselves, but in him. The faith that we have for salvation rests in Jesus Christ and him alone.

We remember our own failures and sins. Herman Melville, author of *Moby Dick,* rebelled against the doctrine of human depravity and went to live among the Africans to prove that it was not true. But he found sin there too. Scripture is right when it asserts that "all have sinned, and come short of the glory of God" (Rom. 3:23). But then we remember God's grace in salvation. Salvation comes about because of the grace of God in Christ.

Conclusion

True believers reveal their faith through their joyful lives and worship God in spirit and in truth.

SUNDAY MORNING, MARCH 21

Title: The Stilling of the Storm

Text: "And he was in the hinder part of the ship, asleep on a pillow: and they awake him, and say unto him, Master, carest thou not that we perish? And he arose, and rebuked the wind, and said unto the sea, Peace, be still. And the wind ceased, and there was a great calm" **(Mark 4:38–39).**

Scripture Reading: Mark 4:35–41

Hymns: "Guide Me, O Thou Great Jehovah," Williams
           "Face to Face with Christ," Breck
           "O They Tell Me of a Home," Alwood

Offertory Prayer: Loving Father God, thank you for the privilege of letting us come into the throne room to thank you, to praise you, and to confess our sins that we might experience cleansing. Thank you for giving us the privilege of being colaborers with you in helping men and women, boys and girls to turn from the life of no faith and waste that they might come and walk and talk with you.

Help us to give our bodies as living sacrifices into your service. Help us to be your love and your grace day by day in our contact with those who are in need. Accept our gifts and add your blessings to them. In Jesus' name we pray. Amen.

Introduction

The miracle of the stilling of the storm is recorded in all three Synoptic Gospels (Matt. 8:18–27; Mark 4:35–41; Luke 8:22–25). Mark, who seldom dates his material, is careful to note: "And the same day, when the even was come, he saith unto them, let's pass over unto the other side" (Mark 4:35). It had been a busy day for our Lord. The scribes who came down from Jerusalem had made a blasphemous accusation: "He hath Beelzebub, and by the prince of devils casteth he out devils" (3:22).

Jesus' mother, brothers, and possibly sisters came to see him, hoping to take him home. When Jesus was told that they were outside seeking him, he said, "Behold my mother and my brethren! For whosoever shall do the will of God, the same is my brother, and my sister, and mother" (Mark 3:34–35).

Leaving the crowded house, Jesus went to the seaside and got into a boat, from which he taught the multitude. He had taught by parables in the house, and now he taught by parables at the seashore (Mark 4:34). It had been an extremely busy day, and he desired to cross to the other side of the lake (v. 35). The eastern shore would be a delightful, refreshing change. It would be his only way to escape the crowds. While crossing the lake Jesus and his disciples encountered a storm. Jesus was asleep on a pillow in the stern of the ship. The fearful disciples awoke him, crying, "Master, carest thou not that we perish?" (v. 38). The Bible says, "He arose, and rebuked the wind, and said unto the sea, Peace, be still. And the wind ceased, and there was a great calm" (v. 39). Then he asked his disciples, "Why are ye so fearful? how is it that ye have no faith?" (v. 40).

The disciples were faced with the wind of circumstances without and the waves of doubt and fear within. After the storm was calmed by Jesus, the disciples said, "What manner of man is this, that even the wind and the sea obey him?" (Mark 4:41).

Let's see the great truths in the miracle of the stilling of the storm.

I. The miracle of the stilling of the storm tells us of the work Jesus performs.

Mark tells us that Jesus had been teaching, preaching, working miracles, and saving souls. One word in Mark occurs again and again—"straightway," which means immediately and indicates that our Lord was a busy man. He was the toiling Savior. He moved among people as swiftly as a sunbeam, and even today his outflow of love, grace, and mercy is continuous. Jesus had a compassionate heart, and he worked because he knew time was short. Jesus' love moved his divine hand.

II. The miracle of the stilling of the storm tells us of the cry Jesus hears.

Fear that drives us to Jesus is not wrong. Only when the ship began to fill with water did the disciples cry, "Master, carest thou not that we perish?" (Mark 4:38).

It is surely time to call on the Lord when we find that the more we try to keep afloat the deeper we sink into the sea of iniquity and failure. Peter said, "Cast all your anxiety on him because he cares for you" (1 Peter 5:7 NIV).

III. The miracle of the stilling of the storm tells us of the needs Jesus meets.

Jesus toils in the face of physical wants. He did not sleep the sleep of indifference. He slept the sleep of exhaustion. He experienced the pressure of human fatigue. He denied his need for sleep to help his disciples. He is never too tired to help.

IV. The miracle of the stilling of the storm tells us of the fear Jesus alleviates (Mark 4:40).

Jesus asked, "Why are ye so fearful?" Although Jesus is in the boat, it is not always smooth sailing. It is, however, safe sailing. Jesus rebuked the disciples' fearfulness. They should have felt secure with him. The psalmist said, "He maketh the storm a calm, so that the waves thereof are still" (Ps. 107:29).

We are fearful when our faith in Jesus is faulty. Fearfulness, like a weed, springs up out of the soil of weak faith. Someone has said, "There are three hundred sixty-five 'fear nots' in the Bible—one for each day of the year."

V. The miracle of the stilling of the storm tells us that Jesus rebukes faithlessness (Mark 4:40).

When we hear Jesus ask his disciples, "How is it that ye have no faith?" (4:40), we naturally wonder where was their faith? Did they think the boat would sink with him in it?

The disciples had not yet come to believe that Jesus was the Lord of nature. They had accepted him as the Messiah, but they didn't understand all that that encompassed. How like us in our troubles they were! Let's ask the Lord to increase our faith.

VI. The miracle of the stilling of the storm tells us of the peace Jesus brings.

Jesus said to the raging sea, "Peace, be still." And "the wind ceased, and there was a great calm" (Mark 4:39). When Jesus helps the needy, all the resources of heaven and earth are at his beck and call.

Jesus saves us from the storms of life, from the wrath of God, from the power of sin, from fear, and from perishing. He fills us with the peace of God. He said to his disciples, "Peace I leave with you, my peace I give unto you; not as the world giveth, give I unto you. Let not your heart be troubled, neither let it be afraid" (John 14:27).

VII. The miracle of the stilling of the storm tells us of the person Jesus is.

The disciples said: "What manner of man is this, that even the wind and the sea obey him?" (Mark 4:41).

A. *Jesus is human.*
   1. He was fatigued.
   2. He was asleep.
B. *Jesus is divine.*
   1. He rebuked the storm.
   2. He is the master of every situation.
C. *Jesus is the only Savior (Matt. 1:21; Luke 19:10; John 3:16; Acts 4:12).*

Conclusion

Jesus is sufficient for all the events of life. He is also sufficient for our sins and able to take us to heaven. Trust him! Receive him as your personal Savior!

SUNDAY EVENING, MARCH 21

Title: The Great Lift-off

Text: "And it came to pass, while he blessed them, he was parted from them, and carried up into heaven" (**Luke 24:51**).

Scripture Reading: Acts 1:9–11

Introduction

The launching of manned spacecraft is a popular attraction. People travel for miles to Cape Kennedy to see launches, and millions more watch them on television. There is an exceptional thrill about these events.

One of the most spectacular lift-offs, however, was witnessed by only eleven men. Forty days after Jesus' miraculous resurrection, he led his disciples to Mount Olivet, where he ascended into the clouds.

We make much of Jesus' incarnation, and rightly so. We make much of his life on earth, his death on the cross, and his resurrection from the dead. Again, these matters should be stressed. But his ascension into heaven is an event of the most momentous importance. Let's see what truths we can glean from Jesus' ascension.

I. The Ascension assures us of Jesus' finished work.

A. *A completion.* Jesus' ascension showed that he had finished his work. The Lord had come to Bethlehem from the throne of glory to seek and to save, to reveal God, and to destroy the work of the devil. The Ascension marked the completion of a wondrous ministry.

Jesus had traveled throughout Palestine seeking those who rebelled against God. In his teachings, interviews, and miracles, Jesus demonstrated God's heart, the assurance that God is for people and wants every person to have a relationship with him through his Son. After Jesus died on the cross for sinners and rose from the grave, he continued for the next forty days to teach the disciples about the kingdom of God (cf. Acts 1:1–8). He emphasized worldwide evangelization and assured them of his continued presence through his Holy Spirit. Then he ascended, completing his earthly ministry.

B. *A coronation.* Jesus' ascension resulted in a coronation. The One who identified with human beings now became identified in heaven. God highly exalted him and gave him a name that is above every name (cf. Phil. 2:5–11).

When Jesus arrived in heaven, according to the Bible, there was a great coronation. The Bible repeatedly states that when Jesus reached heaven he sat down at the right hand of God. This indicates that his work on earth was finished. "When he had by himself purged our sins, [he] sat down on the right hand of the Majesty on high" (Heb. 1:3). He was crowned with glory and honor (cf. Heb. 2:9). God both recognized and rewarded Jesus' completed ministry.

II. The Ascension teaches us of Jesus' continued ministry.

A. *The office of great High Priest.* The New Testament reveals that when Jesus ended his earthly work he took on a new ministry as our great High Priest. Jesus is able to fulfill this role because of his essential deity and his true humanity. As God he is able to strengthen; as man he is able to sympathize.

B. *The ministry of the great High Priest.* In heaven Jesus sits at the right hand of the Father. He is thoroughly qualified to be High Priest and to make intercession for us (see Rom. 8:34; Heb. 7:25). He can identify with and is concerned especially with the needs of his people on earth. "For in that he, himself hath suffered being tempted, he is able to succour them that are tempted" (Heb. 2:18).

III. The Ascension predicts Jesus' future return.

A. *A promised return.* Jesus' ascension was linked directly to the promise of his return. Two angelic messengers announced that Jesus would return in the same manner as he had departed. He ascended personally, and he will return personally. He was seen when he ascended, and he will be seen when he returns to earth.

B. *A prediction of universal reign.* Jesus ascended into heaven to begin his universal reign. Paul said, "He must reign, till he hath put all enemies under his feet" (1 Cor. 15:25).

When Christ returns again, believers will reign with him. Charles Wesley expressed this in the lines of a hymn.

> *Changed from glory into glory,*
> *Till in heaven we take our place,*
> *Till we cast our crowns before Thee,*
> *Lost in wonder, love, and praise.*

Conclusion

It is fitting that we pause to think of Jesus' ascension. The marvel of his ministry on earth amazes us. The thrill of his ascension challenges us to trust him. We can follow the King who reigns. If we do, we will reign with him forever.

WEDNESDAY EVENING, MARCH 24

Title: A Matter of Profit and Loss

Text: "But what things were gain to me, those I counted loss for Christ. Yea doubtless, and I count all things but loss for the excellency of the knowledge of Christ Jesus my Lord: for whom I have suffered the loss of all things, and do count them but dung, that I may win Christ" **(Phil. 3:7–8).**

Scripture Reading: Philippians 3:4–11

Introduction

Profit is one thing we know about in our day. Profit is used as a motive, a basis for action. It might be expressed by "What's in it for me?"

Jesus had something to say about profit. He showed that in the mad rush for gain, for power and prestige, something else is of the utmost importance—the realization of salvation and growth in him. He expressed it in words that we all can understand: "What shall it profit a man, if he shall gain the whole world, and lose his own soul? Or what shall a man give in exchange for his soul?" (Mark 8:36–37).

In Paul's autobiographical section of Philippians, he claims that if anyone could count on his position in the flesh for right standing with God, it should be him. But he discounts that for faith in Jesus Christ.

I. Some profit is really loss (vv. 4–6).

Paul discovered that all for which he had worked were not really profits when judged by the standard of God's will for his life. The problem was that they had promoted pride. As reflected in the life of Paul, we can see some of the things in which we might have an inordinate pride, a pride that can lead to a fall.

A. *The pride of family.* Paul could stand before any of his antagonists and match pedigrees. He could point to his family with pride. But, like Paul, in the end each one of us must stand alone; we must make our own mark in life.

B. *The pride of faith.* Paul's background was that of a Pharisee, the most religious of all the Jews. His faith was without question. That was all settled—settled, that is, until he met Christ on the Damascus Road.

C. *The pride of achievement.* Paul set forth an impressive list of achievements. He had achieved more than others his age. The greatest achievement of all, however, is faith in Christ.

D. *The pride of morality.* Paul could even take great pride in morality. But our own righteousness becomes as filthy rags in the presence of Christ who is righteousness himself.

II. Some loss is really profit (vv. 7–11).

Paul had a great pride in his attainments, all the things he counted as profit, until one day on the road to Damascus they were all swept away and he discovered the greatest profit—faith in Jesus Christ as Savior.

Accepting Christ as Savior and Lord is the most important decision any person can make. Bill Glass, an evangelist and former All-American and All-Pro football player, once expressed it before the Baptist World Congress in Miami, Florida, as a decision he could not sidestep. He was face to face with Christ and could not sidestep him. He had to decide whether Jesus was what he claimed to be or the greatest liar in the world. Neither can any one of us sidestep that decision.

What do you profit by the acceptance of Christ? Through Paul's testimony you can see that there are a number of significant things you gain.

A. *You gain a new sense of values (v. 8).*
B. *You gain a new position (v. 9).* "Be found in him" is the way the apostle expressed it. It describes a new relationship that we have with Christ.
C. *You gain a new fellowship (v. 10).* The word "know" here refers to intimate personal knowledge and fellowship. It means to know by experience.
D. *You gain a new hope (v. 11).*

Conclusion

Goethe once said, "Choose well—your choice is brief yet endless." You have been offered the opportunity to choose. What's in it for you? Life.

SUNDAY MORNING, MARCH 28

Title: The Death of Jesus—A Revelation!

Text: "He was oppressed, and he was afflicted, yet he opened not his mouth: he is brought as a lamb to the slaughter, and as a sheep before her shearers is dumb, so he openeth not his mouth. He was taken from prison and from judgment: and who shall declare his generation? for he was cut off out of the land of the living: for the transgression of my people was he stricken. And he made his grave with the wicked, and with the rich in his death; because he had done no violence, neither was any deceit in his mouth" (**Isa. 53:7–9**).

Scripture Reading: Isaiah 53:1–9

Hymns: "Beneath the Cross of Jesus," Clephane
"At Calvary," Newell
"The Old Rugged Cross," Bennard

Offertory Prayer: Heavenly Father, we are deeply grateful for our Savior's sacrifice in our behalf. With a renewed excitement on this Lord's Day, we lift our voices in praise to you. As we give ourselves through this offering, we do so with generous and thankful hearts. Use these gifts to send the gospel around the world. In the name of Jesus Christ we pray. Amen.

Introduction

Historical records have revealed both the good and bad of humanity. Accounts of people's deeds have shown again and again the hatred that exists among people.

We are shocked when we read accounts of past wars. On bloody battlefields and in prisoner-of-war execution chambers, humanity's deeds of horror have been exposed. The remembrance of torture and genocide in World War II prison camps still produces nightmares in many hearts.

People also show hatred and vengeance in one-on-one situations. What would hateful people do if they had an opportunity to attack God himself? We have a record of how humanity would treat God if it could. The death march of Bataan did not reveal the hell within people as much as did the death march to Calvary. Auschwitz and its gas chambers did not expose as deep a hatred as did the cross and its nails. People destroying people is evil. But humanity seeking to eliminate God is even more demonic.

Using hindsight, let us look at four facets of Jesus' death on the cross.

I. It revealed the hell in humanity.

Jesus' crucifixion is viewed from the perspective of humanity's involvement in a horrible act. The people responsible for his death were representative of people of all times.

There has always been a rebellion against God. Lucifer and a following of angels rebelled and lost their place in heaven. Adam and Eve rebelled and then responded by hiding from God. Jonah tried to run away from God. Sarah dared to laugh at God's promise. The people of the first century went so far as to put Jesus to death. This final act revealed the evil in the hearts of all people.

A. *Annas and Caiaphas (John 18:12–13).* Religious leaders instigated the death of Jesus. Their hearts were so filled with jealousy that they dared to go to the extreme to destroy him.

B. *Judas (Matt. 26:14–16).* Jesus shared his intimate life with a man named Judas for approximately three and one-half years. This familiarity did not erase the evil in Judas's life, which surfaced when the betrayer sold the Savior for the price of a slave.

C. *Mob (John 19:15–16).* The world is swayed by the political ideology that the majority must always determine the ruler. Rightness is not always encased in the deeds of crowds. Such was the situation with an unruly mob who cried out, "Crucify him, crucify him!" Though hidden in a multitude, it was individuals who revealed the hatred in their hearts for the Man of Sorrows.

II. It revealed the holiness of Christ.

What is so amazing about Jesus' trial and crucifixion are the comments the enemies and nonpartisans made about him. Each comment sustained his absolute holiness.

A. *Pharisees (Matt. 9:11).* Though the Pharisees dogged Jesus' every step, they could never secure a more serious charge against him than that he ate with publicans and sinners.

B. *Pilate (Luke 23:4).* Pilate had Jesus' life closely scrutinized from a legal perspective, but still he had to conclude, "I find no fault in this man."

C. *Judas (Matt. 27:4).* Judas had substantial opportunities to know Jesus in a very human relationship. Though he denied Christ, he had to admit, "I have betrayed innocent blood."

D. *Thief (Luke 23:41).* People often expose the truth in their communications just prior to death. In this circumstance, one of the thieves being crucified with Jesus cried out, "This man hath done nothing amiss."

E. *Centurion (Matt. 27:51–54).* The executioner always sees the pleading victim in his weakest moments. The centurion responsible for carrying out the death penalty against Jesus concluded, "Truly this was the Son of God."

III. It revealed the happiness of the recipients.

The irony of the cross is that through the agony experienced by Jesus, multitudes throughout the ages have been granted happiness.

A. *Barabbas is released (John 18:39–40).* At least three men besides Jesus were scheduled to be executed at the same time. Pilate, however, spoke of the custom of releasing one prisoner from death in commemoration of the Passover Feast. He gave the mob a choice of prisoners to be released (Matt. 27:17)—Barabbas, who was probably the most evil of all the prisoners, or Jesus, who was without guilt. They called for Barabbas. The sealing of the death sentence upon Jesus obviously made Barabbas very happy.

B. *The body of Jesus is released (1 Cor. 15:54–55).* Jesus suffered excruciating pain on the cross. His body was tormented to the ultimate degree. His death totally released him from all pain.

C. *People are released spiritually (Rom 5:6, 8–10).* The Bible teaches that people are enslaved to sin, burdened by their own evil. When they accept the work of Jesus Christ on the cross, they are saved from both an inner and an eternal hell. Their souls are made happy through Jesus Christ.

IV. It revealed the honor of God.

Jesus' death on the cross brought to light the honor and glory due to our majestic God. For him to give his only begotten Son to save sinful humanity proves that he is due all glory.

A. *Jesus is glorified (John 17:1).* As Jesus envisioned the hour of his sacrifice, he recognized that this would also be the crowning hour of glory and honor. He was about to do something no one else could do and was convinced that the outcome would be victorious.

B. *God is glorified (John 17:4–5).* God planned the way for people to have eternal life, and this plan called for the death of Jesus. Saved people would give God the glory. Therefore, Christ's death was the means by which God would be glorified.

C. *Humanity is glorified (Rom 8:30).* When people form an affinity with the person of Jesus Christ and his death and resurrection, they also share in his glory.

Conclusion

Jesus' death revealed much to humanity, but the most significant revelation of all is the way to salvation. Through his death we live! Praise his holy name!

SUNDAY EVENING, MARCH 28

Title: The Great Comeback

Text: "But the day of the Lord will come as a thief in the night; in which the heavens shall pass away with a great noise; and the elements shall melt with fervent heat, the earth also and the works that are therein shall be burned up" **(2 Peter 3:10).**

Scripture Reading: 2 Peter 3:1–15

Introduction

Early in World War II, President Franklin D. Roosevelt ordered General Douglas MacArthur to leave the Philippine Islands and go to Australia. MacArthur regretted the order, but he promised the people, "I shall return." The people of the Philippines clung to his promise.

In 1945 MacArthur waded ashore the Philippine Islands and declared, "I have returned." He had fulfilled his promise.

During Jesus' earthly ministry, he spoke of his return to earth. He indicated that after his death, burial, resurrection, and ascension, he would return in a glorious manner. Some day Jesus will fulfill that promise.

I. The Lord's coming fulfills a promise.

A. *The Old Testament prophets anticipated a "day of the Lord."* Though these seers did not have all the details, they expected God to have the final word.

B. *Jesus promised his final return to earth.* The theme of the Lord's return prevails in his teachings and in his parables. One can hardly question Jesus' certainty that he would return to earth.

C. *Other New Testament writers promised the Lord's return.* Paul spoke frequently of Jesus' second coming (see 1 Thess. 1:9–10; 2:19; 3:13; 4:13–18; 5:23), and Peter also predicted the Lord's return (see Acts 3:20; 2 Peter 3:1–15).

II. The Lord's return accomplishes a purpose.

A. *The Lord will return to judge the world.* His first coming was to save the world. His final coming will be to judge the world. The basis of the judgment is one's relationship to him.

B. *The Lord will return to actualize the fullness of the kingdom of God.* The kingdom of God is a reality now. Yet the time will come when we know the kingdom of God in its fullness.

C. *The Lord will return to reorient the world.* Peter said that the present, sinful order will pass away and there will be a new heaven and a new earth. Though some of Peter's language may be figurative, the message is clear. When Jesus returns he will reorient the whole cosmological structure.

III. The Lord's return encourages preparation.

A. *The Lord's return encourages readiness.* Peter urges us to be ready for the Lord's return. Jesus insisted upon readiness: "Therefore be ye also ready: for in such an hour as ye think not the Son of man cometh" (Matt. 24:44). There will be no other opportunity for redemption. Destiny will be decided when the Lord returns. We must trust in him now for salvation and grow in his ways.

B. *The Lord's return encourages godliness.* Peter said, "Seeing then that all these things shall be dissolved, what manner of persons ought ye to be in all holy conversation and godliness...?" (2 Peter 3:11). Knowing that our Lord is coming challenges us to live by his principles.

C. *The Lord's return encourages service.* In almost every mention of the Lord's return, there is a mention of service. In light of the fact that much needs to be done before his return, Christians should work with zeal.

Conclusion

Jesus is going to come back to earth. He came the first time despised and rejected. His second coming will involve every person who has ever lived. For many his return will be disastrous because they will not be prepared. You need to be ready for the great comeback!

WEDNESDAY EVENING, MARCH 31

Title: Secrets for a Mature Life

Text: "Brethren, I count not myself to have apprehended: but this one thing I do, forgetting those things which are behind, and reaching forth unto those things which are before, I press toward the mark for the prize of the high calling of God in Christ Jesus" **(Phil. 3:13–14).**

Scripture Reading: Philippians 3:12–16

Introduction

Across the river from where I live there is an institution that must be the saddest place in the state. It is the state institution for mentally retarded people. Some of them are hopelessly and helplessly retarded. Mature in years, they are immature in mind. Some of them have spent their entire lives in the institution unable to perform even the simplest of things for themselves. I think sometimes of the hope that was represented by their birth. Their families hoped for a child that would someday be mature and take his or her rightful place in society. But it would never be.

Likewise, when we were born again, Jesus hoped that we would grow up in Christlikeness to be mature Christians.

The word "perfect" shows up in verses 12 and 15 of our text. Among other things, it can mean "mature." Paul, then, in this passage is giving us some secrets for a mature life.

I. A wise forgetfulness is a secret for a mature life.

When Paul said "forgetting those things which are behind," he was referring particularly to his past achievements. This does not mean that he was ashamed of his past achievements; it just means that he would not allow them to lull him into complacency. They did not count for very much in his Christian experience, as he had stated in verse 8.

A. *We ought to forget our successes.* Many athletic teams have gone down to defeat because they went into a game with their past successes on their minds. Having succeeded before, they assumed that they would succeed again and thus did not play up to their potential.

The same thing can happen to Christians. Having resisted temptation before, they may wrongfully assume that because of their past successes they are immune to the problems before them.

B. *We ought to forget our failures.* By the same token, we should not dwell on our failures. To have failed once does not make a person a failure. Wisely forgetting the times that we have failed, we can look positively to Christ for strength.

C. *We ought to forget our sins.* When sins are forgiven, the Bible promises that they are removed from us as far as the east is from the west. Having been forgiven of sins, we must accept that forgiveness and no longer dwell on our past.

II. A proper anticipation is a secret for a mature life.

Paul was able to talk about "reaching forth unto those things which are before. . . ." He had a proper anticipation in life for things that were good and Christlike.

What is the aim of your life? Paul was able to say, "This *one* thing I do" (emphasis added). All of his life was moving toward the goal that he had in Christ.

Full fellowship with Christ is the goal before us. But often other things divert us from that goal. Someone has observed that barnacles give promise of being free swimmers when they are born but soon attach themselves to pilings or ships and never swim freely in the ocean. We must have a vision for serving Christ so that we don't get caught up in the cares of life and miss his best for us.

III. A steady effort is a secret for a mature life.

As impatient persons we want instant gratification or success. Often that same idea is carried over into our spiritual life. We must learn to be content with God's timing. He blesses even our smallest efforts and keeps us headed in the right direction. Paul stressed that he pressed forward toward his goal. He was making a steady effort toward Christlikeness.

The story of the race between the tortoise and the hare is old and familiar. Thinking that he could easily win the race, the hare bounded ahead then rested. But the tortoise steadily moved on until he crossed the line before the hare, winning the contest. Our Christian life is not lived by sudden bursts of speed. We must make steady efforts toward the mark of Christlikeness.

Conclusion

These are some of Paul's secrets for a mature life. Let's try to follow them in our own lives that we may attain the maturity to which Christ has called us.

Suggested preaching program for the month of

APRIL

■ **Sunday Mornings**

Continue the series "Our Great Redeemer and Our Great Redemption."

■ **Sunday Evenings**

A series of expository messages based on the first three chapters of the book of Revelation is suggested. The theme is "The Triumphant Christ and the Church Triumphant."

■ **Wednesday Evenings**

Continue the series "A Pathway Through Philippians."

SUNDAY MORNING, APRIL 4

Title: As Sure As You Can

Text: "Now the next day, that followed the day of preparation, the chief priests and Pharisees came together unto Pilate, saying, Sir, we remember that that deceiver said, while he was yet alive, After three days I will rise again. Command therefore that the sepulchre be made sure until the third day, lest his disciples come by night, and steal him away, and say unto the people, He is risen from the dead: so the last error shall be worse than the first. Pilate said unto them, Ye have a watch: go your way, make it as sure as ye can. So they went, and made the sepulchre sure, sealing the stone, and setting a watch" **(Matt. 27:62–66).**

Scripture Reading: Matthew 27:62–28:15

Hymns: "One Day," Chapman
"He Lives," Ackley
"Because He Lives," Gaither

Offertory Prayer: Heavenly Father, we are thankful for the opportunity of worship you have given us. We realize this is possible only because our Lord burst forth from the tomb to be triumphant over death. Because he lives, we worship a living Lord.

Father, remind us of the joy of expressing our faith in a tangible manner. May we give with hearts filled with Christian enthusiasm. And may the world see our faith by the joyous works we perform before you. In Jesus' name we pray. Amen.

Introduction

The resurrection of Jesus Christ is the badge of authority for the Christian faith. On Calvary he suffered and died for the sins of humanity. There were three crosses on that Good Friday. What gave validity to the life and words of the man on the central cross? The Resurrection. When he arose from the grave, the world had to acknowledge that all of his former words and deeds were true.

Jesus' resurrection did not happen without resistance from the enemies of righteousness. They remembered that Jesus had said he would rise from the dead, and they remembered it *before* it occurred. Thus, they sealed his tomb (Matt. 27:63). It is sad to note on the other hand that the disciples did not remember Jesus' words until *after* his resurrection (Luke 24:8). With the dread of a potential resurrection of Jesus Christ in his enemies' minds, they proceeded to try to prevent any incident that might lead people to believe that the Resurrection actually occurred.

I. Attempts to prevent Jesus' resurrection.

In Matthew's account we see paltry people struggling against eternal truth. They imagined the Lord to be a deceiver and the disciples to be cunning men with a scheme to make the Resurrection appear to be real. They took it upon themselves to try to prevent an event that would make the populace think that Christ was raised from the dead.

A. *Religionists in ignorance and malice.* The religionists had come to Pilate out of hatred and ignorance seeking to destroy Jesus (Matt. 12:14). Now that he had been killed, they were going to see that his deathly defeat remained a reality. They approached the cowardly Pilate knowing that they could manipulate him.

B. *Pilate in uncaring complacency.* Pilate had seen and heard enough about this Jesus Christ. He certainly did not want a rumor circulating about Jesus' resurrection, so he gave the chief priests and Pharisees a detachment of soldiers, concurred in their efforts to secure the tomb, and issued the weakest statement of encouragement the world has ever known. He said, "Make the tomb as secure as you know how" (Matt. 27:65 NIV). What a scene of futility—mere men seeking to secure a tomb that God himself had declared would be opened (Matt. 16:21–22; 17:22–23; 20:18–19).

C. *Soldiers in regimented obedience.* The soldiers acted with regimented obedience as they sought to carry out Pilate's command. They went to the grave site and made sure the rock was sufficiently placed in the tomb's entrance. They then sealed the rock, thus making it a trespass against the law of the

Roman government for the tomb to be opened. Then, to make certain the edict was enforced, the soldiers stood guard by the tomb.

II. Attempts to deny the Resurrection.

The soldiers' attempts proved futile. God moved, and his Son arose from the tomb eternally victorious over death. Jesus' prophecy had been undeniably fulfilled. The soldiers appointed to guard the tomb ended up heralding his resurrection (Matt. 28:11).

A. *Conniving religionists.* Attempts to prevent Jesus' resurrection had failed. A second scheme must now be launched to try to cover up what these Christians claimed was fact. The conniving religionists called for the god of money to combat the God of life. They hatched a plot where the soldiers were made the "fall guys." They claimed that the disciples came and stole Jesus' body while the soldiers slept.

B. *Bribed soldiers.* Money and promised amnesty from punishment persuaded the soldiers to go along with the sinful ploy. It was just another day's work with a little extra pay for them. So what if their character was compromised? Didn't the money justify their deeds?

C. *Puppet politician.* The puppet politician Pilate was in the "back pockets" of the religionists, and they knew it (Matt. 28:14). After all, they were the ones who had encouraged him to secure the tomb in the first place. Why should he become overly concerned at this new turn of events? He could be persuaded.

III. Attempts to obscure the Resurrection.

You and I cringe when we read this story of those who tried to prevent and then deny the Resurrection. We rejoice in the victory wrought through Jesus Christ over the forces of evil. Yet an even greater attempt is being made against the Resurrection today. It is impossible to deny the fact of the living Lord. It is insanity to pretend the Resurrection didn't occur. Thus, the powers of darkness have unleashed another attack—an attack to try to obscure the meaning of Christ's resurrection.

A. *Terms used.* When most people think of Easter, they think in terms of eggs, bunnies, candy, and new clothes. It is not a denial of the Resurrection, but rather a diversion. The excitement that the average child experiences at Eastertime is not founded in the fact of Christ's resurrection, but in the expectation of an Easter basket, an egg hunt, a new suit or dress, and a visit to Grandmother's house.

B. *Commercial preparation.* Easter is one of the most lucrative times of the year for manufacturers and merchants. Candy, toy, and clothing sales rise as people try to keep up with their friends and neighbors by providing the best gifts for their children and the most fashionable clothing for the entire family. Is the Resurrection being denied? No. Obscured? Yes.

C. *Holiday instead of "holy day."* To ancient Christendom Easter was the holy day that celebrated the resurrection of Jesus Christ. Easter has now become an extra-long vacation weekend. The holy day has become a holiday.

IV. The real purpose of the Resurrection.

A. *Authority of Christ.* The main purpose of the Resurrection was to reveal the authority of Jesus Christ. He conquered death by his release from its clutches. His resurrection validated all of his teaching while on earth.

B. *Dignity of humanity.* The Resurrection gives dignity and worth to humanity. People, as temporal beings, are faced with extreme limitations. When they receive eternal life by accepting the resurrected Christ as Savior, these limitations of time and space are removed. They are made victors over death through Jesus Christ.

C. *Determine destiny.* Finally, the resurrection of Jesus Christ actually determines the destiny of humanity. Paul says in 1 Corinthians 15:22, "For as in Adam all die, even so in Christ shall all be made alive." As individuals associate themselves with the living, resurrected Christ, they are given a new life. Old things are passed away. All things are become new.

Conclusion

This is an excellent time to reconsider your opinion about the resurrection of Jesus Christ. Is it a simple fact characterized by the worldly trimmings of eggs, bunnies, and new clothes? Or is it a moving force that has caused you to know beyond a shadow of a doubt that you, too, have conquered death through him?

SUNDAY EVENING, APRIL 4

Title: The Triumphant Christ for the Church Triumphant

Text: "And in the midst of the seven candlesticks one like unto the Son of man" **(Rev. 1:13).**

Scripture Reading: Revelation 1

Introduction

The book of Revelation is the revelation that God gave to Christ, who in turn sent it by his angel to John the apostle, who delivered it to the seven churches in Asia. It is a book of prophecy (v. 3), a book that declares "the time is at hand" and that there are "things which must shortly come to pass" (v. 1). It is Christ's message to his churches concerning what to know and be and do to be prepared for the future events of prophecy, especially the next future event—the coming of Christ for his church, an event that could occur at any time. Christ will descend from heaven and call to himself both dead and living believers. Should knowing that Christ could come at any moment make any difference in our lives and in the church? This is really what the book of Revelation is all about.

Revelation describes the triumphant Christ for the church triumphant. It beautifully depicts the church triumphant in heaven but also pictures it on earth. Revelation assures us that God has a plan for his churches and thus he sends a special message to them. He is still building the church spiritually, adding to it, beautifying it, preparing it for the marriage supper of the Lamb. If the church is to be triumphant, it must have a vision of the triumphant Christ.

I. The times prepare for the vision.

John's condition is described in verse 9. He was suffering tribulation under the Roman Empire. He was exiled from Ephesus to Patmos to hard labor because of his testimony for Christ and his preaching of the Word of God. He was being persecuted by Domitian, the Roman emperor, at a time when many Christians were suffering for their faith.

The times in which John lived were times of persecution and apostasy for many. The anti-Christian spirit was at work. Such times are described in 1 Timothy 4:1–3 and 2 Timothy 3:1–5. It is in times of desperation that we need to see the triumphant Christ. In John's distressing times, he was worshiping, praising, and adoring the Lord on the Lord's Day. He was not complaining and moaning about his condition; he was giving glory to Jesus Christ. This is how we should respond in times of trouble.

II. The Holy Spirit inspires the vision.

In verse 10 John says, "I was in the Spirit on the Lord's day." He was worshiping the Lord under the influence of the Holy Spirit. It is always in that atmosphere that we see the living Christ. We do not see him when we are living a life of sin and selfishness; we see him when we are worshiping in the Spirit, for the Holy Spirit reveals Christ to us. In John 15:26, Jesus says, "The Spirit of truth. . .shall testify of me." The Holy Spirit also glorifies Christ within us and among us. He fills us with Christ and presents Christ to us triumphant and victorious. He shows us who Christ truly is (John 16:15).

If we want to know more about Jesus, we must allow the Holy Spirit to minister to us. We must not resist him or grieve him; we must let him teach us and guide us into all truth. A key statement to the seven churches and thus to us is: "He who has an ear, let him hear what the Spirit says to the churches" (NIV).

III. The Lord Jesus Christ reveals the vision.

Jesus is the triumphant Christ, the ascended, reigning, victorious Christ.

A. *He reveals himself in the symbols of his function.* In verse 13 Jesus' long, flowing garment describes his dignity, judicial authority, and kingly presence. He is wearing the dress of a priest, a king, and a judge.

B. *He reveals himself in the symbols of his character.* In verse 14 "his head and hair were white like wool, as white as snow" (NIV) pictures him as the Ancient of Days as in Daniel's vision. He is the eternal One, honored in all his greatness.

"His eyes were as a flame of fire" (v. 14) refers to Jesus' full knowledge. His eyes see and know with full discernment. He searches and judges our lives and motives as individuals and as a church so that we never escape his view.

"His feet like unto fine brass, as if they burned in a furnace" (v. 15) speaks of two things. "Brass" represents God's judgment of sin. All the instruments in the outer court of the tabernacle were made of brass because they had to do with God's judgment of sin. His "feet" represent the triumph he has over all his enemies. As Ephesians 1:22 indicates, he has "put all things under his feet."

Although there have been many messages and messengers in times past, all like "many waters," one great voice has the eternal message of God (v. 15). It is like one great river pouring over the falls after gathering its waters from many streams.

In verse 16 the sword is the Word of God, as identified in Ephesians 6:17. "Out of his mouth" refers to the power of the message of Christ that is preached and delivered.

"His countenance" describes the glory of his presence, the light of his life. We too may have our Patmos, but when we see Jesus Christ in his glory, we will never want to walk in darkness again.

Conclusion

The Lord Jesus Christ is someone we can see with the eyes of our spirit and with the eyes of our understanding. He is someone with whom we may communicate, because he speaks to us (v. 12). And he is someone to whom we respond in worship and submission (v. 17). Just as he laid his right hand on John, so he lays his hand of love, compassion, and encouragement on us today. He is the triumphant Christ who makes the church triumphant.

WEDNESDAY EVENING, APRIL 7

Title: What to Imitate

Text: "Join with others in following my example, brothers, and take note of those who live according to the pattern we gave you" **(Phil. 3:17 NIV)**.

Scripture Reading: Philippians 3:17–21

Introduction

It has been said that imitation is the sincerest form of flattery. If this is true, then many people are showing flattery to others in the clothes they wear, the lifestyles they choose, and the things they pursue. There is much imitation going on.

One of the great problems with this, of course, is that the models that are imitated are often not the best. Rather than imitating the best things about them, people may imitate the worst elements of their lives. There is no question that we will imitate others, the issue is what we will imitate.

The apostle Paul gives us some good advice in this area: "Join with others in following my example, brothers, and take note of those who live according to the pattern we gave you" (Phil. 3:17 NIV). Paul's exhortation may sound very egotistical, but we must remember that Paul was the leader of these people. He could point to himself and his fellow leaders as examples of true Christians.

The problem Paul was writing to the Philippians about was distortion of Christian liberty. Previously he had dealt with the problem of legalism. Now he suggested that they follow his example.

I. There is a positive imitation we are to follow.

If we imitate Paul as he follows Christ, we will ultimately be imitating Christ himself. "Follow me" is the original invitation given by Jesus himself. The early Christians had no New Testament and no tradition or experience to guide them. Therefore, the example of leading Christians was extremely valuable. Inevitably the Christian life became a version of Follow-the-Leader with each ultimately copying Christ.

Paul amplified this thought in 1 Corinthians 11:1 when he said, "Follow my example, as I follow the example of Christ" (NIV). Every time Paul admonishes us to follow him, it is with the understanding that we are really to imitate the Lord Jesus Christ. And as we imitate Christ, others may imitate us. I know of a student who found faith in Christ when he went to a church and observed his science professor—in whom he had great confidence—worshiping Christ. We, then, are to imitate Christ that we may serve as worthy examples to those who might imitate us.

II. In this imitation there is a specific opposition we are to make.

In verses 18–19 Paul identifies some people as "enemies of the cross." They were people who had perverted the gospel in some way, and Paul had opposed them. We are to imitate Paul in opposing people who pervert the gospel of God's grace.

Paul S. Rees characterized these individuals in *The Adequate Man* ([Westwood, N.J.: Revell, 1959], 88–89):

A. *The disguise they wear.* Posing as the gospel's friends, they practice as its foes.
B. *The doom they face.* "Their end is destruction" (v. 19).
C. *The deity they serve.* Their "god is their belly" (v. 19).
D. *The disgrace they bear.* Their "glory is in their shame" (v. 19).
E. *The disposition they display.* They "mind earthly things" (v. 19).

III. In this imitation we have a definite hope.

Said the confident Paul, "We look for the Savior, the Lord Jesus Christ; who shall change our vile body, that it may be fashioned like unto his glorious body" (vv. 20–21).

A. *It is the hope of the return of Christ.* As Philippi was a colony of Rome with Roman citizens, we are subjects of the kingdom of God, and we await the return of our Lord.
B. *It is the hope of the redemption.* Jesus promised that he would change our bodies to be like his glorious body.
C. *In this hope there is sufficient power.* The power of God to change us is expressed in verse 21.

Conclusion

We would do well to imitate Christ as Paul did.

SUNDAY MORNING, APRIL 11

Title: The Living God—The Living Jesus

Text: "And the Word was made flesh, and dwelt among us, (and we beheld his glory, the glory as of the only begotten of the Father,) full of grace and truth" (**John 1:14**).

Scripture Reading: John 1:1–14

Hymns: "Standing on the Promises," Carter
"Blessed Assurance," Crosby
"Wonderful Words of Life," Bliss

Offertory Prayer: Heavenly Father, we praise you for giving your Son, Jesus Christ, to bear our sins on the cross. We are amazed at his leaving the safety of heaven to attack the stronghold of hell for our sake. Thank you for allowing us to help bear the financial burden of your work across the world. May this offering be an expression of our love to you. In Jesus' name we pray. Amen.

Introduction

A scan of the Old Testament quickly reveals that God was active in his relationships with people. The concept of God being alive was awesome to the inspired writers, for they knew that the nations around them worshiped gods of wood and stone. The author of Hebrews declared, "It is a fearful thing to fall into the hands of the living God" (10:31).

This living God so revered by the saints of ages past had a plan for people's salvation that involved placing himself in subjection to and limitation of flesh and blood. He accomplished his plan by sending his Son, Jesus Christ, to earth to be born of the Virgin Mary.

There are several facts to be considered as one ponders the reality of Jesus Christ becoming human. The passage of Scripture that succinctly records the event is John 1:14: "The Word was made flesh, and dwelt among us, (and we beheld his glory, the glory as of the only begotten of the Father,) full of grace and truth."

I. His birth and physical development.

Jesus' life developed naturally even though he was conceived supernaturally.

A. *Genealogy.* Family lineage is very important to the Jewish mind. Jesus' earthly family background is recorded in two different Scripture passages (Matt. 1:1–16 and Luke 3:23–38). This gave a certain credence to his history as far as the Jewish mind was concerned.

B. *Birth.* A young Jewish maiden named Mary was selected by God to be the human instrument for the birth of his Son. The most sacred and awesome act of God in relation to humanity took place as the Holy Spirit blessed this precious virgin with the gift of the Christ child.

C. *Development.* The child Jesus grew physically in accordance with the laws of human nature that God had established for the Garden of Eden. It is amazing to realize that what he had decreed to be a sufficient manner of growth for Adam was also an acceptable procedure for his own precious Son.

II. His emotional structure.

The Bible uses human language to express the activities and emotions of God. At times the language is inadequate to represent God's character completely. But Jesus literally took upon himself the emotional structure of a human.

A. *Anger.* Jesus is spoken of in Mark 3:5 as expressing anger. He was upset with certain "accusers" who were challenging his authority to serve people on the Sabbath.

B. *Compassion.* Our Lord had a deep love for people. As he moved across the countryside, his heart overflowed with compassion (Matt. 9:36) on the multitudes. He viewed them "as sheep having no shepherd."

C. *Displeasure.* Jesus was not a supersentimental type. On occasion he directly displayed displeasure with the immediate circumstances. Such a case was when his own disciples attempted to prevent parents from bringing their young children to him (Mark 10:14).

D. *Sorrow.* Jesus is especially remembered for his deep concern and brokenheartedness for his followers. The scene at Lazarus' grave (John 11:35) is made sober by the tears of the Master prior to the beckoning of Lazarus back from the tomb.

E. *Sensitivity.* Christ exhibited keen sensitivity when he entered Simon's home (Luke 7:36–50). Jesus was aware of the slurs heaped on a poor, sinful woman, and he used this victimized person to teach a great lesson on forgiveness.

F. *Loneliness.* In one prophetical passage, Isaiah depicts the Messiah as "despised and rejected of men" (Isa. 53:3). Due to the nature of his life and ministry, Jesus experienced a grave loneliness.

III. His bodily limitations.

The first thought one has about God is that he is omnipotent. In light of his character and purpose, God knows no limits. When Jesus emptied himself of his heavenly attributes and came down to earth as a baby in Bethlehem, he accepted the bodily limitations of humankind.

A. *Weariness.* Jesus approached Jacob's well after a long journey. His body was weary. In this condition a new avenue of service was opened to him (John 4:1–42).

B. *Sleepiness.* After a feverish day of service, Jesus took advantage of a boat ride to rest his body. Even in this limitation an opportunity to share with his disciples arose (Matt. 8:23–27).

C. *Hunger.* The physical well-being of Jesus was dependent on the intake of food. Satan tried to take advantage of this need by tempting Jesus to turn stones into bread (Matt. 4:3).

D. *Thirst.* Jesus' agony on the cross was intensified by a gnawing thirst. The natural chemistry of his body cried out for the same nourishment required in others.

E. *Time and space.* Prior to coming to earth, the spiritual presence of the Messiah was without limit. His entrance into the realm of humankind made him a temporary captive to time and space. The fact that he could be in only one place at a time spelled pathos to his heart in his desire to serve more people (Luke 4:40–44).

IV. His spiritual development.

Jesus Christ was God in the flesh. In his human form he developed spiritually. This progression involved relating to people and their plight more than his own spiritual development and personal edification.

A. *Baptism.* Jesus asked John the Baptist to baptize him (Matt. 3:13). He developed a greater affinity with the ritualistic needs of humanity. Also, at Jesus' baptism God gave a public declaration of his relationship with Jesus. This recognition could not go undetected by John the Baptist and possibly by others present.

B. *Temptations.* The Lord went through agony as the devil tempted him in light of his messianic ministry (Luke 4:12). These were genuine trials. In his temptation Jesus drew closer to the hearts of the people he came to serve.

C. *Transfiguration.* A strange incident commonly identified as the Transfiguration (Matt. 17:1–13) occurred in the life of Jesus Christ. It was in this experience that Jesus visibly revealed his godhood to a selected few. Again God announced his relationship with the Christ.

This spiritual pilgrimage led Jesus and his followers to an awareness of the awesome presence of the Almighty. Both Jesus and his disciples needed this confidence for the events that immediately faced them.

Conclusion

The capstone of Jesus' humanity was his physical death. He was aware that his impending death was to be temporary (John 14:1–4), yet he felt a human fear of death (Luke 22:42). Finally, he was involved in the ultimate physical event—he died (Luke 23:46). His total humanity was sealed by his death.

What was the reason for Christ's humanity? It was God's way of sharing himself to redeem sinful humanity. Has this experience been in vain as far as you are concerned?

SUNDAY EVENING, APRIL 11

Title: The Lord of the Lampstands

Text: "Among the lampstands was someone 'like a son of man,' dressed in a robe reaching down to his feet and with a golden sash around his chest. . . .The mystery of the seven stars that you saw in my right hand and of the seven golden lampstands is this: The seven stars are the angels of the seven churches, and the seven lampstands are the seven churches" **(Rev. 1:13, 20 NIV).**

Scripture Reading: Revelation 1:10–20

Introduction

Revelation 1–3 is a vision John had showing the relationship of the Lord Jesus Christ to his churches. The seven lampstands symbolize the seven churches. They may actually have been seven lamps on one lampstand like the lampstand that stood in the ancient Jewish tabernacle (see Ex. 25:31–37).

It gave light for the tabernacle, but it also pointed to Jesus, the Light of the World, lighting all humankind.

The purpose of the lampstand in Matthew 5:15 was to "give light to all in the house." Lampstands, as seen in Revelation 1, are symbols of the light the church is to give today. Jesus Christ is the Light of the World, and as Christ's body, the church is the light of the world. He shines into the world through us (see Phil. 2:15). These seven churches were literally Christ's light where they were. Just as the church at Ephesus was light for that city, so are we for ours, shining the light of Christ where we are.

Jesus Christ is in the midst of these seven churches, who represent not only actual churches but also all the churches of all ages. What he was doing then, he is still doing now. He is walking in the midst of his churches, guarding and guiding them to maturity. He is protecting them and interceding for them. He is challenging and chastising and promising them help so they may know his will. He is Lord of the lampstands!

In these seven letters there are four impressive truths about the Lord's relationship to the lampstands that are common to all the letters.

I. Each is addressed to the angel of the church.

The seven stars are the "angels," possibly pastors, of the churches. Jesus Christ holds these spiritual leaders in his right hand, which designates his power and authority. The term "stars" describes the function of the pastors, which is to reflect Christ's glory. As stars serve to guide travelers and to demonstrate stability, so do the pastors to their spiritual congregations. Each pastor is held securely by his personal relationship with the Lord Jesus Christ, as he "holds" them. Every pastor should stand in awe and humility at this scene.

Jesus Christ recognizes the pastors as spiritual leaders whom he has set in position in the churches. He speaks to the pastor and through the pastor to the people. Both the pastor's privilege and responsibility is described in this vision. The privilege of the pastor is to be held in the right hand of the ascended Lord. The responsibility of the pastor is to listen to the Lord of the church and obey him faithfully. The pastor has dual responsibilities—to Christ the head of the church and to the people, who are the body of Christ. The Lord will use his instrument to deliver his message, but if the pastor is unfaithful, he may remove him or her from the place of privilege and responsibility.

II. Christ declares in each of the letters that he knows their works.

The Lord of the lampstands knows our works. He is constantly reviewing our works to see if they meet his standards. If there is commendation to be given, he gives it. If there is judgment and chastising to be given, he does that. And sometimes it is quite severe! For example, in the letter to Thyatira the Lord says, "I will strike [Jezebel's] children dead. Then all the churches will know that I am he who searches hearts and minds, and I will repay each of you according to your deeds" (Rev. 2:23 NIV).

III. For every church there is an appeal.

The Lord closes each letter with the appeal "He who has an ear, let him hear what the Spirit says to the churches" (Rev. 2:7, 11, 17, 29; 3:6, 13, 22 NIV). It is an appeal to be submissive to the Holy Spirit's ministry. He is the administrator of the life of the church and empowers the church for witness and ministry. He regenerates us and then indwells us at conversion. He fills us and controls us as we confess our sins and yield to him. He matures us in the Christian life so that we manifest the fruit of the Spirit. He speaks to us as individuals and as a church. Our responsibility is to hear, to listen obediently to the Spirit.

"He who has an ear" is an appeal to individuals who compose the body of Christ. Therefore, our response is a personal one. Since we are saved as individuals, we are to respond to the Spirit as individuals. He is waiting for that response.

IV. Every church can be triumphant.

To each church the Lord Jesus Christ states the possibility of being an overcoming church (Rev. 2:7, 11, 17, 26; 3:5, 12, 21). The church triumphant is a reality based on the promises of Jesus Christ. And we as individuals can also be triumphant as we stand on Christ's promises. First John 5:4 says, "For whatsoever is born of God overcometh the world: and this is the victory that overcometh the world, even our faith." To be sure, there will be suffering, persecutions, trials, temptations, and many pressures in our Christian lives, but in all of them there is victory!

Conclusion

When Robert Louis Stevenson was about seven years old, he sat at the window watching the lamplighter light the street lamps one by one. Young Robert was fascinated and silent. His nurse feared mischief since he was so quiet. She called out, asking what he was doing. The child answered, "I am watching a man make holes in the darkness." This is what the Lord and the lampstands are all about—making holes in a dark world with the light of God.

WEDNESDAY EVENING, APRIL 14

Title: The Marks of a Christian

Text: "Do not be anxious about anything, but in everything, by prayer and petition, with thanksgiving, present your requests to God. And the peace of God, which transcends all understanding, will guard your hearts and your minds in Christ Jesus" (**Phil. 4:6–7**).

Scripture Reading: Philippians 4:1–7

Introduction

Isn't it strange how we can characterize and categorize people? We call them country or urban or sophisticated or educated or distinctive because of some observable characteristic. But how would you go about characterizing Christians? They may be rural or urban, educated or uneducated. The outward marks that we often use to characterize people fail us. The marks of a Christian depend on definite character traits.

In the beginning verses of the final chapter of Philippians, Paul gives some characteristics of Christians.

I. Love is a mark of a Christian (vv. 1–3).

A. *It is an inclusive love.* Notice that the love Paul expressed for his fellow Christians in Philippi included the quarrelsome Euodias as well as the helpful Clement.

We are often selective in our love. We love only those people who seem lovable or who love us in return. God is not like that. He loves us all even when we do not deserve to be loved. If we are to love like God, we must let our love reach out to everyone.

B. *It is a concerned love.* Love always expresses concern for the one who is loved. Paul called these people his "joy" and "crown." He was concerned about them even though he was separated from them.

II. Joy is a mark of a Christian (v. 4).

A. T. Robertson called his commentary on Philippians *Paul's Joy in Christ.* Joy is a hallmark of this book, and joy is a sure mark of a Christian.

A. *It is an incessant joy.* Paul said that Christians are to rejoice in the Lord always, not just in good times, but also in the bad.

B. *It is an independent joy.* This joy is "in the Lord," which means that it is independent of life's circumstances. When joy is "in the Lord" it can be experienced and expressed even when there does not appear to be much of a reason for joy.

William Barclay cited the letter of Captain Scott of Antarctica when the chill of death threatened his expedition. He wrote: "We are pegging out in a very comfortless spot. . . . We are in a desperate state—frozen feet, etc., no fuel, and a long way from food, but it would do your heart good to be in our tent, to hear our songs and our cheery conversation" (William Barclay, *The Letters to the Philippians, Colossians, and Thessalonians*, The Daily Study Bible [Philadelphia: Westminster Press, 1957], 89).

III. Gentleness is a mark of a Christian. (v. 5).

Gentleness marks the person who is willing to give up something that could rightfully be considered his or hers. Such people know when to use mercy.

Why? Because the Lord is at hand. Everything Christians do they do with the understanding that the Lord is present with them. Seeking to live out Christ's life on this earth, they will act with gentleness toward others.

IV. Peace is a mark of a Christian (vv. 6–7).

Nowhere is the peace that we have in Jesus Christ expressed quite so forcefully as in these two verses. Whatever the circumstances, the Christian must not be crippled by anxiety. Bad situations can be met with prayer and praise. And where prayer and praise exist, there is the promise that the peace of God will keep the hearts and minds of Christians.

The term "guard" in verse 7 is a military term. God's peace will stand guard over Christians. A Christian missionary was on a ship during a time of war. After tossing for much of the night, he remembered God's promise of his presence and decided that it was not necessary for them both to stay awake, so he slept.

Conclusion

How do you tell who the Christians are? Look for the marks we have discussed today.

SUNDAY MORNING, APRIL 18

Title: Jesus Christ—Flesh and Blood

Text: "And he came to Nazareth, where he had been brought up: and, as his custom was, he went into the synagogue on the sabbath day, and stood up for to read. And there was delivered unto him the book of the prophet Esaias. And when he had opened the book, he found the place where it was written, The Spirit of the Lord is upon me, because he hath anointed me to preach the gospel to the poor; he hath sent me to heal the brokenhearted, to preach deliverance to the captives, and recovering of sight to the blind, to set at liberty them that are bruised, to preach the acceptable year of the Lord. And he closed the book, and he gave it again to the minister, and sat down. And the eyes of all them that were in the synagogue were fastened on him. And he began to say unto them, This day is this scripture fulfilled in your ears" **(Luke 4:16–21).**

Scripture Reading: Luke 4:14–30

Hymns: "Lily of the Valley," Fry
           "Jesus Is All the World to Me," Thompson
           "There Is a Name," Whitefield

Offertory Prayer: Heavenly Father, our hearts are overwhelmed by our realization of your personal concern for each of us. Even though there are needs in the lives of others around the world that far surpass the ones we experience, you are still concerned for us. We thank you for this. The thanksgiving we have in our souls now finds a tangible expression through the gifts we offer. May these gifts be acceptable before you. In Christ's name. Amen.

Introduction

As we read the New Testament account of the greatness of our Lord and Savior Jesus Christ, we are awed by his godhood and holiness. He takes on an aura of mysticism and might, and we tend to forget he was flesh and blood as well as power and perfection.

Then we turn to the details of the gospel story. We hear the jeers. We feel the pulsating mob. We fear their denials. We dread their accusations. We are totally surrounded by flesh and blood, and Jesus is one of us.

Jesus returned to Nazareth, the place of his boyhood, to introduce his work to his close friends and family. As was the custom, he entered the synagogue and read God's Word from Isaiah 61:1–2. He rolled up the scroll, handed it back to the attendant, sat down, and interpreted this passage as being fulfilled within his own life (Luke 4:21).

The Christ of flesh and blood had a profound ministry to fulfill. He must be about his "Father's business" (Luke 2:49). Only as flesh and blood could he accomplish his present task as described in the passage from Isaiah that he read in the synagogue.

I. Preaching of the Gospel.

The gospel of God did not find its completion until the death and resurrection of Jesus Christ.

A. *Preach the good news.* Jesus felt the responsibility to proclaim a message of forgiveness and peace to the guilt-ridden and anguished generation of his day.

B. *Power of God.* Paul interpreted this "good news" as being a source of spiritual power. Sinful humanity is weak and insipid. The good news comes as a powerful intervention to rescue people from their wayward condition.

C. *Poverty of recipients.* Isaiah maintained that the recipients of this good news are the poor of the world. This poverty obviously refers to a spiritual bankruptcy that is found in every heart outside of Jesus Christ. The good news, when received by "the poor," extends to them wealth in Christ Jesus.

II. Healing of the brokenhearted.

Our God refused to view humanity only from his heavenly throne. Rather, he came down in the form of his Son and literally took upon himself flesh and blood.

A. *Heal.* In that Christ had experienced people's frailties, he was able to personally understand what was required in the healing process. Though Christ never sinned, he knew the human need to be created anew.

B. *Heartbroken.* Surely God suffered untold heartaches from the portals of heaven. But, as Jesus in the flesh, he was able to experience this from a human perspective.

C. *Help.* God does give the needed help to a person's broken heart. Through the compassion of Christ, the repentance of the sinner, and the aid of the Holy Spirit, the person finds his or her ruptured heart mended.

III. Deliverance of the captives.

Jesus Christ is the world's greatest liberator, but he is not indiscriminate in releasing people. He ministers only to hearts filled with repentance.

A. *Deliverance in general.* The deliverance performed by Christ is twofold—first, spiritual release and, second, physical release. It is available only to individuals who, recognizing their enslavement, are willing to repent and accept the freedom found in Christ.

B. *Deliverance in spiritual dimensions.* The Bible infers that a sinner is a prisoner of his or her own lusts and ungodly sins. Christ has offered each prisoner of Satan an opportunity to escape. This is spiritual deliverance.

C. *Deliverance in physical dimensions.* When people yield to the righteous life of Christ, their old habits of sin are crushed and they receive newness of life.

IV. Recovery of sight.

Every physically blind person who has accepted Jesus Christ as Savior has not automatically had his or her sight restored. The concept involved is spiritual sight.

A. *Recovery.* God wants to protect every one of his children from having to grope about in spiritual darkness. His heart cries for each to be recovered to the life of "lightness."

B. *Blinded.* This refers to the spiritual condition of those outside of Jesus Christ. If people are not walking in Christ's light, they are abiding in the darkness (or blindness) of sin.

C. *Sight.* When individuals let Jesus Christ into their heart, they receive spiritual 20-20 vision. New insights are given. Their eyes are opened to a brand new world.

V. Liberating the bruised.

No person may be held captive to sin without experiencing certain consequences.

A. *Liberating.* Jesus desires that every person everywhere be freed from the consequences of sin. He wants humanity to know freedom from the debilitating effects of sin.

B. *Bruised.* Sin degrades the body and leaves it scarred and mangled. Look at the scars that alcohol, drugs, and illicit sex leave. Look at the results of sin on bodies, minds, and families.

C. *Restoration.* Christ struggles to restore the bruised to a place of wholeness and happiness.

VI. Preaching the year of the Lord.

The Bible declares that through the foolishness of preaching those who believe will be saved (1 Cor 1:21).

A. *Preaching.* Our Lord believes in the value of preaching. He established this method of proclaiming the truth to reach the multitudes. His example is worth following.

B. *The acceptable year of the Lord.* This phrase indicates that the time of God's truth has now appeared. It is now the proper time to yield to the revelation of the Father.

Conclusion

Jesus maintains that this prophecy is now fulfilled within him. Tragically, his own hometown rejected his message. The flesh and blood Christ, rejected by his own, turns to us seeking receptive hearts. Does he find one in you?

SUNDAY EVENING, APRIL 18

Title: When Christ Calls Back His Church

Text: "Unto the angel of the church of Ephesus write . . ." **(Rev. 2:1).**

Scripture Reading: Revelation 2:1–7

Introduction

In these last days, Christ is calling his church back to himself, truly to be the church he desires it to be. The church at Ephesus had that opportunity and so does ours.

The church was located at the capitol of the province of Asia, a city that was a commercial and religious center. Ephesus was called "The Light of Asia." It was an ending point for a great system of Roman roads that constituted the trade route westward. It was famous for the Temple of Diana, one of the seven wonders of the world. And it was the hotbed of every false religious cult and superstition. In this city filled with paganism God planted a church that became a powerful gospel light throughout Asia.

The church at Ephesus had a great Christian background, with the apostle Paul as its originator. During a two-year period, he evangelized the whole province from this church. Timothy labored there, and the apostle John served as pastor before and after his exile to Patmos in his later years. Some of the most important parts of the New Testament are associated with Ephesus—the gospel of John; 1, 2, and 3 John; Revelation; Paul's epistle to the Ephesians; and Paul's letters to Timothy.

To this great church the Lord Jesus Christ gives a strong call. Let's look at three aspects of the church.

I. The Lord of the church.

The same triumphant Christ who is described in chapter 1 is giving his message here. He is the Christ of the churches, the Lord of the lampstands. Notice where he is and what he is doing. He is in the midst of the seven churches and is doing two things. First, he is holding the seven stars—the messengers or pastors of the churches—in his right hand. "Hold" is a strong word that means "to hold authoritatively." The pastors were held in divine protection and under divine control. How encouraging it is to be secure in Christ's hand (John 10:28–29)! Second, he is walking among the seven churches, not just standing. This speaks of his presence in his churches then and now. Matthew 28:20 is still strong with meaning: "Lo, I am with you alway, even unto the end of the world." Christ is administering the churches, revealing himself to them, reproving them, loving them, and ministering among them.

II. The life of the church.

The Lord of the church knows the life of the church. The word "know" emphasizes that he has an absolutely clear vision of all that is happening in the churches. He sees us clearly.

A. *The church is commended for being active and energetic.* The church had many activities, as seen from their "works." They were in business for the Lord. They were not like the church that, in its year-end report, listed no baptisms, no new members, and no gifts to missions, and added at the bottom a note that said, "Brethren, pray for us that we will hold our own."

B. *The church is commended for its labor.* The word used here for their works means toil and working at a cost. It is the type of toil required for a spiritual harvest (John 4:38). We tend to take the Great Commission lightly, but it requires blood, sweat, and tears.

C. *The church is commended for its patience.* Things were not easy for this church in this pagan city, because they were confronted with all kinds of trials. Nevertheless, they were patient. They accepted their difficult situation triumphantly.

We need to remember that patience is developed through trials. Do you want patience? Do you pray for it? When you do, watch out! The Lord will test you by giving you difficult situations. This is how patience grows.

D. *The church is commended for its sensitivity to evil.* They could not "bear them which are evil." The word "bear" has the idea of refusing to let evil have control. This is God's will for the church in all ages.

E. *The church is commended for its spiritual discernment.* John says they "have tried them. . .and hast found them liars." First John 4:1 says, "Beloved, believe not every spirit, but try the spirits whether they are of God." This is necessary lest there be "wolves in sheep's clothing," as Jesus warned.

F. *The church is commended for its endurance.* In verse 3 Jesus said they had "persevered and. . .endured hardships" (NIV) for his name. How do we endure? By the motivation of the name of Jesus Christ. It is his saving, sufficient, victorious name that enables us to keep on serving him.

G. *The church is commended for its determination.* They hadn't fainted, and they wouldn't quit. They purposed to accomplish God's goals in God's time regardless of the opposition.

In light of these commendations, the church at Ephesus was a great church! It possessed commendable qualities, but it still needed to be called back to Christ because one aspect of church life was missing, the most essential characteristic—love. Something had happened in the life of the church that had left them cold, mechanical, and routine. They were not experiencing the love of God as they once had. They had left their first love. It can happen to any Christian, so the Lord of the church is calling us back to our first love.

III. Lessons from the church.

Three lessons may be drawn from this situation.

A. *A church can sin away its opportunity.* Jesus warns, "or else I will come. . .quickly, and will remove thy [lampstand]." He is not speaking of his second coming here. He is talking about coming in special judgment on the church. This later happened at Ephesus. May it never happen to us.

B. *The one thing that Jesus wants for his church above all else is love.* Why was Ephesus such a great church as seen in Acts 19 and 20? What makes the church the church? What makes it the mighty, moving, meaningful body of Jesus Christ? It is filled with love!

Love is Jesus' new commandment (John 13:35). Love is poured into our hearts by the Holy Spirit (Rom. 5:5) and cultivated as the fruit of the Spirit (Gal. 5:22). Love is the more excellent way of the Lord (1 Cor. 13). Without love, we are nothing.

C. *Love can be renewed in our hearts.* Verse 5 says, "Remember. . .repent. . .and do." We can have the fresh touch of love upon our lives. "Remember" how it used do be in your life, in the happy days. "Repent!" Realize the need in your heart, confess the wrong in your life, turn your life over to Jesus Christ, and let the Holy Spirit fill you with love. "Do" the first works in the power of the Spirit and return to the Lord. Take whatever steps you need to take to make sure things are right with him and everyone in your life.

Conclusion

This is the call of Christ to his church today! As Vance Havner once said, "The church needs to take time out to tune up." Lord, renew our first love in our hearts!

WEDNESDAY EVENING, APRIL 21

Title: A Promise of Peace in Problem Times

Text: "And the peace of God, which passeth all understanding, shall keep your hearts and minds through Christ Jesus" **(Phil. 4:7).**

Scripture Reading: Philippians 4:6–7

Introduction

He was a man who had everything—a devoted wife, four lovely children, a comfortable home, two cars, and a job that paid a substantial salary. But he was an emotional wreck. He needed a pill to go to sleep, a pill to wake up, a pill before meals, and a pill to stop his hands from shaking. He was subject to panic attacks that made his legs go numb and his chest tight and gave the feeling that the whole room was spinning around. Soon he could not bring himself to go to work or meet friends or even leave the house. After suffering a nervous breakdown, a psychiatrist gave him drugs and shock treatments, but he only felt worse as a result.

On his doctor's advice he went to visit his brother in another city. While visiting with friends of his brother, he felt an attack coming and tried to leave the house. Blocked by the hostess, he sat down and blurted out the whole story. He ended despairingly by saying that no one could help him. The brother's friend said that someone could: Jesus. He told him his own story of how Christ had delivered him from emotional agony. They read some Scripture, had a prayer, and then went to dinner.

The man grew in his newfound Christian faith and never had another panic attack. He found peace by believing Philippians 4:7, a promise passed on to us by the apostle Paul for peace in problem times.

I. The problem: anxiety.

The New International Version translates the opening phrase of verse 6: "Do not be anxious about anything." Anxiety is not quite the same thing as worry or fear. Worry or fear may have a basis, but anxiety often begins from within.

We have a biblical example in Martha, the sister of Mary and Lazarus. When Jesus visited with them, she was anxious and troubled about the serving of the meal. She was so anxiety ridden that she could not enjoy the company of Jesus while he was in her home. Anxiety often marks people's lives. Their faces show it, actions express it, and words betray it.

II. The answer: prayer.

Paul gives us an answer to anxiety: prayer that recognizes God, opens the heart to God, and gives thanks to God. Notice the specific things said about prayer in the face of anxiety:

A. *It is an inclusive prayer.* "In everything" (NIV) is the way Paul expressed it. Nothing that concerns Christians is too inconsequential to take to God in prayer.

B. *It is a prayer of praise.* Supplications are made with thanksgiving. Prayer begins with praise to God.

A pastor told of an old man, nearly blind, who lived in a tenement in New York's East Harlem. When the pastor visited him, they made their way through the stale stench of a moldy building to a single room on the top floor. The ceiling sagged, and dark brown paper hung in shreds from the dirty walls. When they sat on the bed that took up most of the space, the old man got his Bible. It fell open to Psalms. The psalms he read were psalms of praise, not psalms of comfort. When the old man read those expressions of praise to God, he would say, "Alleluia! Glory! Alleluia!" and never pay any attention to the scratching of a rat behind the wall.

III. The result: peace.

A. *The kind of peace.* It is a peace that transcends all understanding, a peace that has to be experienced before it can be understood.

B. *The extent of the peace.* This peace will stand guard over the believer's heart and mind.
C. *The source of the peace.* This peace is "through Christ Jesus."

Conclusion

Problem times will come, but we have a promise of peace.

SUNDAY MORNING, APRIL 25

Title: Touching the Living Christ

Text: "She said, If I may touch but his clothes, I shall be whole" **(Mark 5:28).**

Scripture Reading: Mark 5:25–34

Hymns: "Blessed Be the Name," Wesley
"The Great Physician," Hunter
"I Love to Tell the Story," Hankey

Offertory Prayer: Holy Father, we come today to worship you in Spirit and in truth. We come bringing our hearts and minds praying that we might be open to every impression that can come to us through your Word. We come bringing tithes and offerings as symbols of our desire to be completely dedicated to you. Bless these gifts to the advancement of your kingdom and to the good of humankind. Through Jesus Christ we pray. Amen.

Introduction

Christianity is a religion based on miracles. The living Christ performs a miracle in the heart of everyone who will trust him. We need to reexamine the great miracles that he performed during his life that we might experience similar miracles today.

The healing of the woman with the issue of blood is a miracle within a miracle. All three Synoptic Gospels record it (Matt. 9:20–22; Mark 5:25–34; Luke 8:41–48).

Jairus, a ruler of the synagogue, came and fell down at Jesus' feet and asked that he come and heal his twelve-year-old daughter who was dying. As Jesus went with Jairus, the people crowded him. It was then that the woman with the issue of blood touched him and was healed. Word came that Jairus's daughter was dead. But Jesus raised her from the dead and made her well.

Consider the woman with the issue of blood, the woman who had hemorrhaged for twelve years (Luke 8:43). She had spent all her money on doctors, and they had not been able to cure her (Luke 8:43). She was healed by showing faith in Christ (Luke 8:44–48). Scripture says that she was healed immediately (Matt. 9:22; Mark 5:29).

Let's seek from this miracle the truths God has for us.

I. The woman who touched Jesus had heard of him, and this inspired her to act (Mark 5:27).

This woman, who legend says was Veronica, a woman who later handed Jesus her handkerchief to wipe his face when he was on the way to the cross, had heard of Jesus. What had she heard? If we glance back chronologically, we will see certain things that had taken place of which she may have heard. For instance, Jesus had raised Simon Peter's mother-in-law from her sickbed, cleansed a leper, raised the son of the widow of Nain from the dead, cast out demons, and stilled a storm on the lake.

No doubt this woman had heard of these things. She felt sure that Jesus could heal her if only she could touch him. Hearing of Jesus inspires hope!

II. The woman who touched Jesus had an imperfect faith, but the main thing is that she did have faith.

Let's thank the Lord for the genuineness of faith even though it appears imperfect.

Jesus asked, "Who touched me?" (Mark 5:30). The disciples thought Jesus was talking about the curious crowd who crushed him. But the word that Jesus used means "grasped." The question was: "Who grasped me?" Jesus knew that power had gone out of him as the woman likely grasped the *kraspendon,* a tassel bound with blue attached at each corner of the garment he wore (Num. 15:37–39). Perhaps the woman thought there was healing in the garment, but healing was in Christ himself (Mark 5:30).

III. The woman who touched Jesus found that he had time for her.

In Leviticus 15:19–27 we find careful instructions as to how persons suffering from any form of the woman's malady were to be treated. She was to be segregated from the company of worshipers for so long as it continued. She was excommunicated from the temple and the synagogue. By the law of the rabbis, she was divorced from her husband. She was shut out from family life, ostracized by society, reduced to poverty, had an incurable disease, and was dying.

The woman who touched Jesus was hopeless and felt that if only she could touch the tassel on Jesus' garment, she could be healed. To her utter astonishment she found that she was not only healed but that Jesus actually had time for her. Jesus is never too busy to have time for you!

IV. The woman who touched Jesus found in him what people could not supply.

The woman with the issue of blood had been to physicians, and they had pronounced her incurable. The Great Physician, however, had what she needed—a miracle. The Lord Jesus Christ has what we need, and he is able to supply all our needs (Phil. 4:19).

V. The woman who touched Jesus found that she had to tell the truth and confess Christ publicly.

The woman who touched Jesus and was healed thought she could carry away the blessing without Jesus even knowing she had touched him. But Jesus asked, "Who touched my clothes?" (Mark 5:30). The question was designed to bring the woman to a public acknowledgment of the blessing she had received. Jesus knew the difference between the jostle of a curious mob and the contact of a soul in need. The woman needed more than a cure; she needed to become a confessor. This she did as she came forward. She "fell down before him, and told him all the truth" (Mark 5:33).

Jesus said to the woman who touched him: "Daughter, thy faith hath made thee whole; go in peace, and be whole of the plague" (Mark 5:34). She found healing, courage, peace, and adoption into the family of God. She believed and she confessed. She was healed by the touch of trust and was strengthened by the confession of her lips.

Conclusion

Hear what God's Word says: "Whosoever therefore shall be ashamed of me and of my words...of him shall the Son of man be ashamed" (Mark 8:38). "For with the heart man believeth unto righteousness; and with the mouth confession is made unto salvation" (Rom 10:9).

Put your trust in the One who can make you whole. Confess him publicly! Confess him now!

SUNDAY EVENING, APRIL 25

Title: The Church Christ Crowns

Text: "Be thou faithful unto death, and I will give thee a crown of life" **(Rev. 2:10).**

Scripture Reading: Revelation 2:8–11

Introduction

It is interesting what people look for when they join a church. What do you look for? Would you have joined the church at Smyrna?

The city of Smyrna was called "the Beauty of Asia" and was the second most notable city in Asia next to Ephesus. A city of many thousands called Izmar is still there today. It, too, has a Christian church. Smyrna was a wealthy commercial center noted for an herb from which myrrh came. The word

Smyrna itself means "myrrh." Myrrh is a sweet perfume used in embalming the dead, so the word is related to suffering and death. It is especially appropriate for the church at Smyrna because it was a suffering church.

This church that the Lord Jesus Christ promises to crown was in a city noted for its wickedness and opposition to the gospel of Christ. Smyrna also was a center for emperor worship and had a temple built to Tiberius Caesar. Many Jews, who were opposed to Christians, lived in the city. They constantly harassed the church. Some special qualities, then, were needed for a church in such hostile surroundings. Of all the seven churches, this is the one the Lord says he will crown. Three things will help us to understand why.

I. The Lord of the church.

Jesus identifies himself as "the first and the last, which was dead, and is alive." This description emphasizes two things.

A. *His person.* Jesus is "the first and the last." He is the eternal One. He has always existed and always will. He is Lord of time and eternity.

B. *His work.* Jesus "was dead, and is alive." "Was dead" speaks of his death on the cross. Philippians 2:5–9 describes how he became subject to death, even the death of the cross. "Is alive" refers to his resurrection and his triumph over death and rejection.

As the Lord of the churches, he is walking among them, being with them, speaking to them words that they need to hear. To the church at Smyrna he speaks words of great encouragement, such as, "Where you are going, I have already been" and "I will make you victorious over all these times you face." Death could not defeat him, and neither will second death hurt them or anyone like them.

II. Life in the church.

Jesus says to the church at Smyrna, "I know. . . ." Thus, the sympathetic Christ assures them of his true understanding of their needs and his ability to supply them. Let's focus on four things he knows.

A. *Their tribulation.* The Greek word here for "tribulation" basically means "pressure." It is to suffer affliction, to be troubled and put under pressure. Vine says it is the type of pressure that comes from without, from circumstances or the antagonism of persons. The picture is of a heavy millstone grinding wheat into flour or pressing juice from grapes. Thus, we can see that the church at Smyrna was under heavy pressure and intense tribulation.

We may not especially like it from a human point of view, but tribulation is an essential part of spiritual growth. Romans 5:3 says, "Tribulation worketh patience. . . ." According to the words of Jesus, we may overcome tribulation and live cheerfully (John 16:33).

B. *Their poverty.* In the New Testament there are two words for poverty. One means to barely make a living; the other means to have nothing, to be utterly destitute. This second word describes Smyrna. Why were they poor? For one thing, most Christians in the first century were poor; and second, they were poor because of persecution. They were plundered and deprived of a way to make a living. Many were wiped out financially by people who reported them to the government as heretics.

But Jesus says something beautiful about this church: "You are rich." They were poor, but they were rich! They were so spiritually rich that being materially poor didn't defeat them.

C. *The blasphemy.* The word "blasphemy" is comprised of two words meaning "to injure" and "speech." Therefore, blasphemy is speech that injures. The Jews were slandering these believers in Christ. They were poisoning the minds of the people against Christians so that persecution resulted.

D. *Future sufferings.* Jesus spoke of the things that the church would suffer. Things would get worse before they got better. The worst was yet to come—imprisonment, tribulation, suffering, and death.

When we think about what this church faced, we realize how important it was that they remembered that Christ the Lord was not dead but alive, walking among them. He was with them! He was holding up the pastor with his right hand of authority. There is hope when we turn our eyes upon Jesus!

III. Lessons from the church.

A. *The people of God have an enemy to face.* He is referred to twice in this letter. In verse 9 he is called "Satan," or adversary. As an adversary he opposes or resists; he is an enemy to the church. In this situation the tactic he uses is blasphemy or slander. The synagogue at Smyrna was slandering the church at Smyrna (v. 9), but the one really behind this was Satan himself. Let us never forget it! Satan is our enemy, and we have to stand against him in hand-to-hand combat (cf. Eph. 6:10–19).

In verse 10 the enemy is called "the devil," or accuser. He can afflict with physical suffering; he oppresses people (Acts 10:38); and here he is about to cast some into prison.

The devil is not dead. Today he is still alive and powerfully at work. He is still stealing, killing, and destroying all that he can, whether it is our testimony, personal relationships, families, the church, or America. But our victory is in the Lord of the church, Jesus Christ himself!

B. *Suffering may come to Christians.* Smyrna had suffered intensely already and would be facing "ten days" of suffering. This represents a brief intense time of suffering; and in a larger sense, it describes prophetically that period of history when the church passed through persecution.

Foxe's Book of Martyrs describes ten pagan persecutions when hundreds of thousands of Christians died for Christ's sake.

Suffering for Christians is a reality. Why do we suffer?

1. Suffering disciplines us (1 Cor. 11:30–32; Heb. 12:3–13).
2. Suffering prevents our being proud (2 Cor. 12:7).
3. Suffering teaches us (Rom 5:3–5; Heb. 5:8).
4. Suffering builds a better testimony for Christ (Acts 9:16).
5. Suffering heals others (1 Peter 2:24).

C. *There are two qualities that will cause Christ to crown the church.* The first one is fearlessness. "Stop being afraid!" (v.10). It is not God's will that we be fearful (2 Tim. 1:7). It is Satan who inspires fear in us toward ourselves, toward himself, toward others, and toward the future. The second quality is faithfulness. "Be thou faithful" (v. 10). The church was already loyal, and they are to remain loyal, even if it meant death.

How Christ honors loyalty! When we are loyal it means that we are using adversity to confirm our commitment to those whom God has called us to serve. It means to confirm rather than quit or compromise. We are to be loyal at all times, under all circumstances, to the very end.

Conclusion

Polycarp, pastor of the Smyrna church, suffered death for Jesus Christ. He was commanded to say, "Caesar is Lord," but instead he said, "Jesus is Lord." He said, "Eighty and five years have I served him, and he has done me no wrong." So they took him, bound him, and burned him at the stake. As he died he glorified Christ by saying, "Jesus is Lord! Jesus is Lord!" It is this kind of life and this kind of church that the Lord Jesus Christ crowns!

WEDNESDAY EVENING, APRIL 28

Title: Inspiration for Noble Living

Text: "Finally, brethren, whatsoever things are true, whatsoever things are honest, whatsoever things are just, whatsoever things are pure, whatsoever things are lovely, whatsoever things are of good report; if there be any virtue, and if there be any praise, think on these things" (**Phil. 4:8–9**).

Scripture Reading: Philippians 4:8–9

Introduction

This is an age of gracious living. But is it a time of noble living? We have learned much about making life different, but we have learned little about making different lives. Perhaps the situation was summed up well by General Omar Bradley, who said that we have become nuclear giants and ethical infants.

How can we learn to live nobly? Paul made an appeal for noble living near the close of his letter to the Philippians.

I. We have a personalized pattern as an inspiration for noble living.

Paul gave us a pattern for noble living in his own life. In Philippians 4:9 he tells his readers to do "whatever you have learned or received or heard from me, or seen in me" (NIV).

Notice the principles that make up the pattern (v.8).

A. *Things that are true.*
B. *Things that are honest or honorable.*
C. *Things that are just.*
D. *Things that are pure.*
E. *Things that are lovely.*
F. *Things that are gracious.*

What are we to do with the six great pieces that make up this personalized pattern? Two things.

First, we must think on them. The word used in verse 8 actually means to calculate as builders do when they take careful measure before they begin to build. The second thing is suggested in verse 9. We are to do these things.

In Plato's *Republic* there is a passage in which Socrates points out that it is not what youth is privately taught concerning virtue that most influences youth, but what is applauded in the assembly and the marketplace. We may give lip service to all of the virtues listed above, but unless we think about them until they become a part of our lives and then do them, we will not change our lifestyle or positively influence others.

II. We have a peace-giving presence as an inspiration for noble living.

Did you notice what Paul said would be the result of following this pattern? "...and the God of peace will be with you." What a strong inspiration that is. To know that the presence of God, that presence that gives comfort, assurance, and security will be with us throughout life, surely gives peace.

We think of peace negatively: Peace is the absence of trouble. But the peace of God is a positive matter that has to do with right relationships with him and with others.

With trust in God we do not have to be constantly beset with worries. Most of our worries never happen anyway. But even if they do, God's presence is with us in peace.

Conclusion

We are inspired to live nobly. We have a pattern to guide us and a presence to strengthen us as we do so.

Suggested preaching program for the month of

MAY

■ **Sunday Mornings**

The church can be no stronger than the homes that make up its membership. Therefore, the church must do all it can to enrich family living. The suggested theme for a series of messages concluding on Father's Day next month is "Would Christ Be Welcome in Your Home?"

■ **Sunday Evenings**

Continue the series "The Triumphant Christ and the Church Triumphant."

■ **Wednesday Evenings**

The suggested theme is "The Prayers of God to His People." At first glance this may seem like an irreverent theme, but the thesis of this series of messages is that prayer is a dialogue between God and his people rather than a monologue in which his people only talk to him.

SUNDAY MORNING, MAY 2

Title: Would Christ Be Welcome in Your Home?

Text: "Now as they went on their way, he entered a village; and a woman named Martha received him into her house" (**Luke 10:38 RSV**).

Scripture Reading: Luke 10:38–42

Hymns: "Glorious Is Thy Name," McKinney
       "He Keeps Me Singing," Bridges
       "What If It Were Today?" Morris

Offertory Prayer: Heavenly Father, we have come together as your children into a place dedicated to prayer and worship. We pray today for the faith that will make it possible for each of us to experience the living presence of Jesus Christ. We come bringing our faults and failures in need of forgiveness and bringing our words of praise and thanksgiving. We come with our tithes and offerings that we might share in your work. Help us this day to give our minds as well as our bodies into your service to the end that others might experience your love and come to know Jesus Christ as Savior. In Jesus' name we pray. Amen.

Introduction

A common wall plaque found in souvenir shops bears the inscription: OUR HOUSE IS OPEN TO GOD, FRIENDS, GUESTS, AND SUNSHINE. That is a pleasant thought. Would Christ be welcome in your home today?

Christ was welcome in the home of the two disciples who lived in Emmaus (Luke 24:28–29). The Christ who revealed himself to be alive to those early disciples lives today and wants to come into your home just as he came into their home.

At the home of Peter, Christ healed Peter's mother-in-law (Mark 1:29–31). He also encouraged hope and delivered those who were under the control of demons. He revealed who he was and what he had come to accomplish.

Christ was also welcome in the home of Zacchaeus (Luke 19:1–10). In this home Christ was the self-invited guest who came to make some changes in Zacchaeus and his household. Zacchaeus listened and responded and rejoiced over the great changes that came about because of Christ's presence.

The New Testament records three visits of Jesus' to the home of Mary, Martha, and Lazarus. There were probably many more.

I. Jesus' three visits.

These three visits of our Lord to the home of his friends were typical but also significant.

A. *Jesus came to the home of Mary, Martha, and Lazarus on a casual occasion when he was unexpected (Luke 10:38–42).* We know that Jesus was unexpected on this occasion because Martha would have had things ready if she had known he was coming.

 1. Perhaps Jesus was a self-invited guest on this occasion as the living demonstration of the grace of God. We can assume that Jesus invited himself into the homes of people because, by doing so, he could bring God's blessings to them.

 2. Perhaps Jesus had a standing invitation at the home of Mary, Martha, and Lazarus. It would be beautiful to think that he did.

B. *Jesus came to the house of Mary and Martha at a time of sorrow (John 11:1–44).* On this occasion our Lord demonstrated his resurrection power and called Lazarus forth from the grave and thus restored the beloved brother to the grief-stricken sisters.

 If you and I want Jesus to come to us in our times of sorrow, he needs to have a standing invitation into our homes at all times.

C. *Jesus came to this home in a time of celebration (John 12:1–3).* Mary and Martha were preparing a feast for their friends, and Jesus was invited. It was indeed a happy time, and a festive spirit prevailed.

Do we forget or ignore the Christ in our times of celebration and happiness? By all means, we should invite him on such occasions.

II. The purpose of Jesus' visits.

A. *Jesus came, not to be served, but to serve (Mark 10:45).* Our Lord was not one who sought to crash a party. He did not intrude where he was unwelcome. He would never cause embarrassment. On the contrary, at the wedding in Cana he provided wine for the guests so that the host would not be embarrassed (John 2:1–11).

B. *Perhaps Jesus came into this home to fulfill his personal needs.*
   1. Our Lord, though he was divine, was yet human and needed nourishment. On two of the occasions when he visited, we read of his eating with his hosts.
   2. Our Lord needed human friendship. He selected the twelve apostles in order that they might be with him.
   3. Our Lord needed encouragement. He was aware of the imminence of his death by crucifixion, and the costly ointment that Mary poured on him was a special sign of devotion that would strengthen him as he faced death (John 12:7).

C. *Jesus came to this home to teach the loving ways of God.*
   1. Mary sat at Jesus' feet and listened to his teaching while Martha prepared the meal (Luke 10:39–40).
   2. At some point Martha learned who Jesus really was (John 11:27). Jesus wants to come into our home to teach us the loving ways of God.

D. *Jesus came into this home to correct and rearrange their priorities.*

   Our Lord told Martha that "one thing is needful." Evidently Martha was preparing a feast of many dishes, and our Lord was declaring that only a simple meal was necessary.

   Our lives would be much more harmonious and productive if we would draw up a list of things that need to be done and arrange them in the order of importance. We could begin with number one and complete it and then move on to number two.

E. *Jesus came into this home with sympathy in the time of their sorrow (John 11).*

F. *Jesus came into this home with power to give new life.*

Conclusion

Jesus was welcome in the home of Mary, Martha, and Lazarus.

We read in the New Testament about a rich young man who admired Jesus but who neglected to welcome him into the home of his heart. His priorities would not permit Jesus to enter in. On the other hand, we read about a man named Zacchaeus who let Jesus come into his house and change his whole life.

What about you? Christ wants to come into your heart to be your Lord. In love and power, he wants to reverse some things in your life and reorganize some other things. He wants to use, enrich, complete, and empower your life.

Is Jesus welcome in your home? Will you invite him to come in today?

SUNDAY EVENING, MAY 2

Title: Christ's Call for Moral Courage

Text: "And to the angel of the church in Pergamos write. . ." **(Rev. 2:12).**

Scripture Reading: Revelation 2:12–17

Introduction

Jesus Christ delivered seven special messages to seven special churches in the first century of Christian history. Those messages have been relevant for every church in every period of history and are still significant for us today. Just as Christ was equipping churches then, so he is equipping churches now.

He is calling us to his best. His will for us as his church is that he be our first love, just as he desired for Ephesus, and a deep loyalty, such as Smyrna expressed. His special word to Pergamos is a call to moral courage. As we will see, this church needed this message, but in our day and time, what church doesn't? Follow the progression of thought in Christ's call to his church by noticing seven words.

I. Christ.

First of all, we see Christ with a sharp, double-edged sword. This is in contrast to the revelation of himself to Smyrna. Here we see the ascended Christ engaging in spiritual warfare against the enemy with the sword of the Spirit, the Word of God (cf. Eph. 6:10–18). His Word is the instrument that is "quick, and powerful, and sharper than any two-edged sword" (Heb. 4:12). The Word cuts two ways—going and coming. It produces death but also life; it delivers judgment but also grace.

II. Conflict.

Pergamos was a church confronted with constant conflict. Notice where the church dwelled: "even were Satan's seat is." The word "seat" is the Greek word for throne, so these Christians were living where Satan had great power. Four idolatrous temples were built there, as was a world-famous altar to Zeus. Three temples were dedicated to Roman emperors, and Caesar worship was forced.

Satan was in the "driver's seat" in Pergamos. He was having his way as the enemy of Christ and the church. He is still in the "driver's seat" today in many places. He must have many of his hosts working on America, because his throne is more evident all the time. We are allowing more and more filth in the land and demonstrating less and less faith as Christians. Evil is bold in our time. This is where we live, just as the church dwelled in Pergamos. This is exactly where the body of Christ ought to be—in the big middle of hell itself—proclaiming the gospel of Jesus Christ!

Satan can set up his throne in a nation, city, home, church, school, or person's life. He can set up his throne in sports, in television, and in the literature of our day. Just be aware of this reality and the conflict that is being waged!

III. Conviction.

But I also see conviction in the church. There was something special about most of the Christians in Pergamos. For one thing, they were "holding fast" to Jesus' name. The present tense of the verb emphasizes how loyal and determined they were. They refused to say, "Caesar is Lord," and were confessing, "Jesus is Lord."

They "[had] not denied" the faith of Christ. They were in close personal relationship with him. The church was engulfed in evil, yet it was standing true. One man, Antipas, especially stood out as a symbol of faithfulness, in that he died for his faith. He stood alone even though it meant death.

We need to remember that the temptation to deny Jesus is a reality. Yielding to pressure of the crowd, going along with the group, or just keeping silent about your relationship to Jesus amounts to a denial of him. The call is to stand alone in your faith and confess him as Lord.

IV. Confusion.

Although the church had some strength of conviction, in it was a confusion that expressed itself in the condition of the church.

First, there existed in the church "the doctrine of Balaam." Numbers 22–24 and 31 tell the story of Balaam's subtle counsel that led the children of Israel into sensuality, carnality, and lust. In the church there were some "Balaamites" who were influencing others to sin against God by compromising their relationship with Jesus Christ. Christians were being confused about eating meat offered to idols and committing fornication. They were conforming to the world rather than being transformed by the renewing of their minds.

How should we live today—by society's standards, no standards, or Christ's standards? The call of Jesus Christ seems clear enough even though the air is filled with moral confusion.

Second, there was confusion about "the doctrine of the Nicolaitans." Some say the Nicolaitans were "the playboys of the day"; others say the doctrine was just another expression of the doctrine of Balaam; and a third view is that this term refers to a class of people who exalted themselves above others. Whatever the precise view is, we know for certainty that the Pergamos church represents the church married to the world and that the living Christ uses his sharp sword against it.

V. Courage.

This letter sounds out a call for moral courage in the church. The church was allowing worldly members to go unchecked. It was permissive instead of powerful. Jesus spoke against their lack of courage. He expected the church to discipline itself and to do whatever was necessary to make the body healthy and strong.

VI. Call.

What is the church to do? Repent (v. 16). We are to repent of our moral impurity, our moral weaknesses, and our lack of moral leadership and courage. We are to repent personally, as families, and as a church. There is no way out of moral bondage apart from repentance, so we are to get our house in order. And it should not take forever to do it!

VII. Conquest.

Conquest speaks of victory, and this is what the Lord promises to those who overcome. Conquest is dependent on obedience to the person and ministry of the Holy Spirit. "He that hath an ear, let him hear what the Spirit saith unto the churches."

Conclusion

Those who respond to this call for moral courage are given "hidden manna"—that is, they have that secret source of spiritual food, fellowship with Christ himself through the ministry of the Holy Spirit. They are also given a "white stone" with a "new name." Some see the white stone as a symbol of full acceptance by the Lord; others view the stone as a crystal clear diamond, like the Urim on the breastplate of the high priest. This would mean that just as the Urim was the means by which God's will could be found, so the white stone means that the one who possesses it can have wisdom to know God's direction in everything he or she faces.

There is no need to live in confusion when the Lord has promised wisdom and victory to those whose lives are lived in moral courage. Do you need moral courage? If so, submit your life to Christ and you will overcome!

WEDNESDAY EVENING, MAY 5

Title: The Prayers of God

Text: "Now the LORD said to Abram, 'Go from your country and from your kindred and your father's house to the land that I will show you'" **(Gen. 12:1 RSV).**

Scripture Reading: Genesis 12:1–4

Introduction

The Bible is a divinely inspired record of God's self-disclosure to humanity. In a unique way, God began his progressive self-disclosure in his choice of Abraham as the father of the faithful. The rest of the Bible is a progressive explanation of what God did after he first communicated with Abraham.

Almost without exception we think of prayer as a human activity directed toward God. Have you ever thought of prayer as a divine activity directed toward humankind?

Do you think of prayer as a monologue in which you come into God's throne room to talk to him about your problems and needs? Is this your total concept of prayer? Do you also realize that prayer is a dialogue in which we communicate with the eternal God who has revealed himself as a loving Father and in which he communicates with us?

I would not be irreverent at all by talking in terms of the prayers of God to us. We pray to God in the hope that he will answer. The Bible is a record of God's petitions, requests, promises, and plans for us.

The account of Abraham's call records one of the great prayers of God and reveals that prayer is a dialogue in which God communicates with us.

I. Prayer is a divinely initiated experience.

Perhaps we have thought of prayer as something we do on our own initiative. A close study of the Word will convince us that prayer is a divinely initiated experience. It is the Father God who moves us to pray and who creates within us a hunger for fellowship with him.

Stephen declares that it was God who took the initiative in communicating his will to Abraham. Stephen said to the people of his day, "Brethren and fathers, hear me. The God of Glory appeared to our father Abraham, when he was in Mesopotamia, before he lived in Haran, and said to him, 'Depart from your land and from your kindred and go into the land which I will show you'" (Acts 7:1–2 RSV).

How and when did God initiate this experience? We cannot know for certain.

Did God speak to Abraham during the silence in the darkness of the night, or while he was in deep meditation and contemplation, or while he was busy at work? We just do not know the answer to this question.

The overwhelming truth is that God initiated the process of communication. Does it not follow that God initiates our experiences with him even as an earthly parent hungers for meaningful communication with a child who is now at a distance?

II. In this prayer experience Abraham received some strong commands.

"Go from your country and your kindred and your father's house to the land that I will show you."
A. *God's command called for him to leave his country.*
B. *God's command called for him to leave his kindred.*

We are to understand this in terms of the total environment rather than his immediate family, for his father accompanied him part of the way and his nephew Lot went with him all of the way. Abraham evidently had a strong responsibility for this nephew.

The call to separateness continues to be true today, for Christ is the great divider. If we would be his true disciples, we must give to him our undivided love and loyalty (see Luke 9:57–62; 12:49–53).

III. In this prayer experience Abraham received some clear promises.

In every commandment that comes from God there is either an implicit or explicit precious promise. Some of us want to claim the promises without meeting the conditions, but the commandment and the promise are always tied together.
A. *"I will make of you a great nation."*
B. *"I will bless you, and make your name great."*
C. *"You will be a blessing."*
D. *"I will bless those that bless you, and him who curses you I will curse."*
E. *"By you all the families of the earth shall bless themselves."*

A close study of these commandments shows that they contain more than a promise; they also contain a commission. God elected Abraham and his descendants by his own sovereign grace for a redemptive purpose. He planned to use them to be a blessing to the whole human race.

God did not choose Abraham as a reward for something that Abraham had done or would do. He chose Abraham that he might be fruitful and productive and that he and his descendants might be useful in the divine purpose of redeeming people from the waste of sin.

As we look at the commandments of God, let's also take note of his precious promises. We must not miss the promise if we are to have the courage and faith to respond to the commandments of God.

IV. Notice Abraham's response to this prayer experience: "So Abram went, as the LORD had told him" (Gen. 12:4).

Abraham answered the prayer that God offered to him with an affirmative response. He moved in trusting obedience to the will of the God who approached him, chose him, and promised to bless him.

Conclusion

When you feel a need for prayer in your heart, recognize it as the divine initiative by which God is drawing you into his throne room to communicate his grace, guidance, and help to you.

Realize that in the prayer experience God is going to bless you that you might be a blessing. Let's rejoice not only that we have the privilege of talking with God but also that he wants to talk with us.

SUNDAY MORNING, MAY 9

Title: The Mother a Child Needs

Text: "Train up a child in the way he should go: and when he is old, he will not depart from it" (**Prov. 22:6**).

Scripture Reading: Proverbs 31:10–31

Hymns: "When Morning Gilds the Skies," Caswell
"Make Me a Blessing," Wilson
"O Master, Let Me Walk with Thee," Gladden

Offertory Prayer: Our Father, this is a special day in our lives, the day we give special recognition to our mothers. Thank you for our mothers. We are grateful for the influence they have had on our individual lives, as well as on the lives of our neighbors and friends. As we worship you in our giving, we ask that you will help us to express our gratitude beyond that of lip service and give as you have given to us. In the name of Jesus we pray. Amen.

Introduction

All normal, conscientious Christian parents want to see their child succeed. It is their hope that their child will exceed in the good things of life, such as Christian virtues—love, forgiveness, kindness, and helpfulness—profitable and honorable occupations, well-adjusted and harmonious home lives, and productive Christian service.

The question that looms high in a Christian parent's mind is, "What can I do to help my child be such a person?"

Most productive people are what they are not because of inherited traits but because of their training. Any child can develop the characteristics that underlie productivity provided that he or she is given the basic conditions for the development of self-esteem. This is where the mother serves the child.

I. The basic of all essentials for a mother is to instill in her children an early acceptance of Jesus Christ as Savior.

A. *Jesus uses some powerful words to emphasize this.* Matthew 19:13–14 has a strong warning about prohibiting children from coming to Jesus and an equally strong command that they be brought. Parents are to take heed.

B. *All mothers need to glean some basic information in regard to child evangelism and also guard against certain erroneous philosophy.* Children can and do become Christians. They need to make this decision early in life, and most who do remain more loyal to their Lord and his church than those who wait until later.

Mothers need to guard against being a hindrance to or holding back a child who desires to accept Jesus as Lord.

II. Another basic condition for the development of self-esteem is to have nurturing parents.

A. *A nurturing mother is one who is affectionate.* The root meaning of the word *affectionate* is "to lay hold of; to act or impress." Affection is the verbal and physical expression of love. Each child needs to be told frequently and under various conditions that he or she is loved. A mother should say "I love you" so much to her child that there is never any question in the child's mind about the love the mother has for her own. Children also need to be touched and held close so that their little bodies feel the warmth of their mother. These affectionate relations are never to cease even though their expression changes with age.

B. *A nurturing mother is one who has empathy toward her children.* Empathy is the projection of one's feelings over to another. This is done by listening. A mother should make sure she takes the time needed to hear what her child is saying. Never consider a conversation to be too childish to listen to. Empathy is also shown by being slow to give pat answers. Giving an inappropriate answer may be worse than having none. All the feelings of a child should be considered. None is too insignificant. A mother is never to degrade her child.

C. *A nurturing mother is one who sets high standards for her children in precept and example.* Jesus said, "Be ye therefore perfect, even as your Father which is in heaven is perfect" (Matt. 5:48). This is a high and noble standard for living. Mothers should have nothing less. A mother is to live the example as well as to teach the right things. She should always hold righteousness and wholesomeness before her children.

III. Self-esteem is realized when the child has authoritative parents.

A. *Authority is defined as being entitled to obedience or acceptance.* A Christian mother will conduct herself in such a way that obedience comes easily to her children. She should avoid a dictatorial attitude and live in such a way that she is accepted as an authority. This includes training and discipline.

B. *A mother's authority is derived from the Lord, directed to the child with tender love, and seasoned with kindness and consideration.* Testimonies from children themselves support the idea that they want this kind of authority exercised by their parents. Testimonies from law enforcement personnel give evidence that authority is a must for a child to develop self-esteem and, consequently, become productive.

Conclusion

Being a mother is a challenging role. But God doesn't give any of us more than we can handle. Rather, he supplies everything we need. Let every mother make a new commitment to him. Ask the Holy Spirit to take control of your life. Then act in obedience and set the example.

SUNDAY EVENING, MAY 9

Title: A Cleansed Church
Text: "Unto the angel of the church in Thyatira write..." **(Rev. 2:18).**
Scripture Reading: Revelation 2:18–29

Introduction

The letter to the church at Thyatira is the longest letter to the church located in the least important city. It contains the strongest commendation, yet it has the severest warning of all the letters.

The seven letters to the churches in Asia Minor reveal God's will for the church. If the church of Jesus Christ is to be the church triumphant, it will be a church where love is warm and fresh and Christlike. It will be a church that possesses the quality of loyalty, even unto death if necessary. It will be a church that will not compromise or be conformed to the world. It will be a church cleansed of all its moral impurities, as Jesus demands of the church at Thyatira.

It is God's will for the church that it be clean. Ephesians 5:25–27 says, "Christ also loved the church, and gave himself for it; that he might sanctify and cleanse it with the washing of water by the word, that he might present it to himself a glorious church, not having spot, or wrinkle, or any such thing; but that it should be holy and without blemish." We cannot possibly be ready for the coming of Christ apart from living a cleansed life. The letter to Thyatira is a call from the living Christ to his church then and now to be cleansed. What is involved in such a call?

I. The person of Christ.

In verse 18 Christ identifies himself as "the Son of God," thus speaking with authority. His "eyes like unto a flame of fire" suggest his penetrating insight into the church. He has the capacity to see who we really are beneath the surface. Only Christ knows what a life and a church are really like. He sees behind the closed doors of our lives, knows what we do when no one is around, and knows our inward motives.

As seen before, Christ's "feet like unto fine brass" refer to his judgment on the church. Brass is symbolic of judgment, and all things are under his feet, so he judges the church by his authority. The Lord Jesus Christ speaks to us in the same firmness when he calls for cleansing in our lives.

II. Praise for the church.

In verse 19 Christ praises the church with strong words of commendation for its way of life.

A. *He praises its works in that it is an active body of Christ.* They are not lazy.
B. *He praises its works of love.* This is agape love—God's love in them and their love for God and one another.
C. *He praises its works of faith.* This refers to their faithfulness, and it is their love that results in faithfulness.
D. *He praises its works of ministry.* This is love in action—acts of ministry in kindness and tenderness to other members of the body.
E. *He praises its works of patience.* They accept their difficult situation from God without giving him a deadline to remove it.
F. *He praises its works of progress.* These works are more at the last than at the first. They are growing spiritually. Their works are commendable, but there is something wrong!

III. The problem in the church.

The problem in the church is introduced in verse 20 by the word "notwithstanding." There are a few things to note about this problem. First, not all the church was involved in it. Some of the people in the church were truly devoted to Jesus. Second, the problem was associated basically with one person, a prominent woman named Jezebel, who called herself a prophetess. She was teaching others a way of life displeasing to the Lord of the church (v. 20).

The character of the woman is seen in her name, Jezebel. As Jezebel of Old Testament times was an immoral woman intent on destroying the worship of God's people (1 Kings 16:31; 2 Kings 9:22), so was this woman in the Thyatira church. She was in a place of leadership and was influencing others to commit immorality. She was stubborn, defiant, and just downright unwilling to respond to spiritual warnings (v. 21). She was a "teacher" of the deep things of Satan (v. 24) and a "seducer" of other Christians to violate God's commands (v. 20). She was not submissive to the revealed mind of Christ for the church concerning fornication and eating meat offered to idols (Acts 15:28). This church truly had a problem!

How is it possible for this to occur in a church for whom Christ had such strong commendation? One answer is that Satan transforms himself into angel of light (2 Cor. 11:13–14). Another answer is that false teachers dress up in Christian clothing to deceive the church (Matt. 7:15). We need to be spiritually alert.

The problem in the church was not this woman only; it was also the attitude of the church itself. The church was too easy going and lacking in discipline.

IV. Punishment in the church.

The Lord of the church had given instructions and warning, and now it was time for correction. He could not allow Jezebel's influence to continue. Verses 22 and 23 describe her punishment. Verse 22 says that he will cast her "into a bed," that is, afflict her with some illness or disease. The word "bed" is used for a couch for the sick. Next, he will bring "great tribulation," some heavy pressure that will be in the form of punishment. Finally, he will bring death to all her followers (v. 23). There is no way to escape the eyes of the Lord and the reach of his hand upon our lives!

V. Purity in the church.

So what does God's Word say about purity in the church? From Ephesians 5 come some directions. We are to walk in love, not lust (vv. 2–3). We are to walk as children of light, not children of darkness (vv. 8–9). We are not to have fellowship with the unfruitful works of darkness; rather, we are to reprove them (vv. 11–12). First Thessalonians 4 says we are to seek the most thorough moral purity. First Corinthians 6:18–20 calls us to the full dedication of our bodies to the Lord as temples of the Holy Spirit. Second Corinthians 6:17–18 says that we are to live separated lives, touching no unclean things. Any way you look at it, Christ's body is to be characterized by moral purity.

Therefore, we are to look upon moral impurity as a cancer in the church that must be dealt with. And the only way it can be dealt with is to so fear the Lord that we hate evil. And when we hate evil, we will confess and repent of our sins, taking any necessary steps in cleansing and restitution. Doing so will set the church free!

Conclusion

When the church responds in repentance and obedience to the Spirit, three promises from Christ come into reality. First, there is the promise of no other burden: "I will not impose any other burden on you" (NIV). The truth already given is enough. The principle of God's Word by which they are to live has already been given. Second, there is the promise of victory over enemies. "Power over the nations" is given by which they shall be ruled with a rod of iron. Both now and in the future, as believers who overcome, we share in Christ's authority over the world. And third, there is the promise of the presence of Christ himself: "I will give him the morning star." Jesus Christ is the Morning Star! We overcome in him as we are obedient to his works.

A cleansed life and a cleansed church are Christ's way to victory. He wants every believer, spiritual leader, and family to live clean lives. "He that hath an ear to hear, let him hear what the Spirit saith unto the churches."

WEDNESDAY EVENING, MAY 12

Title: Abraham: The Altar Builder

Text: "Then the LORD appeared to Abram, and said, 'To your descendants I will give this land.' So he built there an altar to the LORD, who had appeared to him" **(Gen. 12:7 RSV).**

Scripture Reading: Genesis 12:1–7

Introduction

God's call to Abraham was the beginning of God's great plan to redeem and bless the world through a chosen people. The work that God began in Abraham will not be complete until Jesus Christ returns to the earth.

God took the initiative and approached Abraham with a plan for his life. He communicated his will to Abraham and in a real sense offered prayers to the heart of this man whom he had chosen to be his servant. It is interesting to note the response that Abraham made to the prayer of God.

I. Abraham responded positively to God's request.

"So Abram went, as the LORD had told him" (Gen. 12:4).

A. *It is of tremendous importance that we hear what God has to say to us.* A sin that is rebuked repeatedly is the sin of refusing to hear God's voice.

B. *We should listen to hear God's message to our hearts.*
   1. We should listen as we study God's Word.
   2. We should listen as we offer prayers to the heavenly Father.
   3. We should listen to the gentle leading of the Holy Spirit.

4. We should listen to the wise counsel of Christian friends.

C. *Obedience was Abraham's response to God's plea.* This should be our response when a clear impulse comes to us from the Word of God and from the Holy Spirit within.

We need to listen, hear, and obey as God communicates his will to us.

II. The Lord appeared again to Abraham.

In response to Abraham's faith and obedience, the Lord appeared to him again with a message of comfort and assurance. "Then the LORD appeared to Abram, and said, 'To your descendants I will give this land'" (Gen. 12:7 RSV).

Many who consider themselves to be true worshipers of God want the fulfillment of God's promises before they take a step of faith and obedience. It is significant that God really comes through when we are obedient to his revealed will. It is not accidental that Luke records in the story of the ten lepers that "as they went they were cleansed" (Luke 17:14). In compassion the Lord had given a command to these ten pitiful men. It was their response of faith and obedience that made it possible for God to heal them.

There would be more miracles in the lives of modern-day disciples if we would give instant and joyous obedience to the clear commands of our Lord.

III. Abraham built an altar to the Lord at Shechem (Gen. 12:7).

Abraham was discovering the faithfulness as well as the generosity of God. Because God had communicated his will to Abraham, a desire for fellowship with God welled up in his heart.

An altar served a number of important functions. We should build altars along the pilgrimage of our spiritual life.

A. *An altar provided a place for prayer.*

B. *An altar provided a place for offering praise to God.*

C. *An altar provided a place for serious heart searching and self-examination.*

D. *An altar provided a place for dedication and rededication to God's will (Gen. 13:4).*

E. *An altar provided a place for sacrifice (Gen. 22:9).*

F. *An altar provided a place for remembrance.*

Conclusion

How many altars have you built? Most likely the number will be determined by the number of great experiences you have had with God along life's way.

Let's put forth an earnest effort to be obedient as the Lord reveals his will to us. Let's rebuild some altars.

SUNDAY MORNING, MAY 16

Title: The Scriptural Role of Husband and Wife

Text: "Wives, submit yourselves unto your own husbands, as unto the Lord. Husbands, love your wives, even as Christ also loved the church, and gave himself for it; Nevertheless let every one of you in particular so love his wife even as himself; and the wife see that she reverence her husband" **(Eph. 5:22, 25, 33).**

Scripture Reading: Ephesians 5:22–23

Hymns: "God, Give Us Christian Homes!" McKinney
"O Perfect Love," Gurney
"O God in Heaven, Whose Loving Plan," Martin

Offertory Prayer: Heavenly Father, our homes are under a lot of pressure today. Husbands and wives are taxed to their limits. They need a special portion of your grace. Let your spirit flow upon them and enable them to fulfill their respective roles according to divine plans and human needs. In Jesus' name. Amen.

Introduction

One of the biggest threats to our society is the disintegration of husband and wife relations. Divorce statistics continue to be appallingly high. Surely there is a dire need for men and women to get back to the biblical roles for husbands and wives.

In our Scripture passage there are two characteristics that each partner is to have toward the other.

I. The first consideration is the relation of a husband to his wife.

A. *A husband is to love his wife (Eph. 5:25).* This love is far greater than any love apart from the Christian experience. There are four different Greek words that are translated "love," but only three are found in the New Testament. *Eros* is mainly sexual love and is often used to refer to sex apart from marriage. *Phileo* refers to brotherly love. It carries with it a connotation of friendship and warmth. We get such words as philosophy (love of wisdom) and philanthropy (love of man) from it.

The word found here for the husband's love is *agape.* This is the strongest, dearest, and most tender love that can be known. It is loving with the mind and will and can be exercised only by a Christian. It is the product of the Holy Spirit. It means treating one's spouse as God does and seeking the highest and best for one another.

Paul gave two standards for a husband's love for his wife. He is to love his wife as Christ loved the church (Eph. 5:25). Christ gave himself for the church. He sustains and empowers the church and abides within the church. This is the kind of love a husband is to have for his wife. Since only a Christian can have this kind of love, it is essential that a Christian marry another Christian. The husband is also to love his wife as he loves himself. This is in no way condemning one's love for self; rather, it is a standard for loving one's spouse.

B. The husband is to cleave to his wife (Eph. 5:31). Some translations have "joined." The literal meaning of the word is to be glued to her. If you were referring to metal, you would probably use the word weld. This is a word that identifies the husband so closely with his wife that there is nothing apart from Providence that can separate them. They become one in the home, in intimate relations, and in goals and purposes in life.

II. The second consideration is the relation of a wife to her husband.

A. *A wife is to submit to her husband (Eph. 5:22).* To submit means to yield or defer to the opinion or authority of another. The context of the Scripture is a wife's relation to her husband and his being a Christian man. It is referring to a husband acting toward his wife in the same spirit that Christ acts in relation to the church. The writer of Ephesians states that this submission is to be in everything (Eph. 5:24). A wife is to be at one with her husband. When he acts in the Christian spirit, she is to respond to his authority in everything.

B. *A wife is to respect or reverence her husband (Eph. 5:33).* Respect means to hold in esteem. A woman should honor her husband by her words and actions. A woman should speak words of praise, encouragement, and support and should do things that will build up her husband. Many marriages could be saved, some could be strengthened, and all could be happier if wives would take this command of God seriously.

Conclusion

God's plan for husbands and wives is the best. If only men and women could abandon their selfishness and prejudice and follow God's plan, they would be happier. Homes would be havens for all who live there, and the kingdom of God would be advanced.

SUNDAY EVENING, MAY 16

Title: A Church Awakening

Text: "I know thy works, that thou hast a name that thou livest, and art dead. Be watchful, and strengthen the things which remain. . ." **(Rev. 3:1–2).**

Scripture Reading: Revelation 3:1–6

Introduction

Sardis has been considered one of the richest and most powerful cities in the world. It was an aristocratic city and at one time the home of King Croesus, who was known for his vast wealth.

In John's day Sardis was nothing like its past history, but the people were living in the glories of the past. And as in most cities of the day, idol worship and its attending immoralities characterized the city. This influence was so strong upon the church that Jesus had almost nothing good to say. And time was running out for the church at Sardis. The Lord's message to the church was "Wake up!" Notice three key words.

I. Identification.

Jesus is identified as "he that hath the seven spirits of God" and "the seven stars." Since seven is the number for completeness, "the seven spirits of God" describe Christ in the fullness of his power. The church needed a renewed ministry of the Holy Spirit in the church, so they needed to turn their eyes upon Jesus Christ in all the fullness of his power.

"The seven stars" are the pastors of the seven churches, and they are under Christ's control in relationship to the churches. Here is a vision of Christ, the head of the church, having the seven spirits of God and the fullness of the Spirit, in direct personal relationship with the pastors, who in turn serve as his messengers to the churches. This is a living relationship!

II. Evaluation.

Without delay Jesus evaluates the situation of the church. "I know thy works, that thou hast a name that thou livest, and art dead."

Sardis was, along with the other churches of its times, an active church. It was well organized and carried on its business. One educator said of this church that it counted nickels and noses—offering and attendance. Outsiders saw the church as alive and well, but Jesus knew from the inside of the church that it was spiritually dead.

Is this like the church of our day? Busy yet neglecting the most important things? The life of the church is Christ in us, indwelling us and filling us by his Spirit. John 6:63 says, "It is the Spirit that quickeneth. . .the flesh profiteth nothing." Romans 8:2–10 tells us that the life of the believer, therefore the life of the church, is the Spirit of life in Christ Jesus. So where the Spirit of the Lord is, there is no death!

Sardis was in spiritual trouble. It was a church that was losing its saltiness. It had a form of godliness but denied the power thereof. Jesus tells it like it is when he says, "You are dead!" How do we know when a church is dying? What are the signs of death? There are several.

A. *A church is dying when it fails to fulfill the works of the Lord.* "I have not found thy works perfect before God" (v. 2). The word for "perfect" is not the usual one; it is a word that means "fulfill" or "complete." A church is spiritually dying when it allows the works of God to go unfulfilled. Jesus said, "My meat is to do the will of him that sent me, and to finish his work" (John 4:34) and "I must work the works of him that sent me" (9:4).

B. *A church is dying when it loses its awareness of God's presence.* This is expressed in the words "before God" (v. 2), that is, in the sight of God, before his eyes. When the presence of God is no longer real, then true worship and motivation are missing.

C. *A church is dying when it forgets its unique nature.* "Remember therefore how thou hast received and heard. . ." (v. 3). Death is not far off when we forget that we truly are the body of Christ, the people of God. We are a people on a mission—a divine, eternal mission. Drifting from this and neglecting salvation is dangerous to the church (cf. Heb. 2:3; 2 Peter 1:8–9).

D. *A church is dying when it begins to live carelessly.* "Thou hast a few names even in Sardis which have not defiled their garments" (v. 4). Only a "few"! This means that most of the church members were living morally defiled lives. Defiled garments describe clothing smeared with filth. Here it specifically means moral filth. Their lives were morally dirty, meaning that they had impure thought lives, activities, and habits. Their consciences were dead! And that is dangerous!

E. *A church is dying when it is unprepared for Jesus' coming.* "I will come on thee as a thief, and thou shalt not know what hour I will come upon thee" (v. 3). The truth of Jesus' coming is all throughout the Bible, and when we preach it, teach it, believe it, and practice it, it stirs the church to life. When it is neglected, something is missing.

F. *A church is dying when fellowship with Christ is lost.* The "few" promised to walk with him (cf. 4). This means that many were not walking in fellowship with Jesus Christ, as 1 John 1:7 challenges. Not walking with him means missing the blessings of spiritual fellowship with him.

G. *A church is dying when it fails to confess Christ openly.* The Lord says that he will speak the victorious person's name openly before the Father. This indicates that the others were not confessing Christ before people as Matthew 10:32–33 teaches. Was it fear that prevented their witness? A sign of a living and Christ-honoring church is that it shares Christ with others.

No wonder the message to every church is to wake up and live!

III. Stimulation.

Jesus speaks one sentence of evaluation to the church and the rest of his message is given to stimulating their spiritual life. "Stimulate" means to excite to activity or growth and to animate or arouse. Christ is calling the church to wake up!

We need a spiritual awakening today. And as this letter teaches, it is possible to have spiritual renewal in the church. How does Jesus stimulate a church to life?

A. *By imperatives*. He gives a series of commands that demand response: "remember" (v. 3), "be watchful" (v. 2), "strengthen" (v. 2), "repent" (v. 3), and "hold fast" (v. 3).

B. *By memory*. Remember what you have received. Remember your deliverance and the joy of first fellowship with Jesus. Memory is a vital part of the Christian life.

C. *By warning*. If the church does not respond, Jesus says, "I will come on thee as a thief" (v. 3). His coming is a blessed hope, but if we are not watching, it will be an event of terror and surprise.

D. *By example*. "Thou hast a few names" speaks of some who have remained true. They are a challenge to the others to come back to Christ.

E. *By encouragement*. There is hope yet for the church. Christ promises it to them, but they must follow his directions. They must wake up spiritually.

F. *By his Spirit*. "He that hath an ear to hear. . . ." How is the church awakened? By individual members of the body cooperating with the Holy Spirit.

Conclusion

Is it worth it? Yes, the promises of Jesus make it worth it all. We have a renewed fellowship and victory in Christ by being "clothed in white raiment." We have the promise assured us of our names never being removed from the Book of Life. We have the promise of being confessed before the Father and his angels. If there is rejoicing in heaven over one sinner repenting, there will likewise be rejoicing over the confession of the believer who lives victoriously in Christ. Just as life is really not worth it without Christ, neither is the Christian life worth it if you are not experiencing God's best. So wake up, O church of God!

WEDNESDAY EVENING, MAY 19

Title: God's Promises to Abraham

Text: "After these things the word of the LORD came to Abram in a vision" (**Gen. 15:1 RSV**).

Scripture Reading: Genesis 15:1–6

Introduction

Our heavenly Father always initiates our spiritual experiences. In doing so, he does not degrade our human dignity but shows us his gracious redemptive activity in our behalf. If we see our hunger for the Bread of Life as divinely initiated, it will add excitement and expectancy to our study of God's Word. If we can understand that our deep inward desire to go to God's house to meet with his people is in reality the work of his Spirit within our hearts, we will be encouraged to a greater faith and be enabled to have a greater love for our Father God.

The book of Genesis provides illustration after illustration of how God approaches his people and communicates his love and will for their lives.

I. God comes with a command (Gen. 15:1).

The word of the Lord came to Abraham in a vision. This most likely was a dream of such vivid reality that it communicated with his innermost being in a very convincing manner. In modern terminology we would declare that God communicates not only with the conscious mind but also with the sub-conscious mind and that he seeks to communicate with us while we are awake and while we are asleep.

God seeks to communicate with us through our personal experiences along the way of life, through national crises and events of international significance, through the natural normal events of life, and during our moments of deep personal meditation and serious thought. God wants to speak with us supremely through his Word as we come to know Jesus Christ and the power of the Holy Spirit.

God came to Abraham with a command: "Fear not." In many instances, one's initial intimate experience with the invisible God is indeed frightening, because people are sinners and God is holy. Often a high spiritual experience is preceded by an awesome encounter with God in which sin is dealt with radically in the life of the worshiper (Isa. 6:1–6).

Repeatedly our Lord spoke to his disciples saying, "Fear not." God does not want to frighten us. He comes to quiet our fears.

II. God comes with a promise.

"Abram, I am your shield; your reward shall be very great" (Gen. 15:1). The God of Abraham makes great promises to his servants. He not only makes promises but also keeps them.

One of the most important reasons for studying God's Word is to discover the promises God makes to his people that are universal in application. We can enter into the promises made by God to Abraham provided we have yielded ourselves to God's great redemptive plan in the world today.

A. *"I am your shield."* Shields take many different forms, and their purpose is to protect people from injury. A shield was an important piece of armor to the people in the ancient world. Later they built walls around their cities that served as shields. God declared that he would be Abraham's personal shield. He is the greatest shield anyone could have.

B. *"Your reward shall be very great."* Some wrongly think that eternal life is a reward given by God for faithful service, that heaven is a reward from God. The truth is, eternal life is the gift of God. The rewards that God bestows are in addition to his gift of eternal life.

Jesus spoke often about rewards. He urged people to lay up treasures in heaven where neither moth nor rust corrupt and where thieves cannot break through and steal (Matt. 6:19–21). He declared that those who give even the most humble service in the name of a disciple will never lose their reward (Matt. 10:42). He affirmed that upon his return to the earth he will reward all people according to what they have done for God and for others (Rev. 22:12).

The greatest reward God gives us is his presence and the assurance of his love along the way. God himself was Abraham's greatest reward.

III. The human response to God's approach.

It is interesting to note how Abraham responded to this visit by God.

A. *Abraham asked questions of God (Gen. 15:2–3).*

B. *Abraham listened to God (Gen. 15:5).* Many of us make a serious mistake by doing all of the talking in prayer. Prayer should be a dialogue in which we not only talk but also listen. In reality it is much more important to hear what God has to say to us than it is to voice our requests and needs to him.

C. *Abraham believed the Lord (Gen. 15:6).* Faith is taking God at his word. Faith is believing that God is and that he rewards those who diligently seek him (Heb. 11:6).

Conclusion

If you want to receive the blessings of God, respond to the great truth that he is seeking to communicate. Take time to listen and learn from him. He loves you.

SUNDAY MORNING, MAY 23

Title: The Scriptural Role of a Parent

Text: "And, ye fathers, provoke not your children to wrath: but bring them up in the nurture and admonition of the Lord" **(Eph. 6:4).**

Scripture Reading: Ephesians 6:1–4

Hymns: "Abide with Me," Lyte
"Great Is Thy Faithfulness," Chisholm
"I Need Thee Every Hour," Hawks

Offertory Prayer: Father, we recognize that the privilege of being parents is a gift from you. As parents, we thank you for our children. We also realize that being the right kind of parents is a grave responsibility. It is too much for us alone. We need your help. We claim your promises of wisdom, strength, and insight. We ask for leadership, direction, and help. We confess our weaknesses and failures, and we ask you to forgive us. In Jesus' name we pray. Amen.

Introduction

The parent-child relationship is one of the most intimate known to humankind. It is in this relationship that the child receives the love, affection, and security that he or she needs for good self-esteem and adjustment in life.

Conscientious parents want to do what is right for their children. Parents are wise when they seek information from the inspired Word, because the Bible is the best-known source of parental guidance. Parents would be wise to heed the insightful lessons found in today's Scripture passage.

I. Parents are not to provoke their children to wrath (Eph. 6:4).

A. *This is a warning against the misuse of power.* Child abuse is ordinarily thought of as parental abuse of small children or those unable to defend themselves. This passage of Scripture cautions against such abuse. It also goes further in warning parents against injustice or severity in any case. Such parental behavior makes a child indisposed to filial obedience and honor.

There are numerous ways such injustice can be administered. Adults are often committed to cultural traditions. They must be careful not to force their children to comply with outdated customs that are not supported by Scripture. Forcing children to comply with old-fashioned customs can embarrass them, build resentment, and cause rebellion. Another danger parents face in being overly severe with their children is to exercise so much control over them that they are insulted. This type of control says to a child, "I do not trust you nor do I have confidence in you." The normal reaction to such control is loss of respect and rebellion.

Parents should always be on the alert to give encouragement. Failure to do so causes insecurities and frustrations beyond many children's ability to handle. Encouragement needs to be issued in word and in action over both big and little things. It needs to be done in times of success and in times of failure. Rewards can be used for encouragement.

B. *There is also a warning against soft or careless ways that will cause a child to disrespect authority.* This can be called the cruelty of neglect. A child is spoiled when there is no restraint. Such restraint demands time and care.

A story is told of a little girl whose day was a tale of various misbehaviors that were accompanied by corresponding scolding from her mother. Finally the girl sat down and said, "I wish my dad would come home and *make* me behave." Children need and want parents to show authority. In fact, parents can provoke their children's wrath by not being authoritative.

A church youth director was in the presence of a teenage girl and her mother. The girl was saying all kinds of ugly things to her mother. When her mother left, the girl turned to the youth director and asked, "Why does my mother let me talk to her like that?"

II. Parents are to raise their children in the nurture and admonition of the Lord (Eph. 6:4).

A. *Nurture is also translated as discipline, the total training and educational process of children.* Education in the widest sense includes the development of mind and character. Discipline, by the use of commands and admonitions—and sometimes punishment—cultivates the mind and morals, correcting mistakes and curbing passions. All Christian parents should seek divine leadership in counseling their children against faults and oversights. Instruction instills virtues by teaching doctrines and duties.

B. *Admonition is also translated as instruction, training by word of encouragement.* But it is also training by word of reproof and by word of blame when those are required.

A reading of the Scripture passage will disclose that discipline and instruction are to be done "in the Lord." Parent-child relationships are incomplete without the Lord as the third partner, because his Word and his Holy Spirit serve as guides for raising children. Furthermore, our Father God is our pattern for good parenting.

We are to train our children by teaching them the ways of the Lord. Daily Bible reading and prayer should be a common practice from infancy. Use of the proper age level Bible story books can instill in children a great love and respect for the Word. Regular church attendance will provide children with an extended family of Christian peers and mentors. It will also build into children a discipline that will make churchgoing a normal thing to do all their lives.

Conclusion

Serving the Lord in any capacity is an awesome responsibility, but to fulfill the role of a parent as presented in this verse of Scripture is almost beyond one's ability to comprehend. Parenthood demands a close walk and constant communion with God. It calls on each parent to learn from mistakes, grow in knowledge, and develop into maturity. The Lord sets the standards for parenthood and also supplies the grace to meet them.

SUNDAY EVENING, MAY 23

Title: The Church with the Open Door

Text: "And to the angel of the church in Philadelphia write. . .I know thy works: behold, I have set before thee an open door, and no man can shut it" **(Rev. 3:7–8).**

Scripture Reading: Revelation 3:7–13

Introduction

Two of the seven churches, Smyrna and Philadelphia, do not need to be told to repent. To the other five it is necessary for the Lord to say, "Repent or else!" The Philadelphia church is the one that knows the favor of the Lord, the one the Lord is uniquely blessing. It truly is triumphant—alive and well—in the world. The church that is like it today is the same. This letter has three emphases.

I. The Lord who blesses.

As in all the letters, the pastor of the church and the people are challenged to turn their eyes upon Jesus. This letter points out three things about Jesus.

A. *His person.* Verse 7 describes Jesus as "He that is holy, he that is true." These are divine qualities that describe his character. Thus, we are not to think of Jesus irreverently as "the man upstairs," but as holy and true, the living Christ! We should respond in awe of him as John did in chapter 1.

B. *His position.* Jesus' position is expressed in the sentence, "He that hath the key of David." This expression refers to the covenant that God gave through David and fulfilled in Jesus Christ. The phrase is used in Isaiah 22:22, where Eliakim is called the chief steward of the royal household and is in charge of the palace and relations with the king. His official position was one of great power and authority so that he could open and shut doors of access to the king.

Jesus Christ is the King of Kings, and he has absolute authority. He holds the keys to all of the doors in heaven and earth (see Matt. 28:18–19; Eph. 1:19). He gives us the keys of the kingdom (Matt. 16:19). His authority is sovereign, final, and absolute! Let us never forget to whom we belong and whom we serve.

C. *His administration.* The words "he that openeth and no man shuteth, and shuteth and no man openeth" describe Jesus' administrative activity. It is he who directs his churches and who blesses or withholds his blessings. He opens and closes doors. In the light of Jesus' administration, there is faith, hope, victory, and praise.

II. The church that Jesus blesses.

The church of Philadelphia describes the church that may have the blessings of the Lord upon it.

A. *It is a church that is not dependent on size.* The Lord does not automatically bless a large church; nor does a small church have an inside track with God. The church at Philadelphia had a "little strength" (v. 8). It was probably small in size, not large and influential. This affirms to us that it is not size but spirit that counts. There is hope for every church!

B. *It is a church that is already moving.* "I know thy works." It was already active and evidently had the right motives and attitudes. It was not like Sardis; it was alive and stirring.

C. *It is a church that is obedient.* Verses 8 and 10 indicate that these people had kept the Word of the Lord at some crisis time in their existence. This means that obedience is our part, but the blessings are his. The commands of Christ are vitally important to his church (cf. Matt. 28:18–20; John 13:35; 14:21; 1 John 3:23).

D. *It is a church that stands true to Christ.* The name of Jesus Christ was not denied (v. 8). Tests come, but we are to stand true to him. Denying Jesus is a serious matter as attested by the bitter tears of Simon Peter. We may deny him with words, looks, activities, or even silence. Denial may take place in your home, at work, at school, in your neighborhood, or in your social life. Be true to Jesus' name! Prove your love for him with your life.

E. *It is a church that is faithful to what it has.* Verse 11 says, "Hold that fast which thou hast." Some people think of faithfulness in terms of what they will have in the future or what they will do when certain things happen. A college student says, "I will tithe when I graduate and get a job." No, begin now with what you have!

"Hold fast" is a present imperative, so the Lord is emphasizing how important it is to keep on holding fast. The Lord blesses the church that is faithful to its opportunities. And this is how he also will bless your personal life. The danger that we face is having our crown for faithfulness stolen from us.

III. The blessings that Jesus bestows.

Jesus says, "I have set" (v. 8) and "I will make [or give] them" (v. 9) as indications of blessings that he will give the church. What are they?

A. *He gives an open door (v. 8).* The idea of an open door is found in the New Testament in several places. Jesus is the door to the Father (John 10:7–9), but this is not what is meant here. Acts 14:27 tells how God opened "the door of faith" to the Gentiles. "A great door for effective work" was opened for Paul according to 1 Corinthians 16:9 (NIV). The door for preaching the gospel is referred to in 2 Corinthians 2:12 and Colossians 4:3. These references carry the idea of a good opportunity for evangelistic and missionary effort.

What is "the door" here? The key to its interpretation is found in verse 9, where it refers to the opposition that the church is experiencing from "the synagogue of Satan," adversaries and false accusers of the believers. The Lord says, "I will make them come and fall down at your feet and acknowledge that I have loved you" (NIV). He is about to give these opponents to the church as converts. These new converts will worship before the believers' feet and acknowledge the truth of Christ. Thus, the door is an open door of evangelism, victory, and spiritual conquest.

Moreover, this is the door we are to enter today as Christ's church. We are to occupy for Christ every territory of the opposition. We are to appropriate his victory and live Christ-enthroned lives. What a door!

B. *He gives future deliverance (v. 10).* "I also will keep thee from the hour of temptation." This verse is referring to a specific period of time. Revelation 6–19 describes a time of God-ordained tribulation that will come upon the entire world and all the earth's inhabitants. Believers will be delivered from this tribulation when Christ comes to catch away his church to be with him. This is Christ's promise to Philadelphia and to us!

C. *He gives eternal rewards.* In verse 12 Jesus promises eternal position, identification, citizenship in God's city, and exaltation with Christ. These blessings are not experienced automatically. They are dependent on our response to the ministry of the Holy Spirit (v. 13).

Conclusion

The Lord still gives conquest to his church today in opening doors of victory. Adoniram Judson is just one illustration of this. In 1813 he was interdicted in India because of the East India Company. He then went down to Rangoon in Burma, where for six years he labored without a convert. But God was in him and with him. In the terrible war of 1824–26 between England and the Burmese, Adoniram Judson was placed in a filthy prison and fettered with five pairs of chains. He was sick with fever and suffering from the excruciating jungle heat. He was almost destroyed by the terrible treatment of his keepers but was fed, nurtured, and kept alive by his faithful wife. He lived to see the day when thousands of natives turned to saving faith in Christ Jesus.

WEDNESDAY EVENING, MAY 26

Title: Abraham: Visited by God

Text: "The LORD appeared to him by the oaks of Mamre, as he sat at the door of his tent in the heat of the day" (**Gen. 18:1 RSV**).

Scripture Reading: Genesis 18:1–8

Introduction

Prayer is a divinely initiated experience in which God is eager to communicate with and bestow blessings upon his worshipers. The experiences of Abraham, the father of the fruitful, provide us with many illustrations of the fact that prayer is a dialogue between the Father God and his needy and obedient children.

I. God came to Abraham at high noon, "in the heat of the day" (Gen. 18:1).

Isn't it wonderful that our God doesn't limit his activity to the Sabbath or Lord's Day? Isn't it great that the Lord doesn't limit his activity to the early morning or to the darkness of the night? Here we have an instance of God coming to Abraham at high noon. Every segment of the day is open to divine visitation.

A. *Perhaps Abraham had been praying.* Perhaps he was hungry for fellowship with God. Perhaps he had questions that were disturbing his heart or doubts or fears that were upsetting him.

B. *The sovereign God visits a subject.* Abraham was the Lord's servant and was trying to be obedient and fulfill the Lord's purpose for him. To such a person as this the great God of the universe came for a visit at high noon. He will come to us if we are seeking to do his will.

II. Abraham recognized the Lord when he came (Gen. 18:3).

Throughout the Old Testament we have many incidents in which we have a description of how God came to communicate with and to minister to his people. Sometimes he came in the form of an angel, a great leader, or a prophetic spokesperson. At other times he came in the great events affecting the nation's life.

Our Father God is seeking to communicate with us in a variety of ways—by his Word, by his Holy Spirit within us, and through other people.

III. Abraham prepared a feast for the Lord (Gen. 18:4–8).

In our Scripture passage we have a description of generous Eastern hospitality. Abraham was serving as a host to the guests who came to him. It is no accident that this passage closes with a description of a feast. Revelation 3:20, where Christ is standing at the door knocking, describes God's initiative in seeking to communicate with his church.

A. *Let's prepare the way in our hearts for a time of fellowship with God.*

B. *Let's open up the gates of our souls so that the Lord can come in.* Let's prepare a feast and have fellowship with him.

IV. The Lord consented to eat at Abraham's table (Gen. 18:8).

The Lord will bless your heart and home with his presence if you provide for him. It is interesting to note what happened during this feast.

A. *The Lord repeated his promise of an heir for Abraham (Gen. 18:10).*

B. *The Lord reminded them that there was nothing too hard or too miraculous for him to do (Gen. 18:14).* We all need to be reminded of our Lord's precious promises and plans for our lives. He will share them with us if we prepare a feast for him.

Conclusion

The Lord may come to you at high noon, in the early morning, or late at night. Be open for a divine visit to your heart. God will come seeking fellowship with you.

SUNDAY MORNING, MAY 30

Title: The Children's Scriptural Role to Their Parents

Text: "Children, obey your parents in the Lord: for this is right. Honour thy father and mother; which is the first commandment with promise; That it may be well with thee, and thou mayest live long on the earth" **(Eph. 6:1–3).**

Scripture Reading: Proverbs 3:5–7; 4:1–4

Hymns: "O Happy Home Where Thou Art Loved," Spitta
       "Happy the Home When God Is There," Ware
       "O Thou Whose Gracious Presence Blest," Benson

Offertory Prayer: Our heavenly Father, the children of this generation live in a time in which it is hard to be true to you. We pray that you will help them take the words of God seriously. Grant that they may see and understand that the wisdom found in the Bible is yours. Help them to make time to study the

Bible and meditate upon it. Enable them to find specific messages for themselves. Let your words become living orders for them. In the name of Jesus we pray. Amen.

Introduction

Much is said in sermons and articles about the role of parents. Possibly too much responsibility is placed on parents and not enough on children. This message is intended to help children see their role in family life as it is found in God's Word.

I. Children are to obey their parents in the Lord (Eph. 6:1).

A. *The phrase "in the Lord" establishes the sphere of this obedience.* Parents have a high calling to raise their children in God's ways. Likewise, children have a great responsibility to obey their parents as they would Christ. Parents are to follow Christ's example and be servant leaders for their children rather than flaunting their power over them. Children, in turn, are to respect this authority.

Some key thoughts in the word "obey" are "execute the orders of," "be controlled by," and "follow the guidance of." According to the text, children are to execute the orders of their parents so long as those orders are in the Lord. It means doing what their parents say. The text also confirms that children are to be controlled by their parents and are to follow their guidance.

In obeying their parents, children give recognition to authority. Authority gives the right to determine or settle issues. Parents are to set rules, and children are to comply. This will help children develop responsibility, maturity, and sound judgment. Children's background and experience do not give them the input and knowledge they need to act correctly at times. This is where obedience accepts the maturity of parents. Authority and obedience are essential to peace, harmony, and wholesome relations in the home. Absence of authority leads to anarchy.

B. *Children are to be obedient both in and out of their parents' presence.* Legalism alone would never produce peace and harmony in the home as God intended. Therefore, when obedience is applied only while in the presence of parents, it is not obedience at all. Authority, judgment, and control should be a part of a child's life at all times.

II. Children are to honor their father and mother (Eph. 6:2).

A. *Honoring parents is a command for children of all ages.* Adults are to honor their parents too. This principle applies even when parents are old, senile, cantankerous, and hard to get along with.

Honoring parents means giving them due credit for what they have done. It recognizes the hardships, sacrifices, and anxieties through which parents go for their children. Once children are away from home, they need to stay in touch with their parents. Honoring them means acknowledging them and guarding against demeaning them. This is a hard task when one feels frustrated, outdone, or inconvenienced. Honoring parents also means giving them encouragement and hope when they are in a nursing home, hospital, or just alone. Honoring parents is providing help for them. This help may come in the form of financial aid. Children who are scripturally honoring their parents must be willing to sacrifice if necessary to provide their parents' material needs. Or help may be in the form of performing household duties, holding a feeble hand, or helping a parent walk. Honoring parents means treating them with deference, respect, kindness, and courtesy.

B. *Honoring parents should be the natural disposition of children.* Obedience is duty. Honor portrays character and is a Christian virtue that comes from the enabling power of the Holy Spirit. It is closely associated with docility and patience. It takes genuine love and humility to carry out this commandment of God.

Honoring parents carries with it a promise that things will go well with those who are obedient and that they will live long on the earth (Eph. 6:3). This is quality and quantity living—the life Jesus came to give (John 10:10; 3:16).

Conclusion

The text of our message is precise and demanding. It takes the best in us and challenges us. But it is also rewarding. All children, once they are old enough to be responsible, should take God at his Word. They should obey and honor their parents.

SUNDAY EVENING, MAY 30

Title: Laodicea—A Church on the Fence

Text: "And unto the angel of the church of the Laodiceans, write. . ." **(Rev. 3:14).**

Scripture Reading: Revelation 3:14–22

Introduction

The letter to the Laodiceans was special to them, and because of its timeliness, it is special to the church of today.

The city of Laodicea was extremely wealthy. It was destroyed by an earthquake in A.D. 60 but would receive no help from the Roman Empire. The two chief articles of trade in Laodicea were woolen cloth and eyesalve, products for which Laodicea was known throughout the world. Jesus referred to this fact in Revelation 3:18. Also, the hot springs of Hierapolis were near Laodicea. The water that flowed into the city was lukewarm and unpleasant in taste.

The Laodicean church received no commendation from Christ. It faced the dangerous possibility of no longer being useful to the Lord of the church. He warned, "I am about to spit you out of my mouth" (v. 16 NIV). The church of Laodicea was about to become a spiritual castaway (1 Cor. 9:27). Although it was not lacking materially, it was useless as a spiritual body. Once a thriving church, now it was on the fence, useless to Jesus Christ and the world around it.

To the church in this condition the vision of Christ is extremely important. He is "the Amen," the word of affirmation that means "I believe," or "That's right!" So Jesus Christ is *the* answer, the affirmation of God. He is also "the faithful and true witness" to all that he is and does and says. He is not on the fence. He neither exaggerates nor minimizes; he is absolutely true. And this is how we are to be. Added to these two expressions is the fact that Christ is "the beginning of the Creation of God." He is the first cause; all things are the result of his power. He is the source of life and divine energy. So the Christ who is so envisioned has something to say to his church. Since this is the last church, think about this letter from two perspectives.

I. It has a special message for the church today.

A. *Laodicea illustrates for us the plan of God for the church.* God's plan and purpose for the church is for it to be on fire, zealous, and accomplishing Christ's goals. And this is what Laodicea wasn't doing.

B. *Laodicea describes the peril of a church coming to a point spiritually that it is no longer useful to Jesus Christ.* Notice the description of the church in verses 15–17.

1. Laodicea had lost its purpose. It had little or nothing to live for in a relationship to Christ. The church illustrates the three types of people in every church: the spiritually cold, hot, and lukewarm. The third type is neutral, indecisive, and on the fence. They have no enthusiasm or driving purpose. They are unmoved and unconcerned. This describes millions of Christians today.

2. Laodicea had lost its perspective. They said they were rich and therefore had need of nothing. But Jesus said they were spiritually ignorant, "wretched, and miserable, and poor, and blind, and naked" (v. 17). What a deplorable condition! How deceived we can become! The threat to the church was wealth, which made them independent and proud. The evil of becoming self-sufficient can happen to any life or church. We truly need the Lord!

3. Laodicea had lost its power. The power of the church is the person of the Lord Jesus Christ through the ministry of the Holy Spirit. He is its fullness. But at Laodicea, Christ was on the outside of the church knocking and seeking to enter (v. 20).

How does a church or an individual turn Christ away? It isn't done all at once. It is done gradually, step by step, until one day he begins to deal with the offender in judgment.

II. It has a special message of hope for the church.

Hope for the church is found in several factors.

A. *Christ's counsel (v. 18).*
1. "Buy of me gold tried in the fire." Identify yourself with Christ in a vital tested and victorious faith.
2. "White raiment." Christ's clothing for believers is pure and holy.
3. "Anoint thine eyes." The Holy Spirit anoints our eyes to see the things of God.

B. *Christ's compassion (v. 19).* "I love..." means that Christ still loves the church. What hope that is! He still loves us today.

C. *Christ's chastening (v. 19).* "I rebuke and chasten." He disciplines the church by instruction, warning, and correction, just as loving parents do for their children.

D. *Christ's commands (v. 19).* "Be zealous." Shake off your complacency. Be enthusiastic and earnest. Burn with zeal. "Repent." Change your mind, attitude, and life.

E. *Christ's coming (v. 20).* "I will come in to him." If we want Jesus, he will come in. He never goes where he is not wanted or invited. His "coming" here is for fellowship; it is not his coming again. To "sup" together refers to the meal that the family enjoys when they spend time together. This is what the church needs—time with the Lord Jesus Christ so that we can get to know him!

F. *Christ's conquering (v. 21).* "To him that overcometh" means that the church, the people of God, are to be victorious! He gives us the privilege of sitting with him on his throne now (cf. Ephesians 1 and 2) and for eternity.

Conclusion

The message of the Lord Jesus Christ to his church then and to us now is a special message of readiness for his return. The Laodicean church was not prepared for the coming of the bridegroom for his bride. Just as Christ wanted the Laodiceans to get off the fence, so he wants us to get off the fence today. Instead of being dull, insensitive, and complacent, Christ calls his church to be alive, awake, and alert! Be ready to welcome him!

Suggested preaching program for the month of

JUNE

■ **Sunday Mornings**

Continue the series "Would Christ Be Welcome in Your Home?" through Father's Day. On the following Sunday begin a new series based on Romans 12–16 called "The Practice of Genuine Religion."

■ **Sunday Evenings**

The suggested theme is "The Doctrines of Our Faith." The doctrines of our faith form the same function for our spiritual life that our skeletal system does for our physical life. There is a great need to strengthen the members of our congregation in their understanding of the teachings of the Christian faith.

■ **Wednesday Evenings**

Continue the series "The Prayers of God to His People."

WEDNESDAY EVENING, JUNE 2

Title: When God Talks to Himself

Text: "The LORD said, 'Shall I hide from Abraham what I am about to do, seeing that Abraham shall become a great and mighty nation, and all the nations of the earth shall bless themselves by him?'" **(Gen. 18:17–18 RSV).**

Scripture Reading: Genesis 18:1–33

Introduction

The words of our text have been described as "God's soliloquy." God is pictured as being in perplexity regarding what he should do about a situation that brought agony to his heart.

We can draw a number of conclusions from God's experience with Abraham.

I. God holds inquests into the moral condition of nations and cities and churches.

Nothing is hidden from God. He is not only the God of love but is also the God of justice and righteousness. He cannot tolerate sin.

Ruth Graham has been quoted as saying that if God lets America escape from his judgment on its unbelief, immorality, and wickedness, on the Judgment Day he will have to apologize to Sodom and Gomorrah. Perhaps this is an overstatement, but it speaks of a side of God's nature that we need to be reminded of repeatedly.

This experience in Abraham's life reveals that God will disclose to his people what is due to happen unless changes are made in the direction in which cities and nations are traveling. The case of Nineveh and Jonah dramatically illustrates that entire cities can make great changes and turn to God.

II. God is open to sincere and earnest prayers of intercession (Gen. 18:22–23).

This experience in Abraham's life reveals one of the most dramatic illustrations of intercessory prayer in all of Scripture. We find this man of God earnestly pouring his heart out to God, who heard and answered in a gracious and wonderful manner.

III. A mighty minority has preserving power.

God was willing to spare the city of Sodom if only ten righteous people could be found there. Ten would provide a basis of hope for the entire city. If there were ten who would band together and seek to bring about a spiritual and moral change, then there was hope for the whole group. This reveals that the wicked are benefited by the presence of good people.

IV. Our God is a consuming fire (Gen. 19:24–28).

There is a limit to divine grace and patience. When nations, cities, or individuals pass the point of redemption, God deals with them in terms of justice. History records accounts of governments and individuals who descended to the level of becoming such a disease that God performed radical surgery and eliminated them from the face of the earth. Sodom and Gomorrah had so degraded themselves that there remained no hope for their redemption.

May God preserve our nation from a catastrophe like that which befell ancient Sodom and Gomorrah.

Conclusion

God is a God who communicates. Let's listen and really hear. Let's do his will.

SUNDAY MORNING, JUNE 6

Title: The Children's Role to Each Other in Family Life

Text: "Who are my brethren?" (**Matt. 12:48**).

Scripture Reading: Matthew 12:46–50

Hymns: "Love Is the Theme," Fisher
"Share His Love," Sullivan
"Down at the Cross," Hoffman

Offertory Prayer: Heavenly Father, the Bible teaches us that every good and perfect gift comes from you. Children are one of the choicest of all gifts. We thank you for them. For their love, their challenge, their fellowship, and their meaning to us, we give thanks. As we worship in our giving, may we give according to the will of God. In Jesus' name we pray. Amen.

Introduction

There is an abundance of study material on husband-wife relations and parent-child relations, and many passages of Scripture deal specifically with these relations. However, when a search is made for materials, including Scriptures, for the scriptural role of children to one another, one soon discovers that these resources are somewhat meager. This is not to imply that children's relationships with one another are not of concern to God. Our study of the home would be incomplete without a message on sibling relationships.

I. The two terms for the relationship are "brother" and "sister."

A. *The term "brother" is used in the Bible to describe a very close and tender relationship.* It is one of the closest apart from husband-wife and parent-child relationships. It is used to describe fellow Christians in relation to each other and intended as an example for ideal relations.

B. *The term "sister" is the feminine gender corresponding to brother.* Anything and everything that can be said about brothers' relations can be said about sisters' relations.

II. The dominant words in the relationship are "common" and "help."

A. *One word is "common."* A principle that children in the home must recognize is that they have many things in common. They have the same parents, obligations, loyalties, and goals. The things they hold in common dictate attitudes and behavioral patterns. Children are to love one another, work with and for one another, and have a mutual respect for one another. They should also guard against divided loyalty and demeaning each other.

B. *The other word is "help."* It is our Christian duty to help one another. This is especially true of Christian brothers and sisters. The same blood flowing through their veins demands it, their day-by-day relationships demand it, and Christian principles demand it.

Helping one another is done in word and in action. Brothers and sisters have a relationship to one another that gives them insight into each other's problems and heartaches that no one else has. Consequently, they can be supportive, encouraging, and helpful to each other when no one else can.

III. Brothers and sisters in the Bible show how we should and should not relate to each other.

A. *James and John are examples of how we should relate to each other.* These brothers are referred to as "sons of Zebedee." When reading the Gospels, one finds that they shared alike in family affairs. They both worked with their father at a family occupation in mutual support of their family.

Their whole lives were built around service to their Master. This Christian service shows no conflict with family interests. Their biographies indicate nothing but the very best of relations. When one needed the other, he was right there.

B. *Jacob and Esau are examples of how we should not relate to each other.* Each child in a respective family needs to learn from Jacob and Esau that they should not become divided in family loyalty. All children are to love both parents and never play one against the other.

No brother or sister is to ever take advantage of another. This is especially true when it applies to times of weaknesses. Jacob's taking advantage of Esau on two different occasions resulted in bitterness and separation that took years to heal.

Jealousy and rivalry of parents' love and peers' affection are most harmful. Jacob and Esau taught some strong lessons concerning jealousy and rivalry.

The one thing that can be said for this set of brothers that all children in a family need to learn is that they learned to forgive.

C. *Mary and Martha are further scriptural examples of child-to-child relations.* These sisters had a common tie in their relationship with Jesus. Their personal interests, however, varied. Martha was more inclined toward household chores while Mary was more inclined toward spiritual insight. We can learn from Mary and Martha that preferences, likes, and dislikes do not have to be identical for there to be harmony and happiness in a relationship.

Conclusion

More biblical research needs to be done on sibling relationships. Parents need deep spiritual insights in regard to them. Children need to become Christians early and develop spiritual feelings for one another and always follow divine leadership as they relate to one another.

SUNDAY EVENING, JUNE 6

Title: The Living Word

Text: "All scripture is given by inspiration of God, and is profitable for doctrine, for reproof, for correction, for instruction in righteousness: that the man of God may be perfect, thoroughly furnished unto all good works" **(2 Tim. 3:16–17).**

Scripture Reading: 2 Peter 1:19–21

Introduction

With tonight's study, we begin the exploration of twelve basic doctrines of faith. Because all doctrines have their roots in Scripture, it is fitting that we begin with the doctrine of divine revelation.

What should be one's attitude toward the Bible? Some have made a sacred fetish out of the Bible—worshiping the book rather than the Christ it portrays. Others feel that there is some magical value in having a Bible nearby, regardless of whether it is read or studied. These attitudes are dangerously close to bibliolatry—the worship of the Bible as a book—rather than understanding it to be the divine Word of God and the expression of his plan for people's lives.

Before we can properly assess our attitude toward the Bible, we must discover *what it is.* We call it the Word of God, the living Word, the incorruptible Seed, the Law of life. All of these definitions are valid. But what do we mean by them? In answer, let's consider the Bible as:

I. A specific revelation.

People decide that they are going to "study the Bible" and master its contents just as they would study American history, Gray's *Anatomy,* philosophy, or any other subject. They immediately become frustrated and convinced that the Bible is nothing more than a mass of unrelated material filled with contradictions. What is their problem? It is simply that they are natural people attempting to understand spiritual things. Paul commented on this problem to the Corinthians (1 Cor. 2:14).

On the other hand, when people filled with the Holy Spirit approach the Bible, they find an inexhaustible source of truth opening up before them. They discover an amazing unity and a beautiful symmetry in its message. They see a magnificent interrelationship between its sixty-six books, each making a contribution toward the overall theme of God's redemptive purpose for fallen, sinful humanity, as that purpose is culminated and revealed in Jesus Christ.

A. *What do we mean by the term* revelation? The word itself means "drawing back the veil," signifying that an obstruction must be removed for a person's vision to be complete. It means to make known that which was once concealed from view. Divine revelation is disclosure by God of truths that one could not know otherwise. Therefore, whatever people discover about the truths of God must come by divine revelation.

B. *What do we mean by the word* illumination? If a specific revelation by God to a person is to take place, that person's understanding, which has been darkened by sin, must be illuminated. Spiritual illumination means the bringing of heavenly light into the soul of a person who was born into spiritual darkness and who has lived in that darkness. This is one of the ministries of the Holy Spirit—to illuminate the minds of believers so that they can understand God's Word. In honesty and sincerity, the true believer prays, "Open thou mine eyes, that I may behold wondrous things out of thy law" (Ps. 119:18).

C. *To receive illumination from God in regard to the meaning of the Bible, we must be faithful to the light, or understanding, that we receive.* If the motive of our study is spiritual pride, causing us to be "puffed up" with our intellectual grasp of the Bible, we grieve the Holy Spirit within us. We must carefully apply the scriptural knowledge we receive to our everyday lives.

II. A progressive revelation.

Not only is the Bible a specific revelation of God to humanity, it is also a progressive revelation. When Christians begin a systematic study of the Bible, they discover that it is a gradual unfolding of God plan and purpose.

When children are in kindergarten, they aren't given Shakespeare to read and algebra problems to work. Rather, they learn how to write the alphabet and how to count. The progressive development of their minds and understanding begins there. So it is with God's Word. God started with people, "line upon line, precept upon precept, here a little and there a little," until Jesus came and lived among people, showing them what God is like. God had to start with symbols, or "pictures." The Old Testament is a great picture book filled with symbols that lead us to Jesus as he is revealed in the New Testament.

A. *For example, there is a "scarlet thread" that runs through the Bible.* It begins in the Garden of Eden, where the blood of an innocent animal was shed to provide coverings for the nakedness of Adam and Eve after they had sinned. From that primeval incident, God began to show that people cannot hide their sins from him nor remedy the condition of sin in their lives. Only God can do it. Thus, the "scarlet thread" has woven its way through the Bible. Finally, in glorious climax and culmination, it flows forth on Calvary to fulfill every symbol in the Old Testament.

B. *The New Testament is a book bathed in blood—the vicarious, redemptive blood of our crucified Lord.* Natural people are repulsed by this; the critics of Christianity turn away from it. But without the power of God progressively revealed in the Scriptures, flowing forth in the shed blood of his Son, there is no power to save people from their sins. Therefore, God has progressively "turned on the lights" of understanding. The first promise of God in Scripture (Gen. 3:15) has in it the anticipation of a completed redemption; and the first act of worship looks toward Calvary!

III. An inspired revelation.

In addition to being a specific and progressive revelation of God to humanity, the Bible is also an inspired revelation. Without an acknowledgment of the divine inspiration of Scripture, the Bible becomes little more than an anthology of history, myth, and superstition.

A. *The word* inspiration *is found twice in the Bible—in Job 32:8 and 2 Timothy 3:16.* The Job reference refers to God's authorship of humanity's intelligence, while Paul's word in 2 Timothy means "God-breathed," suggesting that God imparted his Word directly into the minds of the authors.

B. *When we speak of the "inspiration of the whole Bible," we refer to those original documents as they came from the pens of the various authors.* We no longer have the original manuscripts, but of one thing we can be certain: The same Holy Spirit who inspired the writers in the beginning will preserve the truth of the Scriptures! Translators are not inspired in the sense that the original authors were, so their choice of words and phrases may not always be completely accurate.

C. *How was God's Word inspired?* Not by "common inspiration"—or in the same way that human literary geniuses are inspired. Rather, God gave his thoughts to the individual writers, and they then expressed them within the framework of their unique personalities. Holy people of God spoke in old times as they were "moved," or inspired, by the Holy Spirit (2 Peter 1:21).

Conclusion

Since John penned the Revelation, God has not given any new or further revelation to humanity. His will for people and for the ages is contained in the Bible. Everything people need to know to be saved from their sins and to live a Christian life is in God's Word. It tells people that they are lost and condemned in their sin. It also tells people that God loves them and that he demonstrated his love in the life, death, and resurrection of Jesus Christ. All they need to do is accept by faith the message of the living Word of God.

WEDNESDAY EVENING, JUNE 9

Title: God Spoke a Second Time to Abraham

Text: "And the angel of the LORD called to Abraham a second time from heaven" (**Gen. 22:15 RSV**).

Scripture Reading: Genesis 22:15–19

Introduction

God comes repeatedly to his children speaking words of comfort and commission. If God only spoke once, that would be great. But he comes repeatedly desiring to have fellowship with believers (Rev. 3:20). Our text declares that the angel of the Lord came to Abraham a second time. You can be sure that the Lord will come to you again and again to make known his will for your life.

I. The Lord came to Jonah a second time (Jonah 3:1).

The prophet Jonah clearly disobeyed God's will by refusing to obey God's command. This brought God's displeasure and chastisement upon him. We can rejoice that God did not cut Jonah off completely to where there was absolutely no hope for his future. God gave him a second chance.

II. The apostle Peter received a second opportunity and commission (John 21:15–19).

Peter openly denied his Lord. Perhaps his only motive was fear and he was just trying to protect himself. The resurrected Jesus gave Peter a three-fold opportunity to reveal his love and to accept a new commission.

III. The Lord called to Abraham a second time.

The Lord's coming to Abraham was different from his coming to Jonah and Peter. The Lord came to Abraham to express his approval and to reaffirm his promises concerning Abraham's future.

A. *Abraham had proven his faith by his willingness to offer Isaac as a sacrifice.* If we have great faith in our precious Lord, he will come to us again.

B. *Abraham had obeyed the clear command of God.* The Lord comes a second time and a third time and on and on to those who in loving obedience seek to carry out his divine will.

C. *Abraham gave his very best to God.* God will come again and again to speak his words of identification, approval, and commission to those who give themselves to him.

At the time of his baptism, our Lord received divine approval from God. Toward the end of his earthly ministry a voice again spoke from heaven identifying and approving Jesus (Luke 9:35).

Conclusion

Our Lord does not speak just once to those who look to him in faith, love, and obedience. He comes continuously. As we bring our needs, our hurts, and our praises to him, God will communicate with us again and again in many different ways. May he give us ears that can hear and hearts that will respond.

SUNDAY MORNING, JUNE 13

Title: Christ in Your Home

Text: "And again he entered into Capernaum after some days: and it was noised that he was in the house" (**Mark 2:1**).

Scripture Reading: Mark 2:1–12

Hymns: "Have Faith in God," McKinney

"He Leadeth Me," Gilmore

"Take Time to Be Holy," Longstaff

Offertory Prayer: Our Father, we pause to thank you for your wonderful gifts to us. Help us to be mindful that everything we have, every good and perfect gift, is from you. You have been most generous toward us. Today as we give our tithes and offerings, help us to be grateful for your great love toward us in the giving of your Son in our place on the cross. In Jesus' name. Amen.

Introduction

The Jesus of history wants to be the Christ of our present-day experience. If we want to experience the benevolent and powerful presence of Jesus Christ, we must let the Christ who once lived, died on the cross, and conquered death come to live where we live today.

We can let this living Christ speak to us from the mountainside as he did in the past.

As Christ spoke to his disciples while onboard ship in the midst of a storm, so we can let him speak to us in the storms that threaten us.

As Christ's disciples listened to him in the temple, so we need to listen to him when we go to the place dedicated to prayer and worship.

Christ will speak to us in dialogue as individuals as he did during his ministry if we will but put ourselves in the middle of these passages as recorded in the New Testament.

Today let's listen to Christ and look at him while visiting a home. It is possible that these words that were spoken and the event described took place in the home of Simon Peter (Mark 1:29–31). While there Christ ministered to Peter's mother-in-law. He brought healing to one who was sick and in pain. Christ specializes in bringing healing into the home. He is eager to bring relief from pain and suffering. Is there need for healing and health and relief in your home?

I. Invite Christ to come into your home.

We can assume that Jesus entered Simon Peter's home by invitation. He was welcome there.

The events surrounding the healing of the man sick with a palsy may have taken place while Jesus was in Simon Peter's home. Wherever it was, we can assume that Jesus was in the home by invitation.

A. *The entire family should invite Jesus Christ into the home.*

B. *Many times Jesus enters the home because of the invitation of one individual.* It may be the wife or husband. In many instances a child comes to have faith in Jesus Christ. By dwelling in one individual's heart, Christ comes to live in a home; and by means of that individual's Christian testimony, a companion can experience conversion, a parent can receive the gift of faith, and children can come to know the Lord Jesus Christ.

II. Christ carries on a spiritual conversation in the home (Mark 2:2).

In the last phrase of verse 2 we read, "And he preached the word unto them." This phrase could leave a false impression. The word translated "preached" is not the word that refers to a proclamation or official announcement. It is not the word that refers to evangelism and announcing the Good News. Rather, it is the word that means "to speak, talk, converse." It literally means that our Lord carried on a conversation with the people in the house concerning spiritual matters.

It is possible for the living Christ to so dwell within us that in our conversations we can discuss spiritual things and encourage each other's faith and experience the presence of the living Christ as we do so. We must not labor under the impression that the living Christ is limited to the place of public worship and to the altar dedicated to him. We would be wise to give Christ an opportunity to converse with us. Some suggestions have been offered.

A. *We should engage in a sincere prayer of thanksgiving at the table before meals.*

B. *We should memorize verses of Scripture that contain great truths about God, and these should be repeated from time to time so that they can be written on the walls of our memory.*

C. *We can read selected passages from the Bible and discuss the meaning of these passages within the family circle.*

D. *We can sing a familiar hymn on appropriate occasions.*

E. *We can pray together in a family circle with hands joined from time to time.*

F. *We can read or tell a bedtime Bible story to children.*

G. *We can encourage private daily Bible study for each family member. Christ will join in these times of conversation and dialogue if we will let him.*

III. Christ encouraged hope while in the home.

Many people came to the home in Capernaum where Jesus was. It was impossible to conceal his presence in the home. If we let him live in our home today, his presence will affect us, and the results will become known to those about us. People will be drawn to the house in which Christ dwells as is described by the passage of Scripture we have read today.

A. *Some came to see Jesus out of mere curiosity.*

B. *Many sought to enter the house because they needed the help Jesus could give.* His very presence was a basis of hope. Some of them were hoping for a revolution against the tyranny of Rome. Others came because they felt a great need for a fresh and loving word from God.

C. *Four men came bringing a friend, hoping for the return of his health, happiness, usefulness, and productivity.*

D. *The helpless one was brought on a palette for the return of that which he had lost.* When Christ is permitted to dwell in a home, he imparts hope for something better in the hearts of all who live within that home.

IV. Christ announced forgiveness while he was in the home (Mark 2:5).

A. *Jesus met the man's spiritual need before giving attention to his physical need.*

　　1. The two needs may have been vitally related.

　　2. Jesus recognized the spiritual need of the man to be of primary importance.

　　3. In other instances Jesus met the physical need as if it were of primary importance.

B. *Unforsaken and unforgiven sin always creates pain and sickness.* Sin is a cheater and a robber. Sin separates peoples from their highest and best self. It literally cripples them and keeps them from becoming what they are capable of being.

C. *Christ specializes in forgiving sin.*

　　1. Christ deals with us in mercy and love as well as in power.

2. When Christ forgives he removes the pain created by our alienation from him.

3. When Christ forgives he restores a warm relationship with the repentant one.

It could be that the greatest need in your home is the need for forgiveness. Do mother and father need to forgive each other for some act or attitude of unkindness? Do parents need to have a forgiving attitude toward children who have disappointed them and perhaps disobeyed them?

Forgiveness that is full and free and forever can bring about health and happiness that nothing else can bring.

Conclusion

Christ revealed who he was in the home. He revealed that he was the Son of Man, the Promised One of God, the Lamb of God who came to take away our sins. He was and is the Lord over all. In this passage he assumed the role of God in forgiving sin. He made illness and pain disappear.

Christ can make a great difference in your heart and home. He wants to communicate with you day by day. He wants to encourage hope and enable you to meet the crises and responsibilities of life with courage. He will deal with your sin problem. You must make him the Lord of all if you want to know life in its fullness.

Invite Jesus to make his home in your heart. He will bring heaven into your life in the here and now, and he will take you to heaven in the hereafter. But you must first invite him into your heart and into your home.

SUNDAY EVENING, JUNE 13

Title: The Almighty God

Text: "God is a Spirit: and they that worship him must worship him in spirit and in truth" **(John 4:24).**

Scripture Reading: Psalm 19

Introduction

God is constantly confronting humanity with his reality. Everywhere people turn, they are faced with unmistakable evidence of a greater power. In spite of atheism, materialism, rationalism, and agnosticism, prophets and apostles in both the Old and New Testaments were certain that God "is, and that he is a rewarder of them that diligently seek him" (Heb. 11:6). Job said, "I know that my Redeemer liveth" (Job 19:25); Paul said, "I know whom I have believed" (2 Tim. 1:12); and John said, "We know that, when he shall appear, we shall be like him" (1 John 3:2). The Bible is filled with certainties in regard to God's existence and involvement in human activities.

The Bible does not attempt to prove God's existence; rather, his reality is assumed. There are three areas in which we can trace the footsteps of God.

I. God is in creation.

"The heavens declare the glory of God; and the firmament sheweth his handiwork" (Ps. 19:1).

A. *The universe has an orderliness that cannot be ignored.* The seasons come and go on schedule. Night follows day. There is an intelligence behind all this. These manifestations of nature comprise the effect of a "Cause." That "Cause" is an infinite creator who made it all, set it all in motion, and sustains it. Paul spoke of God as the Cause behind everything when he described him as the One "in [whom] we live, and move, and have our being" (Acts 17:28).

B. *Furthermore, there is a purpose and design in God's creation.* The atheistic belief that life "just happened" is an affront to human intelligence. For example, consider a house. Would an agnostic say, "We cannot determine who the builder of this house is, so we must conclude that it 'just happened.'"? How ridiculous! Rather, he would say, "We cannot see the architect or builder, but we know that there *was* one because here is evidence of his handiwork, the product of his genius." Likewise, there was an intelligent purpose and design behind God's creation.

> *When all Thy mercies, O my God,*
> *My rising soul surveys,*
> *Transported with the view, I'm lost*
> *In wonder, love, and praise.*

II. God is in humanity.

"When the Gentiles, which have not the law, do by nature the things contained in the law, these having not the law, are a law unto themselves: which shew the work of the law written in their hearts, their conscience also bearing witness, and their thoughts the mean while accusing or else excusing one another" (Rom. 2:14–15).

A. *As another evidence of his involvement in his creation, God has placed within people a moral consciousness that makes them capable of responding to their creator.* People were created with an innate knowledge that there is a higher power and with a capacity to know him. But at the same time, God gave people freedom of will, by which they can choose to ignore and repress these inherent tendencies toward God and morality. In so doing, they prove themselves to be fools, because they are asserting that which is contradictory to the very nature of humanity (Ps. 14:1).

B. *When people are born again, a miracle of restoration takes place in which God brings alive these feelings and intuitions about the existence of a divine creator and about people's moral responsibility to abide by his laws.* God is able, because of his love and through the regenerative power of his Spirit, to resurrect those dead feelings. This is the miracle of the new birth.

> *Down in the human heart,*
> *Crushed by the tempter,*
> *Feelings lie buried*
> *That grace can restore.*

III. God is in the Bible.

"The law of the LORD is perfect, converting the soul: the testimony of the LORD is sure, making wise the simple. The statutes of the LORD are right, rejoicing the heart: the commandment of the LORD is pure, enlightening the eyes. The fear of the LORD is clean, enduring for ever: the judgments of the LORD are true and righteous altogether. More to be desired are they than gold, yea, than much fine gold: sweeter also than honey and the honeycomb. Moreover by them is thy servant warned: and in keeping of them there is great reward" (Ps. 19:7–11).

A. *The Bible speaks of God's nature.* "God is a Spirit" (John 4:24). "Spirit" is the highest form of being, and God is essentially and eternally spirit. This means that he is not limited in any way. He is not confined to a human body, even though for thirty-three years he inhabited the physical body of his Son, Jesus Christ. Still, however, God is a person. He has personality; he is not merely an impersonal force that inhabits the universe. His personality is expressed in his love, grace, mercy, pity, and compassion. Because of this, the writer of Hebrews said, "We have not a high priest which cannot be touched with the feeling of our infirmities; but was in all points tempted like as we are, yet without sin" (Heb. 4:15). In other words, God is *God;* he is infinite and perfect in his holiness and power. Yet, because of his inconceivable choice to identify with people and become their Savior, he understands our plight and is willing and eager to save us!

B. *The Bible speaks of God's attributes.*

1. God is *immense.* "Behold, heaven and the heaven of heavens cannot contain thee!" (2 Chron. 6:18). A circle has a center and a circumference. The circumference is the limiting, outer boundary of the circle. God has a center but no circumference! His "center" is everywhere.

2. God is *eternal.* He has neither beginning nor ending. People divide time into past, present, and future, but God knows no divi-

sions like that. He told Moses to tell the people of Israel that he was sent to be their deliverer by him who is the great "I Am." That means God is everlasting, the One who has neither commencement nor consummation!

3. God is *unchanging.* He is the One "who does not change like shifting shadows" (James 1:17 NIV). People change—they start and stop and are up and down. But not so with God. His glory shines with an unvarying and permanent brightness.

Conclusion

In summary, we can say that God is *omnipotent.* This means that he is almighty and has all power. There is nothing within the realm of God's righteous nature that he cannot do. God is *omniscient.* He has all knowledge. Simultaneously, God knows all things—past, present, and future. God's total knowledge is intuitive with him; it is part of his being. God is *omnipresent.* Not only is he everywhere, there is also an added dimension to his omnipresence because he is love. He cares about everything everywhere.

In spite of his inconceivable majesty and power, God "condescends to men of low estate." "But God commendeth his love toward us, in that, while we were yet sinners, Christ died for us" (Rom. 5:8).

WEDNESDAY EVENING, JUNE 16

Title: Walking and Talking with God

Text: "Enoch walked with God; and he was not, for God took him" **(Gen. 5:24).**

Scripture Reading: Genesis 5:21–24; Hebrews 11:5

Introduction

We must not assume that Abraham was the first person to talk with God. We read in Genesis 5, which has been called "the chapter of nobodyism," that there was one great exception—Enoch. His biography is described in capsule form in the words of our text: "Enoch walked with God; and he was not, for God took him." We can assume that if Enoch walked with God he also talked with God and vice versa.

The New Testament text concerning Enoch indicates that "before he was taken he was attested as having pleased God" (Heb. 11:5). The writer could be speaking of the testimony of those who knew Enoch. It could be that they recognized the blessings of God upon Enoch's life in such a way that they were convinced that his life was pleasing to God. Most likely we would be closer to the truth if we believed that in some wonderful way God communicated to Enoch his own pleasure and approval of his life.

I. If we want to talk with God we must walk with God.

A. *To walk with God we must be in agreement with him.* The call to repentance is the call to agree with God concerning life's issues. The call to faith is the call to depend on God and trust him even when we cannot understand.

B. *To walk with God is to deepen our acquaintance with him.* The new birth is but the beginning. The life of discipleship is a life of following him. Toward the end of his pilgrimage of ministry and service Paul was still desiring to know the Lord in a deeper and richer way.

To be acquainted with some people is to experience a lowering of your level of appreciation for them. Not so with the Lord Jesus Christ. The more we walk and talk with him the deeper we will desire our acquaintance with him to grow.

C. *To walk and talk with God will increase our adoration for him.* The first and greatest commandment is to love God with our total being. The more we walk with him and the more we listen to him the greater our affection will be for him.

II. If we want to talk with God we must learn to listen to God.

Matthew Henry said, "None are so deaf as those that will not hear." Throughout Scripture emphasis is placed on listening.

A. *God spoke through Moses to encourage the people to listen (Deut. 1:11–13).*

B. *God spoke through Isaiah to encourage the people of Israel to listen (Isa. 55:3).*

C. *Jesus repeatedly encouraged his disciples to use their ears.* Most of us have never developed the habit of really listening to either man or God. Some of us are too busy, too selfish, or simply unwilling to listen to God.

Conclusion

The poet said beautifully,

Prayer is not an artful monologue
of voice ascending from the sod.
It is a tender dialogue
between the soul and God.

We must be willing to listen if prayer is to be what God intends it to be.

SUNDAY MORNING, JUNE 20

Title: As Your Father Walked

Text: "If thou wilt walk before me, as David thy father walked…" **(1 Kings 9:4).**

Scripture Reading: 1 Kings 9:1–9

Hymns: "Faith of Our Fathers," Faber

"Serve the Lord with Gladness," McKinney

"All the Way My Saviour Leads Me," Crosby

Offertory Prayer: Heavenly Father, you have placed an awesome responsibility on those ordained to be fathers. We thank you for the privilege of being a dad and assume the responsibility that accompanies the privilege. We are told in your word what our role is, and we are also promised strength and wisdom. We claim that promise and look to you for guidance and help. In the name of Jesus Christ our Lord we pray. Amen.

Introduction

A family sociologist asked a group of fifth graders, "What does it mean to be a father?" Some answers were as follows: "It means getting a good job and making a lot of money." "It means going to work in the morning and coming home with a headache." Related answers painted a grim man who works hard, has little fun, feels no joy, and seldom spends time with his children.

It is hoped that this message will enable each father to avoid such a picture and to be the kind of dad his child needs.

I. Each father needs to see the importance of being a dad.

A. *Studies have revealed that fathers most significantly influence their children's sexual identity.* Children who have a good father's image and influence relate well to the opposite sex, whereas those who are not as fortunate are more likely to have trouble relating to the other sex.

B. *Studies have also revealed that fathers most significantly influence the social behavior of their children.* If children are not well adjusted to their parents and do not have good communication with them, they are more likely to succumb to the use of drugs than those who have a good, healthy relationship.

II. Each father needs to understand the strong influence of what the child sees in him and hears from him.

A. *What are some of the things children should see in a father that make for a good influence?*

175

1. Children should see and feel their father's interest in the things in which they are interested, such as games, grades, school, and friends.
2. Children should see their father working. This is difficult under certain circumstances where outsiders are not allowed. But if it can be arranged, it is helpful. It encourages creativity in children and helps them better understand the value of money.
3. Children should see their father express the emotions of love, affection, anger, and fear.
4. Children should see their father at worship consistently and devotedly. This should be seen at home in family worship and at church in public worship.

B. *What are some things children should hear from their father that make for a good influence?*
1. Children should hear their father pray. Specific objects of prayer ought to be mentioned and not just generalities. For instance, missionaries and friends may be called by name. Children should be led to pray for their pastor, the sick, people in trouble, and the lost.
2. Children should hear their father read the Bible. Family devotions will exercise more good influence than most any other one thing. Good family worship will include daily Bible reading.
3. Children should hear their father extol the virtues of others and hear him speak words of encouragement, commendation, and helpfulness. Children should seldom, if ever, hear derogatory remarks, degrading comments, or criticism.
4. Children should hear their father upholding the roles of leadership and authority, such as pastors, school teachers, publicly elected officers, and police officers. They should also hear their father support institutions, such as the home, church, schools, and state, that serve as the backbone of this nation.
5. Children should hear their father say, "I love you," and call them by name.
6. Children should hear their father openly and unashamedly condemning evil, injustice, and wrong.

Conclusion

True fatherhood is an awesome responsibility, but very meaningful and fulfilling. Fathers, take this seriously. Look to your Maker as a source of wisdom and strength. Spend much time in reading your Bible and listening to what your Lord says to you in the written Word. Pray often to seek divine guidance.

SUNDAY EVENING, JUNE 20

Title: The Incomparable Christ

Text: "And the Word was made flesh, and dwelt among us, (and we beheld his glory, the glory as of the only begotten of the Father,) full of grace and truth" **(John 1:14).**

Scripture Reading: John 1:1–5, 10–14

Introduction

Where do you begin when you start to talk about Jesus Christ? If your subject were some outstanding historic figure, you would begin with his beginning—his birth, parentage, and heritage. But with Jesus, there was truly no beginning, for he said of himself, "Before Abraham was, I am" (John 8:59). Therefore, one can begin *anywhere* and start talking about Jesus and never get it all said! But we will attempt to choose some of the most basic facts concerning the Lord Jesus Christ.

I. First, let's examine Christ in his preincarnate glory.

A. *This is a staggering concept for the human mind.* For us, everything has a beginning. But the Bible teaches conclusively that Christ had no beginning; he existed eternally with the Father. John prefaces his gospel with the declaration, "In the beginning was the Word, and the Word was with God, and the Word was God" (John 1:1). He explains in verse 14 that the "Word" is synonymous with Christ. The "beginning" he is talking about is that referred to in Genesis 1:1. In other words, he is saying that Jesus goes back beyond the beginning of the creation of humanity. In John 17, Jesus prayed, "Father, glorify thou me with thine own self with the glory which I had with thee before the world was" (v. 5).

B. *Not only does Christ exist eternally, but John records in Revelation that Jesus came as "the Lamb slain from the foundation of the world" (13:8).* Because God is omniscient, he knew that people would sin even before he created them. Therefore, because God's nature is love, he provided a way for people to be reconciled to their creator before they were made! In that dateless past, "love drew salvation's plan," and "in the fulness of time" Jesus came as the foreordained sacrifice for the sins of the world. Paul said it like this: "When the fulness of the time was come, God sent forth his Son, made of a woman, made under the law, to redeem them that were under the law, that we might receive the adoption of sons" (Gal. 4:4–5).

C. *From the Bible itself, we have abundant evidence concerning the preexistence of Jesus before he was born of Mary.* In fact, both John and Paul ascribe the very works of creation to Christ. John said, "All things were made by him; and without him was not any thing made that was made," speaking of the "Word" that became flesh (John 1:3). Paul wrote, "By him all things were created, that are in heaven, and that are in earth, visible and invisible, whether they be thrones, or dominions, or principalities, or powers: all things were created by him, and for him: and he is before all things, and by him all things consist" (Col. 1:16). Thus, we must conclude by faith that God the Father, God the Son, and God the Holy Spirit have always existed as *one* God in purpose and in equality.

II. Now let's consider Christ and his earthly manifestation.

A. *When we consider the Incarnation, God becoming man, there are two important truths we must hold with all the tenacity faith provides for us.* First, Jesus became at the same time and in an absolute sense both God *and* man. He did not "become God" at his baptism and "cease to be God" at his death. When he was born in Bethlehem, he was God; when he ascended from Mount Olivet, he was God! Second, in becoming flesh, Jesus, though he laid aside his heavenly glory, in no sense laid aside his deity. This had to be true, for his full deity and complete humanity were necessary if his death on the cross was to have redeeming value for humanity.

B. *Our text declares that Jesus "became flesh and dwelt among us." "Dwelt" here means "tabernacled."* Jesus "pitched his tent" as a person among people. In the miracle of Bethlehem, God became what he had never been before. God became Jesus of Nazareth. Furthermore, John says that he was "full of grace and truth." Some say that Jesus was no more than "a good man" or perhaps "the best man who ever lived," but they stop short of admitting that he was God. John declares that Jesus was "full"—the sum total—of "grace and truth." He was the fullness of God's expression of grace and the complete revelation of God to humanity.

C. *Another significant word in this phrase is "truth."* The Greek word for "truth" is formed from the word *concealed,* or *hidden,* with the Greek word *alpha* added to it, giving it the opposite meaning. So "truth" literally means "the unconcealed." Until Jesus came, God Almighty was at least partially hidden from humanity in an aura of majesty and transcendency. He was, for the most part, unapproachable by humankind. Thus, people had a poor, limited concept of God as a personal God. Jesus came and "unconcealed" God; he became the complete revelation of God.

D. *The book of Hebrews says that Christ was "tempted in all points, like as we are" (Heb. 4:15).* Here we see Jesus' humanity in that God allowed Satan to unleash on Jesus the full force of his tempting power. Satan was allowed to do everything he could to deter Jesus from the cross. This was necessary not to see if Jesus was truly God, but to prove that he *was* God.

III. Last, let's see Christ in his present ministry.

A. *When Jesus ascended into heaven from the Mount of Olives, he did not leave behind just a fond memory of himself in the hearts of his followers.* He had told them, "Lo, I am with you alway, even unto the end of the world" (Matt. 28:20). What about his present ministry in heaven? He is completing in heaven the work he began on earth. The phrase "right hand of God," describing Jesus' position now in heaven, is a symbol of his power, authority, and glory. Part of his present ministry in heaven is the preparation of an abode for his church. He said to the disciples, "I go to prepare a place for you" (John 14:2). At the same time, he has kept his promise and sent the Holy Spirit to fashion the church and to prepare it as his bride. Two glorious projects are under way simultaneously: God is preparing heaven for us and us for heaven!

B. *But that's not all.* Christ also intercedes for us. Every Christian has a redeemed soul, but that soul is housed in an unredeemed body that sometimes disobeys and dishonors God. Often we find ourselves crying out as Paul did: "O wretched man that I am! Who shall deliver me from the body of this death?" (Rom. 7:24). On the basis of his completed sacrifice on the cross, Jesus is our intercessor before the throne of grace. He takes our imperfect prayers, perfects them, and offers them to God as "a sweet-smelling savor."

C. *Finally, Christ's present ministry in heaven brings to completion and perfection the three Old Testament offices: prophet, priest, and king.* When Jesus was baptized in the Jordan, the Holy Spirit was manifested upon him "without measure." Therefore, possessing all of the gifts of the Holy Spirit without measure, he has the full knowledge of a prophet, the perfect holiness of a priest, and the absolute power of a king. A *prophet* spoke to people about God and declared God's word to them. Jesus was the very embodiment of that word. A *priest* mediated between people and God; Jesus suffered in humankind's place, satisfied the divine holiness of God, and opened the way for people to be reconciled to God. *Kingship* is one of Christ's eternal prerogatives. He was born a king; during his earthly life, he asserted his kingship and people recognized his claim. His resurrection proved his sovereignty as King of Kings and Lord of Lords.

Conclusion

Now as we anticipate Christ's return, Christians rejoice in the prospective majesty of the Son of God, for Jesus will in reality be crowned King of Kings and Lord of Lords. How do we sing it?

> *Crown Him with many crowns, the Lamb upon His throne;*
> *Hark! how the heavenly anthem drowns all music but its own:*
> *Awake, my soul, and sing of Him who died for thee,*
> *And hail Him as thy matchless King through all eternity.*

WEDNESDAY EVENING, JUNE 23

Title: Am I My Brother's Keeper?

Text: "Then the LORD said to Cain, 'Where is Abel your brother?' He said, 'I do not know; am I my brother's keeper?'" **(Gen. 4:9 RSV).**

Scripture Reading: Genesis 4:1–6

Introduction

The first recorded question from a person to God is, "Am I my brother's keeper?"

What is our responsibility to our fellow human beings? Someone has jokingly said, "Each person has 67 million fourteenth cousins."

One of the great teachings of the Bible is the responsibility of each human being for others. Each of us is a brother or sister.

I. God spoke regarding our mutual responsibility for each other at the dawn of human history.

In this dialogue between the Creator and Cain, who had murdered his brother, we find a divine communication of displeasure concerning Cain's evil deed. The Lord indicated that Cain did indeed have a responsibility toward his brother.

The poet has put it,

> *No man is an island; no man lives alone.*
> *No man lives to himself and no man dies to himself.*

A. *Am I my wife's keeper?* Yes.
B. *Am I my husband's keeper?* Yes.
C. *Am I my child's keeper?* Yes.
D. *Am I my parents' keeper?* Yes.
E. *Am I my neighbor's keeper?* Yes.

II. The Ten Commandments reveal that we are responsible to God for each other.

A. *We are responsible to God.*
B. *We are responsible for parents.*
C. *We are responsible for family.*
D. *We are responsible for neighbors.*

III. God emphasized the importance of personal responsibility through the prophet Ezekiel (see Ezek. 3:16–21; 33:1–11).

The prophet was instructed to accept his responsibility for conveying a message to the hearts of the people even though they would not listen and even though they had stubborn and rebellious hearts that rejected God's will for them (Ezek. 3:6–9).

IV. The parable of the Good Samaritan illustrates our responsibility for others (Luke 10:25–37).

A. *The priest had religion but no compassion.*
B. *The Levite was concerned but refused to get involved.*
C. *Only the Samaritan demonstrated genuine concern for his brother.*

Conclusion

Are we responsible for others? Yes, to the degree that we have the opportunity to minister to them and communicate to them the message that God has entrusted to us for them.

"Am I my brother's keeper?" The answer of God is obvious.

SUNDAY MORNING, JUNE 27

Title: A Call for Consecration

Text: "I beseech you therefore, brethren, by the mercies of God, that ye present your bodies a living sacrifice, holy, acceptable unto God, which is your reasonable service. And be not conformed to this world: but be ye transformed by the renewing of your mind, that ye may prove what is that good, and acceptable, and perfect, will of God" **(Rom. 12:1–2).**

Scripture Reading: Romans 12:1–21

Hymns: "Hark, the Voice of Jesus Calling," March
"Our Best," Kirk
"Make Me a Blessing," Wilson

Offertory Prayer: Heavenly Father, you are the truth. To know your will is supreme knowledge. You are the way. In doing your will is fullness of life. Open our minds to know your will and empower our wills to do it. We pray in Jesus' name. Amen.

Introduction

When victory over Japan was declared ending World War II, the crew on a tugboat in New York harbor blew its whistle so long that they had to wait to get up steam pressure before getting under way. Paul never exhausted the energy of his theological engine in blowing the whistle. He had practical work to do. In Romans 1–8 Paul developed the theme of God's plan of salvation. In chapters 9–11 he confronted the special problem of Jewish unbelief. Romans 12–16, the practical section, exhorts that salvation by grace through faith obligates the believer to consecration to God and to Christian conduct toward others.

For Paul the justification of sinners from the penalty of sin through grace was unthinkable apart from the regeneration that delivered them from the love of sin and resulted in love for the Savior. It is also true, however, that the saved person needs continual exhortation to live the saved life. Dedication is never forced. It must be voluntary. When from his last imprisonment Paul wrote to Timothy, "Wherefore I put thee in remembrance that thou stir up the gift of God" (2 Tim. 1:6), he was probably acknowledging his own need of continually stirring up the fire of zeal for God. This is doubtless true in your experience also. Every saved person needs exhortation as well as instruction for Christian living.

I. Salvation by grace through faith obligates the believer to serve God (Rom. 12:1).

A. *A call for full dedication. "I beseech you. . .that ye present your bodies a living sacrifice."*

  1. "Living." Under the religious system familiar to Paul's readers, animal sacrifices were presented to God and were consumed by fire on the altar. No longer is there need for animal sacrifices. "For Christ is the end of the law for righteousness to every one that believeth" (Rom. 10:4). The call now is to present your bodies a living sacrifice. By "body" Paul probably means oneself. The New English Bible translates "your very selves." All that the believer does in this life he does in and through his body (see 1 Cor. 6:19–20). The tense of the verb "present" indicates that the sacrifice is to be once and for all time: All of oneself for all time dedicated to God.

  2. "Holy." Christians are saints. Paul so addressed them in Romans 1:7. Christians belong to God and thus are holy persons. In the primary sense of the word *holy,* God sanctified them at the time of their salvation—that is, he claimed them as his own. They belong to him. The position of the believer in Christ can be illustrated by a dot within a circle. The believer is completely encircled by God.

  3. "Acceptable unto God." What is the sacrifice that is well-pleasing to God? The author of Hebrews rightly perceived that there is no inherent merit in animal sacrifices: "It is not possible that the blood of bulls and of goats should take away sins" (10:4). Many of the ancient prophets taught that the sacrifice would be acceptable to God only as the worshiper was acceptable. Hear David in Psalm 51:16–17. Hear Micah in Micah 6:6–8. Hear Jesus in John 14:21 and in Mark 12:29–31.

B. *Motive for consecration to God.*

    1. "Therefore, by the mercies of God." "Therefore" is an arrow pointing both backward and forward. God's mercies are many, but preeminently the merciful God through Jesus Christ has provided salvation for all sinful persons and offers it as a free gift of grace to all who believe. This salvation gives the redeemed right standing before God, union with Christ, new life in which the Holy Spirit abides within to give guidance and direction, peace with God, and assurance that he or she will live on eternally with God in heaven. "For the love of Christ constraineth us; because we thus judge, that if one died for all, then were all dead: And that he died for all, that they which live should not henceforth live unto themselves, but unto him which died for them, and rose again" (2 Cor. 5:14–15).

    2. Other motives Paul might have urged:

        a. Enlightened self-interest. Jesus did not hesitate to use this motive in his appeal for persons to give their hearts to God. He urged people, "Lay up for yourselves treasures in heaven, where neither moth nor rust doth corrupt, and where thieves do not break through nor steal" (Matt. 6:20). He repeatedly indicated that heavenly rewards are worth seeking. Hope of reward and the desire to escape punishment are worthy motives but are not the best motives for consecration.

        b. Assurance of salvation. The apostle John wrote, "Hereby we do know that we know him, if we keep his commandments. He that saith, I know him, and keepeth not his commandments, is a liar, and the truth is not in him" (1 John 2:3–4). One who has not dedicated his life to God must necessarily lack assurance.

        c. Power of influence. One cannot have a Christian influence unless he is a Christian. The possibility that the shadow of one's unchristian influence might cause a son or daughter to stumble should be a powerful force to cause one to be a dedicated Christian. "Let your light so shine before men," said Jesus, "that they may see your good works, and glorify your Father which is in heaven" (Matt. 5:16).

C. *Dedication of oneself to God is an act of intelligent worship:*

    "Your reasonable service," says the King James Version, and "your spiritual worship," says the Revised Standard Version. The same Greek word is translated both "reasonable" and "spiritual," and the same Greek word is translated both "service" and "worship." Some people erroneously think that to be spiritual is to be unreasonable. What follies are committed in the name of being spiritual! Anything contrary to reason cannot be of the Holy Spirit, for God is all wise. "For God hath not given us the spirit of fear; but of power, and of love, and of a sound mind" (2 Tim. 1:7).

II. Salvation by grace through faith determines the believer's attitude toward the world (Rom. 12:2).

A. Negatively—"Be not conformed to this world." "Age," the alternate reading of the Revised Standard Version, is an accurate translation. "This present evil world," or "age," is contrasted with the coming age in which God's will will be done (see Gal. 1:3–4 and 2 Cor. 4:4). The tense of the verb means "Stop being fashioned" or "Do not have the habit of being fashioned" by the present world. Phillips, with evident perception, translates, "Don't let the world around you squeeze you into its mould." In this present evil world Christians are salt and light. The world needs the Christians, and probably the Christians need the world. Note Jesus' prayer, "I pray not that thou shouldest take them out of the world, but that thou shouldest keep them from the evil. They are not of the world, even as I am not of the world" (John 17:15–16).

B. Positively—"Be ye transformed by the renewing of your mind." Phillips translates, "But let God re-mould your mind from within." "Transformed" is the same word used in Matthew 17:2 and in Mark 9:2 of the transfiguration of Jesus. In 2 Corinthians 3:18 it is used of a change of believers into the likeness of Christ from one degree of glory to another. The mind of Christ, which is the goal that the Holy Spirit has in mind for redeemed persons, means not only that we think what Christ thinks but also that we have the same spirit that Christ has (read Phil. 2:5–8).

Conclusion: The effects of consecration.

One proves by experience that God's will is good, acceptable, and perfect. The word "proves" here is the same word used by Peter in 1 Peter 1:7 to describe gold that has been tested by refining fire. The experiences of life prove that God's will is good—the supreme good. In the Beatitudes Jesus equates happiness with holiness. "Blessed are the pure in heart! for they shall see God" (Matt. 5:8). One who with sincerity of heart serves God will keep on experiencing his reality and his goodness.

Consecration to God is acceptable—that is, it is well-pleasing to him. One dedicated to God's will has inner peace. One consecrated to God finds that God's will is perfect—that is, mature and complete. Consecration works. It brings the highest degree of personal satisfaction and spiritual achievement. To live life in accord with God's will is both wise and good. Such a life blesses the worshiper, brings good to others, and is acceptable to God.

SUNDAY EVENING, JUNE 27

Title: The Vicar of Christ

Text: "But the Comforter, which is the Holy Ghost, whom the Father will send in my name, he shall teach you all things, and bring all things to your remembrance, whatsoever I have said unto you" **(John 14:26).**

Scripture Reading: John 14:16–26

Introduction

What is a vicar? A vicar is someone who serves as the agent of another. Our word *vicarious* is an extension of the word *vicar.* The death of Christ on the cross was a "vicarious sacrifice"—that is, Christ, though he never sinned, entered into humanity's sinful situation to become the divine substitute, God's agent in providing the once-for-all payment for our sins. As Jesus was God's agent in redemption, the Holy Spirit is God's representative-in-residence on the earth, the "Vicar of Christ." Furthermore, the Holy Spirit did not come to bear witness of himself, but to draw people to Christ.

I. The Holy Spirit's identity.

Even though Jesus has ascended back to the Father and is no longer visible among us, there is a divine person on earth dwelling in and with the children of God. He is the third person of the triune Godhead. A body was not prepared for him, as was true with Jesus. Rather, the Holy Spirit dwells in the bodies of Christians. According to Paul, our bodies are the temples in which and through which the Holy Spirit manifests himself. We must understand that the Holy Spirit is a person just as Christ is a person. We cannot see him, but his personality and presence are equally as real as Christ's.

In John 16:13–14 Jesus tells us seven things about the Holy Spirit that prove him to be a real person: the Holy Spirit comes, guides, hears, speaks, glorifies, receives, and shows. Moreover, Paul tells us in Ephesians 4:30 that the Holy Spirit can be "grieved." Can a power or an influence be grieved? Hardly! Jesus spoke of the Holy Spirit as "he" in John 16. We do not speak of an influence as "he."

The Scriptures concerning the Holy Spirit indicate that he undertook to be obedient to the Father and the Son. The problem we have here is that, in the human realm, "obedience" often suggests inferiority. We conceive obedience to be part of the servant-master relationship. This is why some consider the Holy Spirit of less importance or of a lower station than God and Jesus. But not so: The Holy Spirit's obedience to the Father and to the Son is a willing subordination in keeping with the unity of purpose of the Godhead. As it was proper for Christ to be "obedient unto death," so it is fitting for the Holy Spirit to be God's unseen, obedient servant, speaking of

Christ rather than himself and glorifying the Father rather than his own person directly.

II. The Holy Spirit's introduction.

A. *Jesus said, "But when the Comforter is come" (John 15:26), and again, "When he, the Spirit of truth is come" (16:13).* These words were obviously used of one who was expected to come but who had not yet arrived. But isn't the Holy Spirit referred to in the Old Testament, long before the Day of Pentecost? Of course, but Jesus had something entirely different in mind. Prior to Pentecost, the Holy Spirit had been on earth only as a visitor. He had "come upon" certain people and empowered them to perform miracles or to declare God's Word. But now, according to Jesus, he was coming as a resident to abide forever with those to whom he was given.

B. *Christ said that the Spirit "shall be in you" (John 14:17).* Paul wrote to the believers at Corinth of "the Holy Spirit which is in you" (1 Cor. 6:19). What is the difference between the Holy Spirit *coming upon* a person and *dwelling within* a person? To illustrate, think of the contrast between an old-fashioned sailing vessel and a modern steamship. The sailing vessel is dependent for its movement on an outside power coming upon it. When the wind fills its sails, movement takes place. On the other hand, a steamship is propelled by a power within, a power that is constant, not intermittent like the wind. In the days before Christ came, God's people were like the sailing vessel. Today Christians are like the steamship. Our progress, if we have the Holy Spirit living within us, is dependent upon the power within, not without.

III. The Holy Spirit's intention.

A. *The Holy Spirit plays a very significant role in the imparting of eternal life to believers in the Lord Jesus Christ.* The Bible teaches that all three persons of the Trinity are related to the plan of redemption. The first person becomes the Father of a Christian. Paul said, "One God and Father of all, who is above all, and through all, and in you all" (Eph. 4:6). The life of the second person, Jesus, becomes the possession of a Christian. Jesus said, "I am the way, the truth, and the life: no man cometh unto the Father, but by me" (John 14:6). The third person, the Holy Spirit, brings about the regeneration, the change that comes when a person is born again. In his letter to Titus, Paul said, "Not by works of righteousness which we have done, but according to his mercy he saved us, by the washing of regeneration, and renewing of the Holy Ghost" (3:5).

B. *It is the Holy Spirit who reveals God to humankind.* There are three phases of revelation in which the Holy Spirit is involved. *He makes known the will of God* (which he did in the form of oral prophecy through the prophets of old); *he inspired the written Word* (the infallible revelation of God to humanity); *and he illuminates the Word* (makes it meaningful and intelligible to Christians as they read and study it).

C.   *The Holy Spirit enables Christians.* He is the One who empowers Christians for spiritual service and for day-by-day consistency in their Christian lives. Because of sin, people in themselves cannot please God or serve him acceptably. But the presence and power of the Holy Spirit within Christians makes it possible for them to please God. Sometimes this is referred to as the "filling" of the Holy Spirit. Paul exhorted believers to "be not drunk with wine. . .but be filled with the Spirit" (Eph. 5:18).

D.   *The Holy Spirit sanctifies Christians.* Sanctification runs in two directions: first, it is instantaneous. The moment a person is born into the family of God, he or she is "set apart" to live and exist for a different purpose. Sanctification is also progressive. When people are born again, they begin to grow and daily become more and more like their Lord. Just as children grow and take on more and more of their parents' physical and dispositional characteristics, so Christians should come to resemble their Lord more each day.

Conclusion

We have seen the blessed significance and importance of the Holy Spirit in God's plan and purpose for humanity. The Holy Spirit operates in the lives of believers so that, day by day, they may be conformed to the image of God's Son. This is not completed at the moment of salvation; it is the beginning of a long work of grace. Are you allowing the Holy Spirit to do his assigned work in your life?

WEDNESDAY EVENING, JUNE 30

Title: What Have You Done?

Text: "And the LORD said, 'What have you done? The voice of your brother's blood is crying to me from the ground'" (**Gen. 4:10 RSV**).

Scripture Reading: Genesis 4:8–16

Introduction

The words of our text contain a pointed and painful question to a man who was guilty of great sin. They indicate that God holds us responsible for our actions.

I. The question, "What have you done?" is very personal.

The question is not, "What has your family done?" or "What has your neighbor done?" or "What has the government done?" It is very personal. It concentrates solely on the wrongdoer.

II. The question, "What have you done?" is very present.

The question is not, "What are you willing to do?" or "What do you hope to do in the future?" or "What do you wish to do?" The question is, "What have you done already?"

Many people make the tragic mistake of living either in the past or in the future and failing to live in the present. We need to ask ourselves, "What am I doing right now for God and for others?"

III. "What have you done?" is a very proper question.

A. *God as creator, sustainer, and redeemer has the right to come and ask us, "What have you done?"*
   1. What have you done with Jesus Christ, God's Son?
   2. What have you done with the Holy Spirit, God's gift to every believer?
   3. What have you done with God's Word that he gave to us so that we can know him better and understand his will for our life?
   4. What have you done with the church to which our Lord gave the commission to carry to the ends of the earth the good news of God's love?
   5. What have you done for and with the unsaved people around you?
B. *This question can be proper for each of us.* It can help us realize our stewardship responsibilities, see our tremendous opportunities, and face up to the fact that time is passing swiftly.

Conclusion

Prayer is a dialogue in which we talk to God and let him talk to us. Maybe this is the reason why we do not engage in prayer more often than we do. Perhaps our performance has been so poor that we find prayer to be a painful experience when God comes to us with the question, "What have you done?"

Let's respond to the gracious ministry of the Holy Spirit who is seeking to lead us in the life of faith and faithfulness so that prayer will not be a painful experience. God desires that prayer be a pleasurable and productive experience for all believers.

Let's rejoice in the wonderful truth that our Father God will not hesitate to direct painful questions at us if he deems it necessary. When we expose ourselves to this type of examination, we guarantee that we will not go far astray in our life of discipleship.

JULY

■ **Sunday Mornings**

Continue the series "The Practice of Genuine Religion" after giving a special Independence Day message on the first Sunday morning of the month.

■ **Sunday Evenings**

The message for the first Sunday evening of the month has a patriotic theme. It is entitled "Stewardship of Citizenship." Continue the series "The Doctrines of Our Faith" on the following Sundays.

■ **Wednesday Evenings**

The suggested theme for Wednesday evenings is "The Way of Faith." The messages demonstrate the truth of Paul's declaration that "we walk by faith, not by sight." The messages encourage obedience and faithfulness to God's revealed will even when we cannot see what the end result is going to be.

SUNDAY MORNING, JULY 4

Title: The Christian As a Citizen

Text: "Render therefore unto Caesar the things which are Caesar's; and unto God the things that are God's" **(Matt. 22:21).**

Scripture Reading: Romans 13:1–7; Matthew 22:15–22

Hymns: "America the Beautiful," Bales
"Faith of Our Fathers," Faber
"God of Our Fathers, Whose Almighty Hand," Roberts

Offertory Prayer: Eternal God, holy Father, we thank you for our country. We thank you that it is founded on the great principles of democracy, justice, equality, and freedom. Forgive us when we fall short of the goal. Guide us. Preserve your blessings for us and our children, we pray, in Jesus' name. Amen.

Introduction

"The Christian as a Citizen" is an appropriate theme for consideration on this Independence Day. If Paul thought it was important for Christians in the Roman world to be concerned with duties to government, how much more should we be concerned! They were more subjects than citizens. They had practically no participation in the formation of governmental policies.

What do you think of the statement "People cannot be good Christians if they are not good citizens"? There is no hope for alleviating poverty, establishing justice, and providing political, economic, and educational opportunity for all except through the political process.

I. Government is ordained of God (Rom. 13:1–3).

A. *Note the teaching of Jesus in Matthew 22:15–22.* The Pharisees and the Herodians, united by a common jealousy of Jesus, sought to ensnare him by a trick question. They asked, "Is it lawful to give tribute unto Caesar, or not?" If Jesus answered yes, the people would react because they hated the Roman government. If Jesus answered no, then he would be subject to arrest by the Roman authorities. Jesus did not allow himself to be tricked. He requested a coin and asked them, "Whose is this image and superscription? They say unto him, Caesar's. Then saith he unto them, Render therefore unto Caesar the things which are Caesar's; and unto God the things that are God's" (Matt. 22:20–21). Jesus had given a forthright answer to their question: We have duties to God and duties to the state. These duties should not conflict; what makes people good Christians will also make them good citizens.

B. *Every person is subject to government (Rom. 13:1–2).* Christians are not anarchists. Government is part of God's plan. Paul would not have wanted his statement, "For there is no power but of God: the powers that be are ordained of God," to be pushed to the point that it allowed for the divine right or infallibility of kings. Neither would Paul want his statement, "Whosoever therefore resisteth the power, resisteth the ordinance of God: and they that resist shall receive to themselves damnation," to be pushed to the point that citizens could not revolt against a government that had ceased to be God's servant and had become Satan's. Paul was painting with a broad brush, as he frequently did, and did not take time to note the qualifications and exceptions to his general statement.

C. *Government is a minister of God (Rom. 13:3–5).* God's purpose through the state is to aid the good and to punish the evil. Governments are ordained of God to help citizens accomplish the greatest good for the greatest number and to prevent evil people from profiting at the expense of the community. Assuming that the government fulfills its purpose, one reason for obeying state laws would be fear of punishment; however, for Christians there is a worthier motive—namely, being good citizens is part of being good Christians. God wants Christians to cooperate with other citizens for the accomplishment of his purposes, one of which is living together in peace.

"Let every soul be subject unto the higher powers" (v. 1). The verb translated "be subject" is a military term used of members of an army arranging themselves for battle. The idea is "Draw up yourselves in proper order one to another." Ideally, a private is just as important to an army as a general. Both are necessary for an army to function properly. If the government is to carry out its proper function, all citizens must draw themselves up in proper order.

II. Some duties of citizens (Rom. 13:5–7).

A. *Obey the laws.* Christians are to obey all laws no matter how foolish they may seem. They should obey for conscience' sake whether they think they would get caught for disobeying or not. If the speed limit is fifty-five miles per hour, Christian citizens should not exceed the legal limit. If Christian citizens think the speed limit ought to be changed, they can present their views to their legislators; but until the law is changed, they need to obey. The one exception is when the lawmaking body enters a realm where it has no authority. For example, if the legislature passed a law prohibiting the preaching of the gospel, then loyalty to God would take precedence over loyalty to God's servant, the state. Peter and John faced that contingency when the Jewish Sanhedrin commanded "that they speak henceforth to no man in this name. And they called them, and commanded them not to speak at all nor teach in the name of Jesus. But Peter and John answered and said unto them, whether it be right in the sight of God to hearken unto you more than unto God, judge ye. For we cannot but speak the things which we have seen and heard" (Acts 4:17–20).

A law officer shared this experience. He was arrested for going forty-one miles per hour in a thirty-five-mile-per-hour zone. When he pleaded guilty, the judge asked him, "Why did you not say that you were on call, and the case would have been dismissed?" He replied, "Because, sir, I was not on call." Later in a traffic case before this judge when the officer's testimony and that of a citizen were at variance, the judge was able to accept the officer's testimony as credible. Every person is subject to the law, or else there can be no integrity in government.

B. *Honor those in authority (vv. 6–17).* Honor legislators, judges, and law enforcement officers because they are servants of God who assist us. Frequently they risk their lives and occasionally give their lives in the service of the state.

   1. Pray for them (1 Tim. 2:1–4).
   2. Assist them in their duties.
   3. See that they are compensated adequately.

C. *Pay taxes (v. 7).* In a representative government such as we enjoy, we have a privilege and a responsibility that Paul did not have—we elect the representatives who levy the taxes. Let's insist on a fair tax and pay a fair share.

D. *Vote.* This is a very precious privilege. An honest ballot and an enlightened electorate provide the means whereby political changes can be effected without violence.

E. *Jury duty.* The right of a fair trial before a jury of one's peers will be endangered if citizens refuse to serve.

F. *Defense of country.* Jesus said, "If the good man of the house had known what hour the thief would come, he would have watched, and not have suffered his house to be broken through" (Luke 12:39). We have a right to protect ourselves, our property, and our country from armed invaders.

Conclusion

The home, church, and state are the three institutions that exist by divine approval. Ideally, people can be good members of their families, active members of their churches, and worthy citizens of their country. When home, church, and state occupy the respective places that God in his providence has assigned to them, there is no conflict. When any one of them oversteps its authority, then a person must first be loyal to God. For example, in the home children are to obey their parents in the Lord. A YMCA secretary reported that a thirteen-year-old boy came to him and said, "My mother is a prostitute. She's making me solicit business for her. Do I have to do that?" The man assured the boy that he did not have to obey his mother when she ordered him to do what was contrary to God's law. Similarly, if the church or state steps out of the realm of the responsibility granted to it and binds a person's conscience with regulations that are contrary to God's will, then he or she has no choice but to obey God rather than the law.

Heavy responsibilities rest on all of us in this wonderful land of freedom to see that our homes, churches, and government function properly and fulfill God's plan.

SUNDAY EVENING, JULY 4

Title: Stewardship of Citizenship

Text: "Render therefore to Caesar the things that are Caesar's, and to God the things that are God's" (**Matt. 22:21** RSV).

Scripture Reading: Romans 13:1–7

Introduction

Stewardship is usually thought of only in terms of bringing tithes and offerings to the Lord's house. This is a very limited and inadequate definition of stewardship. It is true that we are stewards of the treasure that comes into our hands. We are responsible to God for the manner in which we earn, spend, save, invest, and give our money. But we are also stewards of time, the precious commodity of which life is made. We may waste or misuse it, or we may use it for the glory of God, the good of others, and our own happiness. Further, we are stewards of the talents and gifts that God has given to us. Some of us are unusually gifted with physical, mental, or artistic talents. We are responsible to God and to our fellow humans for the ways in which we use our talents. And as Christians we are stewards of our testimony. We sin against God, others, and ourselves when we remain silent instead of being true spokespeople for our Lord.

Today, we are going to talk about another form of stewardship—citizenship. We are responsible to God, our country, and ourselves at the ballot box. To abstain from casting our vote is to sin against the highest and best of which we are capable (James 4:17).

I. As Christians we have definite responsibilities toward our government.

Paul gave an ideal definition of the purpose of government as he encouraged prayer for all who were in positions of authority: "I urge, then, first of all, that requests, prayers, intercession and thanksgiving be made for everyone—for kings and all those in authority, that we may live peaceful and quiet lives in all godliness and holiness. This is good, and pleases God our Savior, who wants all men to be saved and to come to a knowledge of the truth" (1 Tim. 2:1–4 RSV).

A. *Government as an organization and institution is from God (Rom. 13:1–4).*
B. *Respect for and obedience to government laws are necessary attributes of Christians (Rom. 13:5).*
C. *Proper payment of taxes is part of our Christian responsibility toward government (Rom. 13:7).* While we may complain about the improper use of tax revenues, we are obligated as Christians to pay our taxes. We are also obligated to work for legislation that will prohibit our tax dollars from being misused.
D. *We are to pray earnestly for all who are in positions of authority in government (1 Tim. 2:1–2).* We do not have to admire or even agree with all government officials. If our government is imperfect and our governmental officials are unworthy, we should pray more earnestly for them so they might change and so the people might be protected from unjust governmental leaders.

II. Good citizenship produces rich rewards for the country.

A. *Homes are safer and society is more secure.*
B. *Political life is on a finer and firmer foundation.*
C. *Cultural life is encouraged and enriched.*

D. *The community's religious life flourishes when citizens are responsible toward God, the state, and themselves.*

III. The responsibilities of Christian citizens.

The New Testament is silent at the point of endorsing a particular form of government. There have been and are now many different forms of government in the world.

A. *Democracy:* government of the people, by the people, and for the people.

B. *Monarchy:* government by one; it began in the interest of efficiency.

C. *Oligarchy:* government by a few; it is justified by the argument that only a few are fit to govern.

D. *Aristocracy:* government by the best. The word *best* can be defined in many different ways.

E. *Plutocracy:* government by the wealthy; it is justified by the claim that those who have the biggest economic stake in the country have the right to rule it.

F. *Theocracy:* the rule of God in the affairs of humanity.

In the United States our form of government is a democracy. No other form of government gives Christians more freedom.

Dr. Foy Valentine has concluded in a pamphlet entitled "The Bible Speaks on Christian Stewardship" (Christian Life Commission of the Southern Baptist Convention), "Government in the United States is organized and operated so that Christians can make a difference. Democracy invites your influential participation in government. Christianity demands it!"

Dr. Henley Barnett, in his book *Introducing Christian Ethics* ([Nashville: Broadman, n.d.], 172–73), says, "Christian citizenship is to be faced and decisions are to be made in harmony with Christian imperatives of love and justice." He offers six ways Christians can take part in government:

1. Study to understand the nature and processes of government.
2. Participate in the selection of public officials in the formation of public policy.
3. Work for the extension of justice, freedom, and equality of all citizens, regardless of race, creed, or color.
4. Serve in places of political leadership for which one is qualified, regardless of the cost and criticism that may be forthcoming.
5. Challenge and criticize any force in society that tends to deny human rights or to run counter to the claims of God.
6. Align oneself with the church and other constructive forces that serve to strengthen the spiritual and moral fiber of individuals and the nation.

Conclusion

How do you respond to Jesus' command to "render therefore to Caesar the things that are Caesar's, and to God the things that are God's" (Matt. 22:21 RSV)? Again, the suggestions of Dr. Foy Valentine are appropriate:

1. Let us give primary obedience to God. God alone deserves sovereign control over our mind, emotions, energy, and will.
2. Let us be obedient to the laws of our country, state, and city. If we consider the laws to be unjust, then let us work through the proper procedures to change those laws. We are not free to be disobedient to the laws merely because they are unpopular or inconvenient.
3. Let us earnestly and constantly pray for all public officials that they might have faith in God and that they might respond to their responsibilities to him.
4. Let us work to establish justice, righteousness, and peace among men.
5. Let us support and preserve and protect freedom.

We must not assume a negative attitude toward government and retreat into solitude with a feeling of helplessness and despair. We must give ourselves in service to God as responsible citizens, not only of the kingdom of heaven, but also of the community in which we live.

WEDNESDAY EVENING, JULY 7

Title: The Crossing of the Red Sea

Text: "Moses said to the people, 'Fear not, stand firm, and see the salvation of the LORD, which he will work for you today; for the Egyptians whom you see today, you shall never see again. The LORD will fight for you, and you have only to be still.' The LORD said to Moses, 'Why do you cry to me? Tell the people of Israel to go forward'" **(Ex. 14:13–15 RSV).**

Scripture Reading: Exodus 14:10–15:2

Introduction

For 430 years God's people had been in bondage in Egypt. After the death of the firstborn throughout Egypt, God's people were thrown out (Ex. 12:33). It is estimated that 1.5 to 2 million people marched out of Egypt (v. 37). What a sight! The day of deliverance had arrived; God's people had been set free.

God led his people through the wilderness by the Red Sea. During the day he went before them in a pillar of cloud, and at night he went before them in a pillar of fire. God revealed to Moses that Pharaoh would pursue God's people. When the Israelites saw the Egyptians march after them, they greatly feared. It was then that Moses said: "'Fear not, stand firm, and see the salvation of the LORD, which he will work for you today; for the Egyptians whom you see today, you shall never see again. The LORD will fight for you, and you have only to be still.' The LORD said to Moses, 'Why do you cry to me? Tell the people of Israel to go forward'" (Ex. 14:13–14 RSV).

At the Red Sea God performed a miracle to deliver his people again from the hands of the Egyptians. The writer of Hebrews describes the crossing of the Red Sea: "By faith the people crossed the Red Sea as if on dry land; but the Egyptians, when they attempted to do the same, were drowned" (Heb. 11:29 RSV).

Many truths about faith can be found in the account of God's people crossing the Red Sea. Let's consider some of them.

I. The source of faith is God.

When Moses and God's people arrived at the shores of the Red Sea, they could see the Egyptians rapidly approaching behind them. God did something unusual to solve this problem. "Then the angel of God who went before the host of Israel moved and went behind them; and the pillar of cloud moved from before them and stood behind them, coming between the host of Egypt and the host of Israel. And there was the cloud and the darkness; and the night passed without one coming near the other all night" (Ex. 14:19–20 RSV).

When Moses came to the Red Sea, he prayed about the problem that God's people faced with the Red Sea in front and Pharaoh's army close behind. His prayer was answered quickly. He was to lift up his rod and stretch his hand over the Red Sea, and Israel was to go forward on dry ground through the midst of the sea.

Surely God is the source and center of our faith. We must trust him and take him at his word. Let's seek his will and then do what he commands us to do.

II. The secret of faith is to fear not and stand still.

When we are surrounded with difficulties and don't know what to do, we should fear not and stand still. The restlessness of the human heart often causes us to rush ahead without God. We cannot dry up the Red Seas of life or annihilate the hosts of Egyptians who plague us. We need God and we must move with him.

The secret of faith is to fear not and stand still. God will act. Isaiah said: "But they that wait upon the LORD shall renew their strength; they shall mount up with wings as eagles; they shall run, and not be weary; and they shall walk, and not faint" (Isa. 40:31).

III. Faith's success is found in going forward and in the Lord's fighting for you (Ex. 14:13–16).

God is great in his mercy. He opens the way where people can walk in faith.

A. *When God speaks we must go forward.* How many people are faithless and discouraged facing some sea of difficulty? They say, "I can't do this" or "I can't do that." No progress is possible unless God speaks. And he does speak!

   1. Go forward in prayer (Matt. 7:7).

   2. Go forward in Christian stewardship (Matt. 3:10).

   3. Go forward in evangelism (Matt. 4:19; 28:19–20).

   4. Go forward in Bible study and teaching God's Word (2 Tim. 3:16–17; 4:2).

   5. Go forward under the Holy Spirit's leadership (Zech. 4:6).

B. *When we remember that the battle is the Lord's he fights for us.* God knows how to fight and win the battle. He can send hail from heaven (Josh. 10:11). The earth can open and swallow up the people (Num. 16:31–35). The angel of death can destroy all night (2 Kings 19:35).

God planned to destroy the Egyptians in the Red Sea. When his people stood on the other shore after passing through the Red Sea, they were speechless. The Israelites had done nothing but obey God's command. God won the victory. The battle was the Lord's—and still is today.

IV. Faith's song is unto the Lord.

"Then sang Moses and the children of Israel this song unto the LORD…" (Ex. 15:1). "Sing ye to the LORD, for he has triumphed gloriously" (v. 21).

There is power in praise. A singing Christian is a victorious Christian. A singing church is a growing, witnessing church. Let's lift our voices to the Lord because we have seen his salvation.

Conclusion

"Not to us, O LORD, not to us, but to thy name give glory" (Ps. 115:1 RSV). "But thanks be to God, who gives us the victory through our Lord Jesus Christ" (1 Cor. 15:57 RSV). "After this I heard what seemed to be the mighty voice of a great multitude in heaven, crying, "Hallelujah! Salvation and glory and power belong to our God, for his judgments are true and just" (Rev. 19:1–2 RSV).

Do you know God? Do you know his mighty power of deliverance?

SUNDAY MORNING, JULY 11

Title: A Call for Christian Conduct

Text: "Be not overcome of evil, but overcome evil with good" **(Rom. 12:21)**.

Scripture Reading: Romans 12:3–21

Hymns: "Anniversary Hymn," Pruden
"Serve the Lord with Gladness," McKinney
"Take My Life and Let It Be," Havergal

Offertory Prayer: Our heavenly Father, author of liberty, we praise you for making us in your image. We thank you for freedom from the penalty of sin and for the freedom to serve that we have in Christ. May we enjoy and allow other people to enjoy all the freedoms consistent with the lordship of Jesus Christ, in whose name we pray. Amen.

Introduction

Paul appealed for consecration to God in Romans 12:1–2. The corollary of dedication to God is love toward other people. Consecration issues in Christian conduct. Romans 12:3–21 appeals for Christian conduct toward others. The passage presents the characteristics of the new person in Christ.

I. Humility (v. 3).

All people are important in God's sight. They are immortal souls for whom Christ died. God in sovereign grace has given everyone gifts to use. All people are to value themselves and their gifts of grace, but they are not to yield to the temptation to overvalue themselves in relation to others. One person is important, but another person is equally important to God. Paul knew the temptation of pride (see 2 Cor. 12:7). Because of God's gracious gifts to him, and because he knew the temptation, Paul warned the saints to think objectively about themselves in relation to others (see 2 Cor. 10:12).

II. Cooperation and dedication (vv. 4–8).

In 1 Corinthians 12 Paul describes the church as the body of Christ, while Christ is the head, or guiding intelligence. Each believer is a member of the body and has his or her place to fill. And each member is necessary to complete the body. All members are to cooperate with other members and obey Christ, the head. God in sovereign grace has given gifts to the members as he wills. Not all have the same gifts. Every gift is important to God and is given for service, so there is no ground for boasting: "For who maketh thee to differ from another? and what hast thou that thou didst not receive? now if thou didst receive it, why dost thou glory as if thou hadst not received it?" (1 Cor. 4:7). Paul lists some of the gifts in our passage from Romans 12.

A. *Prophecy (v. 6).* "If our gift is preaching, let us preach to the limit of our vision" (Rom. 12:6 PHILLIPS). *Today's English Version* has, "If our gift is to speak God's message, we must do it according to the faith that we have."

B. *Ministering (v. 7).* The word for ministering means "deacon service" but is used here in the sense of all Christian service.

C. *Teaching (v. 7).* Jesus was a great teacher. The Sermon on the Mount might also be called the "Teaching" on the Mount, because the Bible says, "He opened his mouth and taught them, saying. . ." (Matt. 5:2). If a person's gift is teaching, he or she should be dedicated to teaching.

D. *Exhorting (v. 7).* "And if our gift be the stimulating of the faith of others let us set ourselves to it" (Rom. 12:7 PHILLIPS). Exhorting is encouraging others' faith.

E. *Giving (v. 8).* "He that giveth, let him do it with simplicity" probably means with single-mindedness of purpose to glorify God, without self-seeking. Thayer's lexicon says, "Openness of heart manifesting itself by benefactions, liberality, free from pretense and hypocrisy."

F. *Ruling (v. 8).* "He that ruleth" would better be translated according to an earlier use of the word meaning "leader," or literally, "the one who stands in front." Those who lead are to do so with eagerness and diligence. This is a good admonition for moderators, Sunday school directors and teachers, and preachers.

G. *Showing mercy (v. 8).* "Those who offer comfort to the sorrowing should do so with Christian cheer" (Rom. 12:8 TLB).

III. Love without hypocrisy (vv. 9–10).

Love is synonymous with God's will. It means to have the attitude that God wants us to have accompanied by the appropriate action.

A. *Love cleaves to the good and abhors the evil.*

B. *God's will toward people is always goodwill.* It is truly a mark of Christian maturity when we can rejoice in honors that come to others more than when they come to ourselves.

IV. Fervency (v. 11).

Do not be slack or lazy in your work for God. Keep the spiritual fires burning and serve the Lord with a heart full of devotion.

V. Optimism (v. 12).

"Rejoicing in hope" (v. 12). Base your happiness on your hope in Christ. He promises that he will be with us until the end of the age and that we will be with him in heaven throughout eternity. "If God be for us, who can be against us?" (Rom. 8:31).

VI. Patience (v. 12).

When trials come—as they did to the early Christians and as they will to us—endure patiently. Keep on persevering in tribulation.

VII. Prayerful.

"Continuing instant in prayer" (v. 12) means steadfastly maintaining the habit of prayer. Jesus did and Paul did, as illustrated earlier in this letter (see Rom. 1:9–10). When other doors are closed, the door of prayer is always open.

VIII. Kindness (vv. 13–21).

A.   *Be helpful (v. 13).* Christians are to give freely to the needs of others in want—especially to other Christians. When Paul wrote this letter to the Romans, he was on his way to Jerusalem with an offering for the poor saints in Judea.

B.   *Be hospitable.* "Given to hospitality" (v. 13). When public accommodations were almost nonexistent, it was very important that Christians open their homes to other Christians. Note this emphasis in 1 Timothy 3:2; Titus 1:8; Hebrews 13:2; 1 Peter 4:9; and 3 John 5–8.

C.   *Bless rather than curse your persecutors (v. 14).* Jesus had taught in the Sermon on the Mount that we should bless those who persecute us (see Matt. 5:11–12, 43–48) and had demonstrated it on the cross when, instead of praying that those crucifying him would be damned, he prayed, "Father forgive them; for they know not what they do" (Luke 23:34).

D.   *Be sympathetic (v. 15).* "Rejoice with them that do rejoice, and weep with them that weep." It is usually more difficult to do the former than the latter.

E.   *"Live in harmony with one another. Do not be proud, but be willing to associate with people of low position. Do not be conceited" (v. 16 NIV).* "In humility consider others better than yourself" (Phil. 2:3 NIV). Do not be haughty in mind or snobbish in attitude, but take an interest in ordinary people.

F.   *"Do not repay anyone evil for evil" (v. 17 NIV).* Jesus positively affirms, "Love your enemies, bless them that curse you, do good to them that hate you, and pray for them which despitefully use you, and persecute you; that ye may be the children of your Father which is in heaven" (Matt. 5:44–45).

G.   *"Be careful to do what is right in the eyes of everybody" (v. 17 NIV).* Not only are Christians to be honest in the sight of God, but they are to be honest in the sight of all people. Although Paul knew that he was honest in handling the offering for the poor Christians in Judea, he took with himself representatives from the churches that had given the money to distribute the offering so that people could see that he was not dishonest. Church treasurers, financial secretaries, and all who handle the affairs of the church ought to insist on having their books audited regularly. They know that they are honest, but they also want the congregation to know that they are honest.

H. *Live at peace (vv. 18–21).* Next in importance to being reconciled to God is peace with one's fellow humans. Jesus taught this in Matthew 5:21–26; 18:15–17; and Luke 17:3–5. Paul knew that it was impossible to live at peace with all people. Some people will simply not be peaceable. Even God cannot make peace with a person who will not repent of his or her sins. But as far as it depends on you, be at peace.

You are never to take your own revenge. God is the judge. Assessing punishment is God's prerogative. When people take this on themselves, they show lack of faith in God. A Christian's ultimate purpose is to win enemies to Christ.

A dish of food sent in a time of bereavement, a word of congratulations, or continued kindness in response to unkindness may cause a person's conscience to be so anguished that he or she will repent and turn to the Lord. The ultimate weapon in the conquest of evil is the gospel. When people accept Christ, they cease to be enemies and become brothers and sisters.

Conclusion

In this remarkable chapter Paul has enumerated many of the characteristics of a Christian. All of these qualities of Christian character and ideal personhood are found preeminently in Jesus Christ (see Rom. 10:4; Matt. 5:17–48). A Christian's goal is to be like Jesus. Let's not be content "till we all come in the unity of the faith, and of the knowledge of the Son of God, unto a perfect man, unto the measure of the stature of the fulness of Christ" (Eph. 4:13).

SUNDAY EVENING, JULY 11

Title: What Is Man . . .?

Text: "What is man, that thou art mindful of him? and the son of man, that thou visitest him?" **(Ps. 8:4).**

Scripture Reading: Psalm 8

Introduction

King David, that magnificent "man after God's own heart," has echoed our amazement in the question he sent toward the heavens: "What is man, that thou art mindful of him?" After all of the disappointment and sorrow the sinful human race has brought to its creator, it is the wonder of wonders that God could have *any* good intentions left toward humanity! People, God's masterpiece of creation, have brought untold misery into the world, yet God has been unspeakably merciful to them. This astonishing truth demands us to search the Scriptures in order to understand something of humans, who are capable of rising to great heights in the worship and adoration of their creator yet sinking to the depths in moral perversion and sin.

I. First, Let's examine the human race in its generation.

"Generation," in this setting, means the act or process of coming into being. There are four words in the Genesis account of creation that are filled with implication: "Let us make man" (Gen. 1:26). Note that God is referred to in the plural—"Let *us* make man." *Elohim* is the plural name for God in the Old Testament, and it brings together all of the mighty, majestic, creative power of God. When the ancient Hebrews wanted to underscore the greatness of anything, they expressed it in the plural form. God focused all of his creative genius on humankind! In regard to the other creation acts, God said, "Let there *be.*" But with humankind, God was personally involved. Therefore, people bear the fingerprint of God—they were made in God's image and after his likeness.

But the human race, in its degenerate effort to deny God's existence, has set forth several theories concerning how humankind came to be. There is the "spontaneous generation" theory that says there was no creator of humanity and that people simply came into being without a cause, or "out of the nowhere into the here." Then there is the popular theory of evolution, which states that humans were originally protoplasm, and, passing through a long series of changes, they evolved into apes, and finally into people. But God caused a subtle difference to exist between humans and animals that placed humans in a different order of creation altogether. God gave animals *instinct,* but he gave humans *intellect.* Because of this, among God's creation only humans are capable of declaring praise and worship and adoration toward their creator.

The Bible, however, gives a different account. First, humankind was created by a divine, direct, and definite act of God. Second, humankind was created in God's image, after his likeness. Third, humankind is spirit—God breathed the breath of life into humans. God is a spirit, and thus fellowship with him is possible through the Spirit. Humankind was created with the capacity for God consciousness.

II. Second, let's consider the human race's degeneration.

Humans were created to live in perfect accord with their creator, to be at peace with themselves, and to live in harmony with their environment. But humanity forfeited this holy and blessed position through sin. Evolutionists teach that humans are "falling upward," that they are gradually shedding the animal tendencies called "sin," and that they will eventually emerge as a pure race with all evil having dropped away through the generative process. But the Bible takes the opposite view. Paul said it plainly in his letter to the Romans: "Wherefore, as by one man sin entered the world, and death by sin; and so death passed upon all men, for that all have sinned" (Rom. 5:12).

Therefore, as a result of their sin, humans lost their original dignity. Sin has weakened humankind's power to dominate nature. Christ was the perfect man, and consequently he had full control over nature. Dr. F. B. Meyer described fallen humanity in this manner: "Man's crown is rolled in the dust and tarnished. His sovereignty is strongly disputed by the lower orders of creation. The earth supplies him with food only after arduous toil. The beasts serve him only after they have been laboriously tamed and trained, while vast numbers roam the forests, setting [man] at defiance." So we must say that Adam's sin resulted in the depravity of humankind, which means that every part of human nature became tainted with sin.

In scriptural summary, we must conclude that human spirits are darkened (1 Cor. 2:14), human souls are debased (Jer. 17:9), human bodies are diseased, human wills are weakened, and human consciences are dulled by sin (1 Tim. 4:2). Therefore, through human degeneration, sin became universal; it was passed to all people and resulted in the loss of communion with God. R. A. Torrey lists five steps in the fall of humanity as it is described in Genesis 3:1–6: (1) Adam was guilty of listening to slander against God, (2) doubting God's Word and his love, (3) looking at what had been forbidden, (4) lusting for what God had prohibited, and (5) disobeying God's commandment.

III. Third, let's observe the human race's regeneration.

This is the greatest part of the study of the doctrine of humankind. We have seen human "generation" in all of its creative splendor; we have seen the "degeneration" of humans as they turned their backs on their creator; now we will see the provision whereby humans can be regenerated—restored to fellowship with their creator. Through sin, people have lost the image and likeness of God in which they were made. But the Bible teaches that this likeness can be recovered (see Col. 3:9–10). If Paradise has been lost, as John Milton declared in his essay, then according to the Bible and because of God's love, it can be regained.

The miracle of regeneration was made possible because Christ, the "true image of the invisible God," took on himself our human nature and weaknesses (except for sin), and made possible our redemption from the consequences of the Fall. In Adam we died; in Christ we are made alive. How does God bring us to this point of regeneration? He makes us aware of our sins through the Holy Spirit's convicting ministry. Then he makes us capable of experiencing godly sorrow, which is a heartbreaking awareness that we have sinned against God, breaking the heart of the creator who loved us and, through his Son, gave himself for us.

The result of this is the new birth, the regeneration by which we are made new creatures in Christ Jesus. Then, once again, believers experience the "divine nature," and they are sealed by the Holy Spirit unto the day of final redemption.

Conclusion

With our human reasoning, we may wonder why God didn't turn his back on humankind and start fresh. Because God is love, he continued working with humankind. He devised a plan so that people could be restored, reconciled, and brought back into fellowship with their creator. This plan was executed through God's Son, Jesus Christ. "What is man, that thou art mindful of him?" People are nothing in themselves; but in Christ they are the "apple of God's eye" and the crowning glory of his redemption plan.

WEDNESDAY EVENING, JULY 14

Title: The Walls of Jericho

Text: "It came to pass at the seventh time, when the priests blew the trumpets, Joshua said unto the people, Shout; for the LORD hath given you the city" **(Josh. 6:16).**

Scripture Reading: Joshua 6:1–27; Hebrews 11:30.

Introduction

The name Jericho means "fragrant." It is also called "the city of palm trees" (Deut. 34:3). Jericho is located five miles west of the Jordan and seven miles north of the Dead Sea and is situated about eight hundred feet below sea level. Jericho stood opposite Mount Nebo (32:49). It was surrounded by walls (Josh. 2:15) and had a gate that was closed at night (v. 5). It was ruled by a king.

Jericho is probably the oldest city in the world. In the winter it became a resort town for people fleeing the colder weather of the Palestinian hill country. The presence of many springs made Jericho a green oasis in the middle of the dry Jordan rift area.

The first account of Jericho in the Bible is in Joshua 6. It is the story of the capture of the Canaanite city by Joshua and God's people. The miracle of Jericho's walls falling down is recorded in verse 20: "It came to pass, when the people heard the sound of the trumpet, and the people shouted with a great shout, and the wall fell down flat, so that the people went up into the city, every man straight before him, and they took the city."

Anyone who believes in God's power to foreknow and his power to act and direct, will have no trouble believing in the miracle of the destruction of Jericho's walls. At a specified juncture on the seventh day, after encompassing the city seven times, the walls fell down. God had worked another miracle for his people. It was fitting that the first time Israel crossed swords with their deadly and dreaded enemies, God intervened to hearten his people, his warriors.

Miracles show us God's power. God is as much with us in our battles as he was with Joshua and his people when they marched around Jericho.

Now let's look at some of the great truths in this miracle for us.

I. The walls of Jericho fell by faith.

The writer of Hebrews said, "By faith the walls of Jericho fell down" (Heb. 11:30). Faith in God is essential to salvation, to those who do God's work, and to the Christian life. We must believe that God is; God is powerful; and God acts. "Without faith it is impossible to please him" (v. 6). "According to your faith be it unto you" (Matt. 9:29). "If thou canst believe, all things are possible to him that believeth" (Mark 9:23).

The hymnwriter John Yates had it right: "Faith is the victory! Faith is the victory! Oh, glorious victory that overcomes the world."

II. The walls of Jericho fell when God's people followed his plan and his leader.

The plan for conquering Jericho was simple. The people were to march around Jericho once for six days. On the seventh day they were to march around Jericho seven times, blow a long trumpet blast, shout with a great shout, and the walls would fall.

God's leader was Joshua. What kind of man was he?
A.   Called by God (Josh. 1:5–6).
B.   Faithful.
C.   Positive.
D.   Filled with God's word (Josh. 1:7–8).

Israel followed God's plan and God's leader. We always have victory when we follow God's plan for our lives.

III. The walls of Jericho fell when God's will was done without questioning.

Six days God's people were to walk around Jericho without speaking a word! On the seventh day they were to walk around Jericho seven times without a word. No reason had been given for this silence. The entire plan for conquering Jericho had been explained to Joshua. He knew what God was doing. "Joshua had commanded the people, saying, Ye shall not shout, nor make any noise with your voice, neither shall any word proceed out of your mouth, until the day I bid you shout; then shall ye shout" (Josh. 6:10).

The hardest thing for Israel to do was to be silent. The grim silence of the people must have been impressive.

Theirs not to make reply,
Theirs not to know the reason why.

How long could we do the Lord's work in silence without questioning?

IV. The walls of Jericho fell for God's glory.

When we have faith to follow the Lord and his plan and leaders, victory will come, and glory will go to God. Only Rahab and her family were spared in the conquest of Jericho.

Rahab's faith led her to break with her sins. God will receive glory when he saves you and when you serve him. "By faith the harlot Rahab perished not with them that believed not, when she had received the spies with peace" (Heb. 11:31).

Rahab was the mother of Boaz, the great-grandmother of King David, and an ancestor of Jesus (Ruth 4:18–21; Matt. 1:5).

Conclusion

Put your faith in our miracle-working Lord.

SUNDAY MORNING, JULY 18

Title: Love Fulfills the Law

Text: "Let no debt remain outstanding, except the continuing debt to love one another, for he who loves his fellowman has fulfilled the law" (**Rom. 13:8** NIV).

Scripture Reading: Romans 13:8–10; Matthew 22:34–40

Hymns: "Great Is Thy Faithfulness," Chisholm
"Love Lifted Me," Rowe
"My Jesus, I Love Thee," Featherstone

Offertory Prayer: Holy and loving Father, your character assures us that no command will be unrighteous or unloving. We thank you for the lovingkindness you have shown us through the sacrifice of your Son, Jesus, on the cross. Please accept as a token of our love the tithes and offerings we now present before you. In Jesus' name. Amen.

Introduction

Paul has called Christians to consecration to God and renunciation of the world. In Romans 12 he discusses a Christian's relationship to other people, and in Romans 13 he covers a Christian's relationship to fellow citizens of the state. Prior to his discussion in chapter 14 about a person's relation to fellow Christians, especially immature Christians, Paul summarizes the whole of one's relationship to others in this principle: "Let no debt remain outstanding, except the continuing debt to love one another, for he who loves his fellowman has fulfilled the law" **(Rom. 13:8 NIV)**. In this statement Paul built on the teaching of Jesus as he frequently did.

I. Jesus teaches the primacy of love (Matt. 22:34–40).

A lawyer of the Pharisees asked Jesus, "Which is the great commandment in the law?" In addition to the Ten Commandments, the scribes found more than six hundred others in the Torah. How could the law be applied in case of conflict? Which of the commandments would take precedence? The scribes often debated this question. It could have been a very practical question, but among them the speculation was usually academic. In this case we are told that the lawyer was "tempting" Jesus (v. 35). Jesus summarized the whole law and the prophets by two quotations from the Old Testament. The first from Deuteronomy 6:5 encapsulated the first table of the law: "Thou shalt love the LORD thy God with all thy heart, and with all thy soul, and with all thy mind. This is the first and great commandment" (Matt. 22:37–38). Then Jesus condensed the second table of the law by quoting Leviticus 19:18: "And the second is like unto it, Thou shalt love thy neighbour as thyself" (Matt. 22:39). And he added, "On these two commandments hang all the law and the prophets" (v. 40).

A. *It is impossible to frame commandments, laws, or rules judiciously enough to cover all circumstances.* Jesus spoke principles rather than rules. A person may sometimes bend or break a rule while remaining loyal to the principle. One who tries to apply the Bible as a rule book is in trouble. Let's illustrate from the second table of the law.

"Honor thy father and thy mother. . ." (Ex. 20:12). Paul interprets the command, "Children, obey your parents in the Lord: for this is right" (Eph. 6:1). The principle is honor to parents. Are there times when a child can disobey his or her parents and continue to honor them? A fine Christian woman had promised her mother that she would never place her in a rest home. Some years passed; the mother became paralyzed; she required twenty-four-hour care, which her daughter could not give. The mother did not even recognize her own children. On the advice of her doctor and pastor, this woman placed her mother in a rest home because it seemed to be the loving thing to do.

Another commandment is "Thou shalt not kill" (Ex. 20:13). The better translation is "Thou shalt not murder." The reference, as the context shows, has no reference to the killing of animals, nor to the taking of life by the state. The principle is reverence for human life. Is it possible that a person could take the life of another and be justified? Is a police officer justified in killing a person who is holding a gun on another officer?

"Thou shalt not steal" (Ex. 20:15). The principle is respect for property rights. Property rights are personal rights. It would be a strict legalist, however, who would condemn a person for stealing in order to feed his or her starving family.

"Thou shalt not bear false witness against thy neighbour" (Ex. 20:16). The principle is integrity. A Christian's yes is yes, and no is no. A pastor visited in the psychopathic ward of a hospital. After the attendant had let him in and locked the door, there was a disturbance at the other end of the ward. The attendant said to the pastor, "Wait until I return." While he was waiting, a wild-eyed man came up and said, "Say, do you have a knife?" Quickly the pastor replied, "Sorry, no." Then he put his hand in his pocket and there found a knife. Did he call the man back and say, "Forgive me; I lied to you"? Of course not.

These illustrations amply show that the Bible is not a law book to be applied without regard to the principles or situations involved.

B. *"Thou shalt love" is Christ's supreme command.* You will love God, your neighbor (including your enemies), and yourself. The Greek word *agape* has become an English word. The dictionary definition of agape love, however, is very inadequate. What is Jesus commanding?

   1. In English love can signify many things.

      a. Love usually brings to mind the attraction of the sexes based on sexual desires. The Greek word is *eros,* from which our English word *erotic* is derived. Sex is one of God's good gifts. Used in accord with God's intention by two who commit themselves in marriage, it is very meaningful. This, however, is not what Jesus is commanding.

      b. Love is also used for that which is pleasing or attractive, gives pleasure, or friendship. We often use *love* in place of *like,* as in "I just love summer." The Greek word is *philos.* Obviously, when Jesus said, "Love your enemies," he was not commanding "like or be attracted to your enemies."

   2. *Agape* is the word for love in the New Testament. It is defined by its usage. Basically it means "good will" or "God's will, which is good." It is the right motive accompanied by the right actions. John 3:16 illustrates this. "God so loved"—goodwill—"that he gave his only begotten Son"—the right action. Agape is God's love (see Rom. 5:8–10; 1 John 4:7–12). Agape is Christ's love (see John 13:1; 15:9–14; Eph. 5:1–2).

C. *The Great Commandment (Matt. 22:37).*

   "Thou shalt love the Lord thy God." This means that we are to have the attitude of goodwill that God desires, accompanied by appropriate deeds. Love is godlikeness, or the will of God. Since God's will is fully revealed in Jesus Christ, to love God is to yield completely without reserve to him as revealed in Jesus Christ—to obey his loving, righteous will in all of life's relationships.

D. *The second great commandment: "Thou shalt love thy neighbor as thyself."*

    1. Thou shalt love thyself. The command is not *eros* or *philos* but *agape*. The command is not "Thou shalt like thyself," but that you shall have toward yourself the attitude God wants you to have, and accompany this attitude with right actions toward yourself. It means that you should consider yourself a person made in God's image, a steward of a God-given life, and that you should use this life in accord with God's will. Since loving God means to do God's will, then loving oneself (which means doing God's will toward oneself) is a corollary of loving God.

    2. "Thou shalt love thy neighbour as thyself." The command is agape. We are not commanded to like our neighbors, but to have toward others the attitude of goodwill God wants us to have, accompanied by the right deeds.

       We will now rejoin Paul as he comments on Jesus' teaching.

II. Paul teaches the primacy of love (Rom. 13:8–10).

Love fulfills the law. Romans 13:10 says, "Love worketh no ill to his neighbour."

A. *Negatively, this means no harm to one's neighbor.* "Owe no man any thing, but to love one another: for he that loveth another hath fulfilled the law. For this, Thou shalt not commit adultery, Thou shalt not kill, Thou shalt not steal, Thou shalt not bear false witness, Thou shalt not covet; and if there be any other commandment, it is briefly comprehended in this saying, namely, Thou shalt love thy neighbour as thyself" (vv. 8–9). We may recall here Paul's teaching in Romans 12:17–21, which reflects Jesus' teaching in Matthew 5:38–48. All of the "thou shalt nots" ever written with reference to others are fulfilled in the positive statement, "Thou shalt love."

B. *Positively, love means goodwill toward our neighbors.* We desire the best for them, so we will compassionately desire their salvation. We will desire for them food, clothing, health, educational opportunities, freedom to worship, citizenship, the right to own property, freedom from fear, and other privileges that a person desires for him- or herself.

Conclusion

Jesus and Paul agree that "love is the fulfilling of the law." If a person interprets some statement of Jesus or teaching of the Bible in a way contrary to love or holiness, he or she has misinterpreted the statement, for God is love and God is holy. He will never command us to do anything contrary to love or righteousness. All of the teaching of the law and the prophets hang on this great truth.

SUNDAY EVENING, JULY 18

Title: The Blight of the Race

Text: "...there is no difference: for all have sinned, and come short of the glory of God" **(Rom. 3:22–23).**

Scripture Reading: Romans 5:12–21

Introduction

The word *sin* has a hiss to it. It chafes us because it is a blow to our egos, our natural tendency to exalt and justify ourselves. People find it easier to rationalize their sins than to admit and confess them. Therefore, sin is a problem that affects everyone. It is the chain that binds unbelievers' souls in eternal darkness; it is the weight that Christians often drag along and keeps them from glorifying God in their lives. Aside from the revelation of God, there is no subject in the Bible that is given more extensive treatment than sin.

I. First, let's examine the nature of sin.

A. *It is important to understand that, although people are born into sin (for David said in Psalm 51:5: "Behold, I was shapen in iniquity, and in sin did my mother conceive me"), they are not born as slaves to sin.* They become sin's slaves by voluntarily yielding to sin. Paul said, "Do you not know that if you yield yourselves to any one as obedient slaves, you are slaves of the one whom you obey, either of sin, which leads to death, or of obedience, which leads to righteousness?" (Rom. 6:16 RSV). People are sinners by birth, but they are not personally responsible for that. Adam's sin passed that condition to everyone. But when people become sinners by practice (as all people do), they are responsible to God for the sins they commit. So, contrary to the belief of some, it is not people's environment that makes them sinners; it is their nature. People's tendency is toward sin, not toward righteousness.

B. *Sin is also the denial of God's right to command.* In the beginning God set boundaries in which people were to live their lives. This is the story of Genesis 3. When Adam sinned he overstepped the boundaries God had established. People, by nature, resent being told that they cannot do something. Prohibitions to natural humans are like waving red flags at an angry bull! Yet God must be supreme, absolute, and unconditional. When people deny God's supremacy, they deny his very existence. The great missionary-statesman Hudson Taylor said, "If he is not Lord of all, he is not Lord at all."

210

C. *The most common word for sin in the Bible means "missing the mark."* It is the word used in Romans 3:23, which describes people as coming short of the glory of God. The word is borrowed from the sport of archery. It describes an arrow that has been released from a bow without sufficient thrust to reach its mark and therefore falls to the ground. God has an ideal, a "bull's-eye," for people's lives. They pull themselves to their fullest height, take an arrow from their quiver, and pull the string of their bow taut. Then, with pride, they let their arrow of self-righteousness, good works, and human decency fly. But the arrow begins to falter and deviate from its course, finally falling to the ground short of its target. Why? Their act of transgression—stepping across the boundary of God's law—produced a weakness, a condition of shortcoming. They cannot hit the mark with their own strength.

D. *To compound the dilemma, people find that they cannot do anything within themselves to remedy the situation.* The Bible confirms this with such statements as, "There is none that doeth good, no, not one" (Rom. 3:12); "All our righteous acts are like filthy rags" (Isa. 64:6 NIV); "All we like sheep have gone astray; we have turned every one to his own way" (Isa. 53:6); "The heart is deceitful above all things, and desperately wicked: who can know it?" (Jer. 17:9). Therefore, even the best of people in God's sight must find a new place to begin—and only the Holy Spirit, through salvation, can bring this to pass.

II. With joy unspeakable we can declare that there is a remedy for sin.

A. *Why does the Bible go to such great lengths to present the horrors, the ugliness, and the ultimate hopelessness of sin?* It is because people will never understand their need for salvation until they comprehend the nature of their sin. There must be a contrast between good and evil, light and darkness, spiritual life and spiritual death established in people's minds. As God's Word reveals the abomination of sin, we should be driven all the more to him because he can deliver us from our sin.

B. *In understanding the remedy for sin, we must first realize that Christ bore our curse.* From Genesis 3 the Bible teaches that sin brought a curse upon sinners. But Paul says that Christ "became a curse for us" on the cross. Christ became sin for us, but he did not become sinful. Though all of humanity's sin was placed on him, he remained the sinless, spotless sacrifice. In no other way could there be hope for humanity.

C. *Not only did Jesus become a curse for us on the cross, he also provided for our cleansing—both initially, when we are born again, and continually.* He alone can take a person's black heart and make it "white as snow." John said, "If we walk in the light, as he is in the light, we have fellowship with one another, and the blood of Jesus Christ his Son cleanseth us from all sin" (1 John 1:7). Jesus keeps the cleansed clean! From the moment a person is born again, there is a continual flow of cleansing in which the person can, ideally, live every moment of his or her life. How? Christians must "walk in the light as he [Christ] is in the light." We receive the light of divine truth through the study of the Bible and by communication with God in prayer.

D. *Christ also remakes us.* The result of sin was the destruction of the Potter's work. When sin came into people's lives, God's handiwork was marred, and his plan for people was ruined. But when a person repents of his or her sins, the Potter takes the broken vessel and reshapes it. To the end of our earthly lives, God works with us, shaping us into the vessel of honor we will become when one day we stand in his presence.

Conclusion

Many times you have seen an apple with a wormhole in it. Did the worm begin to bore the hole in the apple from the outside or from the inside? Without thinking, most of us would say, "Why, from the outside, of course!" But a botanist would tells us that the egg from which the worm came was laid in the apple's blossom, and the worm was hatched in the apple's heart and bored its way out. That is exactly how the "worm" of sin starts its destructive, deadly work in human life. It begins in the heart and bores its way out. So unless the heart is sound, the life will be distorted and mutilated. Accordingly, God begins with the heart. He gives people new hearts upon their confessions of sin and faith in the Lord Jesus Christ.

WEDNESDAY EVENING, JULY 21

Title: The Miracle of Balaam's Talking Donkey

Text: "Then the LORD opened the donkey's mouth, and she said to Balaam, 'What have I done to you to make you beat me these three times?'. . .The donkey said to Balaam, 'Am I not your own donkey, which you have always ridden, to this day? Have I been in the habit of doing this to you?' **(Num. 22:28, 30 NIV).**

Scripture Reading: Numbers 22:22–35

Introduction

The name Balaam means "devouring" or "devourer." Balaam was the son of Beor, from a city in Mesopotamia called Pethor. Balaam was a soothsayer who had the gift of prophecy (Josh. 13:22).

Balak, a king of Moab in Moses' day, hired Balaam to pronounce a curse on the Israelites (Num. 22–24; Judg. 11:25; Mic. 6:5; Rev. 2:14). Balak was terrified by Israel's victory over Sihon and Og. Balak thought Balaam could turn God's favor from Israel to his own nation. Three times Balak sought to buy Balaam, but instead of curses on Israel he heard blessings on Israel. However, in Numbers 31 we learn that Balaam, through his counsel, caused Israel to sin against the Lord (Num. 31:16).

In Revelation 2 John gives us this interesting word about Balaam: "Nevertheless, I have a few things against you: You have people there who hold to the teaching of Balaam, who taught Balak to entice the Israelites to sin by eating food sacrificed to idols and by committing sexual immorality" (v. 14 NIV). Simon Peter said that Balaam "was rebuked for his wrongdoing by a donkey—a beast without speech—who spoke with a man's voice and restrained the prophet's madness" (2 Peter 2:16 NIV).

Now let's examine this miracle and see what God has in it for us.

I. God speaks to people (Num. 22:28–39).

Aside from the serpent in the Garden of Eden, this is the only instance in the Bible where an animal speaks. God used the donkey to rebuke Balaam's weakness.

God continually speaks to humanity and he speaks in various ways. He speaks through:

A. *History.*
B. *Nature.*
C. *Conscience.*
D. *Others.*
E. *The Bible.*
F. *Prayer.*
G. *The Holy Spirit.*
H. *His Son, Jesus Christ.*

There is no question about it—God speaks to all people, sinful and redeemed. Although God speaks in different ways, Jesus Christ is the highest revelation of God we have (Heb. 1:1–3).

II. God speaks to people about their perverse ways (Num. 22:32; 31:16; 2 Peter 2:15–16).

What kind of man was Balaam? He was a soothsayer who loved the wages of unrighteousness. He was cumbered with superstition, covetousness, and wickedness. He was a person who gave evil advice and led people away from the Lord. He could have been a prophet of the Lord. He was capable of the highest service in the kingdom of God had he surrendered himself to God's Holy Spirit. But Balaam wanted to do the wrong thing. Balaam's lifestyle was perverse. He followed a course of life that could lead only to destruction.

III. God speaks to people, and failure to heed his Word results in tragedy (Num. 31:8).

Because of Balaam's advice, the Israelites were seduced into idolatry and all the vile abominations connected with it. In the judgment that followed, no fewer than twenty-four thousand Israelites perished, until it was evident that the nation abhorred idolatry and considered it a great crime against God. By God's command, Israel meted out vengeance upon her seducers, the Midianites (see Rom. 6:23; Gal. 6:7–8).

Balaam's life ended in death. He tried to make the best of both worlds but couldn't do it. People can serve the Lord or they can serve perverse ways. Balaam said: "Let me die the death of the righteous" (Num. 23:10). He didn't get his wish. We read, "Balaam also the son of Beor they slew with the sword" (31:8).

Conclusion

Balaam's epitaph could read: "Balaam, son of Beor, who loved the wages of unrighteousness, got them, and perished!"

"Then the LORD opened the donkey's mouth" (Num. 22:28 NIV). God still speaks. Are you listening? Will you heed his words or will you serve Satan and perish? The choice is yours.

SUNDAY MORNING, JULY 25

Title: Now Is the Time

Text: "Put ye on the Lord Jesus Christ, and make not provision for the flesh, to fulfill the lusts thereof" **(Rom. 13:14).**

Scripture Reading: Romans 13:11–14

Hymns: "Glorious Is Thy Name," McKinney
"He Is Coming," Crosby
"I Know That My Redeemer Liveth," Pounds

Offertory Prayer: Eternal God, creator of all life, we thank you for the gift of life. Above all, we praise you for eternal life. This is life eternal—that we might know you as the only true God and Jesus Christ whom you have sent. We thank you that you have saved us, that you are saving us, and that you will save us. Grant that we may live for you here and live with you and the redeemed hereafter in heaven forever. In Jesus' name, we pray. Amen.

Introduction

Today is the first day of the rest of your life. This present moment in which you now live is like the dawn of a new day. "Now it is high time to awake out of sleep: for now is our salvation nearer than when we believed" (Rom. 13:11).

Salvation is like a resurrection from the dead. "The wages of sin is death" (Rom. 6:23). "And you hath he quickened, who were dead in trespasses and sins. . . .But God, who is rich in mercy, for his great love wherewith he loved us, even when we were dead in sins, hath quickened us together with Christ, (by grace ye are saved;) and hath raised us up together, and made us sit together in heavenly places in Christ Jesus" (Eph. 2:1, 4–6). By justification and regeneration Christ gave people who were dead in sins a new birth that issued in eternal life. This death to sin and being made alive in Christ is represented by baptism, as Paul explained in Romans 6.

The new life in Christ is like the dawning of a new day. A person made alive in Christ who does not grasp the opportunity to live for Christ is like a person who sleeps on after the day has dawned. "Wherefore he saith, Awake thou that sleepest, and arise from the dead, and Christ shall give thee light" (Eph. 5:14).

I. Now is the time to let Jesus Christ be Lord of your life.

A. *"Put ye on the Lord Jesus Christ" (Rom. 13:14).* The illustration seems to be this: The old evil deeds of a person's life before he or she became a Christian are like old clothes that need to be discarded. As an ancient wrapped his robe about him, believers are to enfold themselves in the Lord Jesus Christ—in a manner of life approved by the Lord Jesus. In Ephesians and Colossians, two epistles that Paul wrote a few years later than Romans from his Roman imprisonment, he developed this idea (see Col. 3:1–17; Eph. 4:22–32).

The change of clothes needs to be complete. None of the old, filthy clothes of an unsaved person will look good on one who is saved. "Make not provision for the flesh, to fulfill the lusts thereof" (Rom. 13:14). One who expects to live the Christian life with only partial allegiance to Jesus Christ is in trouble. That person is as ridiculous as one dressed partly in good clothes and partly in dirty clothes. Jesus must be Lord of all or he is not Lord at all. Jesus asks, "Why call ye me Lord, Lord, and do not the things which I say?" (Luke 6:46). Satan may trip up Christians who do not have any plans to continue in the pleasures of sin. When Christians do stumble, they fall toward Christ and find forgiveness. But those who expect to be Christians and plan to go on sinning are already deceived about their condition or are deceiving others (see 1 John 1:5–10).

God forgives and forgets past sins (see Rom. 8:1). Believers also need to forget them. Past sins should not be barriers to putting on the new clothes and living for Christ. "Forgetting those things which are behind, and reaching forth unto those things which are before, I press toward the mark for the prize of the high calling of God in Christ Jesus" (Phil. 3:13–14).

B. *"Put on the armour of light" (v. 12).* Night and day, darkness and light, are metaphors for Satan and Christ, the flesh and the Spirit. The armor of light represents the qualities of character with which Christians should equip themselves to battle for Christ against evil. In Ephesians Paul expanded on this illustration. In Ephesians 6 he describes the armor of a Christian soldier as suggested by the armor of the Roman soldier who was chained to him as he wrote (see Eph. 6:10–20).

C. *"Let us walk honestly, as in the day" (v. 13).* The way Christians ought to live has been depicted as putting on new clothes and as putting on the armor of light and engaging in battle on Christ's side against Satan. A third depiction is that of walking, the way in which we live. A Christian is to "walk honestly," by which Paul means live honorably and decently. A Christian's walk is open, in the day, for all to see.

II. Why put on Christ? Why accept him as Lord?

A. *He is Lord.* Peter preached at Pentecost, "Therefore let all the house of Israel know assuredly, that God hath made that same Jesus, whom ye have crucified, both Lord and Christ" (Acts 2:36). People who do not accept Jesus as Lord find themselves in antagonism to God.

B. *He has a right to be Lord.* "For whether we live, we live unto the Lord; and whether we die, we die unto the Lord: whether we live therefore, or die, we are the Lord's. For to this end Christ both died, and rose, and revived, that he might be Lord both of the dead and living" (Rom. 14:8–10; read also Phil. 2:5–10).

C. *He is worthy.* He is truth, light, and love. He is righteous. Jesus Christ never asks his followers to do anything contrary to truth, love, or righteousness. To accept his lordship is wise and right, in accord with God's will.

D. *The only way to be happy is to accept Jesus' lordship.*

1. An unsaved person can never be fully happy. "Thou hast made us for thyself, O God, and our hearts are restless until they rest in thee." The satisfactions of this world can no more satisfy the longing of the soul than the hog's food could satisfy the need of the prodigal son. "There is no peace, saith the Lord, unto the wicked" (Isa. 48:22).

2. A backslider can never be truly happy. Professing Christians who try to compromise are the most miserable of all people. They have too much religion to enjoy the world's pleasures and are too worldly to experience the joys of a consecrated Christian. That type of person is like the man who, in the Civil War, wanted to proclaim his neutrality, so he wore a blue coat and gray pants. The Confederates shot him in the coat and the Yankees shot him in the pants. Neutrality with reference to Jesus Christ is denial. Jesus said, "He that is not with me is against me; and he that gathereth not with me scattereth abroad" (Matt. 12:30).

3. A consecrated Christian is thoroughly happy. The Beatitudes describe the characteristics of a citizen of God's kingdom, or Christian disciple. Jesus calls this person "blessed" or "happy." In the Upper Room Jesus washed the disciples' feet and spoke with them about accepting his lordship and serving others in his name. Then

he added, "If ye know these things, happy are ye if ye do them" (John 3:17). Think of the most consecrated Christians you know. Are they not also the happiest people you know? Better yet, prove it by your own experience. JOY is Jesus and you with nothing between.

Conclusion

Now is the time. You are not preparing to live; you are living now. The dawn has come. The day of opportunity is now. "We must work the works of him who sent me, while it is day; night comes, when no one can work" (John 9:4 RSV). "Besides this you know what hour it is, how it is full time now for you to wake from sleep. For salvation is nearer to us now than when we first believed" (Rom. 13:11 RSV). Salvation refers to all that God has done, is doing, and will do for believers. Salvation—justification and regeneration—is past (Eph. 2:8–10). Salvation—sanctification and growth in grace—is present (Phil. 2:12–13). Salvation—glorification, the eternal state—is future. Paul expected Christ to return at any time. Christians should be ready to greet him. It is equally true that Christ may come for believers in death. The only day in which people have the opportunity to accept Christ and serve him is before he comes to end the age or before he comes for them at death. Now is the time to prepare for life after death by "putting on the Lord Jesus Christ."

SUNDAY EVENING, JULY 25

Title: The Called Out

Text: "I tell you, you are Peter, and on this rock I will build my church, and the powers of death shall not prevail against it" **(Matt. 16:18 RSV).**

Scripture Reading: Ephesians 2:19–22

Introduction

While he languished in the Bedford jail, John Bunyan had a vision concerning the church. He saw a flame of fire before a door, and a man pouring water on the flame. But the fire could not be quenched. He could not understand, though this man was drenching the fire with water, why it continued to burn. Then, in his vision, he saw a second man, standing just behind the door, who was pouring oil on the fire!

At no time does the New Testament speak pessimistically concerning the church. There is always a note of victory. Jesus said, "Upon this rock I will build my church, and the gates of hell shall not prevail against it." In Revelation there are letters from Christ to the seven churches of Asia Minor, in which he gives scathing rebukes to individual churches. These letters speak prophetically about problems and weaknesses in the institutional church in every generation. But Christ spoke of the body of believers functioning under the Lord's headship, seeking to follow his commands. The New Testament speaks of the church both as a spiritual body—an organism composed of all believers, and as a local, earthly organization of saints. We will divide this study into two major parts—first, the church as an organism, and second, the church as an organization.

I. The church as an organism.

A. *When we use the word* organism *in relation to the church, we are speaking of a body that possesses inner life and is not dependent on human organization.* It is the concept of the church as being the body of all believers in the Lord Jesus Christ. The inner life of this body is the life of God himself, imparted through the Holy Spirit, who lives in every believer.

B. *How did the church begin?* How did it come into being? In studying the Scriptures, particularly the New Testament, it appears that the church passed through three phases, all of which constitute its origin. It is customary to speak of Pentecost as being the birthday of the church, for there the company of believers were constituted for the first time into a spiritual body by the Holy Spirit. Yet both Paul and Peter indicate that the church existed in the mind of God before Pentecost (Eph. 1:4; 2 Tim. 1:9; 1 Peter 1:18–20). Furthermore, the election and conception of the church came before the election of God's chosen people, Israel, because Israel was chosen in Abraham, while the church was chosen in Christ. It is God's church; it was originated by him, and it is dependent on him for support. Paul said, "We are fellow workers for God; you are God's field, God's building" (1 Cor. 3:9 RSV). The church is described as being a field that God cultivates and enriches so that it will produce fruit. The church exists through God, and having existed eternally in his mind, nothing can destroy it.

C. *Second, we move from eternity into time, and we find that although the church existed eternally with God, it came into being foundationally with Jesus Christ— Jesus "founded" the church.* This phase of the church's origin swings on two pivots. First, Jesus said, "Upon this rock I will build my church." This is the foundation of the church—Jesus himself, the God-man (1 Peter 2:4–9). Peter declares that Christ is the cornerstone of the church. The second pivot regarding the foundation of the church goes hand in hand with Christ's deity—his death and resurrection. Among Paul's parting words to the Ephesian elders were these: "Take heed to yourselves and to all the flock, in which the Holy Spirit has made you guardians, to feed the church of the Lord which he obtained with his own blood" (Acts 20:28 RSV). Here Paul combines both the deity and death of Christ in relation to the church. He calls it the church of God, not of man, and the mystery of the church's existence lies in the fact that it was purchased with the blood of Jesus Christ. Jesus added power to his efficacious death when he arose from the dead, sealing the transaction forever. Therefore, in time, Jesus founded the church, which had already existed in God's mind from eternities past, in his deity and death and resurrection. What an impregnable security the church possesses!

D. *The last phase of the origin of the church was the historical beginning on the Day of Pentecost as a united body.* Before the Holy Spirit's coming, Jesus' disciples existed as separate units; when the Spirit came, they were "baptized into one body." On that same day, three thousand more souls were converted and added to the church, and the church grew extremely rapidly in that first century. Then, in Acts 15, the church broadened to receive not only Jews but Gentiles as well. And in Acts 15:14 God's purpose for his church was explicitly set forth: the calling out of a people for his name. So the very word for church in the New Testament is *ekklesia*, the "called out."

II. The church as an organization.

A. *What is an organization?* It is human-made. It may exist as an orderly whole; it may have different parts and functions, just like an organism. But it lacks the inherent, generating life of an organism. Furthermore, an organization can be disbanded or altered or replaced with new parts and new programs without destroying its existence. But with an organism, when any part is removed or altered, there is a mutilation. False members may be added that may function, but even those do not make the body whole again.

B. *Therefore, churches are organizations of believers in the Lord Jesus Christ scattered throughout the earth, having specific tasks defined by the New Testament.* First, a church's function is to promote worship. All of its other missions and responsibilities receive their impetus and effectiveness based on the true worship that exists in the church. In Philippians 3:3 Paul gives a three-fold description of true worshipers: those who "worship God in spirit, and rejoice in Christ Jesus, and have no confidence in the flesh."

C. *Following worship as the church's main responsibility, several other obligations arise in a worshiping church.* The church has an obligation to function under Christ's lordship. Moreover, the major directive of our Lord is the universal proclamation of the Good News of salvation (Matt. 28:19–20). To Peter, Jesus said, "Feed my sheep." It is the pastor's obligation to feed the flock entrusted to his or her care. Pastors must also serve as teachers. In short, all of the church's ministries should emanate from Jesus Christ—as he is worshiped, and as his gospel is preached and taught. A church engaged in these ministries faithfully and compassionately earns the designation as a New Testament church.

Conclusion

A traveler in a European village discovered a beautiful custom. At night he saw people going to church, each person carrying a little bronze lamp. They placed these lamps in sockets by their pews. The soft light of the lamps was the only illumination for the service. If a member was absent, there was a dark space. Today we do not carry lamps to church, but we do send forth light. When we are in the assembly with fellow believers, or when we are about our day-to-day activities, we are sending forth light. What a joy and a privilege to be part of the body of Jesus Christ by spiritual birth and to be part of an earthly church for fellowship, growth, and service to the King!

> *The church's one foundation is Jesus Christ her Lord;*
> *She is His new creation, by water and the word:*
> *From heaven He came and sought her to be His holy bride,*
> *With His own blood He bought her, and for her life He died.*

WEDNESDAY EVENING, JULY 28

Title: Into the Lion's Den

Text: "Then the king commanded, and they brought Daniel, and cast him into the den of lions. Now the king spake and said unto Daniel, Thy God whom thou servest continually, he will deliver thee" **(Dan. 6:16).**

Scripture Reading: Daniel 6:1–28

Introduction

The book of Daniel was written by the prophet Daniel, and he is the principal figure in the book. It is divided into two parts. Chapters 1 through 6 are the historical chapters, and chapters 7 through 12 are the apocalyptic, or prophetic, chapters.

The purpose of the book is not to give an account of Daniel's life but rather to show how God, by his providential guidance, miraculous interventions, and mighty power controls the forces of nature and the history of nations. God controls the lives of his people and the mightiest kings of the earth all for the accomplishment of his divine plans.

Daniel is a book of miracles and records three of the greatest accounts of supernatural deliverance of individuals found in the Bible: the preservation of the three Hebrews in the fiery furnace (Dan. 3:1–10); the insanity and restoration of Nebuchadnezzar (Dan. 4:1–37); and the story of Daniel in the lion's den (Dan. 6:1–28).

Let's look at the story of Daniel in the lion's den and deduce the great truths found in it.

I. Into the den of lions when one has an excellent spirit (Dan. 6:3).

Darius set 120 princes over the kingdom to help him rule. Over the 120 princes were three men to whom they were to give account. Daniel was one of them. It was said of Daniel, "Then this Daniel was preferred above the presidents and princes, because an excellent spirit was in him; and the king thought to set him over the whole realm" (Dan. 6:3).

A high office often provokes envy. Prominent positions are exposed to searching criticism. Divinely given equipment far outstrips ordinary human talent and causes jealousy. Daniel had an excellent spirit, a remarkable spirit. He was a greatly endowed man, and because of it he found himself in the lion's den.

II. Into the den of lions when evil people have their way (Dan. 6:4–9).

The evil men of Daniel's day sought to entrap him. They attacked him concerning his devotion to God's law. They knew Daniel would not stop his praying. The evil presidents and princes got the law of the Medes and the Persians to conflict with the law of God. We see some of the same things happening today concerning prayer in schools, laws desecrating the Lord's Day, and laws destroying the home. Yes, one is in the den of lions when evil people have their way.

III. Into the den of lions when spiritual practices are in conflict with worldly standards (Dan. 6:12–16).

For thirty days subjects in the kingdom were to refrain from asking a petition of any god or man other than King Darius. Surely Daniel would restrain himself and not pray for thirty days. But when Daniel knew the decree had been signed, "he kneeled upon his knees three times a day, and prayed, and gave thanks before his God, as he did aforetime" (Dan. 6:10).

Darius was not Daniel's god. Daniel prayed, asked God for his needs, and gave thanks. His spiritual practices were in conflict with the standards of his day, so into the den of lions he went.

IV. Into the den of lions when one is faithful to God (Dan. 6:4–11).

Daniel was about eighty-eight years old when he stood before King Darius. He was not critical and complaining. He was still living by faith and still faithful to his Lord. Daniel knew that God was in the plan for his life. He was not down; he was up. He was still loving, confessing, and serving his Lord.

V. Into the den of lions with God who can deliver us by faith (Dan. 6:16, 20–23; Heb. 11:32–38).

Faith gets us into the den of lions, but God gets us out. God is able to deliver us from dangerous situations including those caused by our sins.

Listen to what God's Word says: "Daniel was taken up out of the den, and no manner of hurt was found upon him, because he believed in his God" (Dan. 6:23).

Upon seeing that Daniel was safe, Darius wrote: "I make a decree, That in every dominion of my kingdom men tremble and fear before the God of Daniel; for he is the living God, and steadfast for ever, and his kingdom that which shall not be destroyed, and his dominion shall be even unto the end. He delivereth and rescueth, and he worketh signs and wonders in heaven and in earth, who hath delivered Daniel from the power of the lions" (Dan. 6:26–27).

Conclusion

F. R. Havergal wrote:

I could not do without Thee,
I cannot stand alone,
I have no strength or goodness,
No wisdom of my own.
But Thou, beloved Saviour,
Art all in all to me!
And perfect strength in weakness
Is theirs who lean on Thee!

AUGUST

■ **Sunday Mornings**

Continue the series "The Practice of Genuine Religion."

■ **Sunday Evenings**

Continue the series "The Doctrines of Our Faith."

■ **Wednesday Evenings**

Use the gospel of John as a source for the series "The Meaning of Christian Witnessing."

SUNDAY MORNING, AUGUST 1

Title: Inevitable Decisions

Text: "So then every one of us shall give account of himself to God" **(Rom. 14:12).**

Scripture Reading: Romans 14:7–12

Hymns: "Hark, Ten Thousand Harps," Kelly

"Will Jesus Find Us Watching?" Crosby

"Must I Go, and Empty-Handed?" Luther

Offertory Prayer: Our heavenly Father, you are Lord of life here and hereafter. All of us will give account of ourselves to you. Thank you for revealing yourself as a loving father. Thank you for providing the forgiveness of all our sins. Grant that by full confession of our sins, and by full dedication to your will, we may be ready to give account to you of the deeds done in the body. Forgive us of our sins and lead us by your Spirit. Help us to face life, death, and judgment with the assurance of your full salvation, through Jesus Christ our Lord. Amen.

Introduction

We must learn to cooperate with the inevitable. Some factors in life are given. Some decisions are made for us; no one asked us about them. They are "acts of God." Let's note some of these inevitable decisions.

I. Your birth is an inevitable decision.

You did not choose your parentage, your race, nor your sex. Nor can you effect a change in your condition. "Can the Ethiopian change his skin, or the leopard his spots?" (Jer. 13:23). Nicodemus asks, "How can a man be born when he his old? can he enter the second time into his mother's womb, and be born?" (John 3:4). Jesus said, "Which of you by taking thought can add one cubit unto his stature?" (Matt. 6:27). Some things when done cannot be undone. There is no way to unscramble an egg. All the king's horses and all the king's men couldn't put Humpty Dumpty together again.

II. You are sentenced to live.

Each of us is sentenced to live responsibly. There are exceptions to be sure. We do not expect God to hold the mentally ill responsible for a capacity they do not have. And we do not believe that God will hold children responsible for an understanding they do not have. But it is fair to assume that if you are reading this with understanding you are responsible. There is no way to avoid responsibility. Some try to escape by suicide. That action brings them more quickly to the judgment and adds the sin of self-destruction to their other sins. Some may try to escape by indifference, as did the man with one talent in Jesus' parable. He hid his master's money safely in the earth, but he failed to do with it what his master wanted him to do. At the accounting his master called him both a "wicked and a lazy servant." Doing nothing is sin. Trying to escape the responsibility of life by indifference is wicked.

III. You are sentenced to live in relationship to other people.

"None of us liveth to himself, and no man dieth to himself" (Rom. 14:7).

A. *Everyone has a relationship to God.* God created us, placed us in a world that he created, and gave us a spiritual nature like his own. We are people with power to think, will, and act. He gave us the knowledge of right and wrong and a conscience that tells us we ought to do right. He revealed himself in nature (see Ps. 19:1; Rom. 1:18–20; Acts 14:15–17) and in human nature (see John 1:9; Rom. 2:14–16). In a final and complete revelation, he revealed himself in Jesus Christ (see John 1:14, 18; Heb. 1:1–3). God the Holy Spirit invites every person to salvation and warns against rejecting the grace of God. A person's relationship with God may be good or bad, but no one can live other than in relationship to God.

B. *Everyone has a relationship to other people.* There is no way one can live without influencing or being influenced by other people. "A city set on a hill cannot be hid. Nor do men light a lamp and put it under a bushel, but on a stand, and it gives light to all in the house" (Matt. 5:14–16 RSV). Your influence may be good or bad, but you will have influence. It is inevitable that you have relationships with others.

C. *Everyone has a relationship to oneself.* The second commandment, "Thou shalt love thy neighbour as thyself" (Matt. 22:39), is based on the assumption that people will love themselves. All people are responsible for their own choices. Whether they love or hate themselves, their choices concerning their lives are inevitable. People may be good or bad stewards of their lives.

IV. You will appear before God in judgment.

"It is appointed unto men once to die, but after this the judgment" (Heb. 9:27). "For we must all appear before the judgment seat of Christ; that every one may receive the things done in his body, according to that he hath done, whether it be good or bad" (2 Cor. 5:10). "But why dost thou judge thy brother? or why dost thou set at nought thy brother? for we shall all stand before the judgment seat of Christ. For it is written, As I live, saith the Lord, every knee shall bow to me, and every tongue confess to God. So then every one of us shall give account of himself to God" (Rom. 14:10–12).

A. *The solemnity of the judgment.* The account is "to God" (read Matt. 25:31–46; Rev. 20:11–15).

B. *The universality of the judgment.* "Every one of us" shall give account. All people will be gathered before him. All who have ever lived will be present without exception.

C. *The individuality of the judgment.* The account will be "of himself." One who starts confessing the sins of the hypocrites or of others will be silenced. The account will be of "deeds done in the body."

D. *The fairness of the judgment.*

1. The Judge is a "just God." God in Christ is the Judge. He will judge righteously and will not hold anyone responsible for what he or she could not prevent. "Sin is not imputed when there is no law" (Rom. 5:13). God will not condemn me for Adam's sin nor for yours.

2. The Judge knows all the facts. He will not need to summon witnesses and cross-question for the facts. "Neither is there any creature that is not manifest in his sight; but all things are naked and opened unto the eyes of him with whom we have to do" (Heb. 4:13). No one will fool God. "God is not mocked: for whatsoever a man soweth, that shall he also reap" (Gal. 6:7).

E. *The first matter of inquiry will be: What kind of person are you?* Is your heart right with God? Have you repented of your sins? Have you believed in the Lord Jesus Christ? Do you love God? Do you seek first the kingdom of God and God's righteousness? Is your name written in the Lamb's Book of Life?

If the answer is no, one stands under the condemnation of sin and is assigned his or her portion with the lost. Even in punishment, however, the degrees of punishment will take into account the light against which one has sinned, the willfulness, and the magnitude of sins (see Luke 10:12–14; 12:47–48; Gal. 6:7; Heb. 2:2).

If the answer is yes, one's sins are forgiven for Jesus' sake (see Isa. 53:6; Rom. 8:1; Titus 2:14; 1 John 1:7). The redeemed person's destiny is eternal life with God and with the redeemed in heaven.

Rewards and greatness will be on the basis of faithful service rendered while here on earth. One serves God here on earth as he uses his talents and possessions to help others (see Matt. 6:19–21; 25:14–41; Mark 10:42–45).

Conclusion

You were sentenced to be born. You are sentenced to live responsibly, to die, to appear in judgment, and to live eternally in heaven or in hell.

Why not make life worthwhile? Why not take the dread out of death and judgment? Prepare now to live with God and the redeemed in heaven throughout all eternity. Give God your heart now and start living for him. He invites you to begin now.

SUNDAY EVENING, AUGUST 1

Title: The Divine Acquittal

Text: "Being justified freely by his grace through the redemption that is in Christ Jesus: whom God hath set forth to be a propitiation through faith in his blood, to declare his righteousness for the remission of sins that are past, through the forbearance of God; to declare, I say, at this time his righteousness: that he might be just, and the justifier of him which believeth in Jesus" (**Rom. 3:24–26**).

Scripture Reading: Romans 4:1–8

Introduction

In 1512 a young man with deep religious convictions was serving as a professor at the University of Wittenberg. He had entered the monastery of the Roman Catholic Church to become a monk and had been made a university professor. The day came when the young man was sent to Rome to transact some business with the pope. He joyfully began his journey, believing that his church was supreme and that the pope, in his office, was the incarnation of infallibility. When he arrived in Rome, however, he found such corruption in the church that he became deeply troubled. His faith in an infallible church was shaken. Feeling himself to be sinful and rebellious for even thinking these things, he made his way to the cathedral and began climbing the Scala Sancta, the "sacred stairs." As he climbed the stairs, he kissed each step, as was the custom. In a few minutes, a verse of Scripture began to ring out in his memory: "The just shall live by faith!" After serious consideration and much agonizing in prayer, Martin Luther renounced the Roman Church and began preaching the doctrine of justification. "The just shall live by faith," he said, "not by works, not by penance, but by faith!" This same doctrine had been preached many centuries before by the apostle Paul, but it had been lost in the mystic maze of a ceremonial religion. Now the doctrine began to live again. Out of Luther's experience came the Reformation, and Protestantism was born.

I. What, then, is justification?

A. *Justification, or acquittal (a term better understood in our day), is the act whereby God declares sinners "just" or "innocent," as if they had never sinned.* It is more than a pardon; for a pardon frees people merely from the penalty of the sin they have committed, but not from its guilt. Justification takes away all guilt and blame entirely.

B. *However, as a perfect God faced sinful man, there was a problem.* In the Old Testament, the principle of justice had been laid down. Deuteronomy 25:1 says: "If there be a controversy between men, and they come into judgment, that the judges may judge them; then they shall justify the righteous, and condemn the wicked." Thus, by this principle, God himself must administer justice. But how could God be just and at the same time acquit the ungodly? Paul stated the problem in Romans 3:23: "For all have sinned, and come short of the glory of God." The judgment is passed on the entire human race. When God, then, sits in judgment to dispense justice, he must pronounce all the world guilty. How, then, could God save any person? How could he receive sinners into his presence at all?

II. How are people justified?

A. *Let's approach the question first from the negative standpoint.* We are not justified by our good deeds. A person may live the best moral life in the world; he may sell all that he has and give his money to the poor; he may "do unto others as he would have them do unto him" and still fall short of what God requires. This is what Paul meant when he wrote to the Ephesians: "Because of [God's] kindness you have been saved through trusting Christ. And even trusting is not of yourselves; it too is a gift from God. Salvation is not a reward for the good we have done, so none of us can take any credit for it" (Eph. 2:8 TLB).

B. *Second, we are not justified by performing religious duties.* One may pray, join the church, be baptized, attend regularly, pay tithes, receive the Lord's

Supper—and still be lost! These religious acts, all of which are commendable, must be the outgrowth of the experience of one who is already justified in God's sight.

C. *It is difficult for people to understand that salvation costs them nothing.* Yet when we say that salvation is free, we are not saying that it cost nothing. It cost God his only begotten Son, and it cost Jesus his sinless life! Humans deserved death, but Jesus took humanity's place before God and took upon himself the penalty of a broken law.

III. How does justification work?

A. *It is an instantaneous act.* The moment we surrender our hearts to Jesus Christ we are justified, acquitted of the guilt of our sins. Justification is not a progressive act. The work of the Holy Spirit in convicting us of our sins is often a process, sometimes involving a period of time and a chain of circumstances, depending on the individual. But not so with justification! A judge in court says to the defendant, "I declare you innocent of the crime with which you are charged. You are hereby acquitted." What happens? Does the person stay in jail for another week or so? No! He or she is immediately released! Thus, the vilest sinner who repents and exercises faith in Jesus Christ is immediately justified before God.

B. *Justification also is an irreversible act.* The law today doesn't hold a person in jeopardy the second time for the same crime. A woman kills someone in self-defense. The jury acquits the her of the crime and frees her from all guilt, and never again is that woman in danger of prosecution for the same act. So it is when God justifies us—no one can reverse this great act of justification.

IV. What are the blessings of justification?

A. *It brings full and free pardon from God.* It is a pardon that covers all sin— past, present, and future. God doesn't save us on an installment plan. When we come to him through Christ, we are his, and we are justified eternally. The consequences of sins we commit after we are born again are suffered in this life, but the penalty is covered by the blood of Jesus.

B. *Second, justification produces a perfect standing with God.* Sin has marred our relationship with him, but through justification we can stand blameless before God. When God looked at people in the light of his law, he saw the black sin that produced a hopeless condemnation. But when he looks at believers through the blood of Christ, he sees them cleansed of their sins and eternally righteous!

C. *Third, justification brings peace with God.* Paul said, "Therefore being justified by faith, we have peace with God through our Lord Jesus Christ" (Rom. 5:1). This marvelous peace is "a peace that passeth understanding."

Conclusion

Venice is a city of waterways. Over one canal there is a bridge called "The Bridge of Sighs." This bridge leads from a courtroom to a dismal prison where guilty criminals are left to rot and die. Written over the door of the prison are the words, "Abandon hope, all ye who enter here." I can imagine a man being led across this bridge. He has kissed his loved ones good-bye and is looking into the sunlight for the last time. His heart is filled with grief and despair. But when he is halfway across the bridge, a court attendant rushes up to him and cries out, "Halt! I have here an acquittal for you! You are free!" Can you imagine the overwhelming joy this man would experience?

This is an illustration of what happens when, upon one's repentance of sin and faith in Jesus Christ, he or she is forgiven and justified and the stain is forever removed!

WEDNESDAY EVENING, AUGUST 4

Title: The Word and the World

Text: "He came to his own home, and his own people received him not. But to all who received him, who believed in his name, he gave power to become children of God" **(John 1:11–12 RSV).**

Scripture Reading: John 1:1–5, 9–14

Introduction

We can read exciting stories of ancient monarchs visiting their subjects, but these are like comparing a candle to the sun when placed alongside the story of God visiting the world he had made.

God came to the world he had made. Compare this with men holding their self-made gods in their own hands. It is incomprehensible that he who created the universe would live in that universe at a time and place in history. Yet he did just that.

I. His own people did not receive him.

God came to his own home, but the door was slammed in his face.

Israel is certainly signified in this rejection. They had been chosen as his special people and had been told about his coming throughout their history. The prophets had talked about him and the psalmist had sung about him. All of Israel's history had been training to know and receive him when he came. Not only did they not receive him as Messiah, they accused him of doing his mighty works by Satan's power and finally crucified him.

Old Israel's rejection of God, however, is no more serious than the new Israel's rejection of him. Churches are full of people who do not receive him.

It is not that they do not know him or that they disclaim him with their lips; it is a rejection from their hearts.

We have a tendency to live by our own plans, depend on our own resources, make our own decisions, worry about our own failures, and become engrossed in our own fears as if there were no Jesus.

How many people do you know who live as though Jesus had never lived? How much difference is there in the conduct of people in Japan or India, where a very small percentage of the people are Christians, and those who have heard of Jesus all their lives? An even more basic question is, "How much different is my life from those who do not recognize Jesus as the Son of God?" How different is your life from what it would be if you had never known him?

II. Some people received him.

They "believed in his name." This means that they believed in him as a person. John was fond of the word *believe*. He used it thirty-five times in the gospel of John and three times in 1 John. Throughout the New Testament believing is a condition of becoming a Christian. This word cannot possibly be overemphasized. Jesus told Nicodemus that whoever believes in God's Son may have eternal life. He continued, "Whoever believes in him is not condemned, but whoever does not believe stands condemned already because he has not believed in the name of God's one and only Son. . . . Whoever believes in the Son has eternal life, but whoever rejects the Son will not see life, for God's wrath remains on him" (John 3:18, 36 NIV). People responded to Jesus by saying, "Lord, I believe." Paul and Silas told the Philippian jailer, "Believe in the Lord Jesus, and you will be saved" (Acts 16:31 NIV).

What does it mean to believe? It certainly assumes that one believes that Jesus is the Son of God and Savior. But it is much more than that; it is to commit oneself to him in complete surrender. When I said to him, "Lord, if I am ever to be saved, you will have to save me. If I am ever to get to heaven, you will have to get me there. It is in your hands; I'm not going to worry about it anymore," I felt confident that he had kept his word and received me even as I received him.

Conclusion

Because Jesus was in the world and is in the world, you can become a Christian by believing. You can trust him to be the Lord of your life.

SUNDAY MORNING, AUGUST 8

Title: The Importance of Right Motive

Text: "Let us not therefore judge one another any more; but judge this rather, that no one put a stumblingblock or an occasion to fall in his brother's way" (**Rom. 14:13**).

Scripture Reading: Romans 14:13–18

Hymns: "When Morning Gilds the Skies," Caswell
"More About Jesus," Hewitt
"Since Jesus Came into My Heart," McDaniel

Offertory Prayer: Our heavenly Father, we bring to you our gifts of self and substance. We know that no gift is acceptable to you apart from the gift of self. We repent of sin and yield our hearts to do your will. Purify our motives from any dross of insincerity. Forgive us of our sins of commission, of omission, but especially of disposition. Help us to praise you forever, through Jesus Christ our Lord. Amen.

Introduction

Only God can be the final judge. He alone knows all the facts, including one's motives. "Man looketh on the outward appearance, but the LORD looketh on the heart" (1 Sam. 16:7). Since no person can know the motives of another person, it follows that no individual can be the final judge of another person. Jesus says, "Judge not, that ye be not judged" (Matt. 7:1). Paul warns, "Let us not therefore judge one another any more: but judge this rather, that no man put a stumblingblock or an occasion to fall in his brother's way" (Rom. 14:13).

I. If the motive is not right, nothing is.

A. *By right motive we do not mean simply good intention accompanied by procrastination and neglect of duty.* The road to hell is paved with good intentions. By right motive we mean a heart that is right with God and has honest intent, sincerity of purpose, and integrity and that seeks first the kingdom of God and his righteousness.

B. *Outward deeds may appear similar, but the acts differ in moral quality in proportion to the motives.* Note some illustrations.

Two men may court the same young lady. Their attention may seem the same. Both profess affection, bring gifts, and so on. One is courting the girl because he loves her, the other because he wants to secure her wealth by fraud.

231

Two men pray in church. Both prayers outwardly are about the same. One man has prayed from sincere motives; the other has prayed to impress a man from whom he wanted to receive a loan.

A young man was baptized. Some years later he revealed that he had been wholly insincere. He had been baptized to impress a young lady in the church. He later said that he was not a Christian and did not intend to become one. His act of baptism, which had seemed to be a beautiful confession of faith, had really been a blatant act of hypocrisy.

Illustrations could be multiplied, but these are enough to establish the truth that the quality of any act depends on the motive, and only God can know the motives of other persons.

C. *The importance of right motive is always emphasized in the Bible.* Jesus stressed the importance of right motive in his Sermon on the Mount when he said that religious acts, prayer, and almsgiving are to be done with an eye to God's approval rather than human approval (Matt. 6:1–6). Nicodemus was a leading rabbi. His education, wealth, and position were of no benefit in commending him to God apart from a right heart attitude. "Marvel not," said Jesus, "that I said unto thee, Ye must be born again" (John 3:7).

Paul affirms that an unsaved person cannot please God. "They that are in the flesh cannot please God" (Rom. 8:8). Is not this also what Paul means in 1 Corinthians 13? Define love as being synonymous with "a right heart attitude toward God," and Paul is saying that though one has great gifts, bestows his goods to feed the poor, or even gives his body to be burned but does not have a right motive in God's sight, he has done nothing worthy of God's commendation (see 1 Cor. 13:1–3).

When Simon Magus offered money to Peter and John to purchase the power of the Holy Spirit, "Peter answered him, 'May you and your money go to hell, for thinking you can buy God's gift with money! You have no part or share in our work, because your heart is not right in God's sight'" (Acts 8:20 TEV).

II. Even though the heart is right, one will still make mistakes.

All of us make mistakes of judgment. God does not make Christian people infallible. Many people with good intentions do stupid things—as in the popular Dr. Suess story, in which the elephant meant well when she offered to help hatch the ostrich's egg. Good people differ in their likes and dislikes. Some buy; others rent. Some save; others live it up. Some want hymns; others prefer gospel songs. Some want music slow and stately; others want it peppy. Some think a pipe organ is the only suitable instrument on which to praise God; others prefer guitars, trumpets, and drums; still others banish all musical instruments and use only the voice to praise God. Because others cannot know our motives, and because our judgments differ, we must expect to be misjudged by others.

III. What shall we do?

A. *Let each one be sure that his own heart is right with God.* "Every one of us shall give account of himself to God" (Rom. 14:12). You can know your own heart, and you should be harsh in judgment of yourself.

B. *"Let us not therefore judge one another any more: but judge this rather, that no man put a stumblingblock or an occasion to fall in his brother's way" (Rom. 14:13).* One should be charitable in the judgment of others.

1. Assume that the motives of another person are good rather than evil. The executive secretary of a religious denomination offered to buy a property owned by the denomination. When the offer was presented to the board of directors, the name of the prospective buyer was not revealed. Some of the people assumed that the secrecy was in hope that he might get a better buy. Later it was revealed that his secrecy was for the purpose of paying a fair market value price without any favoritism.

2. Be sure to get all the facts. A young lady who was seen coming from a house of prostitution was excluded from her church. The church acted too hastily. Later inquiry disclosed that she had gone in to try to dissuade her brother from committing an immoral act.

3. Make allowances for circumstances. Try to put yourself in the other person's place. A theology professor went to confer with a young married student about his poor grades. He found the young man in the utility room of the housing complex doing laundry. His wife and baby were both sick, and his bills were more than he could meet. The professor immediately took action to help the student bear the burdens that were too heavy for him to carry alone.

4. If you have a problem with another person, you are to go and speak to him or her about it. If you have wronged another or have given someone cause to suspect your motives, the word of Jesus is clear: "If thou bring thy gift to the altar, and there rememberest that thy brother hath ought against thee; leave there thy gift before the altar, and go thy way; first be reconciled to thy brother, and then come and offer thy gift" (Matt. 5:23–24). If you think another Christian has sinned against you, the instructions are also clear in Matthew 18:15–17 and Luke 17:3.

C. *In God's judgment take confidence.* God knows your heart. No matter how much people may misunderstand and malign you, God knows your motives. In the final beatitude in Matthew 5:10–12, one of the reasons Jesus gives for counting happy those who are persecuted for righteousness' sake, reviled, and lied about is that God knows all about it and will reward them in heaven.

Simon Peter by his denials had given others good reason to think that he was not a Christian. In John 21 we find the account of Jesus probing Peter's heart with the repeated question, "Do you love me?" Simon in effect says, "Lord, I haven't acted like it. I have given others reason to doubt my love for you; but Lord, you know my heart; you know that I love you." God knows all about us and still loves us.

Conclusion

As God knows your heart, and you know your heart, can you affirm that your heart is right with God? If your heart is right, you may know that your sins are forgiven, you have eternal life, and the Holy Spirit will guide you into the truth. If your heart is right, mistakes of the head will be forgiven.

If your heart is not right and you claim to be a Christian, then you are a hypocrite. You may be fooling others and yourself, but you are not fooling God. If your heart is not right, you are lost. Nothing you can do will get you right with God unless your heart gets right. Now is the time to get right. God loves you. Christ died to save you. Trust his invitation, "Him that cometh to me I will in no wise cast out" (John 6:37).

SUNDAY EVENING, AUGUST 8

Title: God's Favor at Christ's Expense

Text: "For by grace are ye saved through faith; and that not of yourselves: it is the gift of God: Not of works, lest any man should boast" **(Eph. 2:8–9)**.

Scripture Reading: Ephesians 1:3–12

Introduction

One of the most familiar words in the Christian's vocabulary is the word *grace.* Many years ago a theologian, with tongue-in-cheek, wrote a book entitled *Grace Is Not a Blue-eyed Blonde,* trying to shock us into realizing that we throw around many theological terms and words, not truly understanding what they mean.

The word *grace* and its related words appear in Holy Scripture about two hundred times. The first reference to grace is found in Genesis 6:8, where we read that "Noah found grace in the eyes of the LORD." The final appearance of the word in the Bible is recorded in Revelation 22:21: "The grace of the Lord Jesus Christ be with you all." Indeed, one needs a firm grasp on the doctrine of grace, for it is the foundation on which the other doctrines rest.

I. The conception of grace.

A. *First, let's examine the word itself.* In the original language of our New Testament, the word implies a favor freely done. The word for "gift" springs from the same root. The Greeks used this word to describe favor shown to a friend. When Jesus came and died on the cross, grace leaped from its confinement as an expression only to friends and included enemies as well. As Paul said, "God commendeth his love toward us, in that, while we were yet sinners, Christ died for us" (Rom. 5:8). In the Sermon on the Mount, Jesus had much to say about Christians' relationships with their fellow humans. He said that terribly hard thing: "Love your enemies!" And in his concern that our "love" for enemies would degenerate into an artificial emotion, he said: "Bless them that curse you, do good to them that hate you, and pray for them which despitefully use you, and persecute you" (Matt. 5:44).

B. *We need to understand that grace goes beyond our salvation.* Grace becomes the spring from which all blessings flow from God. In other words, he who saves us by grace also brings us into the sphere of grace and endows us with all the blessings and favors that accompany this divine expression of love. In fact, this attitude of God was hinted at in the Old Testament: "It shall come to pass, when he crieth unto me, that I will hear; for I am gracious" (Ex. 22:27). Similar expressions are also found in Nehemiah 9:17 and Jonah 4:2. Paul wrote in Romans 5 that God abounds in grace. The word translated "abound" means to "exist in superabundance." All of God's dealings with his people are filtered through his marvelous grace! Thus, we can be eternally grateful that God deals with us through grace and not justice.

II. The sufficiency of grace.

A. *How can we say that God's grace is all-sufficient?* It is true simply because grace comes to us from the glorious and transcendent nature of God himself. It is one of his infinite attributes, and it is the result of the eternal counsel and purpose of his will. We must not forget that grace is an act, not just a favor or a gift from God. Grace reveals what God is as well as what he does.

B. *Grace comes through Christ—there is no other way that humankind could have received the grace of God.* Jesus' life on earth was a platform from which grace was displayed. The writer of Hebrews summed it up this way: "But we see Jesus, who was made a little lower than the angels for the suffering of death, crowned with glory and honour; that he by the grace of God should taste death for every man" (Heb. 2:9).

C. *Paul speaks of the riches of God's grace.* What are some of them? When God freely gives sinners eternal life through grace, he credits them with a perfect righteousness. That is, when God observes Christians—sinners saved by grace—he sees them not in their continued imperfections and sins, but clothed in the righteousness that was imputed to them through their faith in Jesus Christ! (Read Eph. 2:19–20.) This elevates Christians to an impregnable position with God. A further provision of God's all-sufficient grace is that it makes us to be "at peace with God" (Rom. 5:1–2). This means that there has been brought about a reconciliation, creating an insoluble bond between God and the redeemed. Also, a vital benefit of God's grace is the believer's accessibility to God through prayer. Christians are enjoined to "come boldly" to the throne of grace to make their requests known of God (Heb. 4:16).

III. The scope of grace.

A. *Paul told Titus that God's grace is for "all men" (read Titus 3:4–7).* Someone has said that if you take the "g" from "grace" you have the word "race." Grace is for all within the human race, for all stand on one common ground—namely, that of being sinners. Jesus said, "For God so loved the *world,* that he gave his only begotten Son. . ." (John 3:16, emphasis added). From beginning to end, the gospel presents the universality of God's saving grace.

B. *There is one thing we must understand clearly about God's grace.* Grace does not imply that God passes by any person's sin or takes it lightly. Sin is so horribly base in God's sight that he can in no way tolerate it. God sees the sinner utterly ruined, hopeless, and helpless. And the triumph of grace is seen at Calvary, where heaven's love and heaven's justice meet. There Christ bore the curse of human sin, and with God's hatred against sin vindicated on the basis of his grace, he can now forgive the sinner!

C. *Grace is God's part; faith is ours.* We simply accept, by faith, the grace of God. We do not grow *into* grace, but we do grow *in* grace. Once we are made sharers of divine grace, it becomes a progressive force in our lives. John says that there is "grace upon grace." Grace is not just a seed in the heart that lies dormant, but a blade, an ear, then the full corn in the ear. As the roots spread, the plant grows!

D. *The scope of God's grace never widens.* As Christians start to grow in grace, they grow in spiritual stature toward God and grow smaller and smaller in their own eyes. Through grace, one grows out of self-conceit, for grace subdues self. Furthermore, growing in grace means that all of the virtues of the Christian life—the fruit of the Spirit Paul describes in Galatians 5:22–23—grow proportionately. As we grow in grace, the growth of corruption is hindered. The flowers of grace prevent the weeds of sin from spreading.

Conclusion

> *O to grace how great a debtor*
> *Daily I'm constrained to be!*
> *Let thy goodness, like a fetter,*
> *Bind my wandering heart to Thee.*

There once was a ship in distress on the high seas because its water supply had run out. The crew was in danger of dying from thirst though there was water all around them. When hope was almost gone, they sighted a ship in the distance. At once they sent up distress signals. The only answer they got, as they signaled to the passing ship that they were without water, was, "Dip it up!" What heartless mockery to tell those sailors to dip up buckets of salt water! They signaled again, but the same answer came back, "Dip it up!"

In despair they lowered a bucket. Imagine their amazement and joy when the water proved to be fresh water! They thought they were yet on the high seas, but they had drifted into the mouth of the Amazon River.

This is the way it is with the grace of God. Countless souls are dying of spiritual thirst today, when all around them there is available the saving grace of God. All they need to do is, by faith, "dip it up"!

WEDNESDAY EVENING, AUGUST 11

Title: The Ideal Witness

Text: "John bore witness to him, and cried, This was he of whom I said, 'He who comes after me ranks before me, for he was before me'" **(John 1:15 RSV).**

Scripture Reading: John 1:19–36

Introduction

How many witnesses does your church have? How many members do you have? That is how many witnesses. "Oh," you say, "I wish that were true. I wish even 10 percent were witnesses." Well, they are. Some of them are just poor witnesses. Since all of us are witnesses, let's look at the ideal witness. I believe you will agree that John the Baptist is just that.

I. John was sent from God.

How many witnesses here are actually helping people know the truth about Jesus? You are a witness for him or against him. Jesus said, "He who is not with me is against me, and he who does not gather with me scatters" (Matt. 12:30).

It is not likely that our Lord is going to send an angel to this city to remind people of his Good News. He is not likely to appear in the sky or make some other spectacular appearance.

If your family, friends, fellow students, coworkers, or neighbors are ever to know the truth about what Jesus desires to do for them, you will have to be a faithful witness.

John was a man sent from God. Your name may not mean "gift of God" like John's, but you are a person sent from God. Jesus said, "As the Father hath sent me, even so I send you" (John 20:21). You have come "as a witness to testify concerning that light [Jesus]" so "that through him all men might believe" (John 1:7 NIV).

Everybody—farmers, barbers, businesspersons, factory workers, students, professionals—can witness. The question is, What kind of witness are you?

II. John introduced Jesus boldly.

The Jewish religious leaders sent priests and Levites to inquire who John was. He used the opportunity to introduce Jesus. He told them that he was not the Christ, not even Elijah or some other prophet, but was a "voice." Jesus was the Word. John was his voice.

Jesus himself came to John to be baptized, and John saw the Spirit of God descend on Jesus and heard a voice from heaven declaring him to be the Son of God. No one had ever declared that before. It took courage as it often does to testify for Jesus.

Polycarp, an early Christian, was burned to death for his boldness in speaking the Word of the Lord. When given a chance to recant, he thanked the Lord for the privilege of being listed with the martyrs. John the Baptist was himself beheaded for sticking by his convictions. You likely will not have to pay that price, but no one is a bold, faithful witness without paying some price.

III. John faded out humbly.

Evangelists have often been noted for their boldness, sometimes for their humility. There is actually no conflict between the two characteristics, for boldness is not arrogance. John was exceedingly bold to declare that Jesus was the Christ. He was humble in saying that Jesus ranked before him. He made it clear that he was only the voice of the real messenger. He insisted that he only baptized with water while Jesus baptized with the Spirit. He even said that he was not worthy of the servant role of untying Jesus' sandals.

John introduced his own disciples to Jesus knowing that they would leave him to follow Jesus. When people tried to make him jealous of Jesus, John answered, "No one can receive anything except what is given him from heaven. You yourselves bear me witness, that I said, I am not the Christ, but I have been sent before him. He who has the bride is the bridegroom; the friend of the bridegroom, who stands and hears him, rejoices greatly at the bridegroom's voice; therefore this joy of mine is now full. He must increase, but I must decrease" (John 3:27–30 RSV).

Conclusion

Ideal witnesses cannot always report a daily success roster, but they can live a daily life of surrender to Jesus. They may not reap a harvest every day, but they will sow every day with the honor and glory going to the Lord of the harvest.

Jesus expressed deep gratitude for John's unselfish ministry: "There is another who bears witness to me, and I know that the teaching which he bears to me is true" (John 5:32). He also said, "Truly, I say to you, among those born of women there has risen no one greater than John the Baptist" (Matt. 11:11).

SUNDAY MORNING, AUGUST 15

Title: Is Right Ever Wrong?

Text: "Happy is he that condemneth not himself in that thing which he alloweth" (**Rom. 14:22**).

Scripture Reading: Romans 14:19–23

Hymns: "Take Time to Be Holy," Longstaff
"Let Others See Jesus in You," McKinney
"Wherever He Leads I'll Go," McKinney

Offertory Prayer: Righteous Father, our Lord Jesus taught that you are spirit, not confined to a particular place. To the Samaritan woman he said, "But the hour cometh, and now is, when the true worshippers shall worship the Father in spirit and in truth: for the Father seeketh such to worship him. God is a Spirit: and they that worship him must worship him in spirit and in truth" [John 4:23–24]. Help us in sincerity of heart and in truth to worship you. We worship you now in the giving of our tithes and offerings as tokens of our thankfulness for your provision. We pray in the name of him who is the way, the truth, and the life. Amen.

Introduction

One of the surest evidences that we are children of God is our purposing to do right. Christians are not as good as Jesus, but we want to be. Jesus said, "My sheep hear my voice, and I know them, and they follow me" (John 10:27).

The question today is, How can one know the will of God? What is right? What is wrong? Sometimes the choices seem equally attractive. For example, a young man who is dedicated to God's service may desire guidance as to whether he should enter Christian service as a vocation or serve God as a layman. Where is the chapter and the verse that will specifically settle this or a thousand other decisions that one is called on to make?

I. Principles that will help in finding God's will.

A. *God's will is personified in Jesus.* The goal is expressed by Paul: "...until we all reach unity in the faith and in the knowledge of the son of God and become mature, attaining to the whole measure of the fullness of Christ. Then we will no longer be infants, tossed back and forth by the waves, and blown here and there by every wind of teaching and by the cunning and craftiness of men in their deceitful scheming. Instead, speaking the truth in love, we will in all things grow up into him who is the Head, that is, Christ" (Eph. 4:13–15 NIV). Jesus is the perfect example of one who did God's will. His prayer was, "Father, glorify thy name" (John 12:28), and "O my Father, if it be possible, let this cup pass from me: nevertheless not as I will, but as thou wilt" (Matt. 26:39). He alone could pray, "I have glorified thee on earth: I have finished the work which thou gavest me to do" (John 17:4). The Father confirmed that the Son is a perfect example. At Jesus' baptism he said, "This is my beloved Son, in whom I am well pleased, hear ye him" (Matt. 17:5).

Charles Sheldon, in his remarkable book *In His Steps,* faced the problems of his day with the question, "What would Jesus do?" An even more valid question would be, "What would Jesus have us to do?" Because he was other than we, he did some things that would not be appropriate for us. For example, he forgave sins, a prerogative that belongs only to deity. His refusal to use power at his disposal to save himself from arrest and crucifixion does not mean that we who are his followers should refuse to defend ourselves.

B. *The great commandment is "Thou shalt love the Lord thy God will all thy heart, and with all thy soul, and with all thy mind.* This is the first and great commandment. And the second is like unto it, Thou shalt love thy neighbour as thyself. On these two commandments hang all the law and the prophets" (Matt. 22:37–40). Love is synonymous with God's will. It is goodwill accompanied by the right actions. One who seeks to do God's will may be sure that anything contrary to love is not in accord with God's will.

C. *Seek the leadership of the Holy Spirit.* Jesus promised the presence and aid of the Holy Spirit. "The Comforter, which is the Holy Ghost, whom the Father will send in my name, he shall teach you all things, and bring all things to your remembrance, whatsoever I have said unto you" (John 14:26). "When the Comforter is come, whom I will send unto you from the Father, even the Spirit of truth, which proceedeth from the Father, he shall testify of me" (John 15:26; cf. John 16:1–16). It is implied that when one seeks the aid of the Holy Spirit to know God's will, one is committed to doing God's will. Obedience is the open door to added knowledge. One of Jesus' most wonderful promises is "If any man will do his will, he shall know of the doctrine, whether it be of God, or whether I speak of myself" (John 7:17).

D. *The Bible is the guidebook.* The Bible is the record of God's revelation of his will. It contains the prophesies of the coming of the Messiah and the historical records of Jesus in the days of his flesh. It also has accounts of the Spirit-led missionary adventures of the apostles and Christians in the first century.

II. How do we apply these principles? Is it ever right to do wrong?

A. *Some decisions are very easy.* "Now the works of the flesh are manifest, which are these," writes Paul in Galatians 5. Then he proceeds to name them: "adultery, fornication, uncleanness, lasciviousness, idolatry, witchcraft, hatred, variance, emulations, wrath, strife, seditions, heresies, envyings, murders, drunkenness, revellings, and such like: of the which I tell you before, as I have also told you in time past, that they which do such things shall not inherit the kingdom of God" (Gal. 5:19–21). Anyone can see that these sins violate the principles that help us to know God's will. Then Paul adds, "But the fruit of the Spirit is love, joy, peace, longsuffering, gentleness, goodness, faith, meekness, temperance: against such there is no law. And they that are Christ's have crucified the flesh with the affections and lusts" (Gal. 5:22–24).

B. *Some decisions are very difficult.* Right and wrong are not so clearly distinguished. Sometimes the choice seems to be the best of several good choices or it may seem to be the least evil of several bad alternatives.

   1. Examples of the best choices:

      If a neighbor asks Johnny to run an errand and about that time his mother calls, "Johnny, come home," Johnny has a difficult choice, but his relation to his mother is such that her call must get the preference.

      A splendid Christian physician had a good practice. He was a wonderful witness for Christ as he talked to his patients about their relationship to the Lord. In fact, he was considering entering the gospel ministry. He sought the counsel of a minister who advised him to be very sure of the Lord's leadership. The doctor sought God's will earnestly and concluded that he could serve better as a good doctor than as a poorly trained preacher.

      In the parable of the Good Samaritan, the priest and Levite did not have a simple decision. There were probably people waiting for them expecting them to conduct services. It would have been good to conduct the services. It would have been better to help the poor wounded man.

A YMCA secretary pointedly lectured a group of preachers to the effect that it was each man's duty to spend an hour each day in physical exercise. His argument was that the preachers would have better health and render a more effective ministry for spending an hour that way. But the pastors must weigh that hour over against the claims on their time for study, counseling, administrative duties, weddings, funerals, hospital visitation, preaching, attending meetings, serving the denomination, family responsibilities, and so on. One cannot do everything and therefore must make choices. One must not let the good become the enemy of the best.

A lighthouse keeper was supplied with oil for his light at regular periods some days apart. In an extremely cold time, he listened to the pleas of some needy persons to share the oil with them. He did. The oil for the lighthouse was not sufficient. The light failed and a ship was wrecked. The good had become the enemy of the best.

2. Examples of choice among evils.

President Truman had a very difficult choice in World War II. Should he order the use of the atomic bomb and kill thousands of people? To do so might end the war (as indeed it did) and save the lives of many more who would have been killed had the war continued.

Every person who has faced the implications of his military service has had to face this question: Which is worse, to kill the enemy in war, or to refuse to fight and then enjoy the life, liberty, and happiness that people who did fight purchased for him?

Conclusion

More questions have been raised than have been settled by this message. Our discussion does lead us to these conclusions, however:

1. God is the Judge. He knows all the facts including the motives.
2. Nothing—that is, no thing—is in itself right or wrong. It is right or wrong because of the use to which it is put and how it affects persons (see Rom. 14:14–15).
3. Love is the test of right and wrong. Is this action motivated by goodwill? If not, it is wrong (see Rom. 14:20–21).
4. One is to seek the highest and best (see Rom. 14:19; "Seek ye first the kingdom of God, and his righteousness," Matt. 6:33).
5. "Whatsoever is not of faith is sin" (Rom. 14:23). A professor asked his wife if his shirt collar was dirty. She did not even look. She said, "If it is doubtful, it is dirty."
6. "Happy is he that condemneth not himself in that thing which he alloweth" (Rom. 14:22).

7. One is accountable to one's own master. Our business is not to judge others. It is rather to live right and to proclaim the principles on which we shall all be judged.

SUNDAY EVENING, AUGUST 15

Title: A Time for Turning

Text: "Repent ye therefore, and be converted, that your sins may be blotted out" **(Acts 3:19).**

Scripture Reading: Psalm 51:1–17

Introduction

No doctrine in the Bible is more important than the doctrine of repentance, for it is the gatekeeper of heaven. Before people can be reconciled to God through his Son, Jesus Christ, they must experience repentance. The experience of David recorded in Psalm 51 is a classic illustration of genuine repentance. One almost feels that he or she is intruding on a scene that is extremely private and personal, for David is writhing in the agony of remorse and sorrow. He has faced sin in his life, with all the veneers of human excuses stripped away. His soul is naked before God, and he sees himself stained and distorted before his creator. We watch in breathless wonder as this helpless man deals with a problem that clearly has no human solution, for he is guilty of sins that put him beyond the remedy provided by the law of his day. It is with stunned amazement that we watch David work through an experience that resulted in the cleansing of his soul and the restoration of peace and joy in his life. As we study the psalm, we can plot David's journey down the highway of repentance.

I. The realization of sin.

A. *Before we observe the "breakthrough" in David's life, the moment when he came to realize his sin, let us set the stage historically.* We look in upon a court scene in Jerusalem with Israel's greatest king sitting on the throne. David had been divinely chosen and anointed for the task of being God's king to rule over his people. He had also become the nation's spiritual leader. He was clean and sensitive, and God had promised him that his house would be established forever. God had blessed him; his kingdom had flourished, and the enemies of Israel had been soundly defeated by David's armies.

B. *But in the midst of all of this victory and luxury, David saw and wanted and took for himself the beautiful wife of Uriah.* Any other king in the world could have done this without a whisper of blame upon him, but David was

Jehovah's anointed! Before the sordid story was over murder was added to the picture as David had Uriah conveniently placed in battle so that he would be killed. Thus, adultery and murder clung like soot to David's soul. For almost a year, David endured the lashing of his conscience. But one day the fearless prophet Nathan came with that brief but powerful story of the neighbor who had one sheep, which was stolen by the man with many. It was a dagger-thrust into the soul of David when Nathan said, "Thou art the man!"

C. *There would be no story to tell if something marvelous had not happened.* Instead of rejecting Nathan's hot words of accusation and ordering the prophet executed for his presumption, the process was triggered that resulted in David's rising again. Someone has suggested that David's sin must have called for a great celebration in the devil's domain, for David must have been the one person in the entire world Satan longed to have in his clutches. And now this great man lay morally and spiritually trapped and bound and ruined! David, the spiritual leader of God's chosen people, was out of the fight!

II. The agony of turning.

A. *David's first reaction, following the shock of Nathan's accusation, was a cry for forgiveness.* "Have mercy upon me, O God," David cried. God is ever monitoring the channel on which people cry for mercy, and he sends instant relief when people call.

B. *Note David's pattern of thought: His first move was to spread out before God his particular and specific acts of sin.* He used three words to describe his sin: *transgression,* which means rebellion, deliberately setting oneself against the will and the law of God, a calculated sin of high treason against the Sovereign of the universe; *iniquity,* that which distorts one's reason; and *sin,* which means "missing the mark," or failure.

C. *Then David used three verbs of action, indicating that he wanted God to do something for him that he could not do for himself.* He said, "blot out. . ., wash me. . ., cleanse me." "Blot out" means to erase from the record; "wash me" indicates David's realization that his whole being was defiled and needed a divine scrubbing; "cleanse me" reflects his desire to be absolutely clean inside and out.

D. *Following this cry for mercy, David sincerely confessed his sin: "I acknowledge my transgressions: and my sin is ever before me."* Nathan had said, "Thou art the man!" Now David is saying, "Lord, I *am* the man!" He assumed all responsibility for his sin; he did not blame his ancestors or even Bathsheba as an accomplice in his sin. He declared that he, and he alone, was responsible for his sin.

E. *In verses 7–9 David prays not only that he might be received into God's presence again, but that he may be fit for God's presence.* As David bared his soul before

God, he saw what a vile, sinful person he had been. Now he wants God to purify his whole sin-defiled being! He wants God to sprinkle hyssop on him. Hyssop was an aromatic oil used to spray those who had had leprosy or some other loathsome disease. Not only did the hyssop serve as a "deodorizer," but sprinkling it was also a symbolic act whereby one was cleansed for God's presence.

F. *David reached the climax of his prayer—the end of his journey down the road of repentance—when he prayed for a new heart and a new life.* In verse 10 David is saying, in essence: "Lord, because of this terrible thing I have done, you must assume your role of creator again for me! I must have a new heart! I have damaged the old one beyond repair. The scars are too hideous. Do your work all over again, and give me a new heart, O God!" Here David lays the foundation for the New Testament doctrine of the new birth. He recognizes the strategic importance of being born again. The heart must be a new one. David's mental, moral, and spiritual self must be renewed by the creative touch of God.

III. The glory of restoration.

A. *A note of positive, ringing assurance appears in David's words:* "Purge me with hyssop, and I shall be clean: wash me, and I shall be whiter than snow" (v. 7).

David's hope lay in the fact that God is a God who keeps his word and who is as good as his promises. When this hope dawns in a person's heart, life begins, for this is a truth to live by and a truth to die by.

B. *What was the natural result of David's experience of repentance and forgiveness of sin?* It was the same first impulse that every saved individual has—to tell others about this glorious newly discovered remedy for soul sickness. Note again his assurance: "Then will I teach transgressors thy ways; and sinners shall be converted unto thee" (v. 13). David vows that the rest of his life will be spent telling others about God's grace and urging sinners to come to the only source of life and cleansing. David will be an evangelist, a seeker of lost people, and an announcer of good news to those who languish in darkness and sin.

Conclusion

In summary, we find that four ingredients constituted David's repentance: *humiliation, contrition, confession,* and *transformation.* The Holy Spirit convicts people and brings them to a state of humiliation, to an expression of contrition, and to the point of confession. Then the grandest miracle of all transpires when, as a result of these preparatory experiences, they are transformed by the power of God.

WEDNESDAY EVENING, AUGUST 18

Title: The Lamb of God

Text: "The next day he saw Jesus coming toward him, and said, 'Behold, the Lamb of God, who takes away the sin of the world'"! **(John 1:29 RSV).**

Scripture Reading: John 1:29–37

Introduction

How did John respond when he saw Jesus coming to him? He cried out, "Behold, the Lamb of God who takes away the sin of the world." Suppose a child—or an adult—came to you and asked, "Why was Jesus called a lamb? I know a lamb is a very young sheep. Why would Jesus be called a young sheep?"

I. The Lamb of God.

The people who heard John should have had some refreshing memories, for the Jews were familiar with the use of the lamb to signify deliverance, cleansing, and forgiveness.

When Israel was being delivered from Egyptian bondage, the firstborn of all Egyptian children were condemned to die. Israel would be spared if they marked their doorposts with the blood of a spotless lamb. They were instructed to kill the lamb, mark their doorposts with the blood, roast the meat, and eat it. We read in the Old Testament about the Day of Atonement when the Israelites killed year-old male lambs without blemish for sin offerings.

John the Baptist was the son of a priest and therefore was familiar with the morning and evening offerings in the temple. The Israelites never ceased these offerings in war or famine. As long as the temple stood, they continued to offer sacrifices. Even in John's time people could be seen going to Jerusalem and toward the temple with their best blemishless beasts to be offered as sacrifices.

The Old Testament sacrifices were symbolic of the price that was to be paid for sin by Jesus on the cross. In his life, suffering, and death, he fulfilled and transcended all these types and symbols. He is the only completely unblemished offering. He is offered for the sins of all who will believe in him, not only the Jews but all people.

II. Sin is humanity's problem.

Sin is an ugly word, a no-no. One must not talk about sin, especially preach about it. It is not so dirty to sin, just dirty to preach about it. We have gotten so used to sin that it doesn't look like sin anymore. We read about it, see it on television, and hear about it until it doesn't look or sound like sin anymore. The world has become sin oriented.

But so much for the world. What about us? We find it easier to think about the sin of others, right? Sin is something someone else does.

A pastor related an interesting conversation he had had with one of his church members. "I was very surprised once when a man suggested to me that he wished I would preach on sin. The thing that surprised me was the that I thought I did. You cannot preach the Bible without preaching sin, and I thought I had been preaching the Bible.

"I went on to tell him that for several weeks I had been preaching a series of sermons on the Sermon on the Mount. I had talked about what a believer is like, about righteousness, love, prayer, and the Golden Rule; I had also talked about what a believer is not like, about covetousness, greed, selfishness, jealousy, and a mean spirit. I enumerated these to him, and he said, 'This is not what I'm talking about. I wish you would preach more often on sins like drinking, adultery, and gambling.' I said, 'You want me to speak on other people's sins, don't you? When I looked out over the congregation last Sunday morning, I did not see two or three drunks in the entire audience. I saw very few people who I think may have been guilty of adultery the past week, and gambling is not a problem in our church. As I looked out over the audience Sunday morning, I saw men and women who had lied for business reasons, gossiped about their neighbors, and criticized others. I saw kids who had cheated on their examinations and parents who had cheated on their income taxes. I just figured I ought to be preaching on the sins our people were guilty of rather than on the sins of people who would never know what I preach about anyway.'"

Haven't you found it much easier to confess other people's sins than your own?

III. Cleansing from sin.

If we are to serve God and be happy Christians, our lives are going to have to be cleaned up (read 2 Tim. 2:20–21).

"Well," you say, "I know there is sin in my life, but what do I do about it?" Jesus said you must do the same thing you do about any other malignancy: Amputate it. But as Paul said in Romans, you can't do it by yourself. Only by the power of the Holy Spirit can you do surgery on sin. Paul emphasizes that if Christ is in control, the flesh is not in control; but if Christ is not in charge of us, the flesh will constantly be gaining control.

Thus, John spoke of the Lamb of God who lifts off our sin and bears it away. Isaiah said, "He bore the sin of many, and made intercession for the transgressors" (Isa. 53:12 RSV). The writer of Hebrews declared, "Christ, having been offered once to bear the sins of many, will appear a second time, not to deal with sin, but to save those who are eagerly waiting for him" (Heb. 9:28 RSV). And Peter wrote, "He himself bore our sins in his body on the tree, that we might die to sin and live to righteousness. By his wounds you have been healed" (1 Peter 2:24 RSV). You see, there is no other name given among men whereby we must be saved.

Conclusion

The only way to have our sins removed is for Jesus to remove them, and he desires to do so. But we must invite him in as Savior and Lord. After we have done this, we need to invite our friends to receive him.

SUNDAY MORNING, AUGUST 22

Title: How Much Should Others Influence Us?

Text: "Wherefore receive ye one another, as Christ also received us to the glory of God" **(Rom. 15:7).**

Scripture Reading: Romans 15:1–7

Hymns: "O Worship the King," Grant

          "Let the Lower Lights Be Burning," Bliss

          "Who Is on the Lord's Side?" Havergal

Offertory Prayer: Our heavenly Father, we rejoice that you know all about us and still love us. We confess to you our sins with full confidence that if we confess our sins, you are faithful and just to forgive us of all iniquity. We pray, O Lord, that our influence may be for good. Help us to win others to faith in you. Help us to edify. Keep us from causing others to stumble. When we can please others and also please you, help us to do so, but if there must be a choice between pleasing you and others, grant that we may say, "Thy kingdom come. Thy will be done in earth, as it is in heaven."

May our tithes and offerings be pleasing in your sight and may they be used to benefit your kingdom. In Jesus' name. Amen.

Introduction

The power of influence one has over others is a tremendous responsibility. Jesus discusses this under the figures of salt and light in Matthew 5:13–16. Christians are the salt of the earth. "Salt is what makes food taste bad when you leave it out," according to a little girl's definition. Salt is also a preservative used to keep food from decaying. God expects Christians to give flavor and zest to life and to be his instruments in keeping the world from going bad.

Christians are also the light of the world. They can no more hide their influence than a city on a hill can be hidden. Christians are to shine the light of their influence in such a manner that people beholding them will glorify God.

But how much should we allow others to influence us? A little girl prayed, "God, help me to do what you want me to do and what everybody else wants me to do too." That must surely be a prayer that even God cannot answer. Paul exhorts in Romans 15:1–7 that we are to be eager to do good to our neighbors in the spirit of Christ. Christians will inconvenience themselves to help others. It is evident, however, that:

I. We cannot do everything others want us to do.

A. *Some people will try to use you for their evil purposes.* "Blessed is the man that walketh not in the counsel of the ungodly, nor standeth in the way of sinners, nor sitteth in the seat of the scornful" (Ps. 1:1), writes the author of Psalm 1. Note the progression: walketh, standeth, sitteth; counsel, way, seat; ungodly, sinners, scornful. We must say the first no to wicked counsel if we are not to find ourselves with sinners.

B. *Those involved in evil always want company.* The cheater feels better if others are cheating too. Paul concluded his indictment of sinners as those "who knowing the judgment of God, that they which commit such things are worthy of death, not only do the same, but have pleasure in them that do them" (Rom. 1:32). We must not be influenced to do evil by the desire to please others.

II. How much should we accommodate our actions to the consciences of others?

Paul urges:

A. *"Him that is weak in the faith receive ye, but not to doubtful disputations" (Rom. 14:1).* Mature believers ought to help strengthen the faith of younger Christians. Don't deliberately engage young Christians in arguments about difficult theological positions or confuse them with obscure Bible passages.

B. *Whether one should eat meat that had been offered to idols was an urgent question in Paul's day.* The Old Testament codes of clean and unclean (which probably were sanitary codes before they acquired religious significance) had been done away in Christ. Paul wrote, "I know, and am persuaded by the Lord Jesus, that there is nothing unclean of itself" (Rom. 14:14). There is no religious reason why one ought not to eat anything that agrees with one's digestion. If the food is harmful, then the concern for one's health is a valid religious reason for abstaining. Paul knew that "an idol is nothing in the world, and that there is none other God but one" (1 Cor. 8:4). He knew that the meat had not been hurt in any way by being offered to an idol. He advised believers to buy food in the market and ask no questions about whether it had been offered to idols. "Eat anything sold in the meat market without raising questions of conscience" (1 Cor. 10:25 NIV). If invited to a feast, they were not to raise any

questions. If, however, there were those who had questions of conscience, Christians were not to flaunt their freedom nor to encourage
them to do what their consciences condemned. If one thought it was
wrong to eat, for him or her it was wrong. "But the man who has doubts
is condemned if he eats, because his eating is not from faith; and everything that does not come from faith is sin" (Rom. 14:23 NIV).

For this reason Christians will not want to do anything that would
cause another to stumble. Paul's arguments in Romans 14:13–23 and
1 Corinthians 10:23–33 will repay careful reading.

C.   *A second illustration Paul used is that of observing certain days and seasons.* He
wrote, "One man esteemeth one day above another: another esteemeth
every day alike. Let every man be fully persuaded in his own mind"
(Rom. 14:5). He had confronted this problem in his letter to the Galatians. "But now that you know God—or rather are known by God—how
is it that you are turning back to those weak and miserable principles?
Do you wish to be enslaved by them all over again? You are observing special days and months and seasons and years! I fear for you, that somehow
I have wasted my efforts on you" (Gal. 4:9–11 NIV). When people insist
on observing certain days, feasts, and so on in order to be Christians,
they are in grave danger of turning from salvation by grace to salvation
by works or ceremonies. This is a grievous error and must be resisted.
Paul later developed his argument in Colossians 2:13–23 that Christ
nailed to the cross the necessity for ceremonial observances. He concludes, "Let no man therefore judge you in meat, or in drink, or in
respect of an holy day, or a new moon, or of the sabbath day: which are
a shadow of things to come; but the body is of Christ" (Col. 2:16–17).

III. This principle is difficult to apply.

To know how far we should allow others to influence us is most difficult. We wish Paul were here. We would like to find out what he thinks.

A.   *Paul seemed to be willing to offend the views of others when principle was involved.*
When the Judaizers insisted on the circumcision of the Gentiles and
determined that they must keep the Mosaic law before they could
become Christians, Paul vigorously opposed them. It was a matter of
principle. His opposition resulted in the Jerusalem Council (see Acts
15:1–32; Gal. 2:1–10).

When Timothy, whose father was a Greek but whose mother was a
Jewess, joined the missionary party, Paul "took and circumcised him
because of the Jews which were in those quarters: for they knew all that
his father was a Greek" (Acts 16:3). When Titus, whose parents were
both Gentiles, accompanied Paul to the Jerusalem Council, the apostle
refused to have him circumcised. In the case of Timothy, Paul did not
think any principle was involved. He thought his concession to Jewish

feelings would make Timothy's ministry more effective. In the case of Titus, Paul did think principle was involved, and he refused to yield to attempts to influence him. It seems logical to conclude that Paul would agree that loyalty to principle is more important than the desire to please others.

B. *Paul, was it only in public that you refused to eat food that had been offered to idols?* Did you use the meat in private? If you refused to eat the meat in order not to offend the men of weak conscience, would you not confuse the immature Christian who had grasped the truth that the meat was unharmed? Would not your conformity to this superstition do more harm than good?

During World War II a Baptist chaplain and the officers at the Bachelor Officers' Quarters sat down to a Friday evening steak dinner. One of the officers of Roman Catholic faith had grave question about eating meat on Friday. The Baptist chaplain was of no help to him, for he had no conscience against eating the steak. The chaplain would have been willing to refrain from eating the steak if it would have helped the Catholic officer. But had the chaplain refused to eat, would that not have been a poor example for the non-Catholic officers? One of the Catholic officers resolved the question by telling his fellow officers that if no other food were offered they could eat in good conscience. So all of the men of all faiths enjoyed the good steaks.

A young preacher, a college student, was pastor of a church. The preacher had no objection to playing Rook, but some of his deacons thought all card playing was wrong. The young pastor attended a college party. The hostess had planned cards as the entertainment of the evening. He quietly informed her of his dilemma, assuring her that he had no objection to the cards, but he would excuse himself from playing. She did not embarrass him. Quickly she changed the whole plan of her entertainment from cards to other games. It was a most gracious Christian act on the part of the hostess.

Conclusion

Here are some conclusions:

Each one must give account of himself or herself to God.

We will seek to win others to Christ and to build them up in Christian faith.

We will not willfully put a stumblingblock in the way of another.

We will be sensitive to the opinions of others.

We cannot allow legalistic Christians to influence us too much, else when we please them, we alienate others from the gospel.

In love and logic we will seek to sustain our own positions. In the long run, we will serve the cause of Christ better by being loyal to the highest we know rather than by compromising to please others.

SUNDAY EVENING, AUGUST 22

Title: The Strategy of the Kingdom

Text: "Go ye therefore, and teach all nations, baptizing them in the name of the Father, and of the Son, and of the Holy Ghost: Teaching them to observe all things whatsoever I have commanded you: and, lo, I am with you alway, even unto the end of the world" (**Matt. 28:19–20**).

Scripture Reading: Acts 1:8–11

Introduction

One of the amazing attributes of the great God we serve is the meticulous way in which he has laid his plans and mapped his strategy for the universe, particularly for the earth and the human race he has placed on it. There is nothing haphazard about God's planning, nothing left to chance. A beautiful demonstration of this is the way in which our Lord Jesus Christ set forth his plan for the establishment and growth of his kingdom. Therefore, if our Lord has planned so carefully and outlined so explicitly, it is imperative that the church implement its role in this worldwide endeavor as God has set it forth in his Word. Every commission Jesus left for the church has been given to individuals and not to the church as an institution. It is far more comfortable for people to get lost in the crowd, to seek anonymity. But Jesus has singled out individuals in his commission to preach the gospel to every creature.

The picture is that of an army moving forward under the orders of a captain. The writer of Hebrews refers to Jesus as "the captain of [our] salvation" (Heb. 2:10). In fact, the militant concept of the church is found throughout the New Testament. It is possible, therefore, to outline the doctrine of missions within this context.

I. Let us see, first, that Jesus, the "Captain of our salvation," has issued orders.

A. *Just before Jesus ascended from the Mount of Olives, leaving behind a wondering group of disciples, he said to them: "Behold, I send the promise of my Father upon you: but tarry ye in the city of Jerusalem, until ye be endued with power from on high" (Luke 24:49).* Before his disciples were to go out to preach and witness, it was imperative that they tarry, or wait for a season. The *New Eng-*

lish Bible maintains the militancy in Christ's command: ". . .until you are armed with the power from above."

B. *The result of their waiting was the coming of the Holy Spirit, the infusion of God's presence into their total beings.* The Holy Spirit's presence within them brought about a wondrous change—the fearful hesitancy with which they had faced life after Jesus' crucifixion became a fearless courage to communicate the good news of salvation through Jesus Christ.

C. *When believers are possessed by the Spirit of God, they have available the power to perform the tasks God has for them to do and the spiritual sensitivity to discern where and what the tasks are!* It is an insult to God and a grief to his Spirit when we go about his work haphazardly and unprepared. We are to tarry until we are armed with his power; then we are to be "at the ready" to go and to do as we are impressed by his Spirit.

II. Not only has our Lord issued orders, he has also provided the equipment for his marching army.

A. *What is this equipment?* The first and foremost weapon believers wield is the *Word*—the "sword of the Spirit." Paul gives us the picture of the Christian's armor in Ephesians 6, and he is careful to specify that our weapon is the sword of the Spirit. The writer of Hebrews tells us that it is "a two-edged sword," which "cuts asunder, both to the dividing of bone and marrow, and soul and spirit." When Satan tempted Jesus in the wilderness, the one weapon our Lord used with expertise was not his personality as the Son of God, or his perfect, sinless humanity, but the Word of God! In answer to each of the three temptations from Satan, Jesus said, "It is written." With all of the assurance of his soul, Paul could say: "I am not ashamed of the gospel of Christ, for it is the power of God unto salvation to every one that believeth" (Rom. 1:16).

B. *The other major weapon for the Christian soldier is prayer.* We sing about prayer, preach about prayer, and teach lessons about prayer; but most of the time there is a deafening silence between God's people and his throne of grace because we have become so prayerless! We are so busy, even engaged in religious activity, that we do not make time to pray. And the paradox of it all is that it is through prayer that we are able to learn to use the sword of the Spirit! Why? Because prayer is the key that releases understanding and discernment concerning what God would say to us through his Holy Word. Then, as we study God's Word, we are able to see ourselves in the light of the Word and discipline ourselves so that we are instantly and momentarily available for God's use. And, incidentally, we are not to do all the talking in prayer. One of the most amazing experiences a Christian can have is learning to be still before God and listening to him with the ears of the soul.

III. Finally, not only does our Lord issue orders that we are to follow and provide the equipment to carry out those orders, he also supplies the motivation for service.

A. *The greatest motivation of all is God's love.* We cannot understand the love of God. There is no way we can ferret out the reason a perfect and holy God expresses such compassion to creatures who are basically evil and contaminated with sin.

B. *Also, the love of Christ is our motivation.* Listen to Paul: "For the love of Christ constraineth us; because we thus judge, that if one died for all, then were all dead: and that he died for all, that they which live should not henceforth live unto themselves, but unto him which died for them, and rose again" (2 Cor. 5:14–15). What is Paul saying? Simply that it is the amazing love of Christ, so beautifully demonstrated in his life and death, that constrains him, or thrusts him forward in his determination to serve his Lord at any cost.

C. *Finally, humankind's need combined with the love of God and Christ ought to motivate us to carry out his mission until he comes.* Paul said: "As it is written, There is none righteous, no, not one: there is none that understandeth, there is none that seeketh after God. They are all gone out of the way, they are together become unprofitable; there is none that doeth good, no, not one" (Rom. 3:10–12). He continues to the end of the chapter describing the terrible need of sinful humans. Christians do not have to leave the neighborhoods where they live to find people in spiritual need. Time is precious and opportunities are fleeting.

Conclusion

Some will accept the Good News, and some will reject it. Some will receive Christ, and others will turn their backs on him. But the strategy of Christian missions is to make available to every living soul the good news that Jesus died to make eternal life possible for all who will receive it. And whose task is it? Not some elaborate organization or well-equipped institution. It is the task of every individual child of God.

WEDNESDAY EVENING, AUGUST 25

Title: Witnesses Multiplied

Text: "Behold, the Lamb of God!" (**John 1:35** RSV).

Scripture Reading: John 1:35–50

Introduction

"That guy witnesses when he doesn't even want to." The pastor was enthusiastic as he spoke of an evangelistic man in his church. What he meant was that his friend was so enthusiastic about helping others become Christians that it was his lifestyle.

John the Baptist never missed an opportunity to introduce Jesus to others by means of a word of testimony. Some responded negatively, but the important thing is that during his short lifetime enough people responded positively that his ministry has continued through the centuries. Every Christian group in the world honors the memory of John the Baptist as an introducer of Jesus. John was imprisoned and later beheaded, but even those experiences of suffering and death contributed to his timeless ministry of introducing Jesus.

One day John was standing with two of his friends. He saw Jesus walking and said, "Behold, the Lamb of God!" His friends heard him say this, and as a result they followed Jesus. These two friends were Andrew and another disciple of John. They had been looking forward to meeting this person who had become a magnificent obsession with their friend John. It is no wonder that when they came face to face with Jesus they immediately left John and began to follow Jesus. True witnesses do not draw people to themselves but to Jesus. Many apparent successes may not be successes when measured by this yardstick and vice versa.

I. Andrew responded to John's witness.

A pastor and a visiting evangelist witnessed to a teenage girl who gladly responded to their words of testimony and accepted Jesus as her Savior. During the evening service she responded to the invitation and came forward for counseling. She then did something a bit unusual. She left the altar and went back into the congregation. After a brief conversation of whispers, she came back to the altar bringing another young lady with her. She had shared with this friend what her new faith meant and had encouraged her to believe in Jesus Christ too. This teenage believer was following the example of Andrew. After Andrew came to know Jesus, he was greatly concerned about his own brother, Simon Peter.

II. Peter responded to John's witness.

Peter, the most well known of all of our Lord's earthly followers, was brought to Jesus by his brother, Andrew, a little-known apostle. He made his greatest contribution through one to whom he witnessed. Because he witnessed to Peter, his own witness was greatly multiplied.

III. Philip responded to John's witness.

The first thing we know about Philip is that Jesus found him and said, "Follow me." The most important thing we know about him is that when Jesus called him he answered. Every person who faithfully witnesses will experience times when their witness is multiplied. These times will compensate for the dry periods.

IV. Nathanael responded to John's witness.

The first thing we know about Philip after Jesus called him is that he "found Nathanael, and saith unto him, We have found him, of whom Moses in the law, and the prophets, did write, Jesus of Nazareth, the son of Joseph. And Nathanael said unto him, Can there any good thing come out of Nazareth? Philip saith unto him, Come and see" (John 1:45–46). Isn't it amazing that Philip, the new convert, was already using the exact language of Jesus? More importantly, he was acting like a person acts when Jesus has come into his life.

Conclusion

Be diligent and faithful in giving your testimony concerning the goodness of God in your life. Share with others what Jesus Christ means to you. As you give your witness for Christ to your acquaintances, some of them will respond positively, and your testimony for Christ will be multiplied as they in turn share the good news of what God has done in their lives.

SUNDAY MORNING, AUGUST 29

Title: The God of Hope

Text: "Now the God of hope fill you with all joy and peace in believing, that ye may abound in hope, through the power of the Holy Ghost" **(Rom. 15:13).**

Scripture Reading: Romans 15:5–13

Hymns: "O God, Our Help in Ages Past," Watts
"He Leadeth Me," Gilmore
"Wonderful Peace of My Saviour," Barratt

Offertory Prayer: Our heavenly Father, we thank you for the many blessings that come into our lives because we believe in you. We thank you for joy and peace in this present life and for hope for the future life. What joy it is to associate ourselves with other believers in your church as we seek to evangelize the lost and to build up the saved. Forgive us of our sins and lead us by your Holy Spirit into areas of useful service. Bless, we pray, our gifts of self and of substance to your glory and to the good of multitudes for whom Christ died. In Jesus' name we pray. Amen.

Introduction

Our text presents God as "the God of hope." Just as God is love, righteousness, truth, life, and light, so also his nature is hope. His hopeful nature is illustrated by his plan of salvation. "God so loved the world. . ." (John 3:16). "The grace of God that bringeth salvation hath appeared to all men" (Titus 2:11). Christ was born a Jew, but he was the Son of Man. His atoning work was no less for the Gentile than for the Jew. Our Scripture reading, Romans 15:5–13, emphasizes this truth. Paul quotes passages from the Old Testament to show that the Gentiles were in God's plan from the beginning. Paul has been pleading that just as Jew and Gentile become one new humanity in Christ, so all people in the church should be united by a common loyalty to Jesus. The weak in the faith and the strong in the faith are to unite in Christ, so also the Jew and the Gentile become one in Christ. "Wherefore receive ye one another, as Christ also received us to the glory of God" (Rom. 15:7).

The God of hope has provided for the salvation of all people. His hope for glory is in the salvation of sinners and in their becoming like Jesus Christ in character. As long as God is, there is hope. Let none despair.

I. Believing brings joy and peace.

"Now the God of hope fill you with all joy and peace in believing" (Rom. 15:13).

A. *The peace that comes from believing.*

1. Peace with God through justification and forgiveness. Recall the earlier chapters of Romans in which Paul has developed the theme that God in grace has provided salvation for all sinners on the basis of faith in Jesus Christ (recall Rom. 3:19–31). This salvation justifies— puts a person in right standing with God—and takes away the penalty of sin. In the latter verses of 1 Corinthians 15, Paul affirms that "the sting of death is sin; and the strength of sin is the law" (v. 56). The law says, "The wages of sin is death" (Rom. 6:23). The person who sins is not good enough to go to heaven and is separated from God by his or her sins. The sting of death is not our fear that God cannot preserve life after the dissolution of the body. This life is not the end of his wisdom, nor of his power or love. The sting of death is that one should meet God without salvation without one's sins forgiven. A new law that God, the Holy Spirit, gives eternal life to those who believe in Jesus overcomes the old law that the sinner must die. "There is therefore now no condemnation to them which are in Christ Jesus, who walk not after the flesh, but after the Spirit. For the law of the Spirit of life in Christ Jesus hath made one free from the law of sin and death" (Rom. 8:1–2).

2. Sons of God. Those who believe in Jesus are adopted as God's children, have eternal life, and have peace with God. Paul exhorts the believers to enjoy the peace they have with God: "Since we have been given right standing with God through faith, then let us continue enjoying peace with God through our Lord Jesus Christ, by whom we

have an introduction through faith into this state of God's favor, in which we safely stand; and let us continue exulting in the hope of enjoying the glorious presence of God" (Rom. 5:1–2 WILLIAMS).

B. *The joy that comes from believing.*

1. Joy in believing in God. Even the atheist must want to believe in a personal God who is omnipotent, omniscient, holy, and loving. A preacher spoke to another about his belief in the security of the believer. "It is very reassuring to believe in God's keeping power," he said. The other man replied, "I should think that it would be. I would like to believe it."

2. Joy in doing the Father's will. As God is love and holiness, his will is kind and right. His will is always best for us and for others. God will never be defeated. What a joy to be aligned with one who will be victorious.

3. Joy in the assurance of God's approval. We rejoice when we can win the approval of our spouse or friends whose opinions we value. How wonderful to hear Jesus say, "Well done, thou good and faithful servant" (Matt. 25:21).

4. Joy in the knowledge of helping one's fellow humans. Jesus teaches that we serve him as we serve others in his name. He commands us to love our neighbors. As the Good Samaritan helped the poor man on the Jericho road, we are to help others. This brings joy.

II. Joy and peace in believing are illustrated perfectly in Jesus.

A. *The Beatitudes (Matt. 5:1–13) of Jesus describe the Christian as blessed, or happy.* The believer is to be congratulated.

B. *Jesus had to defend himself and his disciples for being so happy.* They were like a wedding party (see Matt. 9:14–15).

C. *To the one sick with palsy Jesus said, "Son, be of good cheer; thy sins be forgiven thee" (Matt. 9:2).*

D. *In the twin parables of the pearl of great price and the treasure hidden in the field, our Lord's emphasis is on the joy of forsaking all else to gain the treasure of the kingdom of God (see Matt. 13:44–46).*

E. *To his disciples on the night of his betrayal Jesus said, "These things I have spoken unto you, that in me ye might have peace. In the world ye shall have tribulation: but be of good cheer; I have overcome the world" (John 16:33).*

F. *The author of Hebrews exhorted, "Looking unto Jesus the author and finisher of our faith; who for the joy that was set before him endured the cross, despising the shame, and is set down at the right hand of the throne of God" (12:2).*

III. Believing brings hope for the future.

A. *Part of the present joy and peace of believers is their hope about the future.* The future is as bright as the person and promises of God.

B. *Christians believe that God has plans for his people beyond death.* They believe what Jesus has said. For examples, see John 14:1–6, 19; 17:24; Revelation 1:12–19; 2:7; 7:9–17.

C. *The Christian believes what Jesus has said about his coming again and the consummation of the age.* For examples, see Matthew 24:3, 27–51; 25:1–46. Baptism and the Lord's Supper refer to our Lord's death and resurrection. Paul said he received his account of the Lord's Supper from the Lord. He correctly interprets his purpose when he writes: "For as often as ye eat this bread, and drink this cup, ye do shew the Lord's death till he come" (1 Cor. 11:26).

Conclusion

Paul shared this blessed hope. For examples, see Philippians 1:21–23; 2 Timothy 4:6–8; 1 Corinthians 2:9, 15; 2 Corinthians 5:1–8. He closed his beautiful thirteenth chapter of 1 Corinthians with these words: "So faith, hope, love abide, these three; but the greatest of these is love" (1 Cor. 13:13 RSV). Faith in the sense of believing that God is cannot be forced. If your doubts are great, act as though God were and you will come to know that he is.

Hope cannot be forced. It is the product of faith and love. If you lack faith and if you find it hard to hope, then you can love. Treat others as Christ would have you treat them. Live up to the highest that you know, and you will find that to your love God will add faith, joy, peace, and hope. "May the God of hope fill you with all joy and peace in believing, so that by the power of the Holy Spirit you may abound in hope" (Rom. 15:13 RSV).

SUNDAY EVENING, AUGUST 29

Title: The Ultimate Ownership

Text: "The earth is the LORD's, and the fulness thereof: the world, and they that dwell therein. For he hath founded it upon the seas, and established it upon the floods" **(Ps. 24:1–2).**

Scripture Reading: Matthew 6:16–34

Introduction

The mention of the word *stewardship* does strange things to some people. The reason for this is usually because most people associate stewardship with money. Most people become quite defensive when a minister starts to talk about money, especially if it is their money! Many church members tend to grit their teeth and brace themselves for the pastor's annual sermon on tithing, and with a sigh of relief, they are glad when the annual stewardship emphasis and budget promotion time is over.

However, stewardship is a biblical concept that far exceeds the singular area of money. There is a natural stewardship to which every person must ascribe, whether he or she wants to or not. The farmer must be a good steward of his soil; the cattleman must be a good steward of his cattle; the employer must be a good steward of the potential labor output of his employees. To be derelict in these areas, and many others, would only spell disaster.

But Christian stewardship goes much deeper. It is far more inclusive.

I. Let's begin, then, by considering the basis for our stewardship.

A. *Nowhere in all of Scripture will you find stated in simpler or more beautiful terms the sovereignty of God over his creation than in Psalm 24:1–2.* These verses carry us back to Genesis 1: "In the beginning God created the heaven and the earth." However, if we read Psalm 24:1–2 in its proper context, we will find that David is dealing with a troubling problem that had developed among his people. There are overtones of protest against the idea that God can be limited to a certain area—like Jerusalem, or the sanctuary in which the people believed God was confined. They had closed God up in the Holy City and in the Holy of Holies, and they came at stated times to pay homage to him. They thought they were pacifying him with their ritual and ceremony and formal worship.

B. *Perhaps David's message would be equally as appropriate today as it was in his day, for people have always preferred to contain God and thus delineate God's involvement in human life.* That is why we hear such statements as, "Well, I think religion has its place, but I don't think you ought to let it make a fool of you!" In short, people prefer to "lock up God" in the church. Christian stewardship tears that door down and lets God out of the prison people would make for him. Christian stewardship declares that God is totally God everywhere and all the time!

C. *Furthermore, there is a majesty in David's concept of total stewardship.* David makes a broad and sweeping confession that God's dominion is unchangeable. By right of creation, the entire earth is his; and furthermore, those beings who inhabit the earth are also within the scope of his sovereign governorship. There is an added dimension here, however, that staggers the human mind. This almighty God, with full and complete power and authority to exercise his rights as creator, has given people freedom to choose their destiny. People are free to rebel against or obey him.

II. This leads us naturally, then, to examine the reason for our stewardship.

A. *Perhaps Paul understood Christian stewardship as no other Bible writer did.* He wrote to the Corinthians: "What? know ye not that your body is the temple of the Holy Ghost which is in you, which ye have of God, and ye are not your own? For ye are bought with a price: therefore glorify God in your body, and in your spirit, which are God's" (1 Cor. 6:19–20). All through the Scriptures we find that God works through a human body. It was in a body that man sinned; it is in a body that we sin. It was in a body that Jesus came to earth; it was in a body that he lived triumphantly and overcame sin; it was in a body that he died and rose again. Now, by his Spirit, he comes to live in the bodies of his people. If Christians are truly joined to Christ in daily submission and obedience, they are therefore enabled by God's grace to control their bodies. But this does not happen automatically.

B. *Christians are predestined to arrive one day in heaven, to stand in the presence of God.* That was settled once and for all when we rested our soul in the finished work of Christ on the cross. But still we are stewards of what goes on during the journey! And because we still reside in unredeemed bodies, subject to temptation and sin, our daily lives become battlegrounds where we must fight and strive every day. Thus, we should be driven to our knees, daily, to pray for strength from God, and for submission to his indwelling Spirit.

C. *In short, the Christian body is the sanctuary of the Holy Spirit.* The building in which the church assembles is not a sanctuary. It is merely an assembly room for the people of God. A sanctuary is where God's Spirit abides! What is going on today in your sanctuary, Christian?

III. Finally, having examined the basis and the reason for our stewardship, let's look briefly at the expression of our stewardship.

A. *Peter summed it up perfectly when he said: "As every man hath received the gift, even so minister the same one to another, as good stewards of the manifold grace of God" (1 Peter 4:10).* Peter says that every person has received this gift of grace. But this gift is useful and fulfills its purpose only as it is given away. Just as the manna that fell in the wilderness was not to be hoarded by the people lest it spoil, so the gift of grace God gives to each of his children cannot be hoarded.

B. *And what are these gifts?* They differ from person to person; they are as varied as the ability to sing or play or preach, to communicate the gospel to children, to be a peacemaker, to be able to say the right word at the right time to soothe a troubled heart, to make money and use it for God's glory—and on and on we could go. It is totally unscriptural for one to say that he or she has no gift, for God has expressly declared that he has bestowed upon all of his children a gift to be used, to be given away, for his glory. This, then, is how we express our stewardship—by giving ourselves away in the name and for the glory of Christ.

C. *Peter adds that we are stewards of the "manifold" grace of God.* This could be literally translated "the many-colored grace of God." This means that

SEPTEMBER

■ **Sunday Mornings**

The suggested theme is "The Primary Demand of the Christian Faith." Another good theme for this series of messages is "The Badge of Christian Discipleship," and an appropriate text for this theme is John 13:35.

■ **Sunday Evenings**

"Getting Acquainted with the Twelve Apostles" is the theme suggested for the next three months of lessons. Some information from tradition is added to the scriptural accounts of the lives of these significant men.

■ **Wednesday Evenings**

Continue with the series based on the gospel of John using the theme "Giving a Winning Witness for Christ."

WEDNESDAY EVENING, SEPTEMBER 1

Title: Why Did Jesus Come?

Text: "My hour has not yet come" **(John 2:4 RSV).**

Scripture Reading: John 2:1–11

Introduction

When the gospel of John was being written, the writer looked back through the entire ministry of Jesus and selected the first miracle in Cana for special attention. We will answer the journalistic interrogatives When? Where? What? and Why? as we look at this passage.

I. When?

John told the story of the wedding at Cana at the beginning of his account of Jesus' life. He had written the profound introduction found in the first chapter, which included Jesus' preexistence, the unique presentation of John the Baptist, and the calling of Andrew, Peter, Philip, Nathanael, and the other disciples. The first chapter closes with Jesus promising Nathanael greater signs. The rapid sequence of several signs begins immediately with Jesus turning water into wine.

It was interesting that this first miracle would occur in the unspectacular atmosphere of a wedding in the little town of Cana. The religious leaders of the time expected the Messiah to come in demonstration and power. The devil had tried to get Jesus to perform his first sign by leaping from the pinnacle of the temple.

II. Where?

The first recorded miracle of Jesus took place in Cana of Galilee. Most of John's record centers around Jerusalem, but the beginning of signs is in Galilee. Nathanael was probably quoting a familiar question when he asked, "Can anything good come out of Nazareth?" Perhaps the religious power structure of Judea would have raised the same question about all of Galilee. Cana would not be the likely place to launch a religious crusade. A wedding would certainly not be the choice beginning for a worldwide ministry. Here, however, the Son of God performed his first miracle.

III. What?

Jesus turned water into wine. His mother told him about the need growing out of the depleted wine supply. Mary likely was distressed about the obvious embarrassment to the family. Wine was very important to such an occasion. Replacement was not as easy as replenishing the punch bowl or making another pot of coffee. Mary believed Jesus could help. She knew him better than anyone else did. While she may have been surprised at his initial response, she might not have been as surprised as others. She knew his life was to be different. Jesus was not disrespectful in addressing her as "Woman." His use of the term was likely tender, though there would be some shock to Mary in adjusting to her Son as her Savior, notwithstanding her previous preparation. The question Jesus asked her, "What have you to do with me?" was not spoken in anger or resentment. It was a reminder to her that while his "hour had not yet come," whatever he did from then on would be more related to his heavenly Father than his earthly mother.

The next scene includes Jesus, the servants, and six stone jars used for the Jewish rites of purification. Now the question arises, Would Jesus put wine in the dirty, defiled jars?

He told the servants to "draw some out" and take it to the steward of the wedding feast. The verb "draw out" is the same one used to draw water out of Jacob's well in Jesus' conversation with the Samaritan woman. This would suggest that the servants drew again from the well for the wine. In either case Jesus performed his first sign by turning water into wine to meet a need at a social function.

IV. Why?

A. *He met a need.* Compared to Jesus' total redemptive ministry in the world, it was not a priority matter, but it is interesting that most of the time the

Son of God dealt with the simplest needs with the profoundest words and greatest power. This is encouraging to us when we pray about our needs, isn't it?

Seven signs are usually listed in this section of John: the one we are considering, Jesus' healing of the officer's son (4:46–54), curing of the lame man (5:19), feeding of the five thousand (6:1–15), walking on water (6:16–21), healing of the man born blind (9:1–7), and raising of Lazarus (11:1–44). All of these miracles met the immediate needs of people. This practice characterizes Jesus' ministry.

B. *He was teaching his disciples.* In the first chapter Jesus began calling disciples. He continued until he had gathered about himself twelve. Throughout his public ministry he was teaching them (and us) about himself, the new life, and how to share it.

   1. Maybe the wine represented the new life offered through the Holy Spirit. If so, the contrast between the water and wine would be significant. John the Baptist had said he baptized with water and Jesus baptized with the Spirit.

   2. The six stone jars may have represented the limitations of the Jewish legalistic system. Six is short of the perfect number of seven. The dirty, stagnant, defiled water was compared to the fresh well water used to make the wine. Perhaps filling the pot to the brim might somehow symbolize the manner in which Jesus fulfilled the law and went beyond to provide the supernatural power needed to cleanse people from their sins.

   3. Wine was sometimes associated with joy, not superficial joy caused by drunkenness, but both physical and spiritual joy. This is illustrated throughout the Old Testament.

   4. No doubt the strongest evidence of the purpose of the sign is seen in the following words: "This, the first of signs, Jesus did at Cana in Galilee, and manifested his glory; and his disciples believed in him" (v. 11 RSV).

Conclusion

Jesus' high purpose of bringing people to faith in God reoccurs throughout the gospel of John. John explained that his reason for writing the book was that people might believe (John 20:31). And Jesus gave this as his reason for coming into the world (John 10:10).

SUNDAY MORNING, SEPTEMBER 5

Title: The Command to Love

Text: "You have heard that it was said, 'You shall love your neighbor and hate your enemy.' But I say to you, Love your enemies and pray for those who persecute you, so that you may be sons of your Father who is in heaven; for he makes his sun to rise on the evil and the good, and sends rain on the just and on the unjust" **(Matt. 5:43–45 RSV).**

Scripture Reading: Matthew 22:34–40

Hymns: "How Firm a Foundation," Anonymous
"Guide Me, O Thou Great Jehovah," Williams
"Jesus, the Very Thought of Thee," Bernard of Clairvaux

Offertory Prayer: Holy and loving Father, today we rejoice in the gift of your grace, love, and mercy toward us. We thank you for the gift of forgiveness. We rejoice in the gift of membership in your family and for the gift of the Holy Spirit. We rejoice in the many gifts that you have bestowed upon us in life. We come now in response to your generosity by giving tithes and offerings to you and your work through the church. Accept these gifts as emblems of our desire to be totally available to you in service to those who need your mercy and grace. In Jesus' name. Amen.

Introduction

Jesus Christ came to earth as the supreme expression of God's love for humankind. Foremost in Christ's teachings is his encouragement that we respond to others in love.

The Jewish religious leaders had gone to great lengths in their attempts to detail the requirements of God. In fact, they had developed 248 affirmative precepts and 365 negative precepts that one must keep to be in proper relationship with God and one's fellow humans. Jesus condensed and concentrated all of the real requirements of God into one great word—*love*.

To love God with one's whole being means that we are to relate ourselves totally to God for his glory. To love our neighbors as ourselves means that we are to do all we can to promote their well-being.

The first and greatest commandment says that we are to love God supremely. This is not a totalitarian demand of a tyrannical God. Behind this command can be discovered God's grace as he seeks to help us with the priorities of life. We are to love God supremely rather than our home, our business, our church, or our work.

We are to love our neighbors as we love ourselves. One of the reasons why we do not love our neighbors more is because we do not love ourselves properly. We do not love ourselves properly because we have neglected to love God supremely.

Can love be commanded? Some say it cannot. In trying to answer this question we need to ask, "What kind of love is Jesus talking about when he issues a command that we love our neighbor, our enemy, and one another in the brotherhood of faith?"

I. The three major kinds of love.

A. *We are most familiar with* eros *love.* Romantic love is sensual love, sexual love, and it can be very selfish love. Our sexuality is a part of the good creation of God, and with an appreciation for the goodness of this gift to the human family, we need to recognize that Jesus was commanding something other than this particular form of love.

B. Philia *is the Greek word for friendship love.* It is love based on the worth and loveliness of the one loved. It is a proper and valuable kind of love. However, it was not this kind of love that Jesus was commanding.

C. Agape *love is the kind of love spoken of in John 3:16.* Agape love is sacrificial and self-denying—the Calvary kind of love. It can be commanded and directed by the mind and will of the person who chooses to love.

The love Jesus commanded us to practice toward others, and particularly whose within the family circle, is agape love.

II. The scope of the commandment to love.

A. *We must first and foremost have a proper love for God.* Only when we dedicate ourselves to God and give ourselves to his glory can we possibly have the capacity to properly love ourselves and others.

B. *We must have a proper love for ourselves.* Jesus said, "You shall love your neighbor as yourself." The love we have for ourselves is the measure by which we are to indicate love for others. If for some reason we hate ourselves, we will not have a proper measure by which to love others.

Do you hate yourself? Do you find yourself constantly cutting down yourself? Are you guilty of punishing yourself for past failures and for bad decisions over which you now have no control? Do you dislike the person whose reflection you see most in a mirror? If so, you are depriving yourself of the capacity to really love your neighbor.

Perhaps your greatest need is to accept yourself as God's creation and as the object of his loving concern. Accept his grace and forgiveness, and then forgive yourself of past failures and shortcomings. Begin to demonstrate some agape love toward yourself, and you will discover that the Holy Spirit is enlarging your capacity to love others.

C. *We are commanded to love our neighbor with agape love.* The big question has always been, "Who is my neighbor?" (Luke 10:29). The common answer has been, "The one who lives close to me. The one who is near and dear to me. The one who has been my friend and who has accommodated me." Jesus would have us believe that any person in need of our ministry and service is our neighbor. He illustrated this in the story of the Good Samaritan (Luke 10:25–37).

D. *We are commanded to love one another (John 13:34–35).* We are to love one another because each of us is an object of divine love; we have experienced the love of Jesus Christ. We are to love one another that we might demonstrate the reality of Christ's presence in our lives. Christian love is to be the badge by which we are identified as Jesus' disciples. Without love nothing else really matters (1 Cor. 13:1–3).

E. *We are commanded to love our enemies (Matt. 5:43–45).* This has always been a difficult passage for those who do not understand the nature of the love Jesus is commanding us to put into practice. It is not an instinctual, romantic love. It is not even a friendship, social kind of love. It is the Calvary kind of love with which we are to relate to those who mistreat us. We are encouraged to love as the Father God loves.

1. God's love does not discriminate but pours itself out on friends and enemies alike.
2. God's love is not motivated by human merit or loveliness.
3. God's love is governed by its own character, which is ever self-giving and self-denying.
4. God's love seeks the good of both friends and foes.

F. *A man is commanded to love his wife (Eph. 5:25–33).*

1. The husband is to love his wife as Christ loved the church in sacrificial, self-giving love (Eph. 5:25).
2. The husband is to love his wife as he loves his own body (Eph. 5:28). It is interesting to note that this commandment to husbands to love their wives is not with romantic love but agape love.

Conclusion

God is love. God has loved each of us in the life, death, and resurrection of Jesus Christ. He continues to love us in the here and now. God will continue to love us with an eternal love.

Respond sincerely and steadfastly by faith to God's love as it is revealed in Jesus Christ. Live a life of faithfulness that expresses itself in following him.

SUNDAY EVENING, SEPTEMBER 5

Title: Andrew: Power of an Ordinary Life

Text: "He [Andrew] first findeth his own brother Simon. . . .And he brought him to Jesus" (**John 1:41–42**).

Scripture Reading: John 1:35–42

Introduction

The late Peter Marshall, who gained fame as a United States Senate chaplain, had a sermon on Andrew that he called "The Saint in the Rank and File." The sermon praises the ordinary people of the earth. We do not know Andrew very well—his brother, Peter, gets most of the attention—but we ought to know him. We see a Peter only occasionally in a lifetime, but we see Andrews every day. Andrews are grocers, mechanics, and farmers, policemen, firemen, and postmen. Every church, school, and civic organization has its leaders, but behind the scenes are those who do much of the work and never get the credit. Andrew was an ordinary man.

Andrew lived in Bethsaida of Galilee (John 1:44), where he made his living by fishing. He was mending nets when Jesus called (Mark 1:16–18). Andrew had heard of the preaching of John the Baptist, so he and John went to see him. As John pointed to Jesus, saying, "Behold the Lamb of God," Andrew followed him. It is a great hour in any person's life when he or she comes to Christ, for salvation is life's greatest discovery. In the early church, Andrew was frequently called by the title *protokletos,* which literally means "first called." Andrew was just an ordinary man, but think of what he did for his Lord.

I. He brought a member of his own family to Christ.

Andrew is first pictured in the New Testament in the words, "He findeth his own brother" (John 1:41).

A. *He looked for Simon.* I like to think that maybe Simon Peter was out somewhere on the lake in a boat. Andrew, having made the great discovery, could not wait to share the good news with his brother. Great emotion swept over his soul. He could not keep it to himself. Andrew cupped his hands to his mouth and called, "Simon, we have found the Messiah." Andrew brought Peter to Jesus.

What a brother Peter was. He became the most important of the apostles, a towering personality and a natural-born leader. But think of this: "There would have been no eloquent Peter at Pentecost had there been no humble Andrew in Bethsaida."

B. *Someone has said, "It often takes more courage to tell your own brother than it does a man over in China."* It takes more genuine religion to witness before your own family than it does to strangers.

Oh, that accusing finger, that cynical laugh! "You're telling me about Jesus?" Peter might have said to Andrew. "Remember the time you became angry and cursed like a sailor? Remember that Saturday night you drank too much? Remember that man you have the grudge against? And you're telling me of Christ?" But Peter could not say that. Andrew lived an exemplary life.

You cannot be an influence for Christ if your life is not fit. Andrew probably never preached a sermon, but I believe we can say he lived a better sermon than most preachers will ever preach. Andrew never wrote an epistle, but he was a living epistle, known and read of men. Andrew never performed a miracle, but his life was a miracle of God. We need more Andrews who live their faith each day and are concerned for members of their own family.

At Dwight L. Moody's funeral, his eldest son, W. R., arose and testified, "D. L. Moody won each of his own children to Jesus Christ." That was probably the greatest accomplishment in the life of the famous evangelist.

II. Andrew brought a boy to Christ.

A. *In the second picture of Andrew, we see him down by the seashore.* Multitudes of people had been following Christ. People simply forgot the passage of time as they listened to him speak. It was now late afternoon, and the people were still hanging on to every word.

The babies and children had begun to fret, for they were tired and hungry. It would be three or four hours before they could buy food. Jesus could not dismiss them under such conditions. The children would suffer; others would faint by the wayside. Jesus asked about food; and one answered, "There is a lad here, which hath five barley loaves, and two small fishes" (John 6:9).

How do you suppose Andrew knew about this boy with sardine sandwiches? Andrew loved people, so he found this boy and gave him a friendly hand.

B. *Now, the most important one in that great crowd was the boy, but Andrew brought him.* Had there been no Andrew, there would have been no lad with a lunch.

Do we recognize the importance of leading and developing our young children for Christ? In a certain revival service, I saw a seventy-year-old man and an eleven-year-old boy come to Christ. Everyone wept at the coming of the man; no one seemed to pay much attention to the boy.

We must set a good example before young people will believe in us. The boy had confidence in Andrew. You can't fool young people. They know whether your religion is genuine. When young people believe in a person, it is usually a pretty good test of that person's character. There is a boy here. What are you doing to save him? What are you doing to teach him? Where do you lead him on Sunday? Someone has said, "Neglect the child and you spoil the future; recognize the child and you determine the future."

C. *Andrew was the ordinary man behind the scenes.* Behind Charles Spurgeon was an unknown layman. Behind William Carey was an unknown preacher. Behind Dwight L. Moody was a humble Sunday school teacher. Who can estimate the power of ordinary people dedicated to God's service?

III. Andrew brought members of another race to Jesus.

A. *Some Greeks came to the Feast of the Passover.* Everywhere they heard wonderful reports about Jesus of Nazareth and wanted to meet him. These worshipers sought help from Philip. "Sir," they said, "we would like to see Jesus." Philip introduced the genial Andrew, and together they brought the Greeks to Jesus.

Philip did not take them to Peter. He might have said, "You ignoramus, you know that Jesus came just for the children of Israel." But he brought them to Andrew, and Andrew brought them to Jesus. Jesus was stirred with joy as he saw the Greeks coming. He saw a vision of the future when all races would come to him. He saw Peter at Pentecost, Paul at Antioch, and Philip witnessing to a black man from Ethiopia. He saw Livingstone in Africa, Morrison in China, Judson in Burma and said, "And I, if I be lifted up, will draw all men unto me" (John 12:32).

B. *Each time we see Andrew in the New Testament, he is introducing someone to Jesus.* That is the reason throughout the world there are "Andrew Clubs" composed of men and women who want to win others to Christ. The church needs more Andrews.

C. *Andrew was an ordinary man with extraordinary qualities.*

1. Andrew was great in humility. He did not care who got the credit as long as the work was done. You have known sour saints who became cynical and surly because someone else got the credit. They bitterly resented the fact that another led the parade. Second fiddle is the most difficult part to play in the orchestra of life. Andrew was greatly overshadowed by his brother, but never was there any hint of jealousy or antagonism. This is a quality of a great person. He was a selfless soul concerned only with service.

2. Andrew was great in personal friendships. He had a genius for reaching out to others. People are brought to Christ on the vehicle of friendship.

3. Andrew was great in missionary zeal. He kept pointing people to Christ. This kind of evangelism—friend to friend, person to person—is the ultimate source of strength and growth for the church.

Conclusion

Tradition has it that Andrew took the gospel to Russia, Greece, Asia Minor, and Turkey. He lived to an old age and died a martyr's death, but he died telling others of Christ.

According to tradition, it was in Greece, in the town of Patras, that Andrew died a martyr. When Andrew came to the town, Maximilla, the wife of the governor, was at the point of death. Because of Andrew's ministry to the family in time of crisis, the governor's wife and brother became Christians, but the governor remained hostile to the Christian faith.

The governor was so enraged by the conversion of his wife and brother that he arrested Andrew. Later Andrew was condemned to death. To prolong his agony, he was not nailed—only bound—to the cross to die of hunger, thirst, and exposure.

When faced with the cross, Andrew prayed. A portion of his prayer is as follows: "Hail precious cross, thou hast been consecrated by the body of my Lord. I have ardently loved thee. Receive me into thy arms; and present me to my master that he who redeems me on thee may receive me by thee."

An ordinary life was extraordinarily powerful when lived in the spirit of the cross.

WEDNESDAY EVENING, SEPTEMBER 8

Title: God's House

Text: "You shall not make my Father's house a house of trade" **(John 2:16 RSV).**

Scripture Reading: John 2:13–25

Introduction

A six-year-old asked, "Why do they call church God's house? He is not there." Maybe not. Maybe so.

All four of the writing evangelists tell us of Jesus' cleansing of the temple. One account would justify study. Four accounts emphasize the importance the Holy Spirit attaches to this unique incident.

I. Jesus attended worship services.

Have you heard people say, "I quit going to church because I didn't like the way they did things"? Jesus didn't like the way they did things, but he didn't quit. The son of a pastor said, "My father was a preacher, and I got so disgusted with the way the 'wheels' treated him that I quite." Have you considered how hurt Jesus must have been with the way the religious leaders of his day treated his Father? But he didn't quit. When visiting cities and villages, he went to the synagogue. When in Jerusalem, he went to the temple. On this occasion he went to Jerusalem to observe the Jewish Passover at the temple.

The religious establishment of Jesus' day was cold, callous, legalistic, and exclusive; but Jesus participated. He sought to correct much that was wrong, but he didn't quit.

I have known people who got so pious and self-righteous that they thought they were too good for the church. People who get "too spiritual" for the church might be more "spiritual" than Jesus. That does not suggest, however, that we should not be constantly alert to any necessary changes. We should also act responsibly in trying to correct errors and improve ministries.

The cleansing of the temple was rare behavior for Jesus, and such action would probably be appropriate only for the Son of God.

II. What was wrong in the house of God?

John records Jesus' complaint: "You shall not make my Father's house a house of trade."

A. *Why the traders were there.* On the surface it seemed entirely practical: This was Passover time, and the Jews needed sheep, oxen, and pigeons for the sacrifice. The original idea was for worshipers to bring their own sacrifices, choice animals without spot or blemish. Some, however, came long distances, making it difficult to transport or drive animals and keep them in good condition. One might select the best animal he had and still it might not pass inspection when it got to the temple. Why not buy an animal near the temple? Further, only Jewish coins were to be used to pay the temple tax; thus the necessity for moneychangers. Innocent enough, right?

B. *Perverted worship.* The prophets had long since decried deterioration of the sacrificial system. "What to me is the multitude of your sacrifices? I have had enough of burnt offerings of rams and the fat of fed beasts; I do not delight in the blood of bulls, or of lambs, or of he-goats" (Isa. 1:11–13 RSV). "Thus says the LORD of hosts, the God of Israel: 'Add your burnt offerings to your sacrifices, and eat the flesh. For in the day that I brought them out of the land of Egypt, I did not speak to your fathers or command them concerning burnt offerings and sacrifices. But this command I gave them, 'Obey my voice, and I will be your God, and you shall be my people; and walk in all the way that I command you, that it may be well with you'" (Jer. 21–23 RSV). "The sacrifice acceptable to God is a broken spirit; a broken and contrite heart, O God, thou wilt not despise" (Ps. 51:17 RSV). A person could go through all the ceremony without worshiping God.

Since the people were going through the motions of confessing sin and worshiping out of a sense of duty, culture, and tradition, why not make it as convenient as possible? It is likely that the temple animal inspectors and traders worked together for profit. The moneychangers were probably extortioners. But even if all participants were on the level, when religion follows the line of least resistance, it is no longer worship.

A certain Jewish merchant left his store open on religious holidays to be run by Gentile employees while he went to the temple. He said he could worship better knowing his Gentile competitors were not getting all the business. He then confessed his personal feeling that outward worship was not worship.

III. The purpose of the house of God.

A. *It was to be a "house of prayer."* John does not mention this, but the synoptic writers quote Jesus as saying, "'My house shall be called a house of prayer'; but you make it a den of robbers" (Matt. 21:13; Mark 11:17; Luke 19:46; Jesus was quoting from Isaiah 56:7). Perhaps this is the heart of the offense. When the temple ceased to be the place of prayer, it began to move in the direction of idolatry. What does this say to us about the purpose of God's house today? What does it say to us about the priority of prayer in our worship?

B. *It was to be a center of evangelism.* Go back and read Mark's quotation of Jesus (Mark 11:17). The temple had different areas for different groups. Non-Jews could worship in the Court of the Gentiles. From the time of God's call to Abraham, God had intended his people to be a blessing to others. But the leaders had become selfish, protective, and exclusive. Guess where the traders were trafficking! In the court of the Gentiles! They lost interest in reaching out to other people, and the result was the pollution of the whole process.

Conclusion

When we cease to pray, the place of worship ceases to be a place of prayer. When we cease to evangelize, we cease to be God's people.

SUNDAY MORNING, SEPTEMBER 12

Title: The Positive Nature of Christian Love

Text: "Love is patient and kind" (**1 Cor. 13:4** RSV).

Scripture Reading: 1 Corinthians 13:1–8

Hymns: "Praise Him! Praise Him!" Crosby
"I Stand Amazed in the Presence," Gabriel
"Blessed Be the Name," Wesley

Offertory Prayer: Loving Father, we love you because you first loved us. We thank you today for the gift of your Son, Jesus Christ. We thank you for the gift of the precious presence of your abiding Spirit. We thank you for the gift of new life that causes us to hunger after you and enables us to love you and to love others. Today we come bringing gifts to indicate our love for you and our concern that a needy world experience your grace and love. Bless these tithes and offerings to the end that many people will come to know Jesus Christ as Lord and Savior. In his name we pray. Amen.

Introduction

God is eternal, all-powerful, righteous, and just. But the greatest truth about God is that God is love. Because God is love, it is possible for us to love and to be loving.

It is no accident that our foremost responsibility to God is to respond with love and that our greatest responsibility to our fellow humans is love.

The dictionary's definition of love is shallow as compared with the New Testament definition of love. In the dictionary love is defined as "art of affection, sympathetic understanding, tender and passionate affection for one of the opposite sex, benevolence." Christian love is primarily a moral love, a spirit of unbreakable goodwill and unflinching desire for constructive action on behalf of those who are loved.

Because God is love, he has created us with a desire and need for love. Everyone desires the love of others. Everyone needs to love others.

The apostle Paul emphasizes that love is the greatest of all the fruit of the Holy Spirit—greater than eloquence, intellectual achievement, faith, philanthropy, and even martyrdom. It is love that really counts in human relationships, for it is the greatest helper, healer, and teacher. It is interesting to note how that in 1 Corinthians 13 you can substitute the name Jesus for the word *love*, and it fits perfectly. Jesus is the personification of love.

Today we look at some expressions of Christian love.

I. Christian love is always patient.

Jesus is patient at all times. "Love suffers long."

We live in a day of tense impatience. We are impatient with waitresses, store clerks, family members, and even with ourselves. We have a critical need for patience.

A. *God is a patient God.* He suffers long with people.

B. *Christ is a patient Savior.* He was patient with his apostles. He has been patient with his servants down through the ages.

C. *Christ wants to help us to be patient with others.*

II. Christian love is always kind.

Jesus is kind at all times and in all kinds of circumstances.

If you and I are to be truly loving, we must live a lifestyle of kindness. It has been said that "kindness is a language that the deaf can hear and the blind can see."

A. *Love does kindnesses.* Are you kind to others?

B. *"Be ye kind" is one of the first verses that children learn in Bible school.* It is much easier to quote the verse than it is to be kind to everyone.

C. *On the Day of Judgment we will be rewarded on the basis of our deeds of kindness to the unfortunate (Matt. 25:34–46).*

Jesus was always kind. He expressed kindness at the wedding in Cana, to the widow of Nain, to the crowds he fed, to his mother by providing for her while he was hanging on the cross, and to the thief hanging next to him. May God help us to be kind at all times.

III. Christian love bears up under everything.

The *New English Bible* translates this, "There is nothing love cannot face." Another translator declares that "love knows no limit to its endurance."

A. *Love carries the burdens of others cheerfully.*
B. *Love can overlook the faults of others.* God sent his Son into the world not to condemn the world, but that the world through him might be saved. Perhaps this is one of the reasons why sinners are attracted to Jesus. He loves them in spite of their unlovely ways.
C. *Love never gives up even when the going is difficult.*

IV. Christian love is always eager to believe the best.

A. *Christian love is not suspicious.* Christian love does not act like a detective or a prosecuting attorney.
B. *Christian love is completely trusting.* Because of a great faith in God, we are able to put faith in others.

Jesus could look at a very unstable person like Peter and see in him a solid rock. Jesus could look into a woman of low morals who came to the Samaritan well and see a great witness to his saving power. Christian love has a habit of always looking for the best in others.

V. Christian love never ceases to hope.

Jesus does not give up hope for you and me.

A. *Christian love has a deathless hope in the heart.*
B. *Christian love believes that no person is a hopeless case.*
C. *No situation is without hope if you remember God and the power of his love.*

VI. Christian love endures all things.

Williams translates this verse, "Christian love gives us power to endure anything."

A. *Christian love does not surrender.*
B. *Christian love holds on and keeps on holding on.*
C. *Christian love is more than a passive resignation.* It is a triumphant fortitude in the midst of difficult circumstances. It never gives up hoping, praying, working, and believing.

Conclusion

Christian love is never an accident, nor is it automatic. It is made possible by the love of God revealed in Jesus Christ for each of us. As God's gift to us, love is the first fruit of the Spirit in the heart of believers. It grows to maturity as we nourish it.

During the coming week, let us take Christian love into every relationship of life. Use love as your approach at home, at school, on the job, and in all the difficult questions and problems you face.

God loves you. Respond to his love with faith and commitment. Let his love flow through you and be his blessing to others.

SUNDAY EVENING, SEPTEMBER 12

Title: Simon Peter: The Man Who Became a Rock

Text: "Thou art Simon the son of Jona: thou shalt be called Cephas, which is by interpretation, A stone" **(John 1:42).**

Scripture Reading: Matthew 10: 1–5

Introduction

When I get to heaven, one of the first men I want to meet is Simon Peter. I feel such a kinship with him. I don't know whether I will feel at home with John, who was so strong and loving, or Paul, who was so brilliant and unbending, but I believe I will feel close to Simon Peter. He was a mixture of strength and weakness, of courage and cowardice, of faith and doubt, and of wisdom and foolishness.

Galileans, like Peter, were often quick-tempered, quarrelsome, impulsive, courageous, emotional, and quickly aroused to adventure. Peter was a fisherman who left his nets to follow Christ (Mark 1:16–17). He was married (1 Cor. 9:5) and lived in Capernaum, which was probably Jesus' headquarters. Jesus healed Peter's mother-in-law there (Mark 1:29–31).

Peter was the leader of the apostles. Matthew 10:2 says he was "first," and the word here for first means "chief." He was not the kind of leader most of us want today—a smooth promoter, a skillful organizer, a fellow whom everyone likes. He would seem more likely to blow up than to build up the church. Yet in every list of the Twelve, Peter is mentioned first (Matt. 10:2–4; Mark 3:16–19; Luke 6:14–16; Acts 1:13).

Peter had four names. He was called Simon (Mark 1:16), and Matthew calls him Simon, called Peter. He was also called Simeon (Acts 15:14). You remember that Jesus gave him a new name, Peter (Mark 3:16). The Greek and Aramaic word for Peter is Cephas. Most people had two names in that day, their own names in their own language and their Greek names, since everyone spoke Greek. But here was a man with four names. Jesus called him "the Rock."

I. Peter resembled clay more than he did a rock.

A. *A rock is firmly set, solid, immovable, and silent.* Peter shifted easily and was never silent. He had clay feet, hands, and tongue. He had many weaknesses and made many mistakes. In Simon's becoming a rock, we see the depths and the heights to which creative love will go in making a life.

Bill Nye, famous humorist, checked into a hotel one evening. The night clerk was a rather proud, egotistical man. He was very boastful and arrogant. Nye was so disgusted that he asked, "Do you know you remind me of clay?" The man stood erect and pushed his hair back and said, "You mean the great Henry Clay?" "No," said Nye, "you remind me of just plain, old, ordinary dirt clay."

Jeremiah compared humans to clay being molded by the hand of God.

B. *Few characteristics of rock appear in Peter's early life.*

1. He talked too much. The first time Jesus foretold his coming death by way of a cross, Peter was horrified and protested loudly. Jesus rebuked him. Peter was a loudmouth; he has been called the "mouthpiece of the apostles."

2. He was overconfident. One night a violent storm arose on the sea. The disciples thought they would perish. They looked and saw Jesus walking toward them on the water, and Peter said, "Lord, if it be thou, bid me come unto thee on the water" (Matt. 14:28). Peter started walking on the water. Then he looked around, saw the rolling waves, and began to sink.

   When the disciples were sitting at the Last Supper in the Upper Room, Jesus made a prediction: "All ye shall be offended because of me this night" (Matt. 26:31).

   Peter spoke up, "Though I should die with thee, yet will I not deny thee" (Matt. 26:35).

   His overconfidence and egotism are evidences of his weakness and frailty. If we could only know ourselves! Pride is a great deceiver, and many of us have fallen because we were self-sufficient.

3. Peter misunderstood the way of Christ. Judas and the soldiers came to the Garden of Gethsemane carrying lanterns, torches, and weapons (John 18:3). Judas said, "Hail, Rabbi," and kissed him. One soldier reached out to take Jesus, and Simon Peter pulled his sword and cut off the soldier's ear. He probably was not aiming at his ear, however, but was trying to cut off his head. What courage and strength! Yet Jesus rebuked him because he misunderstood the ways of the kingdom.

4. Peter was impulsive. One evening the disciples began quarreling about who was the greatest in the kingdom. Jesus took a towel and began to wash their feet. He came to Simon Peter. Peter bowed in humility and said, "You shall never wash my feet." Jesus replied, "If I wash thee not, thou hast no part with me." Quickly, Peter swung to the other extreme, saying, "Lord, not my feet only, but also my hands and my head" (John 13:4–10).

Peter and John ran toward the resurrection tomb on Easter morning. John outran Peter; and when he got to the mouth of the tomb, he stopped, but Peter just blundered right on in to see what was there (John 20:3–6). What an impulsive, spur-of-the-moment, variable creature! He was a high-low personality, capable of great heights and great depths! He was like so many of us. One day we are on the mountaintop; the next day we are in the valley.

Jesus called Peter a rock, but Peter seemed to be more like clay— so weak, so variable, so impulsive, so changeable, so full of faults. How did he grow and develop into a rock?

II. Peter became a rock.

A. *Negatively, we can say three things:*

1. Peter became a rock because he did not become offended by a strong rebuke. Do you know that Benedict Arnold, whose name is synonymous with treason, betrayed his country after George Washington mildly rebuked him for two trivial offenses of which he was proven guilty? But Peter could take a severe rebuke and remain loyal.

2. Peter did not let a failure ruin him. Jesus was on trial in the courtroom. Peter stood out in the courtyard warming himself by the fire. Suddenly a young girl came and said, "Thou also wast with Jesus of Galilee," but Peter began to swear and said, "I know not what thou sayest." Immediately the cock crowed (Matt. 26:69–74). Peter failed, but he did not let a failure ruin him. He came back.

3. Peter did not quit because of disappointment. He was disappointed in Jesus. He thought he was to be an earthly Messiah who would lead great battalions. He thought Jesus would overthrow the Roman Empire and free the Jewish people from bondage. He was disappointed, but he did not quit.

B. *Positively, think of some reasons Peter became a rock.*

1. Peter completely dedicated himself to God. On the morning when the resurrected Jesus made breakfast beside the sea, he asked Peter, "Lovest thou me?" Three times he asked the question. Peter passed the love test (John 21:15–17). He promised to be true and to shepherd the flock.

2. Peter gave everything he had in the service of God. After he was filled with the Holy Spirit on the Day of Pentecost, he held nothing back. He preached the message of God, and three thousand were saved (Acts 2:14).

3. Peter was courageous in the midst of opposition. When Peter and John were arrested and warned not to preach again, at the peril of their lives, they went back out saying, "We ought to obey God rather

than men" (Acts 5:29). Peter was courageous in the face of trials and difficulties.

4. Peter was a man of missionary vision. In Acts 10 we see him opening the door of the gospel to the Gentiles. He saw the universal reach of the gospel.

5. Peter laid down his life for Christ. According to tradition, he died as a martyr for his faith.

Conclusion

As Peter, a man of clay with evident weaknesses, became a rock of strength by following Christ, so we can become strong, secure disciples.

WEDNESDAY EVENING, SEPTEMBER 15

Title: What It Means to Be Born Again

Text: "Truly, truly, I say to you, unless one is born anew, he cannot see the kingdom of God" **(John 3:5 RSV).**

Scripture Reading: John 3:1–7

Introduction

There has been more "born again" talk in recent years than in the previous seventy-five years put together. People have written to "Dear Abby" about it. Newsmen, psychologists, and family counselors are just some of the people who have entered the spiritual maternity ward to explore or deplore. You have perhaps been surprised at both the deep insights and gross ignorance displayed in the discussion of the subject.

Most talks, including sermons and books, center on what it means to *become* regenerated. This is exceedingly important for those who have not been born again. But our message today deals with what it means to *be* born again. A book on what it means to be president would not be limited to the election campaign, though one could not be president without being elected. A book on what it means to be married would not stop with the wedding, though there would be no marriage without it. Without criticizing sermons on "how to be born again" (I have preached many), this one deals with the resultant new life.

I. Most people do not believe in the new birth.

Once a person is labeled, the label sticks. We say, "Once a thief, always a thief"; "Once unfaithful, always unfaithful"; "Once a liar, always a liar." One man said, "The only person who allows for change in my life is my tailor. He measures me every time I go to see him."

One of the basic differences between churches and all other organizations and institutions is that church people believe lives can be changed by the power of God. "From now on, therefore, we regard no one from a human point of view; even though we once regarded Christ from a human point of view; even no longer. Therefore, if any one is in Christ, he is a new creation; the old has passed away, behold, the new has come. All this is from God, who through Christ reconciled us to himself and gave us the ministry of reconciliation" (2 Cor. 5:16–18 RSV).

II. What does it mean to be born again?

Some ideas are so intense and abstract that they cannot be expressed in mere words. We, therefore, use symbols. Jesus said, "I came that they may have life, and have it abundantly" (John 10:10 RSV). He, therefore, said to Nicodemus, "That which is born of the flesh is flesh, and that which is born of the Spirit is spirit" (3:6 RSV). He was using the mystery and miracle of physical birth to illustrate how one enters into the new life in Christ.

Paul wrote, "I tell you this, brethren: flesh and blood cannot inherit the kingdom of God, nor does the perishable inherit the imperishable" (1 Cor. 15:50 RSV). Peter wrote, "You have been born anew, not of perishable seed but of imperishable through the living and abiding word of God" (1 Peter 1:23 RSV).

A. *Through the new birth you become the person you are meant to be.* "For as in Adam, all die, so also in Christ shall all be made alive" (1 Cor. 15:22 RSV). Jesus does not want you to be an imitation of someone else. He wants you to be you plus Jesus. "Of his own will he brought us forth by the word of truth that we should be a kind of first fruits of his creatures" (James 1:18 RSV). I have never been first in many things. I was never head of my class in school. I was never a star athlete. I was never given an outstanding leadership award. But I am "best" with Christ if, by his power, I become the person I am meant to be.

B. *The new life is a changed life.* There was never a life so good but that regeneration made it better. An eight-year-old child said after conversion, "I feel so clean now." The mother of a child recently born again said, "We knew something had happened even before he told us. He has been different at home."

The changed life is not mere reformation. You have heard of "flying worms"? That is what a butterfly is. A while ago it was a worm; now it is a beautiful butterfly. When God transforms you, you become a child of God—"old things are passed away."

C. *The new birth means a new relationship with God.* He has removed sin (1 John 3:9; Matt. 22:37). And because you love him, you become more and more like him.

D. *The new life means a new attitude toward others (Matt. 22:39; 1 John 4:7–8, 11).*

Someone spoke concerning a church, "That's not a church; that's a hornet's nest." Someone else answered, "That's not a hornet's nest. Hornets don't sting one another." I don't know whether they do or not, but a New Testament church is to be a fellowship of love because it is made up of people who are born from above.

The following story illustrates the way Christians should treat each other: A teenage girl was in an accident. Her body was crushed, and for days no one thought she could live. She did, but progress was slow. A deacon of the church went to ask if the insurance was still paying the bills. He found it was depleted. He said, "I will find enough people in the church to help me handle further hospitalization." The doctor said, "I will make no charge for my work." Another person paid the family's transportation back and forth to the distant hospital. Another person took care of telephone bills. That is a New Testament church at work.

Conclusion

This message does not cover all there is to being born again, but it is a sample. God help us to give more attention to what it means to be born again.

SUNDAY MORNING, SEPTEMBER 19

Title: What Love Does Not Do

Text: "Love is not jealous or boastful: it is not arrogant or rude. Love does not insist on its own way; it is not irritable or resentful: it does not rejoice at wrong" (**1 Cor. 13:4–6** RSV).

Scripture Reading: 1 Corinthians 13:1–8

Hymns: "All Hail the Power of Jesus' Name," Perronet
"When We Walk with the Lord," Sammis
"All the Way My Savior Leads Me," Crosby

Offertory Prayer: Loving Father, we rejoice in your love, grace, and mercy. We thank you for your patience with us. We thank you for every blessing you have so freely bestowed upon us. We thank you for the privilege of granting to us fellowship in your kingdom's work. Today we bring tithes and offerings that they might be used in advancing your kingdom's work. We pray your blessings on the missionaries, teachers, doctors, nurses, and all who are seeking to communicate your grace to a needy world. Through Jesus Christ our Lord we pray. Amen.

Introduction

It was the lack of genuine Christian, or agape, love in the church at Corinth that called forth from Paul's heart the tremendous description of the importance, nature, and supremacy of Christian love in 1 Corinthians 13.

The church at Corinth had received many great spiritual gifts from God (1 Cor. 1:4–8). Instead of accepting these spiritual gifts with humility and exercising them with love, the members of this congregation had become proud and boastful of their gifts. Instead of demonstrating genuine love, they were permitting attitudes to prevail that hindered their fellowship with God and destroyed their fellowship one with another.

Paul insists that for them to fail at the point of practicing genuine Christian love is to fail utterly and completely. Love is to be the Christian's trademark, or badge of identification. Without genuine love, everything we do is incomplete. The more excellent way (1 Cor. 12:31) is the way of love. Love is the essential medium by which we use the gifts of God and relate to and serve others. Love is the first and the greatest commandment of our Lord (Matt. 22:37–39). Love is declared to be the first fruit of the indwelling Spirit (Gal. 5:22–23), and the command to love is repeated with a magnificent monotony throughout the New Testament. James 2:8 calls the command to love "the royal law," and Paul says that love is a fulfilling of the law because "love does no wrong to a neighbor" (Rom. 13:10). It expresses itself in genuine concern for the good of others.

I. Christian love is never jealous or envious.

Jealousy is basically a selfish concern for oneself rather than a dedication to the well-being of another. There are times when our desire for our own well-being can conflict with what should be our desire for the well-being of others. Jealousy and envy are expressions of selfishness.

We must beware lest we envy those who are gifted in other ways than we and perhaps more fortunate than we.

II. Christian love is never boastful (1 Cor. 13:14).

Love is no braggart; rather, it is humble and grateful for God's gifts and for life's achievements. As Christian love refuses to begrudge the blessings of others, so it is not eager to make a display of its own gifts and achievements.

Christian love never struts with a peacock complex. It is not arrogant or proud. Christian love never responds to others with an inflated sense of one's own importance. Christian love is never puffed up with pride and never walks with a haughty spirit.

III. Christian love is never rude.

A. *Christian love does not behave in a shameful manner at any time.*

B. *Christian love is never blunt or brutal in its comments or in its relationships with others.*

IV. Christian love does not insist on having its own way.

A. *Christian love is never self-seeking at the expense of others.*

B.   *Christian love insists on the well-being of others first.*
C.   *Christian love has a bigness of spirit that puts aside self-assertion and self-preservation in the interest of others' well-being.*

IV. Christian love is not irritable or easily angered, nor does it fly into a rage.

A.   *Christian love is not mean or high-tempered.*
B.   *Christian love is not difficult to live with.*
C.   *Christian love does not irritate or provoke others.*
D.   *Christian love does not lose its "cool."*

V. Christian love is not resentful, keeps no record of wrongs.

A.   *Christian love refuses to tolerate bitterness in the heart.*
B.   *Christian love refuses to harbor hostility toward others but instead practices forgiveness and forbearance.*

VI. Christian love is never glad when others go wrong or when things turn out badly for others.

A.   *Christian love never gloats over the sins and mistakes of others.*
B.   *Christian love never rejoices over the failures or tragedies that befall others.*

VII. Christian love never gives up hope.

It never comes to an end. It never gives up.

Conclusion

Who can practice love on this level? You can, with the help and grace of God.

1. Divine love for us begets love within us.
2. We love God because he first loved us.
3. Real love is the first fruit of the Spirit.
4. We can love God because of the presence of the living Christ in our heart.
5. Christian love is the only force that will really work in life. A poet has said, "Put love in your eyes like light in the skies. Put love in your words like the song of the birds. Put love in your mind and a true love you will find."

SUNDAY EVENING, SEPTEMBER 19

Title: Philip: God Needs Your Common Sense

Text: "Nathanael said unto him, Can there any good thing come out of Nazareth? Philip saith unto him, Come and see" **(John 1:46).**

Scripture Reading: John 6:5–7; 12:20–22; 14:5–9

Introduction

God needs all kinds of people in his service. Here was Philip—cautious and practical. He had seen the Lord but was not jumping up and down with excitement. He quietly went to Nathanael and said, "We have found him, of whom Moses in the law, and the prophets, did write, Jesus of Nazareth, the son of Joseph" (John 1:45). He had the facts and was as careful in his attention to detail as a bank teller, noting the signatures, the date of the check, the amount written. He never overlooked a thing.

Nathanael was rather skeptical. He replied, "Can any good thing come out of Nazareth?" But down-to-earth Philip did not argue or set out a case for Jesus. He simply said, "Come and see." He wanted Nathanael to see for himself.

I. Look at Philip's method.

A. *Philip was not impulsive.* He thought a thing through. When Jesus said, "Follow me," Philip waited to join the others until he had given it some consideration.

The day came when Jesus saw before him a company of hungry people who had followed him to a desert place to hear him preach. It was mealtime, and they were several hours from a place where they could find something to eat. Jesus said to Philip, "Whence shall we buy bread, that these may eat?" (John 6:5).

Instantly, Philip started calculating the probable cost of an adequate food supply for such a great number of people. In a moment he replied, "Two hundred pennyworth of bread is not sufficient for them, that every one of them may take a little" (John 6:7). Common sense told him that they needed bread and there were no bakeries nearby. He had no idea of the miracle Jesus had in mind.

B. *Philip was in Jerusalem on the first Palm Sunday.* There was tremendous excitement over the entrance of the Messiah into the capital city. Certain Greeks, who were earnest inquirers, came up to worship at the feast. They came first to Philip—perhaps because he had a Greek name, *Philippos,* which means lover of horses. They said, "Sir, we would see Jesus." They wanted to know this religious leader who had made such a stir.

Philip was as cautious in his dealings with foreigners as an immigration officer. They were not Jews. They were Greeks. What did the Messiah have to do with them? Therefore, he went off to consult with Andrew.

C. *Philip was in the Upper Room on the night of the Last Supper.* What an hour of high privilege! It was enough to lift any prosaic soul from the level of ordinary feeling to a spiritual mountaintop.

Then Jesus spoke to his disciples the words we will always love: "I am the Way. . .no man cometh unto the Father, but by me" (John 14:6). The disciples saw in his face the glory of the Eternal; but Philip, cautious, matter-of-fact, even in this high hour, said calmly, "Lord, shew us the Father" (v. 8). He wanted to see something more tangible. Many of us are like Philip.

II. Notice the limitations of such a view of life.

A. *People cannot live solely by visible demonstrated facts.* We walk by faith and not by sight. We cannot walk any other way and make progress.

This is true in marriage. No husband knows completely his own wife's love for him and vice versa. Each lives by faith.

The problem with a practical, common-sense method is that it lacks the faith that leaps over chasms of difficulty.

B. *Philip could not picture Christ feeding the hungry multitudes with five loaves and two small fishes.* He recognized the things that were visible and temporal, but he overlooked the unseen and eternal things. This man had difficulty with the miraculous.

We live in the presence of mystery. How can a person cast a handful of seeds on the ground and then a few months later, because that seed has been blessed by sunshine and rain, gather a harvest?

C. *How can these things be?* The matter-of-fact person will miss something of the mystery and grandeur and wonder of life. Just as Philip believed the five loaves and two fish were inadequate to feed the crowd, many people wonder what their meager supply of knowledge, wavering faith, or limited goodness will accomplish in the face of need. Sitting down with a pad and pencil to assess the facts and leaving out Christ, one may well despair.

III. Notice the value of these down-to-earth people for the kingdom of God.

A. *One man looks up at the starry sky and is thrilled with the sight.* He cries out, "The heavens declare the glory of God; and the firmament sheweth his handiwork" (Ps. 19:1).

Another man looks at the same sky and begins to figure out how many millions of miles the sun is from the earth and how many times greater some of those stars are than our globe. Well and good! Poets and singers with their dreams and visions have a rightful place, but so do prudent, calculating mathematicians and scientists. "Man does not live by bread alone," nor strictly by hard facts. And neither does he live by visions, dreams, and enthusiasm alone.

B. *There are people in our churches who might not stand out in prayer meeting.* Their religious experiences are so plain and simple, so lacking in romance, that they would not seem worth relating. They would not have the deep experience of John, the warm and compelling enthusiasm of Peter. Sometimes they feel that they do not really deserve a place in the kingdom. Yet these very practical and matter-of-fact people are exceedingly useful in God's kingdom. They make good administrators and are exceedingly valuable in planning and directing the church's programs. Perhaps best of all, these people, as a rule, are the first to tell how the principles of the Sermon on the Mount can be increasingly realized in the everyday practice of the work-a-day world.

C. *Bear in mind where the prophet placed his climax in his portrayal of spiritual efficiency: "They that wait upon the LORD shall renew their strength; they shall mount up with wings as eagles; they shall run, and not be weary; and they shall walk and not faint" (Isa. 40:31).* Flying, running, and walking are three modes of advance. All have their places, but most work in this world is being done by men and women who walk and do not faint. Practical, down-to-earth people like Philip are not much given to flying or running, but they can walk in the way of everyday duty and not faint. The kingdom of God is advanced on the level ground on which men and women walk humbly with God and keep doing their duties. Heaven be praised for their contribution to the community, the church, and the home!

Conclusion

Philip was not on the Mount of Transfiguration with Peter, James, and John when our Lord was transfigured and his face shown like the sun, but he was there in the valley when five thousand hungry people were fed. He was there to help meet the needs of people.

So, Philip, God needs you, and people like you who possess common sense for the advancing of his kingdom.

WEDNESDAY EVENING, SEPTEMBER 22

Title: The Art of Witnessing Conversation

Text: "Every one who drinks of this water will thirst again, but whoever drinks of the water that I shall give him will never thirst again" **(John 4:13–14 RSV).**

Scripture Reading: John 4:1–26

Introduction

A recent newspaper story told of an expert on the art of conversation who said that conversation is a dying art. He said that electronic entertainment such as television, videos, radio, and computers are filling the time that we used to spend conversing. But perhaps the chief reason that conversation is dying is that we are poor listeners. And we are poor listeners because we are not very interested in other people.

Tonight we approach the art of conversation, not primarily as a means of entertainment, but as a means of witnessing about Jesus. Since Jesus is our example, we will study his conversation with a Samaritan woman who came to Jacob's well to draw water (v. 7).

Jesus was sitting by a well resting but allowed witnessing to interfere with his rest. He not only used his rest time but also skipped his next meal to witness to a larger group.

I. Jesus initiated the conversation.

In initiating the conversation with the Samaritan woman, Jesus combined simplicity with shock. Jesus was sitting by the well with no vessel for drawing water. When the woman came to the well with a water jar, he asked her for a drink. That sounds simple enough, but it was a shocking thing for a Jewish man to ask a Samaritan woman for water. Jews refused to share food and water vessels with Samaritans for fear of ritual contamination. Besides, a Jewish man would not even speak to any woman in a public place. So the conversation began with more shock than simplicity.

Recently a young man said to three Christian friends visiting in his home, "I can't get over the shock. I just can't get over you guys going to all the trouble to come out here to talk with me tonight."

Don't be afraid to initiate a conversation about Jesus. There will be some surprises. A deacon friend got on a plane and initiated a conversation with a man about becoming a Christian. After he talked a few moments, he introduced himself by saying, "I'm L. T. Sloan, a deacon in First Baptist Church, Lake Charles, Louisiana." The other man extended his hand warmly and said, "I'm Harold Graves, president of the Golden Gate Theological Seminary." They both enjoy relating this experience.

Plan ways in advance to begin conversations with people. Plan for the Holy Spirit to give you opportunities and lead you to the best possible beginning.

II. Jesus kept the conversation interesting and understandable.

A pastor listened to a lawyer witnessing to a parole officer. He used their mutuality as a basis for some of his illustrations. A pastor had a veterinarian as a visiting partner. A dog barked at them as they approached the home. The vet knew the dog's name because the dog had been to his animal clinic. This helped to begin the conversation with the owner of the dog. You naturally make conversation flow if you are interested in the other person.

When the Samaritan woman did not at first understand Jesus' symbolic language about "living water," he proceeded to tell her about drinking water that would quench her deepest thirst forever. She used Jesus' own previous words by saying, "Give me this water." Of course, she still did not understand his symbols fully, but she was now eager for the conversation to continue.

III. Jesus made the conversation relational.

Jesus' interest in the woman led him to become more personal in the conversation. Jesus was not trying to chalk up a "decision." He desired to help this disappointed, disillusioned woman find new life. He said, "Go, call your husband and come here." If the woman was at first embarrassed by the suggestion, the compassion of Jesus reassured her. This was no mere man. He was not trying to exploit her, abuse her, or selfishly use her. He was trying to help her. When the woman said she had no husband, Jesus showed complete understanding but also reminded her that he knew a lot more about her life and was still interested in helping her.

IV. Jesus did not allow the conversation to become a religious argument.

The woman recognized that Jesus was leading into a conversation about her spiritual life, and she reminded him that she had a different religion: "Sir, I perceive that you are a prophet," but "our fathers worshiped on this mountain [referring to Mount Gerizim where the Samaritans once had a temple]; and you [Jews] say that in Jerusalem is the place where men ought to worship" (John 4:19–20 RSV). Almost every witnessing conversation takes this turn at some point. "You see, I am a Catholic and you are a Protestant." Jesus did not compromise by endorsing her religion or criticize the Jews for their prejudice. He told her that worship was not limited to some geographical center, but that worship is directed toward God, who is Spirit; and those who worship him anywhere must do so in spirit and in truth.

Whether the woman's reference to the Messiah was an effort at evasion or delay, we do not know. Jesus used it for the most significant word in the entire conversation. She said, "I know Messiah is coming (he who is called Christ); when he comes, he will show us all things" (John 4:25 RSV). He said, "I who speak to you am he." The Spirit of God gives boldness to follow through a witnessing conversation and leads to confession, conversion, and commitment.

Conclusion

Every interesting conversation does not have the dramatic and immediate results of Jesus' conversation with the woman at the well, but there will be some like this one, and that will encourage us to prayerfully develop the art of witnessing. Sometimes the sower of the seed gathers in the harvest. Sometimes it germinates and grows and another will reap the harvest. But we keep on sowing.

We rejoice that this woman not only believed Jesus herself but became a sincere and able witness in bringing others to Jesus.

SUNDAY MORNING, SEPTEMBER 26

Title: A Proper Love for Yourself

Text: "The second is this: 'Love your neighbor as yourself' " **(Mark 12:31 NIV).**

Scripture Reading: Mark 12:28–31

Hymns: "God, Our Father, We Adore Thee," Frazer
              "Take Time to Be Holy," Longstaff
              "More Love to Thee, O Christ," Prentiss

Offertory Prayer: Loving Father, you are so gracious and kind to us. You have blessed us beyond anything that humans could ever merit. We come thanking you not only for spiritual gifts, but also for the beauty of the day and for the very air we breathe. We thank you for the inward disposition that causes us to love you and that creates within us a hunger and a thirst for you. We come today bringing tithes and offerings to give expression to our faith and love and to indicate our sincere desire that others may experience your forgiving grace and come to know eternal life through Jesus Christ, our Lord. Bless these gifts to that end we pray. In Jesus' name. Amen.

Introduction

Many people suffer the pain of self-hatred and live each day with a feeling of intense worthlessness. This lack of a proper love for self makes true love for others impossible.

In the two great commandments of our Scripture reading, we find condensed into capsule form the total duty of man to God and to his fellow humans. These two commandments are invitations that enrich life, not rules that impoverish life.

The measure of our love for self is the measure of love we are to express toward our neighbor. If we have a low view of self, we will have a low and critical view of others. R. Lofton Hudson says, "When a man does not love himself, he cannot love his fellow man: and when he does not understand God's love, he does not know how to love himself" (*The Religion of a Mature Person* [Nashville: Broadman, 1952], 36).

I. Symptoms that indicate the lack of a proper love for self.

A. *Do you have a habitual tendency to belittle yourself?*

B. *Do you find within yourself a refusal to believe in your own ability and worth?*

C. *Do you regularly hesitate to attempt that which is new or difficult?*

D. *Are you characterized by a feeling of loneliness and alienation from others?*

E. *Do you find that you have a tendency to escape from reality through artificial means such as drugs and alcohol?*

F. *Are you characterized by a continuing flight from one place to another and from one situation to another?*

G. *Do you have suicidal thoughts?*

II. Why do people lack a proper love for themselves?

A. *Some experience an absence of love in early youth and come to have hostile feelings toward themselves.* It is important that a child experience the love of parents or other significant persons. Without realizing what is happening, children may conclude that they are unlovable and worthless because they are deprived of love at a time when affection is as necessary as milk. A deficiency of affection in early infancy can lead to mental illness and despair later. Children who are raised without parents often believe that they were rejected because they were unlovable.

B. *Some lack a proper love for self because they were constantly assaulted by insulting criticisms during the formative period of their lives.*

C. *Some form a low opinion of themselves when they compare themselves with others.* The Bible says that those who compare themselves with others are not wise. Each of us needs to recognize his or her uniqueness and appreciate it as a gift from God.

D. *Some have a low opinion of self because they labor under the burden of unresolved guilt.* Guilt can be a blessing from God, or it can be a horrible curse from Satan. When guilt comes from God, it is intended to bring about correction of one's way of thinking and living. Refusing to acknowledge one's personal responsibility for sin leads to a guilt problem that will bring about depression and self-hate down the road.

   Some of us have hated ourselves because we were unwilling to accept God's complete forgiveness of the sins we confessed. Some of us have been willing to accept God's forgiveness but have been unwilling to forgive ourselves. If you are unwilling to either accept God's forgiveness or grant forgiveness to yourself, it will contribute to self-hate, and it may be the result of self-hate.

E. *We can be absolutely certain that our enemy, the devil, will do all that he can to cause us to hate ourselves.* The devil is a liar and deceiver. The name Satan means "accuser." It is part of his strategy to cause people to hate themselves. Hating yourself makes it impossible for you to genuinely love God and others.

III. How can we develop a proper love for self?

A. *To properly love ourselves, we need to recognize and respond to the good news that God loves us as sinners even though he knows all about us (John 3:16; Rom. 5:8).* Nothing is hidden from the piercing, penetrating eye of the all-seeing, all-knowing God. No secrets can be hidden from him. The good news of the gospel is that God loves us and extends his grace and mercy toward us even though we are sinners.

The good news of the gospel of Jesus Christ is that through him God forgives us of all our sins and redeems us from the waste of sin (Acts 10:43; 1 Peter 1:18–19; 1 John 1:1–9).

The gospel is not good advice. It is good news for sinners. If you would love yourself, try to recognize the height and depth and length and breadth of God's love for you.

B. *Accept God's forgiveness and forgive yourself. (1 John 1:9).* God can be depended on to forgive us and to cleanse us from all that separates us from him. By faith let us accept this tremendous gift. By faith let us respond to the truth that God holds our sins against us no longer. Let us accept the truth that God has accepted us into his family as his dear children (1 John 3:1–3).

C. *If possible, make restitution to those whom you have harmed.* Zacchaeus sets the example for restitution (Luke 19:8). Jesus encouraged his disciples to do all within their power to make things right with those who have something against them (Matt. 5:23–24). In some instances restitution is impossible. At that point we must be willing to admit our helplessness and trust God to help us do the best we can in the future.

D. *Evaluate yourself and accept yourself as God made you (Matt. 6:26–29).* Jesus sought to help people overcome anxiety by encouraging them to evaluate themselves from God's viewpoint. He urged his disciples to listen to a sermon by the sparrows and to take a lesson from the lilies. The God who loves the birds of the air and the plants of the field loves us and will help us to be what he meant us to be if we will but trust him day by day and do the best we can. He also suggests that we accept ourselves because the agony of the anxiety will not help us add one inch to our stature or one single hour to the length of our life. Let us guard against looking down on ourselves if we are taller or shorter than we would like to be. By God's grace let us accept and love ourselves as we are.

E. *Dedicate yourself to something bigger than yourself (Matt. 6:33).* The person who is wrapped up in self makes a mighty small package. If we would truly appreciate and respect ourselves, let us give ourselves to the service of our God and to a ministry of helpfulness to others. Doing so will help us appreciate the person we are.

F. *Discipline yourself toward a worthy goal in life (Matt. 7:13–14).* The narrow gate of which our Lord speaks is that solemn moment of decision and commitment in which we choose a goal that is worth the expenditure of our time and energy. The daily voluntary self-control of ourselves toward the achievement of that worthy goal is the road that leads to abundant life in the here and now.

Conclusion

God loves you. He really loves you. He has proven that love in the gift of his Son, Jesus Christ. He continues to manifest that love through the ministry of the Holy Spirit. You can demonstrate your love for yourself by making Jesus Christ the Lord of love, the Lord and leader of your life. Come to him now and mean it with all your heart.

SUNDAY EVENING, SEPTEMBER 26

Title: James: Son of Thunder

Text: "And James the son of Zebedee, and John the brother of James; and he surnamed them Boanerges, which is, The sons of thunder" (**Mark 3:17**).

Scripture Reading: Matthew 4:21–22; 20:20–23

Introduction

James and John were called the "sons of thunder." James usually is mentioned before John as though he were the leader of the two; however, it was probably due to the fact that he was the older brother. He was a fisherman by trade and worked with his father, Zebedee, and his brother, John. He worked some with the big fisherman, Simon Peter, also. The story of his call is very simple. He had heard of Jesus and had possibly heard him speak. One day Jesus passed by when James and John were mending their nets by the seashore. Jesus turned, looked at them, and said, "Come, follow me." Immediately, they left their nets and father and followed him.

We can say three things about James:

I. James was ambitious.

A. *Ambition is a mark of a real man.* In Matthew 20:20 we find James and John coming to Jesus with a request that each be allowed to sit on one side of his throne in his kingdom.

Jesus then asked, "Are you able to drink of the cup that I shall drink of?" They replied, "We are able." We know that they did not fully understand what Jesus was talking about. They never knew he was speaking of death on a cross. They wanted to have an outstanding position, but it seemed they did not understand the real meaning of life.

Have we grasped its meaning in the twentieth century? In watching Arthur Miller's *Death of a Salesman* the audience enjoys the stories that depict ambition and courage in the hero. But Willie Loman, the main character of this drama, spent his years bluffing and pretending. His whole life proved a fraud, and he died in misery. Could it be that this play has appeal because it depicts the lives of so many in our century for whom life has no real purpose? We want greatness, but we have not counted the cost of greatness. We have ambition, but we forget that it takes sacrifice to do important things.

B. *We want to do great things, but we do not want to pay the price for them.*

1. Some churches would like to grow, but they are not willing to pay the price of growth.

2. Some of us would like to see souls saved, but are we willing to become personal soul winners that people might be won?

3. Some of us would like to see more missionaries sent out, but are we willing to give that these missionaries may go?

    People should not accept places of leadership, such as deacon, director, or teacher, unless they plan to give their best to that position. One of our great preachers said to an ambitious young man, "Do not pray for a big church, for God may answer your prayer." He spoke of the heavy burden of such a responsibility.

    Thrones are reached only by the drinking of a cup—a cup of suffering, service, sacrifice, criticism, loneliness, and maybe even death.

C. *James wished for a throne.* Look what he got: years of service, hardship, persecution—and finally, the swish of a headsman's sword. By way of a cross, he gained a crown.

    The world's idea of greatness is a pyramid with man at its peak, sitting on a throne. Jesus' idea of greatness is an "inverted pyramid," the nearer the peak the greater the burden, the heavier the load. At the cross Jesus Christ reached the "peak of the pyramid," as the burden of the world fell upon him. He was crushed by the world's sin.

> *Oh the bitter pain and sorrow that the time could ever be*
> *When I proudly said to Jesus, All of self, and none of Thee,*
> *Yet he found me, I beheld Him, bleeding on the accursed tree,*
> *And my wistful heart said faintly, Some of self, and some of Thee.*
> *Day by day His tender mercy, healing, helping, full and free,*
> *Brought me lower as I whispered, Less of self and more of Thee.*
> *Higher than the highest heavens, deeper than the deepest sea,*
> *Lord, thy Love at last has conquered, None of self and all of Thee.*

II. James was courageous.

James was a "son of thunder," a fearless, peerless prophet of the living God! Luke 9:54 tells us he wanted to call down fire from heaven and destroy a Samaritan city.

A. *James had courage to stand for Christ regardless of parental influence.* His father was evidently a very wealthy man. He had several boats and many hired servants. It is very likely that his sons' leaving the family business to follow Jesus dashed Zebedee's hopes for the future. If Zebedee did not himself come to have faith in Christ—and there is no evidence in Scripture one way or the other—it would have been hard for him to accept his sons' decision. James followed Christ in spite of parental influence.

B. *James had courage to stand up for Christ in the face of hardships and dangers.* Jesus sent out the Seventy as lambs in the midst of wolves. He warned them, saying, "Beware of men. They will scourge you; you shall be brought up before governors and kings. Brother shall cause his own brother to be put to death. Parents will turn against their children and children against their parents. You will be hated by the world." James was true in spite of difficulties.

C. *James had courage to stand in the face of death.* He saw Stephen as he was stoned to death for the preaching of the gospel. Jesus told him that one day he would drink the cup. He had the courage to go on in the face of consequences.

Would you have the courage to stand up for Christ if you were arrested and warned that if you did not deny your faith, you would be killed? Would you have the courage to be true?

When Lenin was asked how the Communist regime came to power in Russia during World War I, he claimed that it was the failure of the masses to stand up for what they believed. He said, "If there had been in Petrograd in 1917 a group of only a few thousand men who knew what they wanted, we never could have come to power in Russia."

Do you have the courage to stand up for Christ in the face of persecution, hardships, and dangers? Are you willing to stand up for Jesus regardless of the cost?

III. James was zealous.

James was aflame with zeal for his Lord. O, for men like that in the church—men throbbing with energy, abounding with enthusiasm, burning with intensity!

A. *James' zeal led him to be faithful.* He was present always with his Lord—at the raising of Jairus' daughter, at the sending out of the Seventy, on the Mount of Transfiguration, in Gethsemane, at breakfast beside the sea, and in the Upper Room just before Pentecost.

B. *James was zealous in spite of little recognition.* Some of us are on fire as long as we are in the limelight. When the light is taken away, the fire goes out. There are only a few words in the New Testament about James. Even his martyrdom seems crammed in the corner of the Bible, but his zeal continued.

New Testament Christians were full of zeal. The flood of persecution could not dampen their enthusiasm. Jails could not hold them. And their death only made the light of Christ shine brighter.

James' zeal led to his death. "Now about that time Herod the king stretched forth his hand to vex certain of the church. And he killed James the brother of John with the sword" (Acts 12:1–2).

Hugh Latimer of England, during the days of Bloody Mary, was condemned to die for preaching the gospel. As he was on his way to be burned at the stake, he thought of the fire and the light. He thought of him who is the Light of the World, of him who came to set fire on earth. He looked out into the crowd standing along the street gathered to watch him being escorted to his death. He saw Ridley, a friend, weeping, and he said to him, "Be of good cheer, Ridley, for by the grace of God we shall light in England this day a candle which shall not soon be put out."

Conclusion

Oh, that all Christians today could have the spiritual ambition, moral courage, and burning zeal of James!

WEDNESDAY EVENING, SEPTEMBER 29

Title: Who Is Christ?

Text: "Jesus said to her, 'I who speak to you am he'" (**John 4:26 rsv**).

Scripture Reading: John 4:7–26

Introduction

A woman called requesting the pastor to visit her son. He was home after his sophomore year in a denominational college. "He says he doesn't believe in God anymore," she said, "and I am so upset I don't know what to do." Such a request often follows an emotional clash and is not a good time for counseling, but what does one do?

Almost immediately Tom said, "Who is Christ? I am sure there must have been a man named Jesus who lived in Palestine, but how can you be sure that he was the *Messiah?* A lot of people have had a Messiah complex. Why all this jazz about Jesus? I think it's naive."

Most pastors know that this kind of rebellious eruption is not usually too critical. It may be an indication of a sincere search for assurance. It may be a backlash against parental discipline. It may be a reactionary response to what one thinks is superficial or inconsistent in the life of a parent. In the case just mentioned, the young man became a fine Christian, and he and the pastor were good friends for twenty years.

Who is Christ? The question is not necessarily unhealthy. Maybe every thinking person at some point raises the question.

I. Jesus himself may provoke the question.

In the passage before us, Jesus initiated the conversation with the Samaritan woman at the well.

A. *Emotionally, the woman had an open sore.* It was like a bleeding ulcer. Life had been one festering disappointment after another. Without defending her or condoning her obvious sins, it is easy to see how she might have felt she had been more sinned against than the offender. At the time Jesus talked with the woman, she had been married five times and was now living with a man to whom she was not married. Most of the important details of her life are unknown, but we do know that she was an unhappy woman.

You perhaps know a dozen like her. Some of them are generous, kind, compassionate people. Others are bitter, resentful, and defensive.

"I don't have a sweeter child among my five," said the tearful mother. "She was always so gentle and seemed to love all the family. Now she has very little to do with the other children. At times she is like a stranger to me. She never has more than one or two friends at a time, and they don't seem to last too long. She says all the rest of the family think they are better than she is, and I know that is not true. I wish someone could help her." Someone can. I know a specialist in that field. The Great Physician now is near, the sympathizing Jesus.

B. *Jesus offered help to the woman.*

1. He began by asking her for help. Jesus rested beside the well, and he had nothing with which to draw water. When the woman arrived with a water jar, Jesus asked her for a drink. He was not bound by the social customs and religious prejudices that would prevent a man from speaking to a woman in public or a Jew from drinking from a Samaritan vessel.

2. The response of the woman was normal—for her. She reacted with uninhibited surprise. She asked, "How is it that you, a Jew, ask a drink of me, a *woman* of *Samaria?*" (John 4:9 RSV, emphasis added).

3. Jesus met the woman's normal response by offering her what he alone could give. He said, "If you knew the gift of God, and who it is that is saying to you, 'Give me a drink,' you would have asked him, and he would have given you living water" (John 4:9 RSV). Jesus knew physical thirst, but he knew of a far deeper thirst and hurt.

   Our physical bodies need food and water. They get hungry and thirsty. But, even more desperately, we need the water that Jesus alone can provide. We may not know where the fountain is. We may not even know about the water, but we are thirsty.

   "Jesus said to her, 'Every one who drinks of this water will thirst again, but whoever drinks of the water that I shall give him will never thirst; the water that I shall give him will become in him a spring of water welling up to eternal life'" (John 4:13–14 RSV).

The woman responded superficially. She said, "Sir, give me this water that I may not thirst, nor come here to draw" (John 4:15 RSV). Jesus does not offer a halfway house. It is not enough to say, "I'll try to do better" or "I think I will start attending church regularly." A major operation must be performed, and it cannot be done in relays. The surgeon does not remove a little of a malignancy today and a little more tomorrow. A superficial experience with Christ may result in an aversion to the Christian faith. Temporary relief may be dangerous.

II. Jesus answers the question.

By helping the woman understand herself, Jesus helped her to understand himself better. She said, "Sir, I perceive that you are a prophet" (John 4:19 RSV). She was still inclined to argue, however. Argument is often a desperate call for help. People argue because they desire an answer. Her next argument concerned their difference in religious beliefs. The woman began to discuss the difference in Samaritan and Jewish worship. Without compromise Jesus proceeded to define true worship, "The hour is coming, and now is, when the true worshipers will worship the Father in spirit and truth, for such the Father seeks to worship him. God is spirit, and those who worship him must worship him in spirit and truth" (vv. 23–24 RSV). The woman then admitted that she knew there is a Christ, and he said to her, "I who speak to you am he."

Conclusion

There may be variations in Christian experience, but there is one inescapable ingredient: The subject must believe that Jesus is the Christ.

Suggested preaching program for the month of

OCTOBER

- **Sunday Mornings**

  The suggested theme is "The Great Singularities of Our Faith." These messages focus on the uniqueness of Jesus Christ and the great salvation that comes through him alone.

- **Sunday Evenings**

  Continue the series "Getting Acquainted with the Twelve Apostles."

- **Wednesday Evenings**

  Continue the messages based on the gospel of John. The theme could be "The Fruit of Being a Witness."

SUNDAY MORNING, OCTOBER 3

Title: No Other God

Text: "God spoke all these words, saying, 'I am the Lord your God, who brought you out of the land of Egypt, out of the house of bondage. You shall have no other gods before me. You shall not make for yourself a graven image, or any likeness of anything that is in heaven above, or that is in the earth beneath, or that is in the water under the earth'" (**Ex. 20:1–4 RSV**).

Scripture Reading: Deuteronomy 6:1–9

Hymns: "Holy, Holy, Holy," Heber
          "Love Divine," Wesley
          "Come, Thou Almighty King," Anonymous

Offertory Prayer: Our heavenly Father, we address you in the name of Jesus Christ, your Son, who taught us how to pray. We stand amazed in the presence of the creator of the universe. It is incredible that we creatures can speak to you. Yet we believe that you sent your Son, Jesus Christ, to invite us to do exactly that. Accept the gratitude of our hearts for your disclosure of yourself and for the peace that you bring to our troubled souls. We bow in your presence because you are God. We often come with many desires and many requests, but these are not an adequate reason for our coming to you. We come to you in prayer on the ground that you are God and we are your creatures. We pray that you will receive us through Jesus Christ our Lord. Amen.

Introduction

Ethical monotheism was given to the world by the Hebrews. The Old Testament is the sacred Scripture for this concept. The first commandment following God's identification of himself says, "You shall have no other gods before me."

The Hebrew patriarchs came out of a land of polytheism. The later Hebrews lived in a constant struggle with pagan religions. The first commandment not only requires that first place be given to God; it also requires that no place at all be given to other deities. Only God is God; all other pretenders are mere idols.

Our subject for today, however, is not of interest only as it regards ancient history. The Hebrews were not the only people threatened by polytheism and idolatry; many modern persons who regard themselves as Christians unwittingly could be accused of having "other gods" before him.

I. Atheism is not our primary problem.

Technically, atheism is the rejection of theism. Theism is the concept of a personal god or deity in the heavens somewhere. There are many people who on the basis of speculative reason have concluded that there is no such supreme being. This is theoretical atheism. While there are some atheists today in this theoretical category, and some of them follow the ethics of Jesus, this is not a major problem in terms of numbers.

Another kind of atheism is often called practical atheism. It designates a lifestyle of people who live as if there is no God. Usually, they do not undergird this way of life by any rational process that has rejected God; rather, they simply live as if there is no God. The classic Bible passage for this kind of atheist is Psalm 14:1. It reads, "The fool says in his heart, 'There is no God.'" The fool has not reasoned out that there is no God; rather, without thinking he lives as if there is no God.

Today's text certainly rules out atheism, but it is far more concerned with a greater threat—idolatry. Our primary problem is "other gods." These other gods do not openly give their names or otherwise identify themselves. Rather, they are content to usurp the place of God in the lives of people without running the risk of betraying their identity and possible rejection.

Idolatry was a constant threat during the biblical period. The prophets of Israel repeatedly condemned the practice of building images of wood, metal, or stone. They ridiculed the absurd practice of bowing down before something one had made with one's own hands.

God has forbidden the worship of idols even though one may worship God in a prior role. The expression "Thou shall have no other gods before me" does not merely rule out idols coming in a sequence before God; it also rejects the idea of tolerating any idols in God's presence.

In our day we are threatened by more subtle forms of idolatry. Most of us are too sophisticated to literally bow down to a stone idol, but many bow down before other material idols. We bow before the wealth we have or hope to acquire. We bow down before the public acclaim we have or seek. We bow in reverence to the materialistic idols of our society without being aware that they are really idols. Even religion can become an idol. Numerous examples can be cited from history in which religion or the church became a substitute for God.

The danger of having idols is much greater than most of us realize. When we give our allegiance to another god, a kind of blindness sets in and we become unaware of our idolatry.

II. God commands that we have "no other gods."

There are many reasons for this command. First, there is no "other" God. One reason is enough to conclude a case if it is a good reason, so perhaps I should go no further.

But we could also add that if we forsake the true God and place a substitute in God's place, we lose the whole purpose for living. Our reason for existence is grounded in our relationship to the God who created us.

Another reason we are to have no other gods is that it would put eternity in the balance. Humans are creatures with a destiny that is not fully realized in this life and on this earth. Belief in God is related to that destiny. The substitution of idols robs us of eternal life.

Further, evil always prevails under the banner of "other gods." Whatever chance we have of achieving justice in this world is dependent on our relationship to God, which governs our relationships with others. When God is not on the throne, evil prevails in individual lives and in human society. The "other gods" under whose banners people live always introduce evil or assure its victory.

III. This command is both a personal command and a challenge.

While it is a law and may hold legal authority, this command is primarily personal. It takes the form of an exhortation and a promise for individuals. It is a challenge for one to recognize the true God and to give one's life to him.

The question is "Do I believe 'in' God or 'about' God?" Many people hold opinions *about* God but give allegiance to an idol. Believing *in* God means trusting him and giving him our entire allegiance.

Can I identify my other gods? To what do I give allegiance? What stands between me and God? What values take priority over my worship and my service? To what do I give my greatest consideration and time? These questions will help us to identify our idols.

Another approach is to ask, "What is first in my life?" Jesus said, "If any man would come after me, let him deny himself and take up his cross and follow me" (Matt. 16:24 RSV). Denying self does not mean doing without something I want. Rather, it means that I cease to occupy the throne of my life and permit God to sit on that throne.

Sören Kierkegaard has defined purity of heart as "to will one thing." What is the one thing in your life and mind that comes first? Jesus said, "Seek first his kingdom and his righteousness, and all these things shall be yours as well" (Matt. 6:33 RSV). Have you and I sought him first?

Conclusion

As we come to the close of this worship service, will you consider the claim of God on your life? There is only one God who made heaven and earth. He seeks our allegiance so that while he blesses us we may be the creatures he created us to be. Is he God in your life? Or do you serve another?

SUNDAY EVENING, OCTOBER 3

Title: John: Son of Thunder Becomes Man of Love

Text: "But Jesus withdrew himself with his disciples to the sea: and a great multitude from Galilee followed him, and from Judaea" (Mark 3:7). "Now there was leaning on Jesus' bosom one of his disciples, whom Jesus loved" **(John 13:23)**.

Scripture Reading: Matthew 4:18–22; Mark 1:19–20

Introduction

Leonardo da Vinci, in his painting *The Last Supper,* pictures John as a rather effeminate person. Such a portrait does not picture the John I imagine, a son of thunder.

Dr. W. T. Conner, one of our great theologians, used to say that if you disagreed with Paul, he would argue with you all day; but if you disagreed with John, he would simply look at you with eyes blazing and say, "You're a liar and the truth ain't in you."

I see John as a young man, the youngest of the Twelve. Probably he was called while still in his teens to be a disciple. Being a fisherman, he was deeply tanned, rough skinned, and rugged. He was the brother of James, and they were called while mending their nets with their father, Zebedee (Matt. 4:20). James and John immediately left their nets and followed Christ.

John was a partner of Peter in the fishing trade (Luke 5:10). One of my seminary professors taught that Peter and John had a great fishing industry, which packed and cured fish and shipped them all over the ancient world. But John became a partner with Peter in fishing for men (Matt. 4:19).

John was a part of the inner circle; everywhere we see him, we see the group of three who were closest to Jesus—Peter, James, and John.

I. John was a son of thunder.

A. *John was a man of great ambition.* Mark tells how John and his brother came to Jesus with a childish request that one be permitted to sit at his right hand and the other at his left in his kingdom (Mark 10:37).

B. *John was a man of violent temper.* The direct route from Galilee to Jerusalem passed through Samaria, and the Jews had no dealings with the Samaritans. On his last journey to Jerusalem, Jesus took that route. He sent messengers ahead to a Samaritan village to make preparations to stay there, but the ancient enmity produced a shut door. Hospitality was refused. The reaction of James and John was immediate and violent. "Lord, wilt thou that we command fire to come down from heaven, and consume them, even as Elias did?" (Luke 9:54).

C. *John was a man of intolerant spirit.* He saw a man who was not one of the apostles casting out demons in Jesus' name. John forbade the man to carry on this deliverance work (Mark 9:39–40). Jesus gently told John to let the man be, for he who was not against them was for them. This revealed an intolerant spirit in John and earned him his name Boanerges, son of thunder (Mark 3:17).

II. John was changed to a man of love.

John became the beloved disciple, the apostle of love. Jesus Christ wrought a miracle in his life. John learned three lessons that helped in this transformation.

A. *John learned from Jesus to love all men.* Following Jesus day by day, John came to marvel at the mercy of God exemplified in Jesus' life. In John 8 we have the story of the woman caught in adultery. Because the Old Testament law commanded it, religious leaders were ready to stone this despised woman. Jesus showed mercy on her.

John learned a lesson in love when he saw how Jesus treated people. No wonder he wrote so much about love. The great love passages of John are the mountain peak passages in the Scriptures. "God so loved the world, that he gave his only begotten Son..." (John 3:16). "We know that we have passed from death unto life, because we love the brethren" (1 John 3:14). "Beloved, let us love one another: for love is of God; and every one that loveth is born of God, and knoweth God" (1 John 4:7).

B. *John learned from Jesus to be humble.* One of the greatest lessons Jesus taught his disciples was when he washed their feet and said, "If I then, your Lord and Master, have washed your feet; ye also ought to wash one another's feet" (John 13:14).

C. *John learned from Jesus to be loyal.* The beloved disciple is mentioned five times in the fourth gospel. The first reference is when John was leaning on Jesus' bosom at the Last Supper. At Jesus' trial we find him in the courtroom with Jesus. At Calvary he stood by the cross. On the morning of Jesus' resurrection, he ran to the tomb. He was also at the breakfast beside the sea.

Following the Resurrection, John shared with the other apostles the fifty days of waiting for the coming of the Holy Spirit. After Pentecost John was placed in prison with Peter for preaching the gospel. During the latter years of John's life, he was exiled on Patmos as a prisoner of the Romans. Tradition says that he was the pastor of the church at Ephesus. When John was so feeble that he had to be carried, he would always say, "Beloved, let us love one another" (1 John 4:7). And his church would ask, "Why do you always say this?" "It is the Lord's command," was his reply, "and if this alone be done, it is enough."

III. Four factors in the transformation.

A. *It was a growing change.* Some people seem to be changed suddenly, overnight, transformed from a thief, a gambler, a drunkard, or an atheist. Time played a great part in the molding of John's life. Time softened the sharp edges of his character and brought out the nobler aspects of his personality. Be patient with the ways of God.

B. *It was a personal desire.* John wanted to be more Christlike, a man of love. You can be what you want to be.

C. *Hardship, sorrow, and suffering played a part in the change.* John saw Christ die on the cross, and he saw his own brother, James, beheaded by a sword. He saw the other apostles bear bitter persecution and trials, and he suffered with other Christians the persecution of the Romans. John was imprisoned on the Isle of Patmos, where he lived through the reigns of twelve Roman emperors, and nearly all of them were persecutors of Christians.

Hardships can work for good to transform our lives. Lloyd C. Douglas, in his novel *The Robe*, describes Marcellus' visit to the village of Cana to talk with a young crippled maiden named Miriam and to hear her sing. Each evening the inhabitants of Cana and the neighboring villages gather around her cot to listen to her inspiring voice lifted in song. She attributes her beautiful voice to her faith in Jesus. Miriam tells Marcellus: "It has completely transformed my life—my singing. It instantly made me over into another kind of person....I was morbid, helpless, heart-sick, self-piteous, fretful, unreasonable. And now—as you can see—I am happy and contented."

Marcellus asks Miriam why Jesus, since he gave her the power to sing, did not also give her the power to walk.

"I do not regret my lameness," answers Miriam. "Perhaps, the people of Cana are more helped by the songs I sing—from my cot—than they might be if I were physically well. They all have their worries, agonies, defeats. If I had been made whole, perhaps they would say, 'Oh, it's easy enough for Miriam to sing and rejoice. Miriam has no trouble. Why shouldn't she sing?'"

"You're a brave girl," declares Marcellus.

Miriam shakes her head. "I do not feel that I merit much praise, Marcellus. There was a time when my lameness was a great affliction—because I made it an affliction. It afflicted not only me but also my parents and my friends. Now that it is not an affliction, it has become a means of blessing."

Conclusion

As John was changed from a violent, thunderous man to the disciple of love, so Christ can change our lives. Such a change may come gradually as we follow the example and spirit of Christ day by day. It will come if we desire it with all our hearts.

WEDNESDAY EVENING, OCTOBER 6

Title: Harvest Time

Text: "Lift up your eyes, and see how the fields are already white for harvest" (John 4:35 RSV).

Scripture Reading: John 4:27–42

Introduction

As I drove through South Louisiana recently, I was reminded that the rice harvest would soon be taking place. I thought of some friends in the rice business: farmers, buyers, millers, and workers. It is a very busy season. I also noticed men working around the cotton gins getting them ready for the cotton harvest. Soon cotton pickers would be in the fields and tractor-pulled cotton trailers would slow down traffic on nearly every road in Louisiana. Then would come the sugarcane harvest. Trucks and tractors would crowd the roads and the cane mills would be working long hours.

Harvest time is a busy time, and it is now or never. All the investment of planting, fertilizing, cultivating, weed killing, and insect fighting will be lost if the harvest is not brought in on schedule. Farming methods have changed since Jesus and his friends stopped off at Jacob's well in Samaria, but the urgency of the harvest has not changed.

Jesus had two main purposes in the events of this passage: meeting an immediate need and teaching his disciples—then and now.

I. Meeting an immediate need.

A notable conversion had occurred. In a short period of time everything in the city of Sychar had changed.

Christian workers in churches have to be prepared for unanticipated spiritual happenings. Occasions arise when all schedules must be changed and immediate opportunities met. At times longstanding programs must be canceled or postponed in favor of unexpected priorities.

A pastor was reporting some exciting recent developments to the deacons in their regular monthly meeting. Some deacons began spontaneously to report similar experiences. Before the meeting was over, everyone present agreed that a revival was about to break forth. They had a special evangelistic effort planned for some months ahead, but the pastor called the evangelist to ask if he could change his plans to come within a few weeks. He could. The deacons were so enthusiastic that they pledged themselves to visit the homes of all church members within the next three weeks. Leaders of church organizations were called together and apprised of the deacons' meeting and developments. They pledged their support. All scheduled activities were canceled. The revival became the number-one priority. Sure enough, it was an unforgettable revival experience.

In our Scripture lesson, the disciples had gone into the city to buy food for a much-needed meal. When they returned, Jesus was so excited about a woman's conversion that he had lost all appetite for food. The woman had gone back into the city to tell of her experience. Now others were on the way to the well to see and hear for themselves. No wonder Jesus said, "I have food to eat of which you do not know." A glorious emergency had arisen, and Jesus met it in a way the disciples and the Samaritans would never forget.

II. Teaching his disciples—then and now.

Jesus had called these men for a period of teaching and training. If we look carefully, we see that priority coming through in all of his ministry, especially in the signs given in the gospel of John. The disciples' preoccupation with routine matters was normal, but they had to learn that normalcy and tradition must never become fixed patterns. It is easy to become frustrated when schedules are interrupted, but history shows that this is usually when revival and life-changing events have been recorded.

Conclusion

Jesus, during his brief life on earth, made plans and announced programs for all of time and all of eternity, but he was always making momentary adjustments to meet needs. He was teaching his disciples accordingly.

SUNDAY MORNING, OCTOBER 10

Title: No Other Name

Text: "There is salvation in no one else, for there is no other name under heaven given among men by which we must be saved" **(Acts 4:12)**.

Scripture Reading: Acts 4:1–12

Hymns: "O for a Thousand Tongues to Sing," Wesley
"There Is a Name I Love to Hear," Whitfield
"He Keeps Me Singing," Bridgers

Offertory Prayer: Our heavenly Father, we rejoice in the privilege of coming to you in prayer. We recall in your Word how you appeared to men such as Moses, Jacob, and Paul. You gave them your name and invited them into prayer and fellowship. We come to you this day bringing our tithes and gifts in the name of Jesus Christ, your Son and our Lord. Amen.

Introduction

When Peter and John went up to the temple at the hour of prayer, a man who had been lame from his birth lay at the gate of the temple. He asked Peter and John for alms. Peter said to him, "I have no silver and gold, but I give you what I have; in the name of Jesus Christ of Nazareth, walk" (Acts 3:6 RSV). This man was healed and went about shouting praises to God. Peter and John were arrested and brought before the rulers. They were asked, "By what power or by what name did you do this?" (Acts 4:7 RSV). Peter's answer was that the healing took place in the name of Jesus Christ of Nazareth and that there is no other name whereby our salvation happens.

In past generations people used the word *name* to mean reputation. They would say about a good man, "He has a good name." Or about an evil man they would say, "He has a bad name." The biblical writers used the term *name* in a different and very specific sense. You recall that one commandment forbids taking the "name of God" in vain. Jesus admonished the disciples when praying to hallow the "name of God." John repeatedly states that salvation comes about by believing in the name of Jesus Christ. Now in the book of Acts, Luke says that a crippled man was healed by the power of the name of Jesus and that "there is no other name under heaven given among men by which we must be saved."

I. The name is synonymous with the person who bears it.

To know a person's name is to know the person.

In the creation story Adam gave names to the various animals. In a sense, the animals did not have their full existence until they were given names, so naming them was a part of creation.

People do not really have existence until they have a name. In a sense, their name continues even after their death. The ancient Egyptians tried to erase the memory of a wicked king by chiseling his name off the monuments he had left. They thought the destruction of the name would destroy the person who wore the name. They did not realize, however, that a name continues even though its written form may be chiseled off the stone monuments.

God is known only when he gives his name. In Exodus 3:14 God gave his name to Moses. After Moses knew the name of God, he was able to tell others about God, was able to come back to God in prayer, and was able to live for God, whose name he knew. To know the name of God is to know God.

It is interesting that in the Bible many people have a change of name when they come to know God. When Jacob met God he became Israel; when Simeon came to faith in Jesus Christ his name was changed to Peter; when Saul of Tarsus came to know Jesus Christ as Savior he became Paul the apostle.

It is also interesting to note that to speak in one's name is to speak as a representative of the person who wears the name and to have a measure of that person's power and authority. To speak of prayer in the name of Jesus is to speak as his representative and with his power.

II. The New Testament writers claimed that Jesus Christ is the full disclosure of God and only "in his name" do we really come to know God.

Jesus Christ came in his Father's name (John 5:43), thereby disclosing what God is like. When Jesus healed people, he claimed that the works of healing were done in the Father's name (John 10:25). Jesus' name was used in the same way as God's name (Acts 4:17–18), and believing in Jesus' name is the same as believing in the Father's name. Those who are saved are the ones who believe in his name (John 1:12).

There is no greater statement than "He who believes in him is not condemned; he who does not believe is condemned already, because he has not believed in the name of the only Son of God" (John 3:18).

The sovereignty of God is acknowledged by confessing the name of Jesus. "At the name of Jesus every knee should bow in heaven and on earth and under the earth, and every tongue confess that Jesus Christ is Lord, to the glory of God the Father" (Phil. 2:10–11).

III. Salvation is known only in the name of Jesus Christ.

Salvation is a relationship in which a sinner is reconciled to God. It involves the forgiveness of sins and the transformation of the sinful nature. Jesus Christ is the source of our salvation. There is no other way we can be reconciled to God and know him. "No one comes to the Father" except by Jesus Christ (John 14:6).

To wear the name of Jesus Christ is to confess that one belongs to God. Christians meet and worship in his name. Their eternal hope is bound up in the name of Jesus Christ.

The seal of eternal salvation is the name of Jesus Christ. The Christians of Philadelphia were promised victory, and it was said that Christ would write his "own new name" on them as a sign of his ownership and the guarantee of their eternal destiny with God. The martyrs on Mount Zion in the book of Revelation are identified by his name on their foreheads (Rev. 14:1), and the saints in heaven will be forever identified by his name on their foreheads (22:4).

What a privilege it is to wear the name of Christ with us. What a signal honor to be identified as a "Christian," which means one who wears the name of Christ because he or she believes in Christ. Salvation is synonymous with wearing this name.

IV. There is no other name that brings salvation.

Jesus Christ has no rivals. Numerous cheap imitations are scattered abroad like counterfeit coins and fake jewels, but the frauds are obvious in their transiency. The name of Jesus Christ lives on.

The name of Jesus Christ is the clear disclosure of God to humans. In his name we have forgiveness of sins and fellowship with the Father. His name marks us as *belonging* to God, seals our salvation, and protects us against our adversaries. His seal gives us the assurance of God's ownership and of eternal life.

Conclusion

The Christian faith is exclusive in that it does not tolerate any rivals or competitors. But, at the same time, it is all-inclusive. The gospel is to be proclaimed to all people. It is God's will that not one should perish but that all should come to acknowledge the truth. The invitation says, "Whosoever will, let him come." We who believe in him know his name and live in his name, but it is also our task to tell his name to others.

It is our privilege to tell other people the glorious good news, "for, 'every one who calls upon the name of the Lord will be saved'" (Rom. 10:13).

SUNDAY EVENING, OCTOBER 10

Title: Nathanael: From Prejudice to Purity

Text: "Philip findeth Nathanael, and saith unto him, We have found him" **(John 1:45).**

Scripture Reading: John 1:45–51

Introduction

The first time we see Nathanael, his heart is filled with prejudice. Prejudice is a strange thing. Where does it come from? Why is it so strong? Are we born with prejudice? Why are all of us more or less biased against race, color, and creed? Yet, in the presence of Christ, we are transformed from prejudice to purity.

Who was this man, Nathanael, anyway? Bartholomew is listed as an apostle in the first three gospels and in Acts. John does not mention Bartholomew, but he does tell of Nathanael. Most scholars identify these two as the same person. Bartholomew is not itself a first name. It is a distinguishing second name. It identifies a man by the name of his father, "bar" meaning "son of." So Bartholomew probably means "Son of Tolmai." In John's gospel Philip is shown leading Nathanael to Jesus. Close friendship with Philip is indicated in each case. Moreover, Bartholomew and Philip are mentioned together each time in the three gospels, so Philip and Nathanael Bartholomew were friends. In the last chapter of John's gospel seven men are mentioned as being present at Jesus' lakeside appearance. Six are known to be apostles. Nathanael is mentioned as the seventh, and it is logical to assume that he was an apostle. We do not know much about Nathanael, but when we put the several verses that we have about him together, his character clearly emerges.

I. Nathanael was a searcher of the Scriptures and a seeker after truth.

A. *The way in which Philip put his announcement is proof of that.* "We have found him, of whom Moses in the law, and the prophets, did write" (John 1:45). The clear implication is that Philip and Nathanael had spent long hours poring over the words of Scripture searching for information on what the Messiah would be like and when he would come.

B. *Nathanael was skeptical at first and said to Philip, "Can there any good thing come out of Nazareth?" (John 1:46).* He could not understand how anything good could come from such poor, despised people who lived around Nazareth.

When the Wright brothers were working on the first airplane, word of their experiments spread about Dayton, Ohio, their hometown. A local skeptic summed up sentiment when he declared, "No man will ever fly, and if any man does fly, it won't be anybody from Dayton. If any man from Dayton flies, it won't be a Wright brother!" The skeptic was wrong on all three counts. A man did fly, he was from Dayton, and he was a Wright brother. Remember what Jesus said: "Only in his hometown and in his own house is a prophet without honor" (Matt. 13:57 NIV). It is hard to think of greatness springing from familiar soil.

C. *Philip was a practical man.* He did not argue with Nathanael or try to plead the case for Nazareth. He merely said, "Come and see." A pound of demonstration is worth a ton of argument. Nathanael, being a true seeker, went to see for himself. The Bible says, "Ye shall seek me, and find me, when ye shall search for me with all your heart" (Jer. 29:13).

II. Nathanael was sincere.

A. Seeing Nathanael approaching, Jesus read his face and his heart, exclaiming, "Behold an Israelite indeed, in whom is no guile" (John 1:47).

In the presence of Jesus, Nathanael is transformed from prejudice to purity to sincerity. Jesus says, "Here is a man who is completely transparent, sincere, and honest—a true, humble man."

It is not always easy to detect sincerity these days. People work so hard at being politically and socially correct that we can't always see past the sugarcoated exterior. An experienced counselor knows that it takes weeks, and sometimes months, of patient listening before he or she will hear an emotionally disturbed person simply and truthfully answer questions about personal relationships. People have been so carefully conditioned to conceal their true feelings and say the polite thing that it is hard to identify the truth.

B. *Take the simple situation of meeting your neighbor early in the day and being greeted with a cheery "How are ya?"* Your reply would probably be something like, "Fine, thanks!" How surprised your neighbor would be if you told him the truth—how poorly you had slept the night before and how you were suffering with a backache and a nervous stomach.

Yes, much communication is designed to conceal rather than reveal the truth. Sometimes real harm comes from deliberate deception and dishonesty. Jesus said, "Let your communication be, Yea, yea; Nay, nay" (Matt. 5:37).

III. Nathanael was a man of prayer.

Hearing himself described as "an Israelite indeed, in whom there is no guile," Nathanael asked, in amazement, "How do you know me?" Jesus replied, "Before Philip called you, when you were under the fig tree, I saw you." This reveals to us that Nathanael was a man of prayer and meditation. In Palestine the houses of common people had only one room, and often when people wanted a quiet place to pray and meditate, they sought privacy beneath the shade of a fig tree. In effect, Jesus was saying to Nathanael, "I saw you at prayer, in your private devotions, in the only secret place you have."

It is not easy to find quiet time for meditation and prayer in our homes these days. We are constantly bombarded by the noise of radio or television or are interrupted by phone calls. Silence is hard to come by.

Arnold Toynbee, after an exhaustive study of the rise of civilization, believes that the creative personalities who founded the great civilizations drew their creative power from quiet time for thinking and meditation. Toynbee illustrates this with Moses on the mountain, Jesus in the wilderness, and Paul's three years in Arabia. It is in the quiet places that strong spirits are developed and great ideas are born.

IV. Nathanael was a man of wholehearted devotion.

He was overwhelmed when he heard what Jesus said. He could not understand how he could know so much about him. "This man knows not only my heart, but all that I do and think," he said to himself. Fully convinced, he exclaimed, "Rabbi, thou art the Son of God; thou art the King of Israel: (John 1:49). Nathanael surrendered and yielded completely. When he discovered Jesus Christ, none but the highest was good enough for him. Nathanael held nothing back but gave his all to God. To be a disciple is to live a life of obedience to God.

Engraved on a slab in the cathedral of Lubeck, Germany, are these words:

Ye call me Master and obey me not,
Ye call me Light and see me not,
Ye call me Way and walk in me not.
Ye call me Life and desire me not.
Ye call me wise and follow me not,
Ye call me fair and love me not.
Ye call me rich and ask me not.
Ye call me eternal and seek me not,
Ye call me gracious and trust me not,
Ye call me noble and serve me not.
Ye call me mighty and honor me not.
Ye call me just and fear me not,
If I condemn you, blame me not.

To accept Jesus Christ as Lord is to live a life of complete obedience and trust.

V. Nathanael was a man of staying power.

Jesus predicted that Nathanael would see greater things than these. "Ye shall see heaven open, and the angels of God ascending and descending upon the Son of man" (John 1:51). Four times in the gospel of John angels came to Jesus—at his baptism, at his temptation, on the Mount of Transfiguration, and in the Garden of Gethsemane. What Jesus was promising was that as Nathanael lived with him, he would see more and more of the communion of the Son with the Father and the Father with the Son.

It was a wonderful promise whose fulfillment brought great joy to Nathanael. Nathanael died from a brutal scourging at the hand of King Astyages in Armenia. In some medieval art he is pictured holding in his hands part of his own flesh. This vivid portrayal of suffering indicates something of his complete devotion to his Lord. He found an honored place among the Twelve, chosen by Jesus.

Conclusion

As we stay close to the Lord, we too can experience such heavenly nearness. Nathanael stayed with the Lord. He was still with the apostles after the agony of the cross. The man whom he called King found a cross for his throne, but Nathanael still believed.

WEDNESDAY EVENING, OCTOBER 13

Title: The Man Believed

Text: "The man believed the word that Jesus spoke to him and went his way" (John 4:50 RSV).

Scripture Reading: John 4:46–53

Introduction

Would you like to know how to have your prayers answered? The story we have just read illustrates it. Would you like to know how Jesus works? Here it is.

The man in the story was a government official of some prominence, perhaps a Gentile.

I. He had heard about Jesus.

Maybe the official had seen Jesus. Perhaps he had heard of the miracle in Cana or of his recent ministry in Jerusalem. More and more people were talking about Jesus, the genius of evangelism. The word *gospel* means "good news." The word *evangelism* means telling the good news. Of course, the good news is about Jesus. Every Christian is to talk the good news, demonstrate the power of the good news, and share financially in sending the good news. A new Christian said, "I just want to talk about Jesus all the time." That's the way it works. If the Capernaum official had not heard of Jesus, he never would have sought nor received his help.

II. He needed Jesus.

Any person with a sick loved one, especially a sick child, can understand and empathize. I recall standing at the door of the hospital emergency room when our eighteen-year-old daughter had been in a serious automobile accident. I remembered the words of the man of our text, "Sir, come down before my child dies." A sense of need for help is a necessary ingredient in prayer. If you were to say to me, "I have no need of the Lord," I would have to say to you, no help is available. If you were to say to me, "I know I need the Lord's help," I would say to you that you have made the first step toward help.

People cannot become Christians until they are convinced of their sin. However, this conviction is not hard to find. Open your Bible to almost any page and you will find the reminder that you have sinned and need the Lord's help. Even if you had never seen a Bible, your heart would tell you that you have sinned.

I have talked with people who knew nothing of Jesus. They have told me that they always felt a sense of need for something but just did not know what it was or where they could receive help. If you feel in your own life a sense of sin and a need for deliverance, this is evidence that the Holy Spirit is convicting you. The next step is yours.

III. This man asked for help.

He knew that he needed help because his child was at the point of death. He had heard of the miracle-working ministry of Jesus and had some faith that Jesus could help him. He did the most reasonable thing a man could do: He sought Jesus out and asked him for help.

This official likely walked the distance from Capernaum to Cana, some twenty miles. Who wouldn't do that in behalf of a sick child? He was sincere in his need. The Bible promises that if you need Jesus and sincerely seek him, you will find him.

You say, "I guess I just don't have enough faith." It is not a matter of faith in your faith. It is a matter of believing him. Call on him with what faith you do have and leave it in his hands.

IV. This man had a hang-up.

The official tried to tell the Lord how to answer his prayer. He said, "Sir, *come down* before my child dies" (emphasis mine). He assumed that Jesus would have to travel the distance from Cana to Capernaum and stand beside the sick child. A woman thought that if she could just touch the hem of his garment she would be healed. Often Jesus was present when he healed the sick, but this was not necessary. Don't presume upon the Lord's methods and don't try to tell him how to answer your prayers. Just let him do it his way.

Jesus knew the man's problem as well as those around him. He knew that they had a habit of seeking for a sign. He said to the centurion for his benefit and for the benefit of those around him, "Unless you [plural] see signs and wonders you will not believe." The people were always seeking for a sign. They were unwilling to take Jesus at his word. He was, therefore, saying to the man, "Don't try to tell me how to heal your son. Go," he said, "your son will live." Just turn yourself over to Jesus and let him do it his way.

V. The man believed.

"The man believed the word that Jesus spoke to him and went his way." Prayers are answered when we come to the place where we are willing for the Lord to do only what he can do and do it in the way only he can do it. You really have faith in the Lord when you are sure that he has answered your prayer in advance.

VI. His need was met.

As the man was going down, his servants met him and told him his son was living. So he asked them the hour when his son began to mend, and they said to him, "'Yesterday at the seventh hour the fever left him.' The father knew that was the hour when Jesus had said to him, 'Your son will live'; and he himself believed, and all his household" (John 4:52–53 RSV).

Conclusion

If you are willing to surrender your will now to God's, you can be sure that he will do his will in your life. Let us bow right now and pray, leaving our lives, our burdens, our future, our sins, our eternity in God's hands.

SUNDAY MORNING, OCTOBER 17

Title: No Other Salvation

Text: "How shall we escape if we neglect such a great salvation?" (**Heb. 2:3 RSV**). "There is salvation in no one else, for there is no other name under heaven given among men by which we must be saved" (**Acts 4:12**).

Scripture Reading: Acts 16:25–33

Hymns: "Revive Us Again," Mackay
        "Amazing Grace," Newton
        "Praise Him, Praise Him," Crosby

Offertory Prayer: Heavenly Father who comes seeking the lost, we express our gratitude to you for saving us. In our sins we wandered away from your presence and became hopelessly lost. But you in your grace came down to seek us. We rejoice in that salvation, and we pray that you will give us grace to share it with others who are lost. In the name of Jesus Christ our Lord. Amen.

Introduction

Salvation is God's gracious work of bringing people back to a right relationship with him. One might say it is God's rescue effort. When people realize their lostness and cry out, "What must I do to be saved?" there is only one answer: "Believe in the Lord Jesus, and you will be saved" (Acts 16:31 RSV). The Bible says that there is salvation nowhere else but in Jesus Christ.

I. Salvation is a rescue from lostness.

Every person who turns away from God or who has not known God is described as "lost." In Luke 15 Jesus tells parables about a lost sheep, a lost coin, and a lost son. In all of these stories the emphasis is on the lostness and a seeker who comes to save. The gospel story is that God in heaven sent his Son, Jesus Christ, into the world to seek and to save the lost. The mission of the church is to go into the world and proclaim the simple story of God's love so that people may be saved from their lostness.

You can understand salvation better if you have been lost at some time. Have you ever been lost in the woods, in a large city, in the desert, or at sea? I once participated in an aerial search for a man lost at sea. Day after day we combed the surface of the ocean looking for a life raft or some wreckage or an oil slick. A man was lost, and we were seeking him. Likewise, God in Christ comes to seek the lost.

II. Salvation is God's work of reconciling lost people to himself.

We need to think of salvation as God's salvation. It is not something others do for us; it is not something we do for ourselves; it is not even something we do along with God. Rather, it is God's work throughout. "For by grace you have been saved through faith; and this is not your own doing, it is the gift of God" (Eph. 2:8).

The parables in Luke 15 stress that the shepherd went looking for the sheep that was lost, and the woman searched for the lost coin. The father of the prodigal son did not go searching for the son but had been the kind of father whom the son could not forget. When the wayward son contemplated a return to the father, he was motivated by the awareness of his father's character. Again, salvation was in the seeker.

Salvation is reconciliation to God—not something we get, but a relationship with God into which we enter. People think too often of salvation in terms of going to heaven, and therefore they think it is something to obtain. A rich young ruler came to Jesus saying, "I have everything else. They tell me you have eternal life. How do I get it?" Jesus told him that if he would enter into eternal life, he would have to give away all of his wealth, take up his cross, and follow Jesus. The young man failed in this not because he had wealth but because his wealth had him. In other words, he depended on his wealth and would not depend on God. Salvation is a relationship of depending on God. It is the acknowledgment that as God's creatures we do not live in our own strength or on our own resources. Rather, we live in the strength of God. So Paul is correct in his statement that salvation is reconciliation to God (2 Cor. 5:14–21).

III. Salvation is from sin and self.

Salvation is release from the power of sin and self. Sin may be described as unbelief or pride. In the first instance, unbelief is distrusting God or ceasing to trust God. Adam and Eve came to distrust God's goodness when Satan prompted them to seek life on their own terms and apart from God. This unbelief may also be seen as pride. Pride is humankind's inordinate love for self or exaltation of self above God. This overweening self-centeredness is the very essence of sin.

Therefore, the only salvation that will deliver us from the tyranny of sin and self is the larger reconciliation to God our creator. All other efforts to break loose from the power of sin and self have met with failure; but Jesus Christ has delivered us from this tyranny (Rom. 8:3).

IV. Christian faith knows "no other salvation."

It is our command and privilege to announce the Good News to every creature. We must offer salvation freely and guard against the temptation to offer people salvation provided they will join our organization or become part of our efforts. Salvation is free in Jesus Christ. We must not add to it.

Further, we must constantly share the gospel because there is no other means of salvation. We are in a seriously responsible position. One night during the Korean War, the ship on which I served as chaplain received a message by radio that an aircraft had gone down in the sea near Okinawa. We were the nearest ship, and we sped to the scene knowing that the pilot could not survive long in the water and that we were the only salvation he could expect. It was dark, but we knew he would have some kind of light or flare with him if he had survived the crash. Fortunately, we were able to locate the pilot floating in a life jacket and holding a flashlight in his hand. I recall all too well the joy both on his part and ours as we pulled him from the water.

We, too, were lost and had absolutely no chance of saving ourselves. But God in his gracious love came seeking and saving us. Then he entrusted to us, whom he has already saved, the message of salvation for others. We will not escape if we neglect this great salvation.

V. Salvation is a joyful experience.

In the parables of Luke 15 every instance of salvation is followed by rejoicing. On the night we pulled the pilot from the water, there was rejoicing not only on his part but also on the part of all the men on our ship who did not even know him. And there was rejoicing on the aircraft carrier when they received our radio message that we had found their pilot and that he was safe. In the church there is rejoicing when someone is saved. It costs us nothing to give away the Good News, and it is like rescuing someone from the depths of the sea.

Conclusion

We are surrounded by lost people, and we have the message of salvation. These lost people have no hope for salvation other than our message. Let us immediately pledge to share that faith and to rejoice when the lost are saved.

SUNDAY EVENING, OCTOBER 17

Title: Thomas: Changed from Doubt to Faith

Text: "Except I shall see in his hands the print of the nails, and put my finger into the print of the nails, and thrust my hand into his side, I will not believe" **(John 20:25).**

Scripture Reading: John 20:24–29

Introduction

We often judge people by one mistake. We never let them forget it. Further, we never let the world forget it. When we think of David, we think of his sin. We forget what a great man he was in spite of his failure. When we think of Jacob, we think of how he stole his brother's birthright. When we think of Peter, we remember his denial. Shakespeare said, "The evil that men do lives after them. The good is oft interred with their bones." This is what happened to Thomas. No doubt, he showed great faith many times, but we remember him because of his doubt. Today when someone is skeptical, we call that person a doubting Thomas. In reality Thomas was one of the most loyal and steadfast apostles among the Twelve. How many times we have wrongly judged someone!

I. We know that Thomas was skeptical by nature.

A. *Thomas believed with much difficulty.* One day when Jesus was preaching far from Bethany on the other side of the Jordan, his friend Lazarus became seriously ill. In great haste Lazarus' sisters, Mary and Martha, sent for Jesus to come and heal him. When word of Lazarus' sickness reached Jesus, he deliberately lingered for two days. The apostles, remembering the threat of mob action on their last trip to Jerusalem, presumed that was the reason. However, at the end of two days, Jesus surprised them by announcing that he was departing for Bethany. They protested, saying, "The Jews of late sought to stone thee; and goest thou thither again?" (John 11:8). Jesus answered, "Lazarus is dead. And I am glad for your sakes that I was not there, to the intent ye may believe; nevertheless let us go unto him" (vv. 14–15). Thomas responded, "Let us also go, that we may die with him"

(v. 16). His comment seems to reveal excessive pessimism. He could see nothing but disaster ahead. Melancholy marked him.

B. *We must hasten to add that some of the most creative spirits who have ever lived have been of this nature.* Georgia Harkness, a theologian and author, describes her personal struggle with depression in *The Dark Night of the Soul.* She tells how she came through the valley to find strength and victory in her experiences. In the Scriptures we find expression of this temperament in Job, David, Elijah, and Jeremiah. If Thomas was melancholy, he had plenty of company.

C. *Again, when Jesus sought to assure the disciples of eternal life, the spirit of Thomas was revealed.* "I go to prepare a place for you. And if I go and prepare a place for you, I will come again, and receive you unto myself" (John 14:2–3). Thomas broke in, "Lord, we know not whither thou goest; and how can we know the way?" (John 14:5). Thomas could not accept things without questioning them. He was a realist who wanted to be sure.

D. *Thomas utterly refused to believe the Resurrection.* Even after the other disciples told him that they had seen the Lord, Thomas said, "Except I shall see in his hands the print of the nails. . .I will not believe" (John 20:25). Thomas had to see for himself. He was the last to concede the resurrection of Christ from the dead.

Have you doubted? Most of us have. The psalmist cried out, "How long wilt thou forget me, O LORD, for ever? how long wilt thou hide thy face from me?" (Ps. 13:1).

Frederick W. Robertson of Brighton, England, described his wrestling with doubt: "It is an awful moment when the soul finds that the props on which it has blindly rested, are rotten, when it begins to doubt whether there is anything to believe at all. It is an awful hour when life has lost its meaning, when the grave appears to be the end, when human goodness is nothing but a name, when the sky above is a dead expanse from which God himself has disappeared." In the darkness of the night, Robertson struggled to find faith. He found it and became one of the greatest preachers in the British Empire.

II. Thomas wanted to believe.

There is a difference between honest and dishonest doubters. Some people just do not want to believe. They prefer a life of ungodliness. They make up excuses and blame others as a cover for their own dishonesty.

This was not the spirit of Thomas. Thomas wanted to believe. He wanted to be sure. Common sense says there are seven thousand stars visible to the naked eye, but astronomers have counted twenty million stars. Thank God someone doubted what could be seen with the naked eye!

III. Thomas found sympathy from Jesus.

A. *Christ blames no one for wanting to be sure.* Jesus did not condemn Thomas for his doubts. Jesus knew that once Thomas fought his way through the wilderness of his doubts, he would be the surest man in Christendom. Jesus never says, "You must have no doubts," but rather, "You must struggle with your doubts until you reach certainty."

Jesus appeared again and said to Thomas, "Reach hither thy finger, and behold my hands" (John 20:27). Jesus spoke to him as a sincere disciple whose faith was weak, not as one with an evil heart of unbelief. Thomas's answer was immediate. He fell down prostrate at Jesus' feet and exclaimed with a warm, passionate cry of joy, "My Lord and my God!" His doubts vanished in the presence of the living Christ like morning mist in the sunlight.

B. *Thomas has given assurance to the world.* His confession was noble—the most advanced, in fact, made by any of the Twelve during the time they were with Jesus. The greatest doubter attained the fullest and firmest belief. Thomas declared his belief in the miraculous by proclaiming, "The One who was dead is alive! This One who was crucified has become my Lord!" He acknowledged Jesus as the Christ.

Where would we be if it were not for the doubters? Galileo dared to doubt that the earth stood still. Columbus dared to doubt that the world was square. The Wright brothers dared to doubt that they could not fly. Revolutionary doubters have changed the world. Thus, Tennyson could say, "There lives more faith in honest doubt, believe me, than in half the creeds." Doubts stimulate one's faith. Without it, faith becomes inactive and stagnant.

A merchant of exotic fish ordered a barrel of goldfish. Upon arrival, he found the packer had included a small catfish. When the merchant complained, the packer explained, "The catfish aggravates the goldfish en route. Otherwise, they would grow lazy, sluggish, and die." Doubt helps keep our faith strong, active, and vital.

IV. Thomas emerged stronger because he doubted.

His faith became strong and vibrant. Tradition has it that he took the gospel to India. Tertullian said about the early Christians, "No man would be willing to die unless he knew he had the truth." They would not have died for a dream. They would not have been loyal to a figment of the imagination. Thomas emerged victorious and became faithful unto death in his witness for God.

Tennyson was one of those who wrestled with doubt until it resolved into faith. His longest poem, *In Memoriam,* is a collection of 131 separate poems written along the way. They describe the agonies through which he passed in his doubts. They climax with this poem of faith:

> *Strong son of God, immortal love,*
> *Whom we that have not seen thy face,*
> *By faith, and faith alone, embrace,*
> *Believing where we cannot prove,*
> *Thou seemest human and divine,*
> *The highest and holiest manhood, Thou,*
> *Our wills are ours, we know not how,*
> *Our wills are ours, to make them thine.*

We emerge victorious as we wait upon God to reveal himself.

Conclusion

Do you have doubts? Keep doing the best you know right where you are. Stay faithful. Keep trusting, following, serving, praying. God will reveal himself. He will show you the nail prints.

WEDNESDAY EVENING, OCTOBER 20

Title: Christian Attitudes Toward Sin

Text: "Jesus said, 'Neither do I condemn you; go, and do not sin again'" **(John 8:11 RSV)**.

Scripture Reading: John 8:1–11

Introduction

It is one thing to have clear-cut opinions about sin and another thing to have a Christian attitude toward persons guilty of sin. The focus of this message is to help us in our attitude toward those who are admittedly guilty of sin.

I. The religious leaders' attitude.

Jesus was in the temple teaching the people when the scribes and Pharisees rushed in with a woman in their custody whom they had caught in the act of adultery. No reference is made to the man. They reminded Jesus that Moses' law commanded that such be stoned. They then asked him, "What do you say?"

The scribes and Pharisees played an important role in the Jewish community. They gave their lives to the study and practice of the law. Their problem was that they usually missed the meaning of the moral law because they were more enamored with their profession than they were with people. They were more legal than loving.

A. *Their attitude toward Jesus.* The scribes and Pharisees' hateful purpose was to bait and embarrass Jesus. It was an apparently good trap, because it would be characteristic of Jesus to show mercy toward the woman. If he "swallowed the bait," they would have him "hooked" in his attitude toward Moses' law, which he said he had come to fulfill. What if he said, "Stone her"? He would be unfaithful to his mission of mercy. Either way they had him.

Why were the Jewish religious leaders always picking on Jesus? Why the continuous envy, jealousy, and scorn? These men should have been more sensitive to the Messiah and his teachings. Would you say that any religious leader who becomes self-centered and defensive begins to lose his sense of mission?

B. *Their attitude toward sin.* Have you ever read in any old church records about people being excluded from the church? I have. I also remember people who spent their lives outside the fellowship of the church rather than embarrassing their families by trying to reunite with the church.

These religious leaders were not hurting because of the woman's sins. They were cold, compassionless, unforgiving, and judgmental. We had better keep an eye on people who enjoy discussing other people's sins.

C. *Their attitude toward the woman.* The attitude of these religious leaders toward the sinning woman was dehumanizing, hard, and ruthless. Their purpose was to manipulate Jesus into incriminating himself, and they felt justified in using the woman as a mere tool in their hands. They had not learned you cannot love God and hate your neighbor.

II. The woman's attitude.

Nothing is said in the story about the woman's background. We do not know if her motive was economic, social, or deliberately sinful. We do not know the woman's attitude toward being caught and being reported. Of course, she was embarrassed. She may have been defiant and openly resentful. She may have appeared bold and aggressive. She may have been weeping, or very cool.

A teenage girl was brought to the pastor by her parents and grandmother. The grandmother had "caught her in the act." Of course, they were all hurt, but the girl was defiant. She was not sorry. "I love him and will do it again," she said. Through the patient guidance of a pastor over a period of weeks, the Lord began to get to the girl. She became a fine Christian girl with a positive Christian influence in high school, did well in college, and now has a happy family. We could hope this was the case with the woman in our story.

III. Jesus' attitude.

The point of the story is Jesus' attitude. Jesus was on the spot. Would he defend the law of Moses so there would be no question about his orthodoxy? Was it enough to say, "The woman brought it on herself; she deserves to be punished"?

Jesus responded to the woman with compassion, tenderness, and concern. Stoning was not the answer. Sin must be punished, but in this case the punishment came wrapped in the same package as the sin. She had already been punished. Now she needed love, understanding, and forgiveness. Jesus never condoned sin, and he never compromised. The physician does not condone disease. He despises it and works to prevent it. But when it is there before him, he treats it. "God sent the Son into the world, not to condemn the world, but that the world might be saved through him" (John 3:17 RSV).

Conclusion

With bowed head Jesus wrote with his finger in the sand. He who "bore our sins in his body on the tree, that we might die to sin and live to righteousness" suffered for this woman's sin also. Sin did not cool his compassion nor freeze the fountains of his love. We wish we knew everything he said to her. We wish we knew what he wrote on the ground. We wish we knew what happened to her. We could also hope that the accusing scribes and Pharisees joined the small group of religious leaders who had begun to follow him. He loved them, too.

Aren't we glad Jesus died to clean us up and make us sons and daughters of God?

SUNDAY MORNING, OCTOBER 24

Title: No Other Gospel

Text: "I am astonished that you are so quickly deserting him who called you in the grace of Christ and turning to a different gospel—not that there is another gospel, but there are some who trouble you and want to pervert the gospel of Christ. But even if we, or an angel from heaven, should preach to you a gospel contrary to that which we preached to you, let him be accursed. As we have said before, so now I say again, If any one is preaching to you a gospel contrary to that which you received, let him be accursed" (Gal. 1:6–9 RSV).

Scripture Reading: Galatians 1:1–10

Hymns: "My Redeemer," Bliss
"To God Be the Glory," Crosby
"O for a Thousand Tongues to Sing," Wesley

Offertory Prayer: Our heavenly Father, we express our profound gratitude to you for the good news of salvation in Jesus Christ. We are so grateful that he was willing to give his life for us and that you raised him from the dead. We express our thanks for that good news, and we pray for your power as we seek to give it to others. For Jesus' sake. Amen.

Introduction

The Christian word *gospel* means "good news." It is the good news of God's salvation in Jesus Christ. The church was ordered to proclaim this good news to every creature in the world. In short, it means simply this: Through Jesus Christ, God has provided salvation from sin for every creature in the world. This is such good news to all creatures that those who believe in him continually proclaim it at every opportunity.

I. The content of the gospel.

Since preachers are known for preaching the gospel, we mistakenly think that everything they preach is the gospel. Regrettably, some preachers do a great deal of preaching yet rarely preach the gospel.

Several passages in the New Testament summarize the content of the gospel. One such passage is 1 Corinthians 15:3–8. Several themes are emphasized in this passage. (1) Paul did not originate the gospel but received it from others and delivered it to the Corinthians. (2) "Christ died for our sins in accordance with the scriptures." (3) "He was buried." (4) "He was raised on the third day in accordance with the scriptures." (5) He appeared to numerous witnesses. In these statements the gospel is summarized. All other teaching is illustration and explanation.

II. The true gospel was challenged early by religious legalism.

Religion is a human construction of religious beliefs and reason by which people try to please God. It includes worship routines, rituals, moral judgments, and doctrinal considerations. Such religious systems provide a helpful structure by which people live, but they often neglect the simple faith in God for which they were created.

The Old Testament religion of Judaism was a preliminary revelation of God through which God prepared his people for the full revelation of the coming of Jesus Christ. That religious system became so deeply entrenched in the minds of its adherents and particularly their leaders that, when Jesus came, they did not wish to submit to his lordship. Some members of the early church in Jerusalem were so deeply committed to the religious rituals of Judaism that they missed the simple beauty of the gospel of salvation by faith in Christ. They sent representatives into the Gentile area where Paul preached and insisted that the Gentile converts had to be circumcised according to the law of Moses and had to keep the other religious require-ments of that law or they could not be saved.

Paul had preached the Christian gospel that Jesus Christ died for our sins according to the Scriptures, that he was buried, that he was raised from the dead, and that our salvation came to us through faith in him. Paul cham-pioned this gospel in his letter to the Galatians and rather fully explained it in his letter to the Romans. The great conference in Jerusalem in A.D. 49 was the scene in which the early church struggled with this understanding of the gospel. The church agreed with Paul that salvation was by faith in Jesus Christ and that he had been preaching the true gospel. However, the church did not completely let go of its additional religious requirements.

This early challenge to the Christian gospel was particularly severe because its proponents could cite Old Testament Scripture for their case. The New Testament had not yet been written. Paul saw the danger of the Christian gospel being perverted by a mixture of legalistic requirements. He saw that the gospel of Jesus Christ was the good news that salvation was avail-able to everyone on the basis of faith in Jesus Christ. He correctly saw that perversions of the gospel in the form of additional requirements would sub-vert the Christian faith.

In the passage before us, Paul insisted that we keep the gospel simple and pure.

III. Salvation is by the grace of God through faith in Jesus Christ.

The gospel Paul preached always stressed the priority of the grace of God in sending Jesus Christ to die for our sins and believing in Christ as the way of salvation. In Ephesians 2:8 he said, "By grace you have been saved through faith; and this is not your own doing, it is the gift of God" (RSV).

No one should understand Paul's gospel to require less of people than the law had required. Paul's gospel understands faith to be the trust, or com-mitment, of one's life to God. It brings about a transformation of the life of the person who believes so that Paul refers to this new person as a "new cre-ation" (2 Cor. 5:17).

John referred to this experience as a new birth, thereby insisting that a Christian is a new person and lives in a new way. Jesus Christ invited people to follow him saying, "My yoke is easy" (Matt. 11:28–30). But Jesus did not mean that the ethical requirements were less; rather, he meant that his fol-lowers followed out of faith and love and that they obeyed him because of their changed nature. In other words, he did not lay down legalistic require-ments that were galling; rather, he endowed his disciples with love out of which they served both God and man.

Martin Luther began the Protestant Reformation by rediscovering Paul's gospel that justification is by faith in Jesus Christ and not by observing the ceremonial law. In Paul's day the ceremonial law included circumcision.

In Martin Luther's day it involved obedience to the rituals and requirements of the medieval church. When Martin Luther rediscovered this true gospel, his own life was transformed and he began to proclaim this gospel so that the lives of others were transformed.

The church is forever in danger of adding requirements to the gospel, thereby changing it. Our Galatians text states in an exceedingly strong fashion Paul's belief that anyone who would preach a contrary gospel should come under a curse. He was so convinced that this is the true gospel that he insisted there is no other gospel.

IV. "Other gospels" continue to challenge the gospel of Christ.

Legalistic religion is a perennial challenger of the true gospel. Even those in the Christian church who have known the joy of salvation by faith in Jesus Christ repeatedly insist on converting Christian faith into a set of rules by which other people are supposed to live. This always leads to frustration on the part of both the rule maker and the rule breaker. Salvation is a personal assurance that people have only when they commit their lives to Jesus Christ in faith.

Then there is always the gospel of good works. The do-gooders reconstruct the Christian faith around the doing of certain good things. No one would argue that these things are not good nor that one should not do good works. The danger comes, however, if we change the order and think of good works as bringing about salvation rather than thinking of good works as the product of salvation.

In the medieval ages the church made the mistake of replacing the gospel with a system of church obedience. The church worked out rules for human living and subjected the adherents to a rather rigid discipline of religious ritual. This replaced the gospel for most of the people in that era. Churches throughout the ages have made the same mistake and come up with a so-called gospel of salvation by obedience to the church. Usually this takes the form of emphasizing certain moral or ethical practices that are urgent at the time. In its attempt to save people from the injury of certain social sins, the church rebuilds its teaching and leaves the impression that the gospel of salvation requires doing certain moral things and avoiding others. This is another gospel, the substitute gospel, a false gospel, and a rival to the true gospel.

V. The Good News must be proclaimed in its purity and fullness.

The gospel of Jesus Christ is the beautiful but simple story that God sent his Son, Jesus Christ, into the world to save sinners. Christ died on the cross for our sins. He was buried. God raised him from the dead, thereby confirming his work in and through Jesus Christ. Sinners hearing the gospel come under the convicting power of the Holy Spirit. If they trust in Jesus

Christ, their sins are forgiven and their lives are saved. This gospel constitutes the preaching of the church and the subject matter that we are to share with unbelievers. It opens the door to eternal life and is such good news that we cannot keep it to ourselves.

Conclusion

If someone were to discover a cure for cancer that would remove forever the fear and threat of that dread disease, every newspaper and radio and television station in the world would proclaim it. It would be the kind of good news no one could keep secret. In Jesus Christ there is even greater good news: the good news of eternal salvation for everyone who believes. That is the gospel. There is no other.

SUNDAY EVENING, OCTOBER 24

Title: Matthew: Your Life Can Be Significant

Text: "As Jesus passed forth from thence, he saw a man, named Matthew, sitting at the receipt of custom: and he saith unto him, Follow me. And he arose, and followed him" **(Matt. 9:9).**

Scripture Reading: Mark 2:14; Luke 5:27–29

Introduction

A feeling of insignificance is prevalent everywhere today. People are overwhelmed by scientific and technological discoveries. It is an age of depersonalization. People are cogs in a machine. But Christ comes to say that life can be significant. Think of the marvelous possibilities of life in Christ for you. Visualize the greatest success that could come to you. Matthew is an example of one who went from feeling insignificant to feeling valued and dignified.

Matthew was a tax collector. Now, tax collectors are not very popular in most countries, but in Palestine this was especially true. Collection of taxes was farmed out by the Roman government. A man would pay the government a fixed sum for the right to collect taxes in a given district; then he would take all he could get.

Further, most tax collectors were Romans. The patriotic loyal Jew refused to hold such an office. Now and then, however, one moved by greed would take the office of tax collector in order to enrich himself. Such was Matthew.

The scribes and Pharisees passed by the tax collectors and would not even look in their direction. Small boys whose actions frequently expressed the thinking of their elders threw stones at them. The more courageous spat on their garments and then scampered into the narrow alleys before they could be caught.

No wonder Matthew felt insignificant. He had a sense of guilt about his work. He was ostracized from his people. He was so despised and hated by others that he began to despise and hate himself.

One day as Matthew sat at the gate scanning his ledgers a shadow fell across his book. He lifted his head to see Jesus Christ looking kindly down at him. There was something in that look—the eyes looked him through and through; and in that glance Matthew saw his destiny.

I. Jesus Christ saw something worthy in Matthew.

A. *Christ saw a man with hidden hungers and divine desires.* The people saw Matthew the sinner; Christ saw Matthew the saint. The people saw Matthew the greedy publican; Christ saw Matthew the author and useful disciple. Christ saw the best in people and was always bringing it out. He called Matthew not for what he was but for what he could become. Christ sees something in you. Your life can be significant!

The gospel of Christ offers hope for all. There is a chance for every person—the most unlikely, unlovely, and sinful—to be the person Christ sees. A life may be covered with the dust and debris of sin, but underneath it all is a soul for whom Christ died.

B. *Never was there a more unpromising disciple than Matthew.* People probably thought Christ's choice of Matthew as a disciple was unwise. In modern times it would be as if the Community Fund elected as chairman a person just released from prison for embezzling funds from a bank.

II. Matthew needed Christ.

A *Matthew recognized his need.* He was sick and tired of his lifestyle and wanted to change. One who is great enough to make life can also remake it. Christ can do for you what no one else can do. He can cure the love of gambling. He can put out the fires of lust. He can take away the love of drink. He can take away lying, cheating, and cursing. He can remove pride and prejudice and jealousy. Many of us have said, "I would give anything to change. I've tried, but I can't." There is hope, for Jesus Christ can transform your life.

B. *Matthew tells the story of his own conversion.* In Matthew 9 Matthew tells how Jesus healed the man who was sick of the palsy, the woman who had been ill for twelve years, and the two blind men; but right in the midst of these great miracles, Matthew tells how he was called to follow Christ (Matt. 9:9).

Do you know yourself? Do you have any idea of the power, glory, and greatness that are latent within you? Christ knows what you can be. The marvelous thing about Christ is that he did great things with the most unlikely people. He saw possibilities in a prodigal son, in a woman taken in adultery, and in a thief dying for his crimes. He was constantly giving people power to become new creatures.

C. *When Christ touches a life, the instruments of evil become instruments for good.* The voice of blasphemy becomes the voice of love; the hand of hate becomes the hand of mercy. Eyes that seek evil become eyes that seek good. Every talent, if properly dedicated, can be an instrument for God's use. A sense of significance comes in doing what we can for the Master.

III. Christ needed Matthew.

A. *The first thing Matthew did when he became a follower of Christ was to make a feast and invite all his friends to meet Jesus.* He did not say, "Come around the synagogue next Sabbath and sit in my pew." He invited them to come to his home the next night and sit at his table. Jesus needed a man like Matthew, for he could use his method of doing Christian work.

B. *In the book of Acts we find Matthew's name on the list of the twelve apostles.* It is thus assured that Matthew remained loyal to Jesus during his lifetime and during the crisis days of the Crucifixion. Matthew had left all to follow Christ—his business, his money, his way of life. None of the apostles had given up more to be an apostle. Matthew, once despised of all men, became the first man to present to the world a written account of Jesus' life and teachings.

C. *According to tradition, Matthew died a martyr.* Tradition has it that he first preached the gospel in Judea to his own countrymen and later was condemned to die for preaching the gospel. He was faithful to the end.

D. *Christ needed a man like Matthew who would work to save the sinful, needy, and neglected.* A few years ago a young minister in a small town near New York City saw that the people who attended his church already believed in Christ and tried to live Christian lives. He was preaching to the converted while he saw the unchurched people go by saying, "We're not good enough. We're sinners." One Saturday the young minister inserted in the town paper a notice that read like this: "You are invited to a sinner's service. The service at the Downtown Church next Sunday will be exclusively for sinners. The saints are all asked to stay away." Do you know what happened? The following Sunday the church was filled to capacity. The young minister told the people they were the ones for whom Christ came, lived, died, and rose again.

Conclusion

Jesus said, "I am not come to call the righteous, but sinners to repentance" (Matt. 9:13). Such a work makes life significant. Let us give ourselves to reaching the poor, needy, sick, abused, addicted, burdened, problem-ridden, and untouched by the church that we may make our lives count.

WEDNESDAY EVENING, OCTOBER 27

Title: Eyes That Cannot See

Text: "Jesus said, 'For judgment I came into this world, that those who do not see may see, and that those who see may become blind'" **(John 9:39 RSV)**.

Scripture Reading: John 9:1–11, 30–41

Introduction

Jesus didn't have much time for idle speculation. It is much easier to philosophize and theorize than to minister or evangelize. Jesus saw the blind man as he always sees people, through eyes of compassion and empathy.

The Bible teaches that all suffering cannot be explained as caused by sin. The issue is not how the man got blind but what God's people were doing about it. Physical blindness is not nearly as serious as covering our eyes with a veil of theological speculation. Self-imposed darkness is the worst kind.

I. Failure to see people.

A. *The disciples saw a blind man.* They did not see him as a child of God. Most people in a certain small town saw Frank Rogers as a drunk. His family was poverty personified. The church bought clothes and brought the children to church. Some of them eventually became Christians. Then Frank's wife became a Christian. Later Frank became a Christian. The total lifestyle of the family began to change. I visited the community twenty years after Frank became a Christian. Frank had died, and his widow was living in a nice brick house across the road from the shack they had once lived in. The children were married and had good jobs. The Lord had not seen Frank as a drunk but as a man who needed help.

B. *The Pharisees saw a healed blind man as a threat to their system.*
  1. Jesus healed him, and the Jews saw a threat to their deteriorated religious structure.
  2. The man was healed on the Sabbath day. The kneading of the mud made with spittle was a violation of exaggerated Sabbath rules. The Pharisees preferred that the man spend his lifetime in total darkness rather than admit traditional darkness on their part.

II. Failure to see Jesus.

The worst form of blindness is to refuse to see Jesus, who came to defy darkness.

A. *The disciples were blinded by their own dullness.* They had already witnessed Jesus' compassion and power many times, but still they had a limited vision.

A newspaper cartoon pictured a man stumbling along in debris trying to find his way with a dim lantern. He could only see a foot or two ahead. Above him in the picture was Christ saying, "I am the Light of the World." He was blinded by his own efforts rather than looking up to Jesus.

B. *The Pharisees were blinded by prejudice.* Jesus was the "true light that enlightens every man." "He was in the world, and the world was made through him, and yet the world knew him not. He came to his own home, and his own people received him not" (John 1:9–11). The Pharisees were demonstrating exactly what John had said. They were so blinded by prejudice that they could not recognize the Son of God when he was among them.

C. *The parents were blinded by fear.* The parents of the man born blind demonstrated unusual insight when the Pharisees came to them with trick questions to entrap them. "Is this your son, who you say was born blind? How then does he now see?" They asked three questions in one. The parents answered two of the questions: "We know this is our son, and that he was born blind." The third question they evaded. "How he now sees we do not know, nor do we know who opened his eyes. Ask him; he is of age, he will speak for himself." They were wise in their evasiveness if they wanted to remain in the Jewish faith, because "the Jews had already agreed that if any one should confess him to be Christ, he was to be put out of the synagogue."

III. The blind can see Jesus.

After working with a blind girl for several days, a missionary decided that blind people may see more than those who seem to see, because they don't see all the obstructions.

Jesus found the man born blind and asked him, "Do you believe in the Son of man?" The man answered, "Who is he, sir, that I may believe in him?" When Jesus identified himself, the man said, "Lord, I believe." Jesus said, "For judgment I came into this world, that those who do not see may see, and that those who see may become blind." When the Pharisees asked, "Are we also blind?" Jesus answered, "If you were blind, you would have no guilt; but now that you say, 'We see,' your guilt remains."

Conclusion

The man healed by Jesus got what he needed most but lost his profession as a beggar, his home, and his church (the Jewish synagogue). He gained eternal life but lost what had seemed important before. The Pharisees kept what they had—blind prejudice, selfishness, and contempt—but lost Jesus and eternal life.

SUNDAY MORNING, OCTOBER 31

Title: No Other Foundation

Text: "Every one then who hears these words of mine and does them will be like a wise man who built his house upon the rock; and the rain fell, and the floods came, and the winds blew and beat upon that house, but it did not fall, because it had been founded on the rock. And every one who hears these words of mine and does not do them will be like a foolish man who built his house upon the sand" **(Matt. 7:24–26 RSV).**

Scripture Reading: 1 Corinthians 10:1–13

Hymns: "The Solid Rock," Mote
"O Jesus, I Have Promised," Bode
"I Am Resolved," Hartsough

Offertory Prayer: Our heavenly Father, we find ourselves afraid in a changing world as we are caused to drift by the pressures and powers of our time. We long for stability and strength in such a turbulent world. In Jesus Christ you provided a rock of salvation on which we build our lives. We pray for your grace to guide us as we build on that foundation in his name. Amen.

Introduction

My father was a carpenter. When I was a small boy, I often went with him to his work and observed him and the other men building. Consequently, building has always had a fascination for me. I enjoyed watching the workmen as they poured the concrete foundation on which they would later build the structure. I noted how they dug down into the earth until they found rock and how they carefully poured or laid a foundation on that rock.

The little parable by Jesus speaks, as all of his parables do, clearly about the importance of building our lives on the right foundation. All of us have seen the lives of men and women fall when they were not built on the right foundation. We have also seen the lives of strong men and women who were able to withstand all pressures that were brought against them.

The apostle Paul, apparently knowing this parable of Jesus and having also observed the importance of the foundation for building, used the analogy in our text for today. Paul said that there is "no other foundation" on which one can build a meaningful life except the foundation of Jesus Christ. Today I want us to consider this exclusive claim.

I. Jesus Christ is the only foundation adequate for everyday living.

Jesus Christ is the immovable rock on which we can build our lives. All else is like the shifting sand that may appear to be firm today, but tomorrow it moves leaving our lives in ruins. The world in which we live changes so rapidly that we are always in danger of falling or being swept away. Jesus Christ, the Son of God, invites us to build our lives on him.

When we speak of building our lives on Jesus Christ, we are not talking about holding opinions concerning Jesus. We are not even talking about reliable doctrinal conclusions about Christ, as important as they are. Rather, we are talking about the personal commitment of our lives to Jesus Christ and the building of our lives on that solid foundation.

In the town in which I lived as a boy, there was a man who lost all of his financial holdings in the Great Depression. He was a broken man. He walked the streets with his head down and his shoulders slumped. He became disagreeable with his neighbors and was unkind to the children who lived near him. Apparently, the foundation under his life was financial success. When the depression came, his foundation was swept away. In the same town there were other people who also lost their possessions but found a way to go on in life cheerfully. The difference seemed to be the foundation on which life had been built.

Today, perhaps as never before, people need to consider what foundation they will build their lives on. Jesus taught and Paul believed that there is no other foundation that will meet all of the pressures of life except the firm foundation of faith in God. This is the starting point for life.

II. Jesus Christ is the foundation of our beliefs.

Faith is our basic commitment to God, the trust of our lives to him. Beliefs are the doctrinal convictions that we hold with our minds. All persons hold to beliefs that support the kind of lives they live. Some of those beliefs are erroneous or very shallow. Some are correct, and others are incorrect. Jesus Christ is the only foundation of beliefs that are adequate to support one in life.

The basic religious belief of all is belief in God. Christians believe the New Testament when it says that our only way of knowing God is through his revelation of himself in Jesus Christ. "God was in Christ reconciling the world to himself" (2 Cor. 5:19). Jesus Christ was the "word made flesh" (John 1:14). God, who spoke in various ways, such as through the prophets, spoke to us by sending his Son (Heb. 1:1–3). In Jesus Christ God was pleased to dwell fully (Col. 1:19). Jesus Christ is the foundation belief of our faith in God.

A person must have some undergirding belief about human nature. This is foundational for meaningful life. Christians believe that Jesus Christ showed us not only what God is like, but also what humans should be like. Jesus exhibited the right relationship with the heavenly Father and with fellow humans. He did not live selfishly but rather gave himself freely to and for others. His life was motivated by an inward dedication to the Father, which sustained him in the right direction through life. The Christian belief is that there is no other foundational belief about humans that is adequate except that derived from Jesus Christ.

One can hardly live right without right beliefs about the world and the people he or she encounters in the world. Those who believe in Jesus Christ believe that God created the world and that he created the people who live in the world. We have the love and care of God over our lives while we are entrusted with the care of God's world under his sovereignty. Because we are all creatures of God and this is God's world, we have dominion over the world and care for our fellow creatures. These beliefs are the only beliefs that are adequate for the kind of life one is called upon to live in this world.

III. This foundation has been laid; we do not lay it; rather, we build on it.

According to the text in 1 Corinthians, there is no other foundation; Jesus Christ is the foundation that has already been laid by God the Father. In other words, God just "is." He is as certain as the law of gravity. He is as much reality as the changing seasons or the earth on which we walk. We do not choose a foundation; rather, we choose only whether we will build on the foundation or whether we will build without a foundation.

Repeatedly the New Testament stresses the exclusiveness of the Christian faith in that the only God disclosed himself fully in the person of Jesus Christ, his only Son. It is not a question of whether or not one can find some good in all religions. It is rather the question of who God is and how we may serve him. The writers of the New Testament were inspired to believe that there are no rivals to Jesus Christ. He is the only complete revelation of God, the only foundation on which we can build our lives.

In Philippians 2:5–11 we have a beautiful hymn that tells us that Jesus, the Son of God, previously existed on an equality with the Father but freely gave up all of that to come into the world, taking the humble form of a servant and giving his life that we might be brought to God. In Galatians 4:4–6 we are told that God, who had disclosed himself in the history of the Old Testament, came in the fullness of time in the person of Jesus Christ, his Son, so that we might receive reconciliation with God and adoption into God's family.

This exclusiveness of the Christian faith is not arrogant. Rather, we are under the orders of God to tell all creatures in the world of this salvation because it is the expression of the supreme love of the almighty God.

IV. The other foundations are not foundations at all.

What appear to be other foundations are but mirages on the desert. For a long time the institutional church assumed full authority over the lives of men and women. It made the claim that to be right with the church was to be right with God. It claimed to be the foundation on which people could build their lives. This claim proved false, for the church alone is inadequate.

Jesus Christ is the foundation. The church is merely a witness to that foundation and is comprised of the family of God in which the people live who have built on that foundation. The church forever exists to hear and proclaim the truth that Jesus Christ is the only foundation for life.

Some people who have had a deep spiritual experience in their religious pilgrimage make this mystical experience to be the foundation of their lives. Without passing judgment on the validity of such experiences, our text would point out "but the foundation of life is faith in Jesus Christ." This faith may or may not be characterized by mystical experience.

Conclusion

We always face the temptation of building our lives on a false foundation. Such mirages may be beautiful and inviting, but they are like the sand on the beach. They shift with the tides, and the house that is built on them, like the house in Jesus' parable, will fall when the waves and the winds beat on it.

Jesus Christ is the foundation for life. You can trust your life to him. There is no other foundation.

SUNDAY EVENING, OCTOBER 31

Title: James: Least Known of the Apostles

Text: "Matthew and Thomas, James the son of Alphaeus, and Simon called Zelotes" **(Luke 6:15).**

Scripture Reading: Matthew 10:1–10

Introduction

There are three men named James in the New Testament: James, the son of Alphaeus; James, the brother of John; and a third James, the brother of our Lord and leader in the early church.

We know almost nothing about James, the son of Alphaeus. There are several things we can assume about him from the Scriptures, however.

I. In the books of Matthew and Mark, the last four apostles to be named are James, the son of Alphaeus; Thaddaeus; Simon the Zealot; and Judas Iscariot.

In Luke 6:15 we find these same four men listed together. Since they are so consistently named together in the Gospels, there must have been some common factor that bound them into a group. Simon, we know, was a Zealot, a fanatical Jewish patriot; Judas Iscariot was probably such a patriot; one Latin manuscript calls the other Judas (Thaddeus) a Zealot.

There is considerable evidence, then, that Simon, Thaddaeus, and Judas Iscariot were all Zealots. Therefore, it is a reasonable deduction that James, the son of Alphaeus, was also a Zealot.

II. Barclay supposes from the records that James and Matthew were brothers.

A. *Mark says, "As he passed by, he saw Levi the son of Alphaeus sitting at the seat of custom, and said unto him, Follow me" (Mark 2:14).* We know, then, that Matthew and Levi are the same person. Since that is so, the name of Matthew's father was also Alphaeus, and Matthew and this James could have been brothers. Since we assume that they are brothers, we can see that there must have been, in the beginning, a wide gulf that separated them. James, as we have seen, was probably a Jewish nationalist of the most fiery type, and Matthew, you remember, was a tax collector, working for the Romans.

B. *The Zealots hated these tax collectors with a terrible bitterness.* Thus, it is not unlikely that James regarded his own brother, Matthew, as a renegade traitor and would have plunged his dagger into his heart if he had had a chance. Then Jesus came and called both of them. In the presence of this common Master, these brothers who had drifted so far apart came together again. The brothers who hated each other were reconciled in Christ. It is a great illustration that Jesus came not only to reconcile men to God, but also to reconcile them to each other.

III. Further, James shows the importance of the Christian family.

A. *The mother of James was one of the Marys who stood by the cross when Jesus was crucified.* Her presence there suggests the possibility that she was one of the group of unnamed women who went to anoint the body of Jesus on Easter morning. Certainly, James had the gift of a godly mother. The record indicates that Joses, another disciple of Christ, was the son of this Mary, the mother of James.

It is probable, then, that the entire family—the parents, Mary and Alphaeus, as well as their sons—were united in love for Jesus Christ. Based on this reasoning, the family of James, like the family of Lazarus, Mary, and Martha, became one of the first Christian families. Great blessings have been bequeathed to the world through families whose common bond is loyalty to Jesus Christ.

B. *I wonder how many of us could testify to the importance of having a good Christian mother or father.*

The Quaker philosopher Rufus Jones had the gift of a godly home. He says, "While I was too young to have any religion of my own, I had come to a home where religion kept its fires always burning. We had very few material things, but we were rich in invisible wealth. I was not christened in a church, but I was sprinkled from morning until night with the dew of religion. We never ate a meal that did not begin with the hush of thanksgiving. We never began a day without a family gathering in which Mother read a chapter of the Bible, after which there would follow a weighty silence. These silences, during which all the children of the family were hushed, with a kind of awe, were very important features of my spiritual development. There was work inside and outside the house waiting to be done. Yet we sat there hushed and quiet, doing nothing. I very quickly discovered that something real was taking place.

"We were feeling our way down to that place from which living waters come and very often they did come. Someone would bow and talk to God so quietly and simply that he never seemed far away."

James evidently came from such a home. Many blessings come from such a Christian heritage. One never gets away from the prayers and faith of a godly mother or father.

IV. The name of James is suggestive.

A. *The Revised Standard Version translates this, "James the younger."* The Greek phrase literally means *micros,* from which we get the English words *microcosm* and *microscope.* Thus, James is identified as James the less, indicating James was small in stature.

B. *If you are small of stature and it has given you problems, you can accept yourself and rejoice.* Some of the great people of all time have been small. Think of the great military leaders who were small of stature: Alexander the Great, Napoleon, John Paul Jones. Think of the great writers who were physically small: John Milton, Alexander Pope, Isaac Watts, Shelly, Keats, and Victor Hugo. John Wesley was just slightly over five feet tall. Raphael, Sir Isaac Newton, and Steinmetz measured about the same. The great Queen Victoria was even smaller of stature. If you are small of stature, you are akin to James, and you can rejoice. You stand in good company.

V. We do not know much about James, but he too served.

A. *He was one of the Twelve.* Therefore, James speaks to us of the ministry of little-known followers of Christ.

Think for a moment, if you will, of the tremendous debt the world owes to the men whose names have never been recorded in human history. We know the names of some of the great writers: Milton, Byron, Keats, Shelley, Lowell, Longfellow, and all the rest, but we do not know the people in the background who helped them to become what they were.

We know some of the giants in the field of music: Beethoven, Bach, Toscanini, but what of those little-known musicians who first captured the sounds in God's symphony of nature and translated them into notes on a music staff.

In science we know the name of a man like Pasteur, who made a great discovery, but he did not stand alone. He relied on an unnamed army of men who had previously discovered certain things that helped him to make his discovery.

Students of history are familiar with decisive battles of the world and the heroic generals who fought them, but battles are never fought by generals alone. Victories are won by the unknown soldiers who gave all they had.

When we get to heaven, I believe some of these people who labored in the background will be more prominent than some of the ones who received much recognition on earth.

Lord Shaftesbury of London, a member of the House of Peers, could have enjoyed the pleasures of the idle rich. Instead, he became the champion of the underdog. He gave his strength to the weak, his gifts to the poor, and his love for all humankind. His well-born, rich friends could not understand him. Why did he not enjoy his fame and wealth? His mother, bent on her own pleasures, turned the rearing of her son over to his nurse. The nurse's name is almost unknown. It was Maria Millis, the nurse, who opened the streams of sympathy and started them flowing from the generous heart of Lord Shaftesbury. Thus, the unnamed and unknown influences of life play a major role in human destiny.

Think of this in the kingdom of God. History records the names of men like Peter, James, and John—the natural-born leaders, the builders, the missionary pioneers. We shall never forget Matthew's gift of writing, Thomas's skepticism, or Simon's patriotic zeal; but what of men like James the Less? Jesus did not overlook these men. He called them, too, to serve him.

Conclusion

Are you one of these? Do you feel that your life is insignificant and inconspicuous? Do you feel it doesn't matter whether you are true or false, faithful or faithless? Believe me, it does. It matters to you, to your loved ones, to your church, and to the everlasting God. He is counting on you!

NOVEMBER

■ **Sunday Mornings**

"A Grateful Response to the Goodness of God" is the suggested theme for a series of stewardship sermons for the month of November. On the last Sunday of the month begin a series focusing on the coming of Christ entitled "Christmas Means Listening to Jesus."

■ **Sunday Evenings**

Continue the series "Getting Acquainted with the Twelve Apostles." On the last Sunday evening of the month, begin a new series entitled "The Mission of the Christian and the Mission of the Church" based on the Great Commission. Let us join with the angels and sing about the coming of Christ. Let us join with the shepherds and tell the story abroad that Christ has come.

■ **Wednesday Evenings**

Continue with the messages based on the gospel of John. The theme could be "Christ and the Crises of Life."

WEDNESDAY EVENING, NOVEMBER 3

Title: He Went Away

Text: "He went away again across the Jordan to the place where John at first baptized" **(John 10:40 rsv).**

Scripture Reading: John 10:40–42

Introduction

We do not live very long before we experience rejection by someone. Some parents I know felt rejection, failure, and guilt when their daughter moved out saying, "I don't like this lifestyle. I want to live my own life. I don't see things like you do." Maybe they were partly to blame; maybe they were not as guilty as they felt. In either case, they felt that the one they loved had spurned their proffered expressions of love and refused the advantages their home offered and settled for what they thought was less. This has been the story of God's spurned perfect love from the beginning.

Jesus was rejected in Jerusalem. John had this in mind in his introduction when he wrote, "He came to his own home, and his own people received him not" (1:11 RSV). Isn't that sad? Jesus offered understanding, compassion, forgiveness, and new life, but they "received him not." This stubborn resistance of the Jews had now reached the breaking point, and Jesus went away from Jerusalem eastward across the Jordan.

Every person who has ever seriously witnessed to others about Jesus has had some taste of this. A group of businessmen meets every Monday morning at 7:00 to pray, report on their witness experiences during the past week, then plan their ministry for the new week. Recently a new group member revealed his disappointment over a friend refusing to hear his testimony. A lawyer in the group spoke up and said, "Remember, Jesus experienced rejection too."

The saddest part of the story is personal. All of us must admit that we have often rejected Jesus. We are horrified at the thought of crucifying him, yet over and over we reject him when he offers to help with our decisions, comfort us in our sorrows, and help us lift our burdens.

Where did Jesus go when he left Jerusalem?

I. He went to a place of holy and fond memories.

"He went away again across the Jordan to the place where John at first baptized" (10:40 RSV). Jesus likely remained there through the winter months between the Feast of Dedication in December (10:22) and the Passover season in March (11:54–55).

Not only should we learn a lesson from Jerusalem and not reject him, but we should learn a lesson from Jesus and sometimes return to sacred experiences of the past.

A. *It may be a joyful worship experience to go back.* All of a mother's children and grandchildren came home for a family reunion. They attended church where the children had been taught the Bible, had first publicly professed faith in Christ, and had worshiped. It was a high and holy experience.

Go back to those early experiences with God. If you cannot go back literally, go back mentally and spiritually. Remain long enough for the renewal you need.

B. *You may hear a great testimony.* Jesus did. Many came to him and said, "John did no sign, but everything that John said about this man was true" (v. 41 RSV).

A pastor's wife showed him a church bulletin from a former pastorate. They were featuring "the deacon of the week." He recalled with joy the remarkable progress the deacon had made during a five-year period as he became a Sunday school teacher, a deacon, chairman of deacons, building committee member, and an evangelistic witness. By reading a few lines from the church bulletin, the pastor went back twenty-five years to rejoice in his testimony of Christian growth. Jesus must have rejoiced in remembering John the Baptist who had said, "He must increase, but I must decrease" (3:30).

II. He went back to a warm reception.

Jerusalem had rejected Jesus, but he was received warmly across the Jordan. One usually wants to give up after a disappointment in witnessing. But the next effort may be just as rewarding as the last was disappointing.

An evangelist says, "I spent several years conducting about thirty evangelistic campaigns a year in as many different churches. Sometimes the biggest disappointments were in places that seemingly offered the best opportunity, and the greatest rewards were in the least likely places.

III. Many believed in him there.

In the same passage in which John wrote, "His own people received him not," he added, "but to all who received him, who believed in his name, he gave power to become children of God" (1:12 RSV).

We are saddened when people reject Christ, but we must not give up in despair. It has been my experience in personal witnessing that for every two people who reject him, one will receive him. Some who reject him today will receive him tomorrow. It is likely that some who rejected Jesus in Jerusalem later received him following the Day of Pentecost.

Conclusion

"Let us not grow weary in well-doing, for in due season we shall reap, if we do not lose heart" (Gal. 6:9 RSV).

SUNDAY MORNING, NOVEMBER 7

Title: How Much Do You Love God?

Text: "Take now thy son, thine only son Isaac, whom thou lovest, and get thee into the land of Moriah; and offer him there for a burnt offering upon one of the mountains which I will tell thee of " **(Gen. 22:2).**

Scripture Reading: Genesis 22:1–14

Hymns: "Trust, Try, and Prove Me," Leech
       "Is Your All on the Altar?" Hoffman
       "My Jesus, I Love Thee," Featherstone

Offertory Prayer: Our Father, help us to recognize that giving is a vital part of worship. May this experience of bringing our money to be used in your work be as much a part of our worship as any other in the service today. May the offering that we bring today be a symbol of the fact that we are giving ourselves to you. Bless each gift, each giver, and each cause that we support through our gifts. We pray in our Savior's name. Amen.

Introduction

Few stories in the Old Testament convey their message as clearly as the account of Abraham's trip to offer Isaac on the altar. We become excited as we move from event to event. Also, if we are observant, we notice the many things that the Holy Spirit omitted in telling us this story. Among these are the personal conversations that must have taken place between Abraham and Isaac as they journeyed toward Moriah.

No way exists for us to know the method that God used in communicating his will to Abraham. Nor is it necessary for us to have this knowledge. Whether God spoke in an audible voice, through a dream or vision, or in some other way is not nearly as important as the fact that Abraham understood God's will and was obedient to it. The basic truth of this story runs like a golden thread throughout the Old Testament. In fact, two outstanding themes from the story continue through the Old Testament. First, God wants the best from us in worship. Second, sacrifice is at the heart of God's plan for humankind, especially in redemption. These two truths, expressed so explicitly in this story, are repeated many times under many circumstances throughout the rest of the Old Testament accounts.

I. God wants us to love him.

God's command to Abraham probably came soon after Abraham's covenant with Abimelech. God's promise to give Abraham an heir had been fulfilled, and nothing seemed in the way of the Lord's redemptive program being worked out through Abraham. But God felt that Abraham needed another test. He wanted the patriarch to be a person of unquestioned faith and to produce a family of like character. The command for Abraham to offer Isaac was actually a command to demonstrate how much love he had for God and how much faith he had in both the resources of God and his integrity to keep his word. When the command came to Abraham to take his son Isaac, the phrase "whom thou lovest" follows and indicates the affection the father had toward the son. Child sacrifice was common among Abraham's neighbors. So this was God's way of saying, "How much do you love me, Abraham? Do you love me as much as the pagan people around you love their gods? If so, are you willing to do for me what they are willing to do for their gods?"

The decision must have been difficult. Yet Abraham "rose up early in the morning" and began the journey. He loved God and wanted to obey as quickly as possible. Prompt obedience is the best demonstration of respect and love. During the Civil War General Robert E. Lee dispatched a note to Stonewall Jackson saying, "At your convenience, I would like to see you on a matter of not much importance." Late that night, although the rain was pouring, General Jackson knocked on the door of General Lee's headquarters. "Come in, man, come in. What on earth brings you out on a night like this?" Jackson replied,

"Your note, sir." General Lee replied, "I said 'at your convenience.'" General Jackson raised his hand in salute and said, "General, your slightest wish is my command, and this general delights in prompt obedience."

II. We never lose what we put on the altar for God.

Abraham's heart must have beat rapidly as he took his son and led him up the mountain. To add heartbreak, he laid the wood upon Isaac. How beautifully we see symbolized the coming event when God the Father would put the cross on his own Son for the world's redemption! Actually, Abraham offered Isaac. The book of Hebrews states the fact emphatically, "By faith Abraham, when he was tried, offered up Isaac; and he that had received the promises offered up his only begotten son" (11:17). When Abraham's will was completely dedicated to the fact that he was going to do it, he had, in his heart, performed the act. God will accept the will even though the deed has not been done, but he will never accept the deed if the will has not truly surrendered.

Although Abraham then offered Isaac, he did not lose him. We never lose what we give to God. We often hear, "You can't outgive God." When we dedicate ourselves and our possessions to God, he gives back, sometimes tenfold, sometimes fiftyfold, and sometimes a hundredfold. This does not mean that God will automatically make us wealthy merely because we become tithers. God can give us many blessings besides material ones. Yet God does have a marvelous way of making the nine-tenths go further than the ten-tenths when the first ten is dedicated to him.

Another strange fact about this matter of "laying upon the altar" is that God often gives back, with extra dividends, that which we give to him. God takes our talents when they are dedicated to him and multiplies them far more than we ever could in our own selfish pursuits. When we, as Hannah did (1 Sam. 1:28), "lend" our children to God, he makes them far greater than had we chosen to push them into the rat race for materialistic things and worldly acclaim. Abraham gave Isaac to God, and he received Isaac back and many descendants through him. A hymn writer said,

> *But we never can prove the delights of his love*
> *Until all on the altar we lay;*
> *For the favor he shows and the joy he bestows*
> *Are for them who will trust and obey.*

Another hymn writer said the same truth a bit differently:

> *Oh, we never can know what the Lord will bestow*
> *Of the blessings for which we have prayed,*
> *Till our body and soul he doth fully control,*
> *And our all on the altar is laid.*

III. True stewardship requires great faith.

Unless we are people of faith, we can never be effective stewards for God. Abraham was a man who literally lived by faith. Every step in his life required that he trust God to the utmost. When he left Ur of the Chaldees, when he left Haran to go to Canaan, when he left Canaan to go to Egypt and then returned to Canaan, when he waited patiently for the seed God promised, and finally when he was willing to offer the seed upon the altar—all of these and many more events in his life required faith. The writer of Hebrews gives another interesting commentary on this great steward of God. He wrote that Abraham believed "that God could raise the dead, and figuratively speaking, he did receive Isaac back from death" (11:19 NIV). This, of course, agrees with the statement of Abraham to the servant, "Abide ye here. . . .I and the lad will go yonder and worship, and come again to you" (Gen. 22:5). To give our possessions to God on a regular, sustained basis requires faith. The real test is, of course, how much we love God. John Oxenham wrote:

> *Love ever gives—*
> *Forgives—outlives*
> *And ever stands*
> *With open hands.*
> *And while it lives—*
> *It gives*
> *For this is love's prerogative—To give—And give—And give—*

Conclusion

This entire story memorializes God's goodness and his promise for the future. To those who trust in him, God gives deliverance in times of extremity. The expression "Jehovah-jireh" means literally "the Lord will provide." Perhaps the nearest equivalent in English is our familiar truism "Man's extremity is God's opportunity." Only those who love the Lord and obey him completely come to know this great truth.

> *Lovest thou Me? I left my all,*
> *My kingly crown, my heavenly hall,*
> *For Bethlehem, for Calvary—*
> *I left it all for love of thee—*
> > *Lovest thou me?*
> *Lovest thou me? Behold the blood,*
> *Blood of the sinless Son of God!*
> *Go, gaze on Calvary's crimson tide!*
> *Behold my hands, my feet, my side—*
> > *Lovest thou me?*

Lovest thou me? For thee I died—
God for the sinner crucified!
O Soul, what thinkest thou of me?
What hast thou done with Calvary?
 Lovest thou me?

SUNDAY EVENING, NOVEMBER 7

Title: Thaddaeus: Apostle with Three Names

Text: "Judas (not Judas Iscariot) said, 'But, Lord, why do you intend to show yourself to us and not to the world?'" **(John 14:22 NIV).**

Scripture Reading: John 14:18–25

Introduction

Jerome called Thaddaeus, Trinomius, which means "the man with three names." In Mark 3:18 he is called Thaddaeus; in Matthew 10:3 he is called Lebbaeus; in Luke 6:16 he is called Judas, the brother of James.

In John's gospel we find that John is careful to distinguish him, calling him "Judas (not Judas Iscariot)." The name literally means "courageous, lively, vivacious." Perhaps his name indicates something of his character. Judas makes no appearance in any of the first three gospels. He appears only briefly in John's gospel. He breaks silence to ask a question at the Last Supper.

Let us look in on the scene in the Upper Room. Jesus sat at the table with the Twelve. He suddenly surprised the apostles by instituting a new observance. Taking bread from the table, he gave it to Judas and to the others, saying, "This is my body which is broken for you" (1 Cor. 11:24). Likewise, he gave them the cup saying, "This cup is the new testament in my blood" (1 Cor. 11:25).

Judas asked, "Lord, why do you intend to show yourself to us and not to the world?'" **(John 14:22 NIV).** What is the meaning of this? More than likely, Judas was a violent and intense nationalist who dreamed of world power. Thus, as the days drew to a close, Judas did not understand Jesus.

I. Love is a true demonstration of power.

Judas asked Jesus for a manifestation of his power. Jesus answered that any manifestation of himself was impossible except to the obedient and loving. When a person gives Jesus love and obedience, the Holy Spirit makes that person's heart his dwelling place. Judas was telling Jesus to go out to the crowds of strangers and dazzle them, if need be, to convince them to follow him. Jesus then told him that the only loyalty that is any good is the loyalty of a loving heart and a surrendered life. Christ reveals himself only to those who love him.

II. Love enables us to see what we could never see otherwise.

Love opens our eyes. One evening, sitting around a campfire in the mountains of western Maryland, a group of young people listened to a young woman describe the birds of the area. She took the names of the birds she had seen in the few days she had been in the camp, described what they looked like, and gave their calls. She paused several times to point out and identify the birds whose songs came across the evening sky. The camp was familiar ground to most of these youth. Year after year they had returned to enjoy the forest, the lake, the playgrounds, and the cottages; but the beautiful birds who made the woods their home had not been noticed by any except the bird lovers. The beauty of nature is seen by the heart of love and no other.

Isn't this true in so many areas of life? What difference love makes in what the eye sees. Those who love see beauty in the natural world, goodness in others, and potential for the best on every hand. Love enables us to see what we could never see before. This is what Jesus was saying to Judas.

III. Love brings forth true obedience.

Jesus said, "If anyone loves me, he will obey my teaching" (John 14:23 NIV). The person of love does not need a thousand rules of do and don't, for love fulfills all the law and the commandments. In Jesus' time on earth, there were many rules and regulations that governed life—so many, in fact, that they became tiresome. There were 623 laws to be kept, and they were so detailed that only the experts could really know right from wrong. When confronted with this situation, "Which is the greatest of the commandments?" Jesus said, "Thou shalt love the Lord thy God with all thy heart, and with all thy soul, and with all thy mind" (Matt. 22:37).

Someone has said, "If you love God, you can do as you please." Paul addressed many of the weaknesses that beset the church at Corinth. The church was divided into four warring factions, each claiming for its spiritual leader Paul, Apollos, Cephas, or Christ. Ugly as church quarrels are, there was an even worse situation, for the Corinthians were tolerating in their fellowship immorality of a type that even pagans condemned. A member of the church was living with his father's wife. Added to this scandal was the fact that Christians were taking one another to court. Even the house of God was not sacred. When gathering to eat the Lord's Supper, some were actually getting drunk.

How did Paul meet this distressing situation? Did he, in anger, disown this wayward church? In the spirit of his Master, Paul poured out his heart in a beautiful hymn of love. "Make love your aim," he urged, "earnestly desire the spiritual gifts" (1 Cor. 14:1 RSV).

Jesus says that our love for God meets the responsive love of God for us. If it is true that God loves all people, the love of God, like the sun, constantly floods the earth and is the source of all life. People can shut out the light of the sun by withdrawing into their houses, closing the shutters, and drawing the blinds, but the person who dwells in self-made darkness does not thereby destroy the sun. The sun forever shines and enters every house the instant blinds and shutters are opened wide.

Even so the love of God surrounds every person. When people throw open the windows of their hearts, love comes flooding upon them. "If anyone loves me, he will obey my teaching" (John 14:23 NIV). The responding love of God awaits the open heart of love.

IV. Other fruit of this loving fellowship with God are peace, joy, and confidence.

Jesus says, "Peace I leave with you, my peace I give unto you" (John 14:27). The peace of Jesus is not release from burdens and conflicts, but an inner resource of strength that gives a place of quietness at the very center of life's hurricanes. Jesus tells his followers, "In this world you will have trouble. But take heart! I have overcome the world" (John 16:33 NIV).

V. Further Jesus promises rejoicing in time of sorrow.

By the promise of rejoicing at the time of death's separation, Jesus does not deny the experience of grief. The feeling of grief and the expression of sorrow are in no wise unbecoming to a Christian. The joy that Jesus promised Christians is the knowledge that beyond the tears of separation is the joy of reunion.

VI. Finally, Jesus says that love can never die.

In just a little while, great nails would be driven into Jesus' hands and feet by Roman soldiers. Yet they would not really have power over him in that he laid down his life in love. A life ruled by love cannot be destroyed; it is eternal.

Paul Geren, in his biography of Peter Strong, relates an experience during the Burma campaign that illustrates confidence growing out of love. One night at dusk three soldiers stood up with him and sang "When I Survey the Wondrous Cross."

Peter asked himself, "What if in the singing of this song, a shell comes over and gets you?" He answered himself, "It would be all right. It would be everlastingly all right. Now, nothing can be lost. Nothing can be forgotten. Nothing can begin. Nothing can end. We have struggled and nothing can unhand us. We have learned, and nothing can rob us. We have begotten, and nothing can deny us."

When they were on the third verse, a shell did come. When it whistled, the quartet hit the dirt as one man, leaving the song awkwardly suspended at the place, "Sorrow and love flow mingled down."

But Peter's heart was beating fast, his breathing was heavy. He realized that the shell did not hit him, but a man behind him. The dying soldier was lying in the arms of a comrade. Peter whispered, "Sorrow and love flow mingled down." But before and after the shell came, he felt "death would be all right, everlastingly all right."

Conclusion

Judas asked for a demonstration of power, and Jesus told him and all generations to come that love is the greatest power, because it will live forever.

WEDNESDAY EVENING, NOVEMBER 10

Title: When Sickness Comes

Text: "Now a certain man was ill, Lazarus of Bethany. . ." **(John 11:1 RSV).**

Scripture Reading: John 11:1–4

Introduction

Perhaps sickness is not the most important subject in the story of Jesus, Lazarus, Mary, and Martha, but it is an important subject for us all. Most people have been seriously sick at one time or another, or at least some of your loved ones have. Should we prepare for it, try to prevent it, or make believe it only happens to others? Most people never think seriously of illness until it comes and never stop talking about it afterward. Some people enjoy talking about their illnesses and others refuse to admit them. Perhaps both have problems.

I. Is there a biblical view of illness?

A. *Saints and sinners get sick.* There is no evidence that Lazarus was sick because of sin. Maybe our guilt produces such erroneous questions as, "Why did God send this on me?" An old *Candid Camera* show featured students being brought into a school counselor's office by twos and told they had been accused of some bad things. The counselor would leave the two alone while he went ostensibly "to talk it over with the principal." In every case boys and girls discussed what it might be and did not deny that they might be guilty. It was only a matter of "What?" Some actually began to "confess" to each other. The Bible teaches that all have sinned, but nowhere does it teach that all suffering is caused by sin.
   1. Some suffering is because of sin (Ps. 107:17; Mic. 6:13; Acts 12:23; 1 Cor. 11:30). We know that some diseases of the heart, lungs, and liver are caused by tobacco and alcohol use. Promiscuous sexual practices may result in sexually transmitted diseases. And there are other illustrations.
   2. Some suffering is not caused by sin (2 Kings 20:1; Job 2:7; Acts 9:36). The cases of sin causing illness are rare in the Bible.

B. *Healing is an expression of love.*
   1. The example of Jesus: "They brought him all the sick, those afflicted with various diseases and pains, demoniacs, epileptics, and paralytics, and he healed them" (Matt. 4:24). When his critics could find no guilt, they accused him of healing on the Sabbath.
   2. The example of the apostles (Acts 3:7; 5:16; 14:10; 19:1–2).
   3. The use of medicine is biblical (2 Kings 20:7; Isa. 1:6; Ezek. 30:21; Luke 10:34; 17:12; 1 Tim. 5:23).
   4. Physicians are biblical. "Those who are well have no need of a physician, but those who are sick" (Luke 5:31). Paul had his own personal physician (Col. 4:14).

II. What is the Christian attitude toward sickness?

A. *Prevention.* The Christian ethic has been the strongest influence in preventive medicine and good health practices. Christian compassion and ministry are normal and scriptural when dedicated to the prevention of disease epidemics, teaching good nutritional practices, and advocating good health habits.

B. *Treatment.* I have never seen greater compassion than that demonstrated by doctors and nurses in mission hospitals. Doctors and surgeons who could have successful practices in the United States literally burn out their lives as missionaries in poverty stricken areas of the world.

C. *Understanding.* Thankfully, we do not live forever in this world of limitations. There is a better world, and it becomes our inheritance through death. Death usually comes as a result of disease, sickness, or accident. Because we do not understand the mystery of life, we find it difficult to understand body deterioration and cessation of health. God does understand, and we must trust him.

D. *Growth.* Just as many people never practice good health habits until after a health scare, most people do not grow much as Christians until they really need the Lord. Most great Christians have suffered much.

Conclusion

When Jesus heard of the illness of Lazarus, he said, "This illness is not unto death; it is for the glory of God, so that the Son of God may be glorified by means of it" (John 11:4). No one wants to get sick, but God may use sickness for his glory.

SUNDAY MORNING, NOVEMBER 14

Title: The First Gift in Stewardship

Text: "They. . .first gave their own selves to the Lord" (**2 Cor. 8:5**).

Scripture Reading: 2 Corinthians 8:1–9

Hymns: "Something for Thee," Phelps
           "I Gave My Life for Thee," Havergal
           "Take My Life, and Let It Be," Havergal

Offertory Prayer: Our Father, we are grateful that we have new life because of the Holy Spirit's presence in us. Help us that we shall never again live as though we were dead. May the Holy Spirit's presence bring constant renewal as day by day we grow in the new life that was begun when he first entered our hearts. As we bring our gifts this morning, may we do more than bring our money. Rather, help us to commit ourselves afresh to living for Christ in the everyday pursuits of life. May we be properly motivated and give in proper measure as you have given to us. We pray in Jesus' name. Amen.

Introduction

Paul loved all the churches with which he worked. Each of them had individual needs and problems. Some were more exemplary than others. Yet a common strain ran through all of them. They were made up of people who had become new creatures in Christ. The greatest changes, morally speaking, were among those who had previously been in the Gentile world worshiping idols and living the immoral lifestyle that accompanied idol worship. Thus a revolutionary change came to many of these people when Christ entered their lives. Some were ostracized economically by their fellow countrymen. This was true, perhaps for different reasons, of both the Jews who accepted Christ and the Gentiles who left their pagan friends for the Christian faith.

Paul, in this letter to the church at Corinth, called special attention to the northern neighbors of the Corinthians who had shown great generosity in supporting God's work even though their resources were limited. Paul emphasizes the importance of learning that a part of commitment to Christ is supporting the work of his churches.

I. Giving is a grace.

Far too often we apologize for asking people to give their money to God's work. Members of a church in an affluent community were once pointing out with pride to a visiting pastor their accomplishments in building a beautiful church and maintaining it. They also showed him other parts of their church program that needed funding. One of the men said, "And, preacher, we never say a word about money at this church. Our preacher never preaches on it." While one can dwell too much on the subject, one wonders what the church might have been able to do by way of mission out-reach if the pastor had challenged the people of that affluent community to give to God the proper portion of their money. In verse 7 of today's Scripture reading, Paul places the giving of money on the same level as the other great virtues. He urges the Christians at Corinth to "abound in this grace [the grace of giving] also."

II. God has a plan.

Even as God has a plan for redeeming lost souls, he also has a plan for financing his work. In the Old Testament the financial requirement is spelled out clearly: The tithe is holy to the Lord. In fact, most Old Testament scholars see three different tithes required at various times by God in sup-port of his work. In addition, special gifts were encouraged and commanded.

The New Testament deals with gifts on the basis of the stewardship principle. Yet nowhere does any writer make the suggestion that less than the tithe is acceptable to support God's work. When denouncing the Pharisees for failing to emphasize spiritual things in their lives, Jesus said, "Woe unto you, scribes and Pharisees, hypocrites! for ye pay tithe of mint and anise and cumin, and have omitted the weightier matters of the law, judgment, mercy, and faith: these ought ye to have done, and not to leave the other undone" (Matt. 23:23). Some who have sought to minimize tithing have pointed to this verse as a basis for their contention. Jesus, however, did not put tithing on a lower level, but rather emphasized what the Pharisees had ignored— righteous living and compassion. He said clearly that the people should tithe. Paul emphasized a "regular program" of giving when he said, "Upon the first day of the week let every one of you lay by him in store, as God hath prospered him" (1 Cor. 16:2). This verse seems to have as its Old Testament background the command of Malachi who said, "Bring ye all the tithes into the storehouse, that there may be meat in mine house, and prove me now herewith saith the LORD of hosts, if I will not open you the windows of heaven, and pour you out a blessing, that there shall not be room enough to receive it" (Mal. 3:10).

God's plan is proportionate, systematic giving with the tithe as a mini-mum. When this is faithfully practiced by members of a church, there will be no problem of adequate funding. In fact, the biggest problem the church will have will be what mission causes to support with the abundance of avail-able money.

III. Personal priority is necessary.

Paul could understand the conceptual thinking of the Graeco-Roman world, and he never failed to put his finger on the real issue. The secret of the Macedonian Christians' practice of stewardship was that they understood what was most important. Paul says that they "first gave their own selves to the Lord" and adds "unto us by the will of God."

No one can or will do much to support God's work financially until he or she has decided what things should have priority. Occasionally we may see an undedicated person give a large gift to a special cause. Unless that person's giving is motivated by a desire to be a part of God's program in a true spiritual sense, such gifts will not continue on a long-range basis. The consistent, even if humble, gift or gifts of those who are genuinely dedicated to God's work will exceed those of the spasmodic and often improperly motivated giver. Years ago someone asked John Wanamaker, "How can you be such a dedicated person? You serve in an important role in government, own and operate a large department store, and yet you find time to be superintendent of one of the largest Sunday schools in the nation. How can you do it?" He replied very quickly, "Years ago I decided to base my life on one verse of Scripture. This is it: 'Seek ye first the kingdom of God, and his righteousness; and all these things shall be added unto you.' I have tried to live by that verse all these years." Only a commitment such as this can serve as the basis for true stewardship. It is the only kind that God will honor and the only kind that will bring true joy to the Christian.

Conclusion

Have you ever taken an honest look at your own motivation for stewardship? We need to remember that God's command for us to bring our money to him is not a way of raising funds for carrying on his work. Rather, it is his plan for developing people. The gift is important. Let no one minimize it. But in the words of the poet many years ago, "The gift without the giver is bare."

SUNDAY EVENING, NOVEMBER 14

Title: Simon: Importance of Christian Zeal

Text: "Simon the Canaanite, and Judas Iscariot, who also betrayed him" **(Matt. 10:4).**

Scripture Reading: Titus 2:1–14

Introduction

The word *enthusiasm* means "God-breathed." I love to see people zealous in the work of the Lord, people upon whom the Lord has breathed his power. There is something magnetic about a person who gets on fire for a cause. Simon was such a man. We know little about him other than his name.

The New Testament calls him Simon the Canaanite (Matt. 10:4; Mark 3:18), and two other places (Luke 6:15 and Acts 1:13) call him Simon; he is called a Zealot in all four places.

The title Zealot tells us much about Simon. The Zealots were a group of hot-headed patriots. Their one goal was the deliverance of the Jewish nation from the hated Roman yoke. They organized an underground movement and sabotaged every plan of the Romans and struck telling blows under cover of darkness.

I. Simon was zealous for his country.

A. *Simon was a member of a band of revolutionaries.* The Zealots blew upon smoldering coals and fanned them to blazing flames. Reaching into the past, they seized upon the dying words of Maccabeus, "My children, be ye zealous for the law, and give your lives for the covenant of your fathers, and call to remembrance the deeds of your fathers which they did in their generation and receive great glory and an everlasting name."

B. *The Zealots were actually founded by Judas of Gamala.* He coined a slogan, "No God but Jehovah, no tax but to the temple, no friend but a Zealot." He gathered a large following of the youth of the land in about A.D. 7 and they fell upon isolated garrisons of Roman soldiers and took the lives of all they captured.

Roman soldiers were dispatched at once to put down the rebellion. Within sixty days the strong arm of Rome had crushed all opposition and put their leader to death. His four sons continued guerrilla warfare until each of them fell in battle or took his own life to prevent capture by the Romans. One garrison fought until the last defender was taken up and put to death by the Romans. Nine hundred soldiers shut themselves up in one fortress and destroyed themselves by fire so the Romans would have only the ashes for their victory. They were zealous unto death for their cause.

C. *Their zeal for their cause and their love for their country are to be commended.* The Zealots were like the Liberty Boys and Minute Men who fought in the early days of the Revolution for the right of self-government. Struggles for freedom are still going on all over the world today.

D. *We see an indirect message from the life of Simon.* Simon's love for his country was a wholesome and noble thing. Every Christian should be a good citizen. One of the tragedies in our own nation is the bad citizenship of good people.

Sir Walter Scott, poet and patriot, spoke for all of us when he wrote:

Breathes there a man with soul so dead,
Who never to himself hath said,
This is my own, my native land!

Whose heart hath ne'er within him burn'd
As home his footsteps he hath turn'd
From wandering on a foreign strand!

So Jesus saw something good in this hot-blooded patriot. If he could harness Simon's passionate zeal, put it on the right track, what a power Simon could become for God and righteousness.

II. Simon was zealous for Christ.

A. *Why was this passionately patriotic Zealot attracted to Jesus?* Was it not because Jesus showed evidences of being a revolutionary? Did he not call some of the perfunctory leaders of his day "a generation of vipers"? Was he not fearless in his attacks on the moneychangers in the temple? Did he not have strange powers over man?

It could be that this powerful religious revolutionary, Jesus of Nazareth, was the man Simon was looking for.

B. *So we notice that Simon was transformed.* His zeal for his country was transformed into zeal for his Lord. Brought under Christ's daily companionship, we can easily understand how that ardent feeling that had flamed out in the revolt against Rome would have value for the unfolding of the kingdom of heaven.

C. *The transformation of Simon gives hope for us all.* The most impossible person may become an instrument in the hands of God. From the stammering Moses to the Roman centurion at the cross, from Saul the oppressor to St. Augustine, from Luther to Franklin Graham, God has demonstrated over and over again what happens when a person links up with the Almighty.

Barclay calls Simon "the man who began by hating and ended in loving." He had a bitter hatred of Rome; he was a fanatic nationalist, but he was transformed into love. He became zealous for Christ and for the salvation of his people. He became an apostle—meaning "one sent forth from the face."

It is said that this was a three-way love, a tremendous realization of God's love for them, an ever-growing love for their Father, and a love for their fellow humans, which counted all people as brothers and sisters and impelled them to seek their redemption. This threefold love was to them such a transcendent reality that they could not become other than zealots—zealots for Christ!

III. The importance of Christian zeal for all.

A. *We can be like Simon.* We can enter into a religion of love and grace and power that will set us afire. Our Lord requires loving zeal.

Long years have passed since the Zealots lived, yet the principle that dominated them continues to operate in the modern world. The love of nation and the desire for freedom arouse people as deeply now as ever. We wonder if Jesus were here today where he would stand.

B. *Simon the Zealot was wiser than many Christians today.* He did not try to change Jesus into a Zealot. Rather, he changed himself into a humble apostle of the Lord. Whether he came to Jesus with blood on his hands or smoke in his cloak we do not know, but we do know he was a man full of zeal for his Lord.

C. *The goal of the gospel of Christ is to produce something of this in the lives of all Christians.* Titus 2:14 tells us that for this end Christ died, giving himself for us "that he might redeem us from all iniquity, and purify unto himself a peculiar people, zealous of good works."

The word translated "zealous" here comes from the word "Zealot." Titus uses this figure to call Christians to be zealous of spiritual duties, of good works.

Be zealous in prayer. If we neglect prayer, the spiritual resources of our souls dry up. Be zealous in Bible reading. We will never be radiant Christians until we develop the habit of reading the Bible every day. Be zealous in church attendance. Absence from worship can destroy your spiritual life. Be zealous in giving. Be zealous in witnessing. This zeal comes from being near Christ. Every day we can open our hearts anew and receive the Spirit. Every day we can open our Bibles and hear again his living words for our hearts.

Conclusion

No person is ever zealous simply because he or she is commanded to be, but when one enters into a relationship of love and the fellowship of power with the living Christ, then obedience is set to music. Love is law translated into melody. Love is caught up on the wings of inspiration. When love for Christ is at the center of our being, cold and formal obedience is replaced by spiritual zeal.

WEDNESDAY EVENING, NOVEMBER 17

Title: When Death Comes

Text: "Then Jesus told them plainly, 'Lazarus is dead'" **(John 11:14 RSV)**.

Scripture Reading: John 11:1–36

Introduction

Often when children are asked to quote a Bible verse, they quote, "Jesus wept," and everyone smiles. The message is missed.

Jesus wept in the presence of sorrow and death. Psychiatrists are not the only ones who have concluded that those who refuse to face reality and restrain their emotions will more likely break under the strain of separation and death.

I. Death is universal.

A wife said following her husband's death, "You would have thought we never expected to die. We never discussed it or made any preparation for it." Obsession with death is unhealthy, but refusal to face it is unreal.

Death visited the home of Mary, Martha, and Lazarus—even though they were dear friends of Jesus. When Lazarus became sick, his sisters sent for Jesus: "Lord, he whom you love is ill." They no doubt felt that he would come to them. They both said the same thing when he finally did come: "Lord if you had been here, my brother would not have died." Whether they were expressing their strong faith or registering some complaint is impossible to know. Frustration and perplexity in the presence of death often results in blaming the Lord.

Mary, Martha, and Lazarus were obviously some of Jesus' best friends, and they had the same reaction of so many: "How could this happen to us?" We are not faulting them. We are seeing ourselves in them. We have experienced or will experience the death of a loved one. We should therefore do all we can to prepare ourselves in advance.

It seems that people accepted death more readily in the past. Our ancestors accepted the reality and talked of a better life to come. They sang "When We All Get to Heaven" and "When the Roll Is Called up Yonder" and other gospel songs of promise and assurance. In our day people have become domesticated on earth to the extent that this is their heaven. This makes death more agonizing when it inevitably comes. Death does not go away because we dislike it or deny it.

A preschooler went with her parents to register for prizes at several retail businesses. On the same day, they visited the funeral home, saw the body of a deceased friend, and signed the register. Her parents did not understand her consternation on the way home until she finally said, "I do not want us to win that casket." However, every home will win one one day.

I should add that this is no reason to protect our children from knowledge of death. Fewer people needed counseling following the death of family members when most children lived on farms and saw death often. During those years, the bodies of family members were kept in the home overnight, and they got somewhat adjusted before the funeral service and interment. Death is real and cannot be escaped by fantasies.

II. Death is progress.

A. *Progress is often painful.* Mary and Martha were not ready for Lazarus to die. This is normal. Even though we understand the inevitability and the temporality of death, it is still painful. With all his understanding of death and his power over it, Jesus wept with relatives when his friend died.

B. *Progress is not always recognizable.* Death is like graduation in school. It is promotion from a lower to a higher life. It is moving from a house of clay to one eternal in the heavens. Jesus' resurrection, his physical appearances, and his teachings indicate the final resurrection to a more, rather than a less, complete life after death.

Our primary problem with death is that it is separation, usually associated with suffering. Jesus enters into this suffering with us just as he did the Bethany family. But he goes further. He assures us that while we are separated from some, we have a reunion with others. He suffered more than any of us at the time of his death, but he makes it clear that every tear shall be wiped away in heaven.

Conclusion

In the resurrection of Lazarus, Jesus not only showed his love, but also his power over death. In his own resurrection, to which this story is introductory, he gives us the benefit of his experience. He said to Martha and to us, "I am the resurrection and the life; he who believes in me, though he die, yet shall he live, and whoever lives and believes in me shall never die" (John 11:25–26).

SUNDAY MORNING, NOVEMBER 21

Title: The Stewardship of Gratitude

Text: "What shall I render unto the LORD for all his benefits toward me?" (**Ps. 116:12**).

Scripture Reading: Psalm 116:1–19

Hymns: "All Things Are Thine," Whittier
"Our Best," Kirk
"Now Thank We All Our God," Rinkart

Offertory Prayer: Gracious heavenly Father, you have blessed all of us far beyond that which we deserve. Both our joys and our sorrows have enriched our lives. To us has been given the assurance of forgiveness and the joy of being members of your redeemed family. We come now to give ourselves to you as we bring our substance. Through our gifts of money, we can render ministries of mercy in your name in places where we cannot go personally. Use these tithes and offerings to tell the good news of the salvation that is in Christ Jesus and to render other deeds of mercy and kindness to those who do not have the privileges that we possess. We pray this in our Savior's name. Amen.

Introduction

This psalm is written against the background of a man who had experienced a severe sickness or some other situation of danger. Having been delivered, he then gave thanksgiving for what the Lord had done and made promises of what he would do in gratitude for his deliverance. An "attitude of gratitude" shows that one is a mature person. Ingratitude has been called the "chiefest of sins." In Dante's *Inferno,* his masterpiece concerning everlasting punishment, he did not put in the pit of hell those whose iniquity had sprung from passion. Rather, the pit of his hell was filled with sullen, ungrateful men frozen in ice. On this Sunday before Thanksgiving, let's reflect on the many goodnesses of God and examine our hearts to see the quantity and quality of our gratitude. Let us look at what the psalmist said he would do in appreciation for all that the Lord had done for him.

I. I will take the cup of salvation.

Until we have seen ourselves as sinners and have received Jesus Christ as personal Savior, we begin at no beginning and work toward no conclusion in developing our lives. A young preacher, mature beyond his years, was riding on a train with a group of military men during World War II. The conversation developed around religious themes, and a very "liberated" preacher expounded some ideas that even unbelievers, if they had any biblical background at all, recognized were untenable. This young man, who was still a ministerial student, replied with several passages of Scripture. One of the soldiers came to the young preacher, who was also in the military, and asked him a word of advice about his spiritual matters. Very wisely, the young man said, "Now before we discuss the matter, let me ask you, am I talking to a saved person or not? In other words, if you have not settled the problem of your personal relationship to Jesus Christ as Savior, the only advice I can give you as the ultimate answer to your need is that you repent of sin and trust Christ as Savior." This young student was wise. Trusting Christ as Savior and becoming a Christian does not mean that we will automatically have all of the answers to life's questions immediately, but it does mean that we will have a working basis whereby we, with the help of our Savior, can resolve the problems. Until people do become Christians, however, they simply do not have the inner working of the Holy Spirit to give them strength for the difficulties of life.

Sometimes we see a preacher or a lay witness trying to scare people into becoming Christians. Paul taught rather that it is the "goodness of God" that leads to repentance (Rom. 2:4). People who can be scared into religion don't usually last long in their commitment unless they learn soon in their Christian life to live by love and faith. When one of our greatest scientists, who was noted for his new approaches and creative thinking, was on his deathbed, someone said, "What are your speculations now?" He replied, "Speculations?

I have no speculations." He contended, "I know whom I have believed, and am persuaded that he is able to keep that which I have committed unto him against that day" (2 Tim. 1:12).

II. I will pay my vows unto the Lord.

The psalmist does not go into detail concerning the vows he had made. Perhaps he had prayed in his crisis and promised that if God would deliver him he would change his way of life in certain areas. In all probability he had agreed with God that he was deficient in his bringing of sacrifices to the altar. A seminary president, who had been a successful pastor, told the seminarians in a chapel service of a professional man who was at the point of suicide because he had lost most of his investments. The preacher sensed the man's need and said, "There's only one hope for you. You have majored on the material and, now that the material is gone, you have nothing left personally by way of resources. If you want deliverance, get down on your knees with me and promise that if God will give you strength for a comeback, you will dedicate a tithe to him of all that he gives to you." The man did it. His entire life was changed. His family life straightened up and his medical practice was as good or better than ever. The president closed with a pungent statement: "Since assuming the presidency of this seminary, I have handed one of his sons two theological degrees from this institution." When we get right with God on the matter of our finances, amazing miracles can take place in other areas of life. But we'd better be careful! When we make vows, we must keep them or we will be worse off than ever before. Jacob vowed a vow at Bethel, but, as far as we know, he stayed twenty years in Haran working for Laban and seemingly ignored those vows. Stewardship is an important part of living. In fact, for the Christian, next to accepting Jesus Christ as personal Savior, it is probably the most important element of our life.

III. I will be your servant forever.

As the psalmist thought about his great deliverance, he probably realized that his life had been lengthened in order that he might fulfill God's purposes for him. Someone said years ago that God keeps us here on earth until one of two things happens. Either we realize the purpose for which he placed us here or we show him one final time that we have no intention of fulfilling his plans for our lives. Perhaps a thought such as this may have been in the background of Paul's statement, "For me to live is Christ, and to die is gain" (Phil. 1:21).

Throughout the psalm, the writer recognizes a relationship between himself and God. Because of this, he has been given certain benefits by God and is, therefore, obligated to render certain services to God. This relationship is so important that God is not yet ready for him to pass on to the other world. He has, therefore, rescued him from the very jaws of death and thus has a claim on his life. The psalmist has become God's servant, but he is also God's friend. God walks with him and, therefore, he must not relax his service to God. The highest concept of servant is not that of a hireling who toils for wages and not even as a slave who is completely owned by God, although the latter is true. Rather, the relationship of friend to friend is the highest motivation for effective service. This is the basis on which the psalmist said, "I will offer to thee the sacrifice of thanksgiving" (v. 17). The psalmist also believed that if a friend is worth having, he is worth serving in the presence of others. This paves the way for Jesus' statement, "Whosoever therefore shall confess me before men, him will I confess also before my Father which is in heaven" (Matt. 10:32). When one accepts all that is involved in being a servant of the Lord, all other matters fit into place.

Conclusion

The underlying theme of this psalm is that gratitude should characterize our life before God. A preacher of another century, Jeremy Taylor, said, "The private and personal blessings we enjoy, the blessings of immunity, safeguard, liberty, and integrity, deserve the thanksgiving of a whole life." Gratitude is, as Theodore Parker said, "a touch of beauty added to the countenance giving an angelic loveliness to the character." The constantly recurring theme of the book of Deuteronomy, "Beware that thou forget not the LORD thy God. . .which brought thee forth" (Deut. 8:11, 14), may have been in the mind of the psalmist as he wrote this hymn. Charles Jefferson once wrote, "Gratitude is born in hearts that take time to count up past mercies." Such a spirit leads one to give one's best to God in all areas of living.

SUNDAY EVENING, NOVEMBER 21

Title: Judas Iscariot: The Company of the Betrayers

Text: "Then Judas, which betrayed him, answered and said, Master, is it I? He said unto him, Thou hast said" **(Matt. 26:25).**

Scripture Reading: Matthew 26:47–50

Introduction

Who was this man Judas? He came from Kerioth, a little village in south Judea. He was the only one of the Twelve who was not a Galilean. He probably was named for Judas Maccabeus, a man who led the Jews in a mighty way in past history. Perhaps Judas was possessed with his ambition—to throw off the Roman yoke of bondage.

Hearing of the Messiah, Judas made his way to Galilee to see him. He saw his great power and miracles, was drawn to him, and then one day Jesus called him to be one of his disciples. Judas became one of the Twelve. He was a fiery little man, a leader, full of zeal, selfish, fanatical, intolerant, and greedy.

I. The treason of Judas.

A. *Judas betrayed Christ, but treason is not a characteristic of Judas alone.* It has inscribed its black mark on people everywhere.
   1. In the Garden of Eden we see Adam and Eve betraying God.
   2. Joseph's own brothers betrayed him.
   3. Ananias and Sapphira betrayed their Lord.
      Woven into the tapestry of the church are the words, "All forsook him and fled." This is the real company of the betrayers.
B. *Jesus made one last appeal to Judas before his betrayal.* Can you visualize the scene that took place at the Last Supper? In those days the guests reclined on low couches, resting on their left elbow with the right hand free for raising food and drink. Clearly, John is at Jesus' right, for he was reclining on his bosom. But the most favored guest was placed at the host's left, for the host would be reclining with his head on the breast of the person on his left. It seems clear that Judas was occupying the place of special honor.
   At one point of the ceremony, some bitter herbs were placed between two pieces of unleavened bread, dipped in the broth, and eaten. That was called the sop. And for the host to personally make up the sop and hand it to a guest was a mark of distinct honor.
   Jesus handed the sop to Judas, then said, "One of you shall betray me." Around the table they asked, "Lord, is it I? Lord, is it I?" When Judas asked, "Is it I?" Jesus answered, "Thou hast said" (Matt. 26:25).
   So Judas went out and made his plans for the betrayal. He knew where Jesus would be—his favorite place of prayer, the Garden of Gethsemane.
C. *So Judas, in the full light of the Passover moon, led the authorities there.* We watch him as he comes into the Garden; soldiers carrying lanterns and staves are with him. Judas approaches Jesus quickly and quietly. He bows down, takes Jesus' hand, and kisses it, saying, "Master."
   A kiss on the hand was the token greeting between a disciple and his teacher. I do not think Judas betrayed Christ at once. He had tried to follow Christ, but his heart had never been able to do it fully. No person ever betrays Christ all at once. There is rarely ever one decisive act to reject our Lord, but an accumulation of small wrongs growing heavier and heavier until the rejection is complete.
D. *Note three aspects of the treason:*
   1. God called Judas to a high and holy place.
   2. Judas chose his own way. Dismiss the idea that Judas was a mere puppet on a string. Jesus chose Judas to a high and holy place, but Judas refused and chose to go his own way.

3. Judas, choosing his own way, went to his own place. His act had consequences. His destiny was determined by his choice. You and I are free moral agents. We make our choices, but they, in turn, make us.

II. The truth about Judas.

A. *Why did Judas betray Christ?*
  1. Was it because of cowardice? The Bible says that the fear of man is a snare. Some do betray Christ because of fear of the crowd. They reject him because they do not have the courage to confess him before people.
  2. Was it because of the love of money? He was a greedy man. One day, at a feast honoring Jesus, Mary broke an alabaster box full of very expensive ointment and anointed Jesus' feet. Judas objected to such waste. He asked, "Why was not this ointment sold for three hundred pence, and given to the poor?" (John 12:5).

     John wrote, "This he said, not that he cared for the poor; but because he was a thief, and had the bag" (John 12:6). Judas was a covetous man who used his position to pilfer from a common purse. Perhaps this greed for money and love of gain were the motives that led him to betray his Lord.
  3. Did Judas betray Jesus because of selfishness? Judas has been described as a zealous patriot. He was a violent, fanatical nationalist, pledged to use any means to drive the Romans from Palestine. He wanted more than life to be free from bondage to Rome.

     Judas saw his dream being crucified. This time he took action. He took vengeance for the death of his dream by betraying the man who had disappointed him. He betrayed him because he wanted to use his power for the achievement of selfish ends.
  4. Did Judas betray Jesus because of rebellion? Was there deep, seething rebellion in his heart against the Lord of life? It is always sin in the heart that causes us to betray our Lord.

B. *Judas could not place the blame on anyone but himself.* Likewise, you and I are responsible for our own sins. Sin is a self-inflicted wound.

III. The tragedy of Judas.

A. *Judas went back to the priests, told them that he had sinned against innocent blood, and besought them to take their money back.* When they would not, he flung it to them and went out and hanged himself.
  1. Here is the tragedy of lost opportunity. Judas cast aside his opportunity to be what God called him to be. One of the saddest passages in the Bible tells of the man who buried his talent in the earth.
  2. Here is the tragedy of a lost soul. To lose your soul is life's greatest tragedy. Some losses can be repaired. We may regain our health, our fortune, or our character, but a soul that is lost is lost forever.

3. Here is the tragedy of a crucified Savior. Judas's betrayal led to Jesus' crucifixion, but when anyone betrays Christ, Christ is crucified afresh and anew.

B. *The whole company of the betrayers has a part in this crucifixion.* Even today when we reject Christ, we crucify him again. Nails are driven into his hands and feet, his brow is crowned again with thorns, and his side is pierced with the sword.

Dr. J. B. Tidwell, my Bible teacher in college, used to tell his students the story of his conversion. J. B. had gone to Sunday school all his life, but still at the age of sixteen he had never accepted Christ. He was timid and could never get up the courage to make a confession. One night after a revival service, his aunt lovingly placed her arms around him and asked, "J. B., did you know that your rejection is breaking the heart of Jesus? It is crucifying him again."

He had never thought of that. His heart was so broken that he could not even go out the front door of the church. He climbed through a window, got on his mule, and started home. There was a full harvest moon that night. As he rode along, his heart became so heavy with the burden of sin that he could not continue.

He got off the mule, walked over to a tree stump, got on his knees, and prayed, "Forgive me, O God, I didn't know my rejection was doing that to Jesus Christ."

Conclusion

Let us open our eyes to the awful consequences of our sins. May we see that sin crucifies Christ today the same as the day when he died on Calvary. Such a vision will drive us to our knees in confession of our wrongs and the acceptance of forgiving grace.

WEDNESDAY EVENING, NOVEMBER 24

Title: Attitudes Toward Jesus

Text: "When the great crowd of the Jews learned that he was there, they came, not only on account of Jesus but also to see Lazarus, whom he had raised from the dead" **(John 12:9 RSV).**

Scripture Reading: John 12:1–11

Introduction

What happens before church may influence worship more than what happens in church. What happened when the Jews were on the way to celebrate the Passover in Jerusalem illustrates the level of deterioration of the whole religious structure at the time. Even more importantly, the story of

Mary anointing Jesus' feet in Bethany illustrates that attitudes toward Jesus not only affect our worship but also determine our lives. Let's look at some of the attitudes found in our Scripture reading.

I. The attitude of the Jews.

Interesting indeed is the early arrival of the Jews in Jerusalem "to purify themselves" (John 11:55) of the contamination they received by associating with Gentiles in their travels. Let us see what else we can learn about the attitude of the Jews.

A. *Curiosity.* They were curious as to whether Jesus would attend the feast. They doubted if he would run the risk of facing his foes. Since the raising of Lazarus, his enemies were after him with greater intensity than ever (John 11:56). Some just wanted to gawk at Lazarus because they had never seen anyone who had been resurrected (12:9). Some of the Bethany crowd were curious to see this Galilean who was causing all the furor. It was a curious crowd.

B. *Hatred.* The Sadducees were determined to put Jesus to death because of the resurrection of Lazarus. They denied and despised the whole idea of resurrection. The religious leaders in general felt so threatened by Jesus that their hatred had become murderous. They also hated Lazarus and planned to kill him too (John 12:10–11).

C. *Belief.* Thank God, notwithstanding the danger involved, many of the Jews were believing in Jesus (John 12:11). Persecution always eventually prompts an evangelistic response.

II. The attitude of Judas.

Selfish attitudes often are clothed in sanctimonious language. Judas criticized Mary's generous gesture by saying the price of the expensive ointment should be given to the poor rather than poured on Jesus' feet. Did you ever hear that kind of argument? It is an almost daily ostentation in legislative sessions, but did you ever hear this kind of hypocritical argument in a church business meeting? John wrote later that Judas was a thief. Obviously, the disciples did not know this at the time. That Judas still had influence is attested by the statement in Matthew (26:8–9) and Mark (14:4–5) that other disciples agreed with Judas that Mary's generosity was wasteful misuse of property. Thankfully the other disciples went no further with Judas in other matters. Anytime a person takes an unchristian attitude, he or she runs the risk of serious embarrassment and hindered witness.

III. The attitude of Mary.

Simon the leper had prepared a dinner in honor of Jesus and Lazarus and had invited the family of Lazarus and the twelve apostles

(Matt. 26:6; Mark 14:3). It was a gracious occasion. No doubt all were deeply moved by what Jesus had done for this lovely family. Mary, with unusual sensitivity and deep perception, "took a pound of costly ointment of pure nard [the spike or head of an East India plant] and anointed the feet of Jesus and wiped his feet with her hair." Mark and Matthew say the ointment was in an alabaster jar and that she poured it on his head. Maybe she poured it on his head and feet. To pour the valuable ointment on his feet and wipe it with her hair was an unusual gesture of humility and openness. This is the part John recalls. The whole house was filled with the fragrance. The Jewish worship had deteriorated to a level of ostentation and formality. Mary's act portrayed pure personal praise. Judas demonstrated selfishness and sarcasm. Mary demonstrated self-sacrifice, loyalty, and love.

Conclusion

Mark summarized Jesus' response to the Jewish leaders, spectators, disciples, Judas, and especially Mary. "Let her alone; why do you trouble her? She has done a beautiful thing to me. For you always have the poor with you, and whenever you will, you can do good to them; but you will not always have me. She has done what she could; she has anointed my body beforehand for burying. And truly, I say to you, wherever the gospel is preached in the whole world, what she has done will be told in memory of her" (Mark 14:6–9 RSV). Those few lines from the lips of Jesus comprise one of the greatest sermons in the New Testament.

SUNDAY MORNING, NOVEMBER 28

Title: The Miracles of Christmas

Text: "Now the birth of Jesus Christ was on this wise: When as his mother Mary was espoused to Joseph, before they came together, she was found with child of the Holy Ghost" **(Matt. 1:18).**

Scripture Reading: Matthew 1:18–25

Hymns: "Hark! The Herald Angels Sing," Wesley
          "Joy to the World!" Watts
          "Ye Servants of God," Wesley

Offertory Prayer: Gracious and loving Father, during this period of the year we are reminded over and over of the lavishness of your gift to us in your Son, Jesus Christ. Today we come bowing before him in reverence and gratitude, bringing gifts of our love. Accept these gifts and bless them to the end that others around the world will come to know Jesus Christ as Lord and Savior. In his name we pray. Amen.

Introduction

The real story of Christmas abounds with miracles—the star that guided the Magi; the angelic appearances; the annunciation by Gabriel to Zacharias of the birth of John the Baptist; the annunciations of the birth of Jesus to Mary, to Joseph, and to the shepherds; the anthem of praise by the angelic choir; the Magi warned in a dream not to return to Herod; Joseph directed by an angel into the land of Egypt and told to depart from Egypt, and warned in a dream against Archelaus, Herod's wicked son and successor; the birth of John the Baptist when his parents were advanced in age; the birth of Jesus, who had a human mother but not a human father.

The birth of Jesus Christ is the most meaningful and unique birth in the annals of time. Christ existed from all eternity; he was in the beginning with God (John 1:1). He said, "Verily, verily, I say unto you, Before Abraham was, I am" (John 8:58).

The miracles of Christmas are manifold, and they have a message for us. Let us hear what they have to say to us.

I. The miracles of Christmas speak of the miraculous conception (Gen. 3:15; Isa. 7:14; Matt. 1:18–25; Luke 1:26–27, 34–38; Gal. 4:4–5).

The angel Gabriel told Mary that the Holy Spirit would come upon her and the "power of the Highest" would overshadow her (Luke 1:35). The figure is that of a cloud. The cloud of glory represents God's power. The miraculous conception is plainly set forth in the gospels of Matthew and Luke. The fact that Luke was a physician gives added meaning to the miraculous conception of Mary by the Holy Spirit. It is a miracle. It is the power of God acting in accord with his laws. "For with God nothing is impossible."

A. *The miraculous conception declares Jesus to be God (Luke 1:35; Matt. 1:23; John 1:14).*

B. *The miraculous conception declares Jesus to be sinless.* He was born without an earthly father. He lived without experiential sin. He declared himself to be sinless when he said, "Which of you convinceth me of sin?" (John 8:46). They could not lay one sin to his charge. Not one blotch, not one mistake, not one error did he commit, for he was sinless.

II. The miracles of Christmas speak of the glorious Incarnation (Matt. 1:23; John 1:14).

Jesus became flesh and dwelt among us. He was God in human flesh—the God-man—not God indwelling a man. He is God and man combining in one personality the two natures of God and man.

The incarnation of Jesus Christ shows humankind's capacity for God. We can know God as he reveals himself through Jesus Christ, the God-man.

III. The miracles of Christmas speak of wondrous salvation (Matt. 1:21; Luke 2:10–11; 19:10; John 3:16; Gal. 4:4–5; I Tim. 2:3–6).

A. *Jesus Christ came to save (Matt. 18:11).*

B. *Jesus Christ came to save sinners (1 Tim. 1:15).*

C. *Jesus Christ came to save by bearing away our sins (John 1:29; 1 John 1:7).*

D. *Jesus Christ came to save by his own blood (Col. 1:14; Eph. 1:7; 1 John 1:7).*

E. *Jesus Christ came to save because no one else can save (Acts 4:12).*

Conclusion

Let the miracles of Christmas speak to your heart. Let the Christ of Christmas be your Savior and your Lord!

SUNDAY EVENING, NOVEMBER 28

Title: God's Plan of the Ages

Text: "God's plan, which he will complete when the time is right, is to bring all creation together, everything in heaven and on earth, with Christ as head. For all things are done according to God's plan and decision" **(Eph. 1:10–11** TEV**)**.

Scripture Reading: Ephesians 1:3–12

Introduction

Paul says that God has an "eternal plan of the ages," the mysteries of which have been made known in Jesus Christ. What was not earlier understood should now be plain to every believer. The purpose of this plan is "to bring all creation together. . .with Christ as head." God's plan has at least five facets to it:

I. There is one God.

A. *The Bible states clearly that we worship one God.* The Bible opens with the words, "In the beginning God. . ." (Gen. 1:1). This sets the tone for the biblical doctrine of the sovereignty of God. Paul explains, "There is. . .one God and Father of all, who is above all, and through all, and in you all" (Eph. 4:4, 6).

B. *God is a living God with whom we have to deal.* Moses at the burning bush questioned God about his name. God answered, "I am who I am. . .say to them, 'I AM has sent me'" (Ex. 3:14 TEV). He is the living one, "the same yesterday, today, and for ever" (Heb. 13:8).

C. *God is a jealous God (cf. Josh. 24:19).* The Old Testament often likens God's relationship with his people to the marriage relationship. It took the wilderness wanderings and exile into Babylon for the Hebrews to learn this lesson of loyalty—one yet unlearned by millions today.

II. There is one world.

A. *It is a world united in the common bondage of sin.* Although divided by diversities, yet as the sons of Adam all people struggle with the common problem of sin.

B. *History is a story of human sinfulness.* Biblical history of Noah's day testifies to early humankind's downfall: "God saw that the wickedness of man was great in the earth, and that every imagination of the thoughts of his heart was only evil continually" (Gen. 6:5). Romans gives an update to the same problem, "When they knew God, they glorified him not as God, neither were thankful; but became vain in their imagination, and their foolish heart was darkened" (Rom. 1:21). There follows a description of the downward route of man into idolatry, spiritual blindness, and gross immorality.

C. *Current news provides a modern commentary.* Paul concludes, "By one man sin entered into the world, and death by sin; and so death passed upon all men, for that all have sinned" (Rom. 5:12). The daily news media speaks this truth in stark, modern language.

III. There is one mediator.

A. *A qualified intercessor.* "There is...one mediator between God and men, the man Christ Jesus" (1 Tim. 2:5). Because he was both God and man, yet sinless, Christ met the demands of the law and could atone for our sins. *The Living Bible* paraphrases, "God is on one side and all the people on the other side, and Christ Jesus, himself man, is between them to bring them together, by giving his life for all mankind."

B. *God's grace brings reconciliation.* "Where sin abounded, grace did much more abound" (Rom. 5:20). "For he is our peace, who hath made both one, and hath broken down the middle wall of partition between us" (Eph. 2:14). God's grace reaches down in Christ to reconcile sinful man to a righteous God. This spiritual reconciliation makes possible reconciliation and fellowship with others of our divided race.

IV. There is one people.

A. *God called a missionary people.* God called Abraham and said to him, "I will make of thee a great nation, and I will bless thee, and make thy name great; and thou shalt be a blessing" (Gen. 12:2). He passed it along to Moses, saying, "Ye shall be unto me a kingdom of priests, and an holy nation" (Ex. 19:6). This missionary call was handed on to other generations of God's people.

B. *The church is the new people of God.* To the body of believers, the church, God gave a similar commission. "Ye are a chosen generation, a royal priesthood, an holy nation, a peculiar people; that you should shew forth the praises of him. . .which in time past were not a people, but are now the people of God" (1 Peter 2:9–10).

V. There is one mission with one message.

A. *Our message is the world's greatest need.* Renowned theologian Karl Barth, when asked for the most profound statement he had ever read, answered, "Jesus loves me this I know, for the Bible tells me so."

Paul says, "For I delivered unto you first of all that which I also received, how that Christ died for our sins according to the scriptures" (1 Cor. 15:3–4).

B. *Bearing the message is our mission.* Jesus spoke to his disciples, "Go ye into all the world, and preach the gospel to every creature. He that believeth and is baptized shall be saved" (Mark 16:15–16). These words were echoed to the church at Corinth: "God, who hath reconciled us to himself by Jesus Christ, and hath given to us the ministry of reconciliation; to wit, that God was in Christ, reconciling the world unto himself. . . .Therefore if any man be in Christ, he is a new creature: old things are passed away; behold, all things are become new. . . .Now then we are ambassadors for Christ, as though God did beseech you by us: we pray you in Christ's stead, be ye reconciled to God" (2 Cor. 5:18–19, 17, 20).

Conclusion

Paul proclaims the plan of the ages, God's purpose for humankind from eternity to eternity. It is God's plan that "the earth may hear his voice" through you. You are to witness personally, participate in the local church, and share your faith to the ends of the earth. The church must find its divine place in missions, in God's plan of the ages. Are you willing to commit your life, ability, spiritual gifts, and financial resources to make a bold new step as your part of a priestly people?

DECEMBER

■ **Sunday Mornings**

Continue the series "Christmas Means Listening to Jesus."

■ **Sunday Evenings**

Continue the series "The Mission of the Christian and the Mission of the Church."

■ **Wednesday Evenings**

Conclude the series of messages based on John's gospel. The theme could be "Events in the Last Week of the Life of Our Lord."

WEDNESDAY EVENING, DECEMBER I

Title: Hosanna!

Text: "Hosanna! Blessed is he who comes in the name of the Lord, even the King of Israel" **(John 12:13 RSV).**

Scripture Reading: John 12:12–19

Introduction

From here on through the rest of the book, every passage in the gospel of John is packed with tension. John himself inescapably recalls it with tension. All the actors in this true-life drama keenly felt the gravity of every moment. Since the wedding in Cana, Jesus had said, "My hour has not yet come." In this chapter he says, "The hour has come for the Son of man to be glorified." The disciples were confused. They "did not understand" what was going on (John 12:16). The Pharisees were getting desperate. They "said one to another, 'You see that you can do nothing; look, the whole world has gone after him'" (v. 19). The crowds were divided into three tense groups: his enemies who were trying to destroy him, the people who had seen the miracle in Bethany, and the ever-present spectators who were looking for excitement.

I. The crowd.

John's account is curiously curt and undetailed as compared to the full and vivid accounts in Mark and Luke. No doubt some of these pilgrims were Galileans with the same delirium as those who had been rebuffed by Jesus a year earlier when they tried by force to make him king. Always there are insecure and superficially eager crowds who are looking for a leader. One reason they respond irresponsibly is that they do not want to assume any responsibility of leadership themselves. They will follow any strong leader at least temporarily.

Some of the most sincere followers of Jesus were there. They had dedicated their lives to him. Martha had said, "I believe that you are the Christ, the Son of God, he who is coming into the world" (John 11:27). The most devoted of his followers had terribly warped concepts as to the kind of Messiah he was. They waved palm branches, which were symbols of power. Palm branches were pictured on coins to symbolize the Maccabean overthrow of the Syrians years earlier. Simon, their leader, had made a triumphal entry into Jerusalem like this one, and Jesus' followers hoped that he would now overthrow the Romans. This mood was further indicated by the cry "Hosanna," which means "Save us now." They were no doubt recalling with some variation a song used to welcome people on the way to the temple to worship: "Save us, we beseech thee, O LORD! O LORD, we beseech thee, give us success! Blessed be he who enters in the name of the LORD!" (Ps. 118:25–26).

II. The disciples.

The undiscerning disciples apparently did not understand the symbolism nor the Lord's response. John remarks that they did understand after Jesus was glorified. Jesus' closest friends were slow in their understanding.

III. Jesus.

Jesus now allowed what he had prevented a year earlier, when at Passover time he had fed the five thousand, and the people had said, "This is indeed the prophet who has come into the world!" When they had been about to take him by force to make him king, Jesus had withdrawn to the mountain by himself (John 6:14–15). Now when the Pharisees rebuffed him by saying, "Teacher, rebuke your disciples," he responded by saying, "I tell you, if they were silent, the very stones would cry out" (Luke 19:39–40).

Contrary to anything he had ever done before, Jesus sent two of his disciples (Luke 19:29–35) to get a young donkey that had never been ridden and used it to symbolize that the hour had now come by riding on the donkey. The donkey symbolized a peaceful reign rather than a military rule. Jesus was a new type of king, with none of the extravagant trappings of royalty, none of the fanfare and pomp that would be expected if he really meant to set up an earthly kingdom. Yet at the same time he allowed a symbol that would be remembered both because it had been prophesied and because it had happened. To us it is a reminder that he is the King of Kings and the Lord of Lords. Jesus was and is never ostentatious, but always humble. It is to be remembered that he is the Son of God with all authority in heaven and earth.

Conclusion

"Therefore God has highly exalted him and bestowed on him the name which is above every name, that at the name of Jesus every knee shall bow, in heaven and on earth and under the earth, and every tongue confess that Jesus Christ is Lord, to the glory of God the Father" (Phil. 2:9–11 RSV).

SUNDAY MORNING, DECEMBER 5

Title: Do You Need to Hear Some Good News?

Text: "The angel said to them, 'Be not afraid; for behold, I bring you good news of a great joy which shall come to all the people; for to you is born this day in the city of David a Savior, who is Christ the Lord'" **(Luke 2:10 RSV).**

Scripture Reading: Luke 2:1–10

Hymns: "Majestic Sweetness Sits Enthroned," Stennett
"The Head That Once Was Crowned," Kelly
"Great Redeemer, We Adore Thee," Harris

Offertory Prayer: Eternal Father, giver of eternal life and bestower of all blessings, we come to offer to you the love of our hearts, the praise of our lips, and the results of our labor as an expression of our worship. We come to thank you for all the good news you communicate to our hearts through the coming of Jesus Christ to be our Savior. Help us as your children and as your servants to share with the angels, with the shepherds, and with the wise men in proclaiming far and wide the good news of the coming of the Christ. In his name we pray. Amen.

Introduction

We live in a day in which there is much bad news. With satellite communication and twenty-four-hour news channels, we are made aware of every crisis around the world on a minute-by-minute basis. Wars, crime, economic disasters, political corruption, personal scandals, and natural disasters contribute to the avalanche of bad news with which we are assaulted every day.

A part of the appeal of Christmas is that it is a message of good news about God.

A.   Christmas reveals to us the God above and behind the world in which we live.
B.   Christmas reveals God in the world in the person of Jesus Christ.
C.   Christmas reveals that God is for the world.

If we miss the good news of Christmas, we have missed the main point, for "the angel said to them, 'Don't be afraid! For I am here with good news for you'" (Luke 2:10 TEV).

I. The good news of Christmas is that our God is the living God.

A. *God is (Heb. 11:6).*

B. *God works.*

C. *God works for good in all things to those who love and trust him (Rom. 8:28).*

D. *God has an orderly procedure in which he is at work in the world and in the hearts of those who trust him.*

E. *Our God is personal.* Jesus reveals this dramatically.

    1. John 1:18.

    2. John 1:14.

    3. Matthew 17:1–8. In his glorious transfiguration experience, the deity of Jesus Christ shone through the veil of his humanity. The disciples of our Lord beheld deity in his humanity. Jesus came to reveal that God is more than just an impersonal power behind the universe. He is the personal God who relates to us as a loving father to needy children.

    4. John 14:9. If you would see and know God, then look into the face of the Christ who came as a baby on that first Christmas morning.

II. The good news of Christmas is that our God is a loving God.

God is love.

A. *God's love for people is unmerited.* God loves us because he is love.

    1. God has loved us in the past.

    2. God loves us in the present.

    3. God always will love us. His love for us is not determined by our attractiveness or performance.

B. *God's love is all inclusive.* The children's chorus says, "Red and yellow, black and white, all are precious in his sight." No person is so high or so low that he or she is not the object of God's love.

C. *God's love is liberating.* He sets us free from passions and emotions that would destroy us.

D. *God's love is personal (John 3:16).* In order for this great verse, which has been called the little Bible, to be really meaningful, we need to put ourselves right in the middle of it. Instead of reading, "God so loved the world," read it "God so loved [your name] that he gave his only Son, that if [your name] believes in him [your name] will have eternal life." Personalize God's great love for you.

Christ's coming to earth, living, dying, rising from the dead, ascending to heaven, and interceding for us assure us that God loves us.

III. The good news of Christmas is that our God has provided for us a leader.

Christ came to be our Savior from sin and the Lord of our life. For him to be both Savior and Lord, it is necessary that we let him be our leader.

A. *Jesus Christ wants to lead you out of all that is destructive, evil, and wasteful.* He wants to lead you out of that which is nonproductive and disappointing into that which will be most productive and satisfying.

B. *Jesus wants to lead you into the abundant life of peace with God and into a right relationship with others.* In the Bible, people begin their existence in the Garden of Eden. The last book of the Bible pictures people in the paradise of God. The Christ who came at Christmas wants to lead you into that heavenly way of life in the here and now as well as in the hereafter.

C. *Jesus Christ wants to lead you through the uncertainty of the present and the complexity of the future.* The psalmist was greatly comforted by the assurance that the Good Shepherd would lead him through the valley of the shadow of death (Ps. 23:4). The message of Christmas is that Christ wants to lead you through your dark and dangerous valleys.

D. *Jesus Christ wants to lead you to the highest and best possible manhood and womanhood.* He wants to lead you up to the highest quality of life in your home, in your work, and in your personal achievements. Between now and the end our Lord wants to lead you upward to that which is highest and best for you and for those about you. He is a competent, compassionate, and consistent leader. You always can trust him to lead you in the right way.

Conclusion

Have you really heard the good news of Christmas? How are you responding to it? Make this your best Christmas ever by believing the Good News and receiving Christ as Savior and Lord.

SUNDAY EVENING, DECEMBER 5

Title: A New Beginning

Text: "I will make of thee a great nation, and I will bless thee. . .and thou shalt be a blessing" **(Gen. 12:2).**

Scripture Reading: Genesis 12:1–9

Introduction

We turn back to Genesis, the book of beginnings, to find God's purpose for his people. God does have an eternal plan for humankind. From the beginning of history, humanity's contribution to that plan has been disappointing. The early chapters of Genesis picture Adam's fall and the failure of society in Noah's day. Following the Flood, God's plan again seemed destined to failure as a result of human disobedience. But in Genesis 12 God chose to begin anew with one man, Abraham.

I. God gave to Abraham both a gift and a promise.

From the long lineage in Genesis 11, in which men lived long, begat sons and daughters, and died, there surfaces a different type of person in Abraham. Little is known about him. But one day the voice of God spoke to Abraham saying, "Get thee out of thy country, and from thy kindred, and from thy father's house, unto a land that I will shew thee" (Gen. 12:1).

A. *Abraham received God's greatest gift.* How or why God came to get in touch with Abraham is lost in God's providence. But, in calling Abraham, God gave his greatest gift—himself. In the New Testament we are told, "Abraham believed God, and it was counted unto him for righteousness" (Rom. 4:3). In response to the love and call of God, Abraham found God's presence in his life. He believed that God would work through him to ultimately bring about divine salvation for humankind.

B. *Abraham also received a promise.* God promised, "I will make of thee a great nation, and I will bless thee, and make thy name great; and thou shalt be a blessing" (Gen. 12:2)—all of this to a man and his wife for whom childbearing seemed an impossible hope. Later God reaffirmed this promise: "Look now toward heaven and tell the stars, if thou be able to number them. . . .So shall thy seed be" (Gen. 15:5).

II. God also made a demand.

A. *God made a covenant with Abraham.* God's gift and promise were part of a conditional contract. God called for Abraham's agreement to fulfill his part of the covenant. A covenant with God is somewhat like a marriage ceremony. As the pastor inquires, "Do you take this man? Do you take this woman?" there is a hush until there is a definite "I do." God calls on man, but he must await a response.

B. *God demands a commitment.* We do not receive God's salvation nor enter into God's purpose and work until we have made a definite commitment. God demanded from Abraham a wholehearted commitment and a strict obedience. There is an entrance fee at the door of Christian service. Salvation is free in that it cannot be bought, but both salvation and service demand the "I do" of self-surrender.

III. God gave a command.

A. *God's command to leave the familiar.* Abraham was called to leave his native land and his father's home. Abraham apparently did not question. It was a call to leave the familiar and go out toward the unknown.

B. *God's call to trust.* To any question of Abraham's, God's only answer was "Trust me." Whether called to leave family and native land or to remain right where you are, God's command is always, "Up and out"—out of self and the conformity of society into a transformed life in Christ. For specific instructions we must trust him one day at a time.

IV. God put Abraham to the test.

A. *Faith is often put to the test.* The Bible nowhere promises Christian workers they will be exempt from hardships and trials. Every believer must face doubt, problems, sorrows, and disappointments. Abraham's commitment to leave home and follow God was only the beginning point.

B. *Abraham faced trials.* Abraham was faced with two great trials, both of which were centered in his call to a missionary life. First, his faith was tested by Sarah's inability to have a child. God had promised a nation, and he did not have a single child. He must have asked, "Lord, why, how, when?" God seemed to have answered back, "I have promised. I will fulfill. Wait for my time." Waiting is often a trial.

Abraham's second trial was even greater. God finally gave him a son in his old age, and the son rapidly was growing into manhood. God spoke again, "Take now thy son, thine only son Isaac, whom thou lovest, and get thee into the land of Moriah; and offer him there for a burnt offering" (Gen. 22:2). For Abraham, the sky fell; the world came to an end. But he obeyed, answering his son's query about the sacrifice with a helpless dependence on God, "My son, God will provide." At the last moment, when the last ray of hope was about to fade, God told Abraham it was enough: "Now I know that thou fearest God" (Gen. 22:12).

C. *Abraham's test has significance today.* God always demands our best. A foreign missionary preached in a small church and gave an invitation for young people to give their lives to God's service. The pastor took up the invitation and extended it. A lovely young woman came striding purposefully forward. The pastor embraced her and cried, "But, honey, I didn't mean you." She was his only daughter. God does not want from you what comes easily. He wants your best.

Conclusion

Abraham could be called the first missionary. Thousands have followed God's call. Now God presents himself to you. Through you he wants to make a new beginning in your home, your church, your community, or on an isolated mission field.

God demands your best because it is part of his plan. When it came time for his own Son to die, there was no substitute. Christ died for our sins. On the basis of that kind of love, God now calls you to make a new beginning in his service. Will you help others find meaning and purpose as they find life in Christ Jesus? As God needed Abraham, so he also needs you.

WEDNESDAY EVENING, DECEMBER 8

Title: Footwashing

Text: "Then he poured water into a basin, and began to wash the disciples' feet, and to wipe them with a towel with which he was girded" **(John 13:5 RSV).**

Scripture Reading: John 13:1–20

Introduction

Most references to footwashing in religious conversations are spoken in jest. "Are you a footwashing Baptist?" The typical jesting answer is "Every Saturday night." This is understandable but unfortunate. It is understandable because through the years there have been groups who practice footwashing as a church ordinance. It is unfortunate because the occasion of Jesus washing the disciples' feet was an exceedingly dramatic and unforgettable moment, and the lesson implied is extremely significant.

1. *Jesus' hour had come.* Many times before he had reminded his disciples and family that his hour had not come. Now he knew that he was soon to depart out of the world and go to the Father. His reactions and responses were, therefore, changed. For the first time he was ready to let the people know that he had come from God and was going to God. The Father had put all things into his hands, and he was acting accordingly. He loved his own who were in the world, and they needed to be prepared for his departure, especially his death.

2. *The devil was dedicated.* His plans to defeat man and defy God were in jeopardy. He had failed in his efforts at temptation but had not permanently retreated. He sought to destroy Jesus by putting it into the heart of one of the inner circle to betray Jesus.

3. *A new community was launched.* Even before Jesus' crucifixion and resurrection he had begun to prepare his disciples for their new relationship in the church and to teach them the kind of fellowship it was to be.

I. Jesus washed the disciples' feet.

Surprisingly, John omitted the institution of the Lord's Supper as described by the synoptic writers. He assumes a knowledge of it and tells of the unusual footwashing incident.

A. *The disciples' feet needed washing after the journey.* There was no servant to perform the menial task, and the disciples did not offer to assist each other. There was a practical need, and Jesus characteristically rose to the occasion.

B. *Jesus exemplified love and demonstrated humility.* Love and humility go together like selfishness and pride. The church is to be a fellowship of love, and members are to be examples of humility. The disciples had been fussing (Luke 22:24) about who would be greatest, and Jesus demonstrated that the greatest would be the lowliest servant.

C. *Jesus was preparing his disciples for his own death on the cross.* He had taught them that he was the Son of God. He was to further reveal his oneness with the Father, but they must learn that he was also the Suffering Servant.

  1. He laid aside his garments (v. 4), just as he was to lay down his life.
  2. He poured water into a basin and began to wash their feet. Perhaps he was symbolizing his work of cleansing them from sin through his approaching death.

II. Peter objected.

Peter often opened his mouth before he thought about what he was saying. He was willing for Jesus to be King but not Servant. He did not know he could not be one without being the other. Because of his impulsive nature, Peter made a rash statement, "You shall never wash my feet." Many people have suffered endlessly because of an impulsive statement they were unwilling to retract. The result has been broken families, divided churches, and saddened lives. My own father had said before his conversion that he would never put his foot inside a church door. He perhaps regretted the statement many times but was too hard-headed to recant. My mother and a wise friend later reminded him that he had not said he would not attend a brush arbor revival. After his conversion, he had no difficulty reversing his statement.

III. Peter changed his mind.

Repentance means changing one's mind. No one ever demonstrated it better than Simon Peter. The new life that begins with decisive repentance continues with daily repentance and renewal. Just as impulsively as he had spoken foolishly the first time, Peter overreacted in the opposite extreme: "Lord, not my feet only but also my hands and my head." Jesus answered profoundly, symbolically, and prophetically: "He who has bathed does not need to wash, except for his feet, but he is clean all over." Once we have had our sins removed in the new birth, we do not need to keep on being born again, but we do need continuous renewal. When Christians sin we do not invalidate all the saving work of Jesus, for the Christian life is a life of growing and maturing faith.

Conclusion

While our culture does not often provide the need or opportunity for washing our brothers' and sisters' feet, it does offer daily opportunities to meet other needs within the fellowship of the church. When we realize the value of servanthood in our lives, we will be able to impact others' lives. The only way we can demonstrate humility with consistency is to love others as God in Christ loves us.

SUNDAY MORNING, DECEMBER 12

Title: The Childhood and the Home Life of Jesus

Text: "The child grew and became strong, filled with wisdom; and the favor of God was upon him. . . .And Jesus increased in wisdom and in stature, and in favor with God and man" (**Luke 2:40, 52 RSV**).

Scripture Reading: Luke 2:39–52

Hymns: "Joyful, Joyful, We Adore Thee," Van Dyke
"Thy Word Is Like a Garden, Lord," Hodder
"Jesus Loves Me," Warner

Offertory Prayer: Holy Father, as the Christmas season approaches, we are overwhelmed with reminders of your generosity and the richness of your gifts to us through Jesus Christ. Today we would imitate the wise men and bring gifts to him who was born and anointed to be our King. We bow down before him in reverence, adoration, and commitment. Bless these gifts that the good news of his birth, death, resurrection, ascension, and coming again might be spread to the ends of the earth. In his name we pray. Amen.

Introduction

Today I am going to bring a Christmas message to the children of the congregation concerning Jesus' childhood and home life. The message will also be helpful to parents and others.

What were Jesus' childhood and home life like? How did his home life differ from that of average American children today? Are there any parallels between Jesus' childhood and that of children now?

The circumstances under which our Lord grew up were very simple in comparison to the modern and affluent society in which many children grow up today. Jesus grew up in a home where poverty, rather than affluence, was known. He grew up in a home in which there were none of the modern appliances and conveniences that have come to be considered as necessities today. However, there are some similarities.

I. The Christ was very fortunate in the parents of his home.

In many respects it is the parents who affect the childhood and home life of a child more than any other single factor. Jesus was fortunate to grow up in a home where Joseph served as the father and Mary was the mother.

A. *Mary, Jesus' mother, was chosen by God for a unique service.* God had chosen to visit the earth in the form of a human being, and he chose Mary, a virgin peasant girl, to be the mother of the Christ child. While Mary performed a unique function, she had characteristics that others can emulate.

 1. Mary was a devout and genuine believer in God.
 2. Mary was pure in mind, body, and motive.
 3. Mary was humble before God, recognizing her dependence on him for everything.
 4. Mary was obedient to the known will of God as he revealed his plan and purpose for her.
 5. Mary was cooperative with the Holy Spirit not only at the beginning but throughout the childhood and lifetime of her Lord and our Lord.
 6. Mary was thankful to God for the privilege of being his servant and responded with joyful submission.
 7. Mary's life was a life of consistent self-control as she sought to be the servant of God. Jesus had this kind of a mother during his childhood, and she contributed greatly toward a happy home life for her family.

B. *Joseph consented to being a father to the Christ child.* While Joseph was not the biological father of Jesus Christ, he fulfilled all of the responsibilities of a loving father.

Having the ability to be the biological father of a child is not nearly as significant as having the disposition and the determination to provide the nurture, guidance, wisdom, and help that a growing child needs in his or her pilgrimage toward maturity.

 1. Joseph listened to God (Matt. 1:18–22; 2:13–14). For Joseph prayer was not just a matter of talking to God. It was letting God talk to him. God communicated with Joseph in dreams. At times perhaps the subconscious mind that continues to function even while we are asleep may be much more open to divine communication than is the conscious mind. Joseph heard the voice of God because he was a genuine believer in God. He believed in the goodness of God's purpose.
 2. Joseph was obedient to God's instructions (Matt. 1:24). Abraham, the father of the faithful, was a man who believed in God and

obeyed God. These two traits go together in the making of a great and good father.

3. Joseph worked with his hands (Matt. 13:55). Our Lord learned to work as a child with Joseph in his carpenter shop. He placed a divine stamp of approval on working with one's hands.

4. Joseph provided Jesus with a model for thinking of God.

Mary and Joseph related to Jesus as mother and father (Luke 2:48). It is interesting to note that our Lord's favorite term for God is "Father." He taught his disciples to think of God as a wise, benevolent, and gracious father. It was from Joseph that Jesus received this model for thinking about God.

II. Jesus' childhood was one of growth.

A. *Jesus experienced physical growth.* There is no evidence of sickness or disease in Jesus' life that hindered him as he grew toward physical manhood. We can assume that Jesus experienced the joys of a healthy developing body.

B. *Jesus experienced intellectual growth.* He increased in wisdom.

1. Jesus learned to read in the synagogue.
2. Jesus learned to write. We read later of his writing in the sand.
3. Jesus learned a trade. He was a carpenter. Every Jewish boy learned a trade during childhood.
4. Jesus learned to work while he was yet a child. He did not grow up with the idea that the world owed him a living.

C. *Jesus experienced spiritual growth.*

1. Jesus studied the Scriptures both in his home and in the synagogue.
2. Jesus regularly attended the synagogue's services (Luke 4:16).
3. Jesus developed a habit of prayer and didn't break it. He talked with God the Father and was open to divine communication.
4. Jesus let the world of nature remind him of the presence, power, and purpose of God.

D. *Jesus experienced social growth.* "The favor of God was upon him. . . .And Jesus increased in. . .favor with God and man" (Luke 2:40, 52 RSV).

1. Jesus learned the art of getting along with family members. Maybe Jesus learned to be a giver rather than just a receiver, a helper rather than a hinderer, and a listener rather than just a looker.
2. Jesus related to his parents in reverent obedience. He recognized and responded to their authority. God has appointed parents to be authority figures in their children's lives. It is sad when a child does not respect parental authority.
3. Jesus related to his brothers and sisters in terms of practicing a persistent spirit of unbreakable goodwill.
   a. He didn't abuse them.

b. He didn't capitalize on their faults.
c. He aided them and did not seek to exploit them.
d. He practiced the golden rule.
4. Jesus learned how to serve and satisfy the needs of others in the carpenter's shop. He lived by the philosophy of being a giver even in his youth.
5. Jesus learned to wait for the call of God to service and to duty. Perhaps there were days when he wanted to move out into the world, but he waited until God called.

Conclusion

How can we follow the pattern of Jesus in his youth and childhood?
1. Recognize and relate to God as your Father.
2. Commit your life to the house and to the business of God.
   a. Jesus worked for God in a carpenter shop.
   b. Jesus lived for God in a redemptive mission.
3. Respond positively to God's helpers.
   a. Parents.
   b. Brothers and sisters.
   c. Spiritual teachers.
4. Let the Scriptures enter your heart and mind and provide divine guidance.
5. Be open to God's invitations.
6. Listen to his voice and respond affirmatively.

SUNDAY EVENING, DECEMBER 12

Title: A Search for Reality

Text: "I heard the voice of the LORD, saying, Whom shall I send, and who will go for us? Then said I, Here am I; send me" **(Isa. 6:8).**

Scripture Reading: Isaiah 6:1–9

Introduction

The demise of a king or ruler is always a traumatic experience. We all remember the emotional waves that swept the nation at the assassination of President Kennedy and the resignation of President Nixon. Such times send people searching for the real amid the superficial and hypocrisy of life.

Another young patriot, Isaiah, faced a similar time. King Uzziah had died. He had started well, made reforms, and formed a stable government. "But when King Uzziah became strong, he grew arrogant, and that led to his downfall" (2 Chron. 26:16 TEV). As a result of his presumption at the altar of

God, he was struck with leprosy. The king finally succumbed to the disease and died in shame and isolation. Seeing his nation falling apart, Isaiah sought to find some verities and realities on which he might depend. His experience guides us in our search.

I. The steps in Isaiah's search.

A. *He was confronted by the living God.* Isaiah sought his answers in the right place. He went to the temple and worshiped. Isaiah "saw also the Lord sitting upon a throne, high and lifted up." The seraphim cried, "Holy, holy, holy, is the LORD of hosts" (Isa. 6:1, 3). Isaiah was confronted by the presence of the living God.

B. *Isaiah faced himself and confessed his sin.* At the sight of God's presence, Isaiah cried out, "Woe is me! for I am undone; because I am a man of unclean lips, and I dwell in the midst of a people of unclean lips" (Isa. 6:5). Standing before the Lord of hosts, Isaiah was overwhelmed by his sin.

Isaiah confessed only one sin, the sin of unclean lips. This was not foul language, but the sin of hypocrisy. The nation's sin was also that of hypocrisy. They had been called to be the people of God; they had jealously kept God's blessings to themselves; they had forgotten their priesthood; they had lost their role as a holy nation. A search for reality must find the truth about ourselves and about our religious institutions.

C. *The Lord cleansed the repentant sinner.* Upon Isaiah's confession, a seraphim took from the altar a burning coal of fire and put it to Isaiah's mouth, saying, "Lo, this hath touched thy lips; and thine iniquity is taken away, and thy sin purged" (Isa. 6:7). God applied the remedy of grace and cleansed one man of hypocrisy.

This type of cleansing must come to God's church. Like Isaiah, we also have played the part of the hypocrite. We talk about missions and we dip into our purses occasionally to give to mission causes, but our hearts and souls are not really in it. We play at church.

D. *Isaiah was faced with a decision and a commitment.* Immediately upon hearing the words "Thy sin is purged," the voice of the Lord came saying, "Whom shall I send, and who will go for us?" The call of God to salvation is always a call to service and to witness.

The decision to make Christ Lord requires a commitment of self to the will of Christ. Isaiah's answer was, "Here am I; send me." Every worship service calls for such a commitment. In the quietness of that moment, the Lord speaks again, "Go, tell." In his own time and manner, God's Spirit will direct how and where you are to go.

II. Isaiah's search for reality points to God's eternal plan.

As he sought to become God's preacher, Isaiah was given a look through the ages to see that his service was a part of a great eternal plan. In this purpose of God, Isaiah was to find life's reality. This revelation was to come by several stages.

A. *Isaiah the servant.* One can visualize this young preacher, fired with a heavenly vision, preaching to worshipers. The elders pat him on the shoulder and say, "That's fine, lad; that's good preaching." But Isaiah knows it is hypocrisy, that the people don't intend to do anything about it, that they are not about to give up their phylacteries, their prayer beads, their rituals for a personal experience with God.

Isaiah was to learn at least two lessons. First, missionary work is full of heartaches. Ministering to people is costly. Second, one person, no matter how dedicated and zealous, cannot win the world alone but can be one voice.

B. *The nation as a servant.* Isaiah also caught a vision of what God intended when he made a covenant with Abraham and Moses. He saw what could be done if God's people, a nation of holy people, actually lived before and witnessed to the pagan nations. But his people had failed to do so. He continued to call them back to repentance of personal and national sins so that they might again become the "people of God." His description of God's vineyard (Isa. 5) speaks to the church today.

C. *A remnant as a servant.* Isaiah was a realist and saw that the whole nation would never turn to God, so he began to proclaim the hope of a remnant. If the whole church will not be a missionary vessel, God can use a small group of the faithful. The world has yet to see what could be done if the whole church were harnessed in power. But with hope Isaiah proclaims, "The remnant that is escaped...shall again take root...and bear fruit" (Isa. 37:31). In every age, God has his remnant that in spite of discouragement remains faithful and brings renewal. Are you among them?

D. *The Messiah, the Suffering Servant.* In the midst of both Isaiah's high hopes and his deepest despair, Isaiah saw that neither he, the nation, nor a faithful remnant held the real answer. God uses individuals, nations, and remnants; they are all his instruments. But the real hope of the world would come as a consummation of God's purpose in the promised Messiah, the Suffering Servant. "He was wounded for our transgressions, he was bruised for our iniquities: the chastisement of our peace was upon him; and with his stripes we are healed" (Isa. 53:5). This provides the central truth and the central figure of God's plan for an individual, a church, and a nation. "God was in Christ, reconciling the world unto himself" (2 Cor. 5:19).

Conclusion

In a world filled with hypocrisy and blasphemy, and in the church where hypocrisy becomes the most damnable of all sins, how does one find reality? Like Isaiah, we find reality when we seek it in a personal encounter with God, a personal commitment of self to him, and when we find our place in God's evangelistic and missionary calling. The church has no purpose for existence apart from this central purpose. As we prepare for Christmas, may we rise up and declare, "Here am I; send me."

WEDNESDAY EVENING, DECEMBER 15

Title: Last Words

Text: "These things I have spoken to you, while I am still with you" **(John 14:25 RSV).**

Scripture Reading: John 13:31–14:31

Introduction

Our Scripture centers around some of the departing conversations of Jesus with his disciples. We will not read the entire passage but will look at some of the carefully worded counsel centered around the questions of three disciples: Peter, Thomas, and Philip. The honest questions reveal surprising vulnerability and ignorance and provoke deep insights and profound truths.

I. Peter's questions.

Jesus had announced his departure and glorification (John 13:31–32). His departure involved death, and death was necessary to his glorification. He had already made the decision to suffer and die; therefore, his glorification was past as well as present and true. Since his actual death was the immediate future, his physical presence with his disciples would be for only a little while. Since they could not go with him until later, he commanded them to maintain the fellowship that had been begun by loving one another (John 13:33–35). Peter could not or would not accept the responsibility involved in the new commandment to love, but asked Jesus two questions and made a rash commitment.

A. *"Lord, where are you going?"* Naively, Peter was thinking of the immediate future. He was an activist who often confused courage with impulsiveness. From our perspective the question was far more profound than Peter realized.

B. *"Lord, why can't I follow you now?"* Perhaps in this question Peter was confusing impatience with dedication. It is often easier to be busy doing "the Lord's work" than it is to make the deeper and more permanent commitment to love and obedience.

C. *"I will lay down my life for you."* Again, Peter responded with emotional impulsiveness that would later mature to courage and boldness. Jesus reminded Peter that this loyalty would not last till morning. No doubt his intentions were the best, but he was later to learn that humility rather than pride produces boldness.

Where Jesus was going and how the disciples of all time could go with him was answered by Jesus in one of the most beloved and oft-quoted passages in the Bible: "Let not your heart be troubled; believe in God, believe also in me. In my Father's house are many rooms, if it were not so, would I have told you that I go to prepare a place for you? And when I go and prepare a place for you, I will come again and will take you to myself, that where I am you may be also. And you know the way where I am going" (14:1–4 RSV).

It is unfortunate that this passage is usually read only at funerals to assure the bereaved of the heavenly home of the deceased. While not discounting this truth, it is wise to remember the context of the discussion, both from the standpoint of Peter's question and subsequent promises of the Holy Spirit's presence with the Lord's disciples after he goes away. I certainly would not detract from the Lord's precious promises about his future return. I would like to point out that because of "another Counselor, to be with you forever," his precious promises are now effective for all believers. He is with us now, and we will be with him forever.

II. Thomas's question.

"Lord, we do not know where you are going; how can we know the way?" We have to thank Thomas for the question, because the answer gives us both an effective evangelistic text and a great passage of comfort. Jesus answered, "I am the way, and the truth, and the life; no one comes to the Father, but by me" (14:6 RSV). The assurance wrapped up in the words "way," "truth," and "life" are as immeasurable as eternity and as available as a prayer. Jesus is revealed as both mediator and friend. The last part of his answer to Thomas prompted the next question: "If you had known me, you would have known my Father also; henceforth you know him and have seen him" (v. 7).

III. Philip's question.

"Lord, show us the Father, and we shall be satisfied."

A. *Idolatry grows out of a desire to see physical evidence of God.* This was a problem of Israel in the wilderness. It is a problem today with those who desire some image they can handle. Some mentalities have great difficulty with anything abstract.

B. *God provides us with everything we need to worship him.* "The Word became flesh and dwelt among us, full of grace and truth; we have beheld his glory, glory of the only Son from the Father" (John 1:14). Jesus' answer to Philip was, "Have I been with you so long, and yet you do not know me, Philip? He who has seen me has seen the Father." He continues in the next several sentences (vv. 10–14) to explain the relation of the Father and Son and presents this relationship as the basis of promised answered prayer.

Conclusion

"If a man loves me, he will keep my word, and my Father will love him, and we will come to him and make our home with him." That is now!

SUNDAY MORNING, DECEMBER 19

Title: Christmas Means Listening to Jesus

Text: ". . .but in these last days he has spoken to us by a Son" **(Heb. 1:2 RSV).**

Scripture Reading: Hebrews 1:1–4

Hymns: "Angels We Have Heard on High," Old French Carol
           "As with Gladness Men of Old," Dix
           "There's a Song in the Air," Holland

Offertory Prayer: Heavenly Father, for all the blessings that you have so abundantly bestowed upon us, we thank you. We thank you for the joy of this season of the year in which we celebrate the coming of your Son, Jesus Christ, in the flesh to reveal to our hearts the God of love and grace. Open up our hearts to receive him. Help us to welcome him in reverence and to bow before him in worship. Help us to give to him the trust and the adoration of our hearts and the loyalty of our lives. In Jesus' name. Amen.

Introduction

Christmas means many things—giving, sharing, loving, singing, and fellowship—but Christmas also means listening to Jesus Christ to hear what he has to say about God. The big question is, "How do you listen when God speaks through Jesus Christ?"

The faith of the Old Testament and the faith of the New Testament is that the God whom we worship is the God who communicates with his creatures. The Bible is a record of God's events of self-disclosure in which he has sought to communicate with people. One way in which he communicates is through his natural creation (Ps. 19:1–4). Some people listen to and learn what God has to say. Another way God communicates is through what we call conscience. People have a sense of oughtness. God communicates through a universal moral law to people's consciences.

The writer of Hebrews declares that "in many and various ways God spoke of old to our fathers by the prophets" (Heb. 1:1 RSV). God spoke through holy men moved by the Holy Spirit. Through Moses, God gave the Ten Commandments, ten great principles by which an ordered and stable society can be regulated, maintained, and perpetuated. These laws are self-executing laws in that to ignore or to violate a single one of them is to break oneself upon them.

Through Elijah, God called the nation of Israel away from the waste and desolation of idolatry and urged them to worship the one true God (1 Kings 18:21–22). Have you listened to the challenge of God through the prophet Elijah? Have you forsaken the false gods that always disappoint? Are you worshiping the one true God with all of your heart?

Through Isaiah, God spoke concerning his sovereign holiness. Isaiah went into the temple to pray at a time when his mind was filled with thoughts of an empty throne because of the death of King Uzziah (Isa. 6:1). As Isaiah bowed in reverent worship, God opened the eyes of his soul and let him see the eternal King sitting sovereign and supreme, majestic and holy, on the throne of the universe. God revealed to the frightened young man that even though Uzziah was dead, Israel's God was still on the throne. The God whom Isaiah saw was a holy God who could not tolerate sin. Isaiah acknowledged his own sinfulness and unworthiness, and immediately one of the seraphim came and purged away the filth of his soul by means of a hot coal taken off the altar. With cleansing there came a call to God's service, and Isaiah volunteered. He heard what God was saying. Have you heard what God was saying through his prophet Isaiah?

Through the rustic shepherd-prophet, Amos, God spoke to northern Israel concerning his own moral character and of the absolute necessity of his people being committed to righteousness and justice. It was Amos who declared that a moral God places moral demands on his people, that a God of integrity requires integrity on the part of his people. Have you heard God speak through Amos?

Through Hosea, God spoke to the nation of Israel concerning his suffering, seeking love. Hosea is the evangelist of the Old Testament, the prophet through whom God revealed that there is hope in God's grace when all hope seemingly has disappeared. In Hosea's domestic tragedy, God revealed his compassionate love for the wayward nation in the person of Gomer, the prophet's wayward wife. How do you listen when God speaks? Have you heard what God was saying through the prophets of old?

The message of Christmas and the message of our Hebrews text declares that in these last days God has spoken through his Son, who was born of a virgin in Bethlehem. Christmas means that we should listen to Jesus Christ as he speaks about God, for it is in Jesus Christ that God has made his full and final self-disclosure.

I. God has appointed Jesus Christ "the heir of all things" (Heb. 1:2).

A. *Jesus Christ is declared to be the goal of history.*

B. *The kingdom belongs to Jesus Christ.* John declares, "The kingdom of the world has become the kingdom of our Lord and of his Christ, and he shall reign for ever and ever" (Rev. 11:15 RSV).

C. *The victory belongs to Jesus Christ (Phil. 2:6–11).* Jesus Christ has bought the decisive battle of history through his coming in the flesh, assuming the form of a servant, taking upon himself our guilt, and dying as a sacrifice for our sins on the cross. God exalted him by raising him from the dead and has lifted him to the position of supreme authority in this world and in the world to come. It is through this One who is "the heir of all things" that God speaks.

II. It is through Christ that "God made the world."

People listen to people of power. Powerful political and military leaders can command a crowd. Those who have power in the world of finance can command the attention of businesspeople. The inspired writer tells us that in Jesus Christ lies the creative power by which the universe was literally called into being. John declares, "He was in the beginning with God; all things were made through him, and without him was not anything made that was made" (John 1:2–3 RSV). In Paul's epistle to the Colossians he declares, "All things were created through him and for him" (1:16 RSV).

III. Jesus Christ "reflects the glory of God."

The word translated "reflects" is a strong word also translated "effulgence." It refers to "the radiance shining forth from a source of light." Just as the radiance of the sun reaches the earth, so in Jesus Christ the glorious light of God shines forth to illuminate the heart and the way of humankind.

IV. Jesus Christ is the very image of the substance of God.

Jesus Christ "bears the very stamp of God's nature." We see the images of great people on our coins. Just as the image on a coin exactly corresponds to the device on the die used to make that coin, so the Son of God "bears the very stamp of God's nature." To see Jesus Christ is to see what God is really like. Paul said to the Colossians, "In him all the fulness of God was pleased to dwell" (1:19 RSV).

V. Jesus Christ upholds all things in "the universe by the word of his power."

Jesus Christ upholds the universe not like the mythological character Atlas who supported the dead weight of the earth upon his shoulders but as one who carries all things forward on an appointed course. Jesus Christ keeps the universe on schedule.

VI. Jesus Christ has "made purification for sins."

A. *Jesus Christ, the Babe of Bethlehem, lived his life, rendered his service, and finally sacrificed himself as an atonement for our sins on a cross.* For us to neglect to hear him speak concerning our need for the forgiveness of our sin is to miss what God is saying through Jesus Christ at this and every Christmastime.

B. *As the perfect High Priest, Jesus Christ has entered into the most holy place as a perfect sacrifice for our sins.* He has borne the penalty for us. On the basis of his sacrificial death for our sin, he is able to offer us the gift of eternal life.

C. *As the One who has conquered death and who is alive forevermore, Jesus serves as our advocate, making intercession for us (Heb. 7:25; 1 John 2:1–2).* It is not enough for us to sing beautiful Christmas carols and rejoice in a baby who was born long ago. Let us listen to what he has to say about God and let us respond to what he has to say about humankind's deepest need.

VII. Jesus Christ has been exalted and enthroned to be our King Redeemer (Heb. 1:3).

A. *Jesus Christ was born to be our King.* He merits the place of lordship in our hearts and lives.

B. *Jesus Christ alone can be our Savior from sin.* He has come offering forgiveness and a new life. Have you heard his invitation, "Come unto me," and responded by making him the Lord of your life?

C. *Jesus is a worthy and competent leader who says, "Follow me."* Have you listened and heard him as he invites you to become acquainted with God?

Conclusion

How do you listen to what God has to say through Jesus Christ? Are you in some pain that makes you too uncomfortable to listen? Have you been injured and are too angry to listen? Are you a fool who is too stupid to listen? Are you a self-sufficient, sophisticated, conceited person who feels no need to listen? Are you so preoccupied with things that you are too busy to listen? Are you too fearful and uncertain to listen? Or are you willing to listen to him now as he speaks words of assurance concerning the greatness of God's love for you and of the wonder of God's plan for your life? Let the Christ of Bethlehem become the King and Lord of your empire. Make him Lord so that you can experience the joy of being what God meant for you to be.

SUNDAY EVENING, DECEMBER 19

Title: Through Sacrifice to Glory
Text: "Sir, we would see Jesus" **(John 12:21)**.
Scripture Reading: John 12:20–28

Introduction

This week we will celebrate the birth of Jesus. However, if we see only a baby in a manger, we have missed the significance of Christmas. The Incarnation involves not only the fact that God became flesh, but it also involves Christ's life of service, crucifixion, and glorious resurrection. All of this is contained in the declaration, "The Word became flesh and dwelt among us" (John 1:14).

The incident about which we have read in our text is recorded only by John. John typically looks beyond the event to a spiritual significance. He saw the coming of the Greeks as a tying together of the many strands of God's eternal purpose. At lease three emphases are made in the simple words of the text.

I. The quest of the Gentiles.

A. *The desire of the Greeks to see Jesus.* These were not the first Gentiles to come to Jesus. There had been others in whom Jesus had found faith, but Jesus saw in this occasion a significant movement. These Greeks were familiar with Judaism. It is likely that they were proselytes, for they had come to the city to worship. But there was something lacking, some uncertainty, some dissatisfaction. They had heard in Jerusalem of Jesus' miracles and had come to learn more about him.

B. *The reluctance of the disciples.* The Greeks likely sought out Philip because he had a Greek name, had come from the cosmopolitan city of Bethsaida, and probably would be sympathetic to their query. Philip, however, reacted with coolness and hesitation. He kept them waiting while he consulted Andrew.

II. The person of their search.

A. *The Greeks sought Jesus.* They came with a specific request that they be introduced to Jesus. They did not come to have Philip or another tell them about Jesus. They sought firsthand experiential knowledge of him. Nothing else is ever sufficient for those interested in coming to know God.

B. *Jesus exulted in their coming.* Jesus' answer to the request placed before him by Andrew and Philip was immediate and spontaneous. "The hour is come!" he exulted. He went on to add, "The hour has now come for the

Son of Man to be given great glory" (John 12:23 TEV). It is as if he had said, "Of course, tell them to come in. This is what we have been waiting for. This is why I came. This is what I have been trying to get across to you." Oh, that God would give his churches the same spirit so that we may zealously and eagerly go out into the ghettos and the slums as well as into the affluent family rooms of suburbia, exclaiming that God loves all.

C. *Jesus saw a new door opening.* It is true that only a few Greeks sought him out, but he looked beyond this to the future generations of Gentiles from every tribe and nation that would make their way to the cross. It is in the future generations that Jesus saw his coming glory. Today there is hardly a nation that has not some who give honor and glory to the King of Kings.

III. A momentous revelation.

The coming of the Greeks did not seem so significant to the disciples, yet Jesus used this occasion to make one of the most profound of all his revelations concerning his death and his Father's purpose in it.

A. *Jesus spoke of sacrifice.* Immediately after hearing of the Greeks, Jesus began to speak of his own sacrificial death. We are not certain whether the Greeks were included in this discourse, but if so, their hearts must have burned within them as they learned that this Jesus whom they sought was the sacrifice for their sins. Jesus used an agricultural illustration: "I tell you the truth: a grain of wheat is no more than a single grain unless it is dropped into the ground and dies. If it does die, then it produces many grains" (John 12:24 TEV). Plainly he began to describe his coming death. A little later he added, "I, if I be lifted up from the earth, will draw all men unto me" (John 12:32).

B. *Jesus spoke of honor.* Jesus said to those with him, "If any man serve me, him will my Father honour" (John 12:26). He said that his ministry involved suffering and death. Then he turned to his disciples and explained, "Whoever loves his own life will lose it. . . .Whoever wants to serve me must follow me, so that my servant will be with me where I am" (John 12:25–26 TEV). This means that believers will be with Christ in heaven, but it also means that they must be with him in suffering as well.

How does Jesus plan to honor his servant? When I was a young man, my father turned over the keys of his store to me and said, "Son, the responsibility for the business is yours for a week." In doing so, he shared his work with me and thus honored me. God honors us by sharing his redemptive work with us. "As my Father hath sent me, even so send I you" (John 20:21).

C. *Jesus speaks of glory.* As Jesus contemplated the next days, he was troubled. He asked himself, "Shall I say, 'Father, do not let this hour come upon me'? But that is why I came, to go through this hour of suffering" (John 12:27

TEV). Then he added, "Father, bring glory to your name." A voice answered, "I have brought glory to it, and I will do so again" (John 12:28 TEV).

Christian glory comes through suffering. God had glorified his name in the life and ministry of Jesus. Now, in the coming suffering of arrest, betrayal, and crucifixion, God would again be glorified.

God continues to be glorified in the salvation of the lost. We share in this by receiving his salvation and praising him for it. We glorify God with Christlike lives and by witnessing. As we bring others to Christ, the process of glorification continues. His glory is reflected in our lives, but glory is always within the shadow of the cross.

Conclusion

It's Christmastime again. Let us put the real meaning of the Incarnation into it. Let's make it a daily observance as we receive God's gifts and commit ourselves to him. Christmas means sharing; sharing demands involvement with others; involvement brings suffering; suffering with Christ brings the glory of a surpassing peace now and an eternal glory of his presence hereafter. Christmas is "missions" and the response to the world's quest, "Sir, we would see Jesus."

WEDNESDAY EVENING, DECEMBER 22

Title: A New Commandment

Text: "A new commandment I give to you, that you love one another; even as I have loved you, that you also love one another" **(John 13:34 RSV).**

Scripture Reading: John 13:34–35

Introduction

As *life* and *light* are key words in the first twelve chapters of John, *love* is the key word in chapters 13–17. Love is not merely advised or exemplified; it is commanded. Christ commanded his disciples to "Go therefore and make disciples of all nations, baptizing them in the name of the Father and of the Son and of the Holy Spirit, teaching them to observe all that I have commanded you" (Matt. 28:19–20 RSV). He commanded them "to preach to the people, and to testify that he is the one ordained by God to be judge of the living and the dead" (Acts 10:42 RSV). The primary emphasis in Jesus' commands is love. In addition to our text we read: "He who has my commandments and keeps them, he it is who loves me; and he who loves me will be loved by my Father, and I will love him and manifest myself to him" (John 14:21 RSV). "If you keep my commandments, you will abide in my love, just as I have kept my Father's commandments and abide in his love" (John 15:10

RSV). "And this is his commandment, that we should believe in the name of his Son Jesus Christ and love one another, just as he has commanded us. All who keep his commandments abide in him, and he in them" (1 John 3:23–24 RSV). John was certainly impressed with Jesus' emphasis on love, so it is no surprise to us that tradition says that love was John's theme in his old age.

I. A new commandment.

Loving your neighbor as you love yourself is not new. The Old Testament taught, "You shall not take vengeance or bear a grudge against the sons of your own people, but you shall love your neighbor as yourself: I am the LORD" (Lev. 19:18). Jesus taught that one must love his neighbor better than himself: "Greater love has no man than this, that a man lay down his life for his friends" (John 15:13). The newness of this commandment was that it was based on the love between Jesus and the Father. "For this reason the Father loves me, because I lay down my life, that I may take it up again. No one takes it from me, but I lay it down of my own accord. I have power to lay it down, and I have power to take it again; this charge I have received from my Father" (John 10:17–18). "I do as the Father has commanded me, so that the world may know that I love the Father" (John 14:31).

The love Jesus is talking about is not saccharine sweet. It is not mere emotion. The love he commands is the kind of love that cost him his life on the cross. No wonder love has been called the greatest thing in the world. When I was a child I heard my preacher cry as he told a story of a dog dying for his master. It would have been a better illustration of Jesus' love if it had been a master dying for his dog. Parents have died for children and children for parents. Husbands and wives have died for each other. A better illustration is one who died for his enemy. "Why, one will hardly die for a righteous man—though perhaps for a good man one will dare even to die. But God shows his love for us in that while we were yet sinners Christ died for us" (Rom. 5:7–8).

Jesus is talking about a new kind of love. To whatever extent church fellowships can approach that kind of love, they will be moving closer to the greatest revolution in Christian history.

II. A new witness.

When an evangelist asked a new convert, "Was there some one thing I said tonight that helped you reach your decision?" the young lady said, "Honestly, I don't remember much you said. It was a telephone call from my parents today. When I saw how much they loved me in spite of the way I have treated them, I said there must be something to being a Christian." Jesus said, "By this all men will know that you are my disciples, if you have love for one another" (John 13:35).

Conclusion

I once heard a great sermon on the parallels between the great commandment and the Great Commission. The preacher's thesis was that loving one's neighbor and trying to lead the neighbor to Christ were equally important. In a sense he was correct, but it would be more correct to say that the Great Commission issues out of the great commandment. We witness because we love. We can go after new members for the church like a businessman goes after customers or like a politician goes after voters, but that is not evangelism. When we go because the love of Christ constrains us, we are evangelists. Not only, however, is love the best *motive* for evangelism, it is the best *method*. If we love, we win.

SUNDAY MORNING, DECEMBER 26

Title: Seizing Our Opportunities

Text: "Look carefully then how you walk, not as unwise men but as wise, making the most of the time, because the days are evil" **(Eph. 5:15–16 RSV).**

Scripture Reading: Ephesians 5:15–20

Hymns:　"Have Faith in God," McKinney
"Must Jesus Bear the Cross Alone?" Shepherd
"Throw Out the Lifeline," Ufford

Offertory Prayer: Heavenly Father, in obedience to your request, we pause today and pray that you will send forth more laborers into the harvest. Help each of us to be willing to take hold and labor in that portion of your vineyard where you would have us to work. We come bringing tithes and offerings of our material goods, thanking you for the privilege and the power to work and to earn. Bless these gifts to the end that others will come to know your love and the light that leads to the life abundant in the here and now. In Jesus' name. Amen.

Introduction

It is interesting to see how our text is translated in some of the modern translations. Montgomery translates it, "See to it, then, that you carry on your life carefully; not as foolish, but as wise men. Buy up opportunity, for the times are evil." Goodspeed translates it, "Be very careful, then, about the way you live. Do not act thoughtlessly, but like sensible men, and make the most of your opportunity, for these are evil times." Moffatt translates it, "Be strictly careful then about the life you lead; act like sensible men, not like thoughtless; make the very most of your time, for these are evil days." Today's English Version translates it, "So pay close attention to how you live. Don't live like ignorant men, but like wise men. Make good use of every opportunity you get, because these are bad days."

Paul is calling upon the disciples of Jesus Christ in the city of Ephesus to walk in a manner worthy of their calling (Eph. 4:1–16), to walk differently from the pagan world about them (vv. 17–24), to walk in love (4:25–5:2). In the first part of chapter 5 he urges them to walk in the light as the sons of light (Eph. 5:5–14). In the words of our text he encourages them to walk with wisdom, seizing every opportunity to render service to God and to others.

Paul issues a call to walk in wisdom over against the folly of a pagan world. Wisdom is not an intellectual achievement but is a mind-set in which one seeks to do only those things that are pleasing to God. We are to "snatch up all the opportunities that are available" for doing God's will. Paul uses the commercial vocabulary of the marketplace to describe the intense activity that he is encouraging them and us to put forth.

Some watch the stock market with intense interest because they are eager to seize bargains. They try to buy at the right time and sell at the right time in order to experience a profit. The apostle is encouraging this type of interest, energy, and ingenuity concerning spiritual opportunities for service. We are to seize an opportunity for service in the same manner that we would seize a bargain in the marketplace. The early Christians outlived, outthought, and outdid their contemporaries. That is what our present generation needs.

This is a call to a serious acceptance of our stewardship of time. Not one of us has as much time as we think we have. It is much later than we think. Our opportunities are rapidly slipping away from us. Each of us has an equal amount of time every day, and each must make the most of it.

A salesclerk gave a customer a sheet of paper on which to try out a new fountain pen. The customer wrote all over the page, *"Tempus Fugit."* The clerk brought him another pen and said, "Perhaps you will like this one better, Mr. Fugit." It really doesn't matter what pen you use, because "time flies."

Orville Kelly was the founder of an organization called Make the Day Count. Kelly founded this organization after discovering he was terminally ill with cancer. The purpose of the organization was to help those who were fatally ill face the realities of both their disease and their remaining time. We need to stress the importance of the present and become intensely aware of the value of life and time. This would help us to learn what really matters and what doesn't.

I. Time is loaned to us to be used in God's service.

A. *Time is very precious.*
B. *Time is passing swiftly.*
C. *Time is very uncertain.*
D. *Time once gone cannot be recalled.*
E. *Time is something for which we are accountable.*

Each moment, as it passes, is the meeting place of two eternities.

II. Make good use of time.

A. *Yesterday cannot be recalled.*

B. *Tomorrow cannot be assured.*

C. *Only today is ours.*

D. *If we procrastinate, we lose the present.*

E. *Someone has said, "One today is worth two tomorrows."*

III. What time is it?

A. *It is time to open your heart to the good news of God's love for you.*

B. *It is time to put your faith and trust in Jesus Christ as Savior and Lord as well as leader and teacher.*

C. *It is time to do the good that your heart tells you you should do.*

D. *It is time to speak to others the words that need to come from your heart and your lips to them.*

E. *It is time to become a giver.* Define your purpose for being in terms of being a contributor and a helper rather than merely in terms of being a pack rat who accumulates things.

F. *It is time to forgive those who have mistreated you or deprived you.*

Conclusion

It is a good time for you to do what the Lord is leading you to do at this moment.

SUNDAY EVENING, DECEMBER 26

Title: Unfulfilled Prophecy and an Unfinished Task

Text: ". . .repentance and remission of sins should be preached in his name among all nations, beginning at Jerusalem" (**Luke 24:47**).

Scripture Reading: Luke 24:44–49

Introduction

First words and last words are important. The world gathered around television and radio and waited in hushed silence as Astronaut Neil Armstrong spoke the first words from the moon. A family draws near a sickbed to catch the last whispered words of a loved one. Likewise, we want to catch the last words of our Lord. Jesus spoke to his disciples and gave them final instructions. What did he say? He spoke of an unfulfilled prophecy and an unfinished task as he placed the disciples firmly in the midst of God's purpose and destiny.

I. Jesus reasoned about prophecy already fulfilled.

Jesus pointed out to the disciples from Moses, the prophets, and the Psalms how God's eternal purpose had been at work throughout history. He likely called to their remembrance the covenants with Abraham and Moses as God had created a missionary nation. He emphasized how the prophets had wrestled with the infidelity of the chosen people and their disloyalty to their missionary calling. He also reminded them of the messianic promises.

Following this exposition of Scripture, Jesus said to his disciples, "This is what is written: that the Messiah must suffer and be raised from death on the third day" (Luke 22:46 TEV). Then he added, "You are witnesses of these things" (Luke 24:48). These prophecies of the Messiah have been perfectly fulfilled in Jesus. No longer is there necessity for making animal sacrifices or priestly rituals. The law with its sacrificial system and rituals has been superseded by God's fulfillment of prophecy in Jesus Christ.

II. Jesus revealed the future.

Not all prophecy, however, had yet been fulfilled. Jesus again placed the future of the disciples and the church squarely back in God's plan of the ages. He called to them, "It is written that in his name the message about repentance and the forgiveness of sins must be preached to all nations, beginning in Jerusalem. You are witnesses of these things" (Luke 24:47–48 TEV).

A. *He reminded them of the content of their message.* On the basis of the fulfilled prophecy in his death, burial, and resurrection, the disciples were to call people to repentance and forgiveness of sins. Jesus calls us back to this simple central message of the Bible.

B. *Jesus recalled them to the extent of their task.* This was unfulfilled prophecy. The gospel "must be preached to all nations." Students of missions today argue about how this may be done or whether it may have already been accomplished, but as long as there are individuals and groups who have not heard the gospel, our task is to go to the nations with the message.

C. *The instrument of missions is a human witness.* To his commission to evangelize the whole world, Jesus added, "You are witnesses of these things" (Luke 24:48). God did not choose heavenly messengers to bear the Good News. His reminder is that the gospel of Christ is to be preached by flesh and blood people—sinners who have found in Christ their salvation. Mass media is a wonderful tool, but the witness must be personal, from heart to heart.

D. *The place to begin is where you are.* Jesus said, "Beginning in Jerusalem. You are witnesses" (Luke 24:47–48). He did not ask his followers to make a pilgrimage to Jerusalem. That is where they happened to be. To preach the gospel to a strange people, in a far land, in a foreign tongue takes on a somewhat romantic aura, but to preach the gospel to the neighbors next door is also missionary work. Both witnesses are necessary, beginning where you are at this particular time.

III. The promise of power.

At the time Jesus spoke, these words were yet unfulfilled prophecy. Joel had prophesied, "And it shall come to pass afterward, that I will pour out my spirit upon all flesh...and it shall come to pass, that whosoever shall call on the name of the LORD shall be delivered" (Joel 2:28, 32). Jesus said, "Behold, I send the promise of my Father upon you; but tarry ye in the city of Jerusalem, until ye be endued with power from on high" (Luke 24:49). On the Day of Pentecost, when the Holy Spirit was given to the church, Peter interpreted this to be the fulfilling of Joel's prophecy and the promise of Jesus. The Spirit has now become a living presence and reality for all believers.

Evidence of the continuing work of the Holy Spirit around the world has been seen and felt in our time. There have been nationwide revivals. For some there has come miraculous outpouring; for others a deep, quiet undergirding of power. The promise is that God will keep on pouring out his Spirit on us and will infill us for the tasks he has set for us to do.

IV. The unfinished task.

The prophecy remains unchanged; some is fulfilled, some is not. The commission to go into the whole world with the whole gospel is the same. The promise of the Holy Spirit and his power remains undiminished. Yet the task is unfinished.

Earlier in Jesus' ministry, the disciples had asked Jesus about the end, and he answered, "This gospel of the kingdom shall be preached in all the world for a witness unto all nations; and then shall the end come" (Matt. 24:14). In a sense, then, our witness is a contributing factor in the final consummation and return of our Lord. The task is yet unfinished.

While Christ tarries, we are given the opportunity to "redeem the time." New millions continue to arise who have yet to behold the old story. At the same time, others die in sin who have never heard. Our task grows weightier instead of lighter as every day passes. Certain lepers said, "We do not well: this day is a day of good tidings, and we hold our peace: if we tarry till the morning light, some mischief will come upon us; now therefore come, that we may go and tell" (2 Kings 7:9).

Conclusion

We stand in the reflected glory of the cross, resurrection, ascension of our Lord. We witness in the glorious power of the Holy Spirit. We exult in the fulfillment of biblical prophecy. Yet there remains before us unfulfilled prophecy and an unfinished task. As we face a new year, let us make evangelism and missions our major emphasis. Apart from these, the church will lose its purpose for existence and will become just another club to join, another function to attend.

Missions is God's eternal purpose. It is not so important that we know the time of his coming but that we be found faithful in his calling.

WEDNESDAY EVENING, DECEMBER 29

Title: The True Vine

Text: "I am the true vine, and my Father is the vinedresser" **(John 15:1 RSV)**.

Scripture Reading: John 15:1–17

Introduction

More than in any other gospel, John wrote with the church in mind. As Jesus prepared for his departure, he prepared his disciples by showing them how he would continue with them through the indwelling Holy Spirit. In so doing he was preparing his church until the end of time. In this preparation as recorded in John 15–17, love is the theme. The familiar vine is the figure used to describe the love relationships. I know of several churches that have called themselves "The True Vine Church." In the light of Jesus' words here it appears to be a most appropriate name for a church. It is another way of saying "Christ's Church" or "Church of Christ." Every New Testament church is a "Church of Christ" or "True Vine Church."

The vine was a well-known symbol for Israel in the Old Testament. In using this symbol Jesus was designating himself the true Israel. In the vine-branch relationship he describes the relationship between himself and the church like the earlier relationship between God and Israel.

I. The church is not alone in the world.

Jesus has said, "I will build my church, and the powers of death shall not prevail against it" (Matt. 16:18 RSV). Elsewhere he is described as the Bridegroom and the church as bride, himself as head and the church as body. A vine and branches are beautiful and vivid figures. The church of John's day faced hatred and heresy. They were being reminded that they were not self-sustaining but their life was in Christ. One can no more destroy the church than Christ's enemies could destroy him. As he was glorified by suffering and death, the church prospers by persecution.

II. The Christian is not alone in the world.

Our Lord assures us of his sustaining love: "As the Father has loved me, so have I loved you; abide in my love" (v. 9). Paul wrote, "Who shall separate us from the love of Christ? Shall tribulation, or distress, or persecution, or famine, or nakedness, or peril, or sword?. . .in all these things we are more than conquerors through him who loved us" (Rom. 8: 35, 37 RSV).

A. *The Christian is kept by Christ.* As the sap flows from the vine to the branch and the branch is kept alive, the life of Christ constantly flows through the Christian. His life is in us living and his love is in us loving. That is the only way we can keep his command to love one another.

B. *The Christian life is lived by Christ.* We cannot live as Jesus commanded us to live in human strength alone. Paul had the problem and said: "I know that nothing good dwells within me, that is, in my flesh. I can will what is right, but I cannot do it. For I do not the good I want, but the evil I do not want is what I do" (Rom. 7:18–19 RSV).

He found the answer: "But you are in the flesh, you are in the Spirit, if the Spirit of God really dwells in you. Any one who does not have the Spirit of Christ does not belong to him. But if Christ is in you, although your bodies are dead because of sin, your spirits are alive because of righteousness. If the Spirit of him who raised Jesus from the dead dwells in you, he who raised Christ Jesus from the dead will give life to your mortal bodies also through his Spirit which dwells in you" (Rom. 8:9–11 RSV).

What can a branch be or do without the vine? There is no foliage, no flower, no fruit. There is no Christian who has not Christ.

C. *The Christian's fruit is produced by Christ.* "As the branch cannot bear fruit by itself, unless it abides in the vine, neither can you, unless you abide in me.... He who abides in me, and I in him, he it is that bears much fruit, for apart from me you can do nothing" (John 15:4–5). If we witness effectively to others, it is Christ witnessing through us. If we lead others to Christ, it is Christ leading them.

D. *The Christian's joy is in Christ.* "These things I have spoken to you, that my joy may be in you, and that your joy may be full" (v. 11).

Conclusion

Our relationships with Christ and with the church are relationships of love. We do not choose those with whom we live and serve in the church. They are chosen for us. Nevertheless, we are to love those whom we did not choose, even to the extent of laying down our lives for them: "This is my commandment, that you love one another as I have loved you. Greater love has no man than this, that a man lay down his life for his friends" (John 15:12–13). "You did not choose me, but I chose you and appointed you that you should go and bear fruit and that your fruit should abide; so that whatever you ask the Father in my name, he may give it to you." Even the answer to our prayers is contingent upon loving others. Therefore, let's love one another.

MISCELLANEOUS HELPS

MESSAGES ON THE LORD'S SUPPER

Title: Lessons from the Cross

Text: "For when we were yet without strength, in due time Christ died for the ungodly. For scarcely for a righteous man will one die: yet peradventure for a good man some would even dare to die. But God commendeth his love toward us, in that, while we were yet sinners, Christ died for us" **(Rom. 5:6–8)**.

Scripture Reading: Romans 5:1–8

Introduction

In expressing his preference for observing the Lord's Supper rather than hearing a sermon, King Henry III of France said, "I had rather *see* my friend than hear of him."

King Henry does not stand alone, for scores of other Christians join his ranks through the centuries testifying of the spiritual blessings received in the experience of the Lord's Supper, which is a memorial to the cross of Christ.

The lessons of the cross tend to be obscured by the rush of our twentieth century. Let us pause in the quietness of these sacred moments and learn the lessons of the cross.

I. The lesson on the love of God.

"God commendeth his love toward us, in that, while we were yet sinners, Christ died for us" (Rom. 5:8).

A. *God's love is sacrificial.* "For God so loved the world, that he gave his only begotten Son; that whosoever believeth in him should not perish, but have everlasting life" (John 3:16). God's love is no empty sentimentality. It is concern in motion, love in action to meet our deepest need.

B. *God's love is unfailing.* "I will be with thee: I will not fail thee, nor forsake thee" (Josh. 1:5). Why is God's love unfailing? Because our needs are unfailing and because unfailing love is a characteristic of God, for "God is love."

C. *God's love is impartial.* This truth was clearly communicated through the cross. The death of Christ proclaims, "Whosoever will, let him take the water of life freely" (Rev. 22:17).

D. *God's love is redemptive.* It is one thing to love a person in deep need. It is quite a different thing to be able to do what is required to meet that need. Through the cross God's love was released in a redemptive manner. Not only does he love us, but his love meets every need we have. "In his love and in his pity he redeemed them; and he bare them, and carried them all the days of old" (Isa. 63:9).

II. The lesson on the dedication of Christ.

"For when we were without strength, in due time Christ died for the ungodly" (Rom. 5:6).

A. *Christ goes a second mile.* "For scarcely for a righteous man will one die: yet peradventure for a good man some would even dare to die. But God commendeth his love toward us, in that, while we were yet sinners, Christ died for us" (Rom. 5:7–8). His dedication leads him to surpass our highest expectation (Rom. 5:7). It is expressed in his redeeming the undeserving (Rom. 5:8).

B. *Christ endured unbelievable hardships.* "He is despised and rejected of men; a man of sorrows, and acquainted with grief: and we hid as it were our faces from him; he was despised, and we esteemed him not. Surely he hath borne our griefs, and carried our sorrows; yet we did esteem him stricken, smitten of God, and afflicted" (Isa. 53:3–4).

C. *Christ refused to compromise.* The jeering crowds tried to get him to compromise. "He saved others; himself he cannot save. If he be the King of Israel, let him now come down from the cross, and we will believe him" (Matt. 27:42).

D. *Christ was faithful unto death.* "When Jesus therefore had received the vinegar, he said, It is finished: and he bowed his head, and gave up the ghost" (John 19:30).

III. The lesson on the seriousness of sin.

"About the ninth hour Jesus cried with a loud voice, saying, Eli, Eli, lama sabachthani? that is to say, My God, my God, why hast thou forsaken me?" (Matt. 27:46).

Sin is such a serious matter and so contrary to the character of God that he could not even look upon his Son as he carried our sins on the cross.

A. *The seriousness of sin is seen in the penalty for sin.*
1. Death. "For the wages of sin is death" (Rom. 6:23).
2. Anxiety. "Neither is there any rest in my bones because of my sin" (Ps. 38:3).
3. Alienation from God. "If I regard iniquity in my heart, the LORD will not hear me" (Ps. 66:18).

B. *The seriousness of sin is seen in the provision for sin.* "The blood of Jesus Christ his son cleanseth us from all sin" (1 John 1:7).

Conclusion

> *In mem'ry of thy cross and shame,*
> *I take this supper in thy name;*
> *This juice of grape, and flour of wheat,*
> *My outward man doth drink and eat.*

Oh, may my inward man be fed
With better wine and better bread.
May thy rich flesh and precious blood
Flow o'er me like a swelling flood.
I thank thee, Lord, thou died for me;
Oh, may I live and die to thee.

Title: A Time for Beginning Again

Text: "And he took bread, and gave thanks, and brake it, and gave unto them, saying, This is my body which is given for you: this do in remembrance of me. Likewise also the cup after supper, saying, This cup is the new testament in my blood, which is shed for you" **(Luke 22:19–20).**

Scripture Reading: Luke 22:19–27

Introduction

Of the many things that the Lord's Supper is, it is a time for beginning again. It can be to the Christian life what a midcourse correction is to a spaceship.

Imagine that it was possible to make a direct shot to the moon without orbiting the earth. Imagine also that there was no opportunity for an in-flight correction. If, in the launching, the calculations were off just one degree, that space vehicle would miss the moon by almost 1.5 million miles! We can begin to understand the importance of a midcourse correction in space travel. To drift off course, ever so slightly, is to miss the goal by a wide margin.

If we are drifting off course in our spiritual lives, the Lord's Supper can be an opportunity for us to make a midcourse correction and get back on track. The Lord's Supper is:

I. A time for a fresh dedication.

A. *To the will of God.* Perhaps some little sin has crept into your life and is causing you to drift off course from God's will. You may be only a fraction of a degree from dead center, but the farther you go with the miscalculation the wider is the ever-increasing distance by which you will miss God's will for your life. The observance of this supper can be that time of in-flight correction that gets you back on course.

   Jesus was always in the center of the Father's will, but he used the occasion of the Last Supper to reaffirm his dedication to that will. "This cup is...my blood, which is shed for you...and truly the Son of man goeth, as it was determined" (Luke 22:20, 22).

B. *To the task of witnessing.* The disciples were about to face the most strenuous period in their ministry. Christ chose the Supper as the climactic moment of his ministry before the cross to impart to them new determination for the trials ahead.

II. A time for self-examination.

"Let a man examine himself, and so let him eat of that bread, and drink of that cup" (1 Cor. 22:28).

Paul's emphasis surely must have been on the word "himself." We do not come to this hour to sit in judgment on others. We are not here to examine the lives of our fellow believers. To partake of this supper in such a manner would be to eat and drink "unworthily" (1 Cor. 11:29).

A. *Self-examination admits sin, whatever it may be and wherever it may be in our lives.* It is simply to be honest about ourselves before God.

Simon Peter's failure to make such a self-examination may well explain his claim, "I am ready to go with thee, both into prison, and to death" (Luke 22:33). I do not think he was hypocritical, nor was he deliberately telling a falsehood. He simply failed to see himself as he really was, and a humiliating denial of Christ followed.

We may save ourselves many spiritual defeats if we will pause and examine ourselves.

B. *Self-examination should result in turning from our sin.* We can accept the encouraging promise that "whoso confesseth and forsaketh [his sins] shall have mercy" (Prov. 28:13).

III. A time for meditation on Christ's death.

One of the main purposes of this ordinance is to meditate on Christ's death. "For as often as ye eat this bread, and drink this cup, ye do shew the Lord's death till he come" (1 Cor. 11:26). Could it be that the reason we do not feel any greater obligation to Christ is that we seldom really meditate on his death? Looking on the broken and bruised body of Christ on the cross will have a sovereign influence on our lives.

IV. A time for humility.

We will never admit our need to begin again as long as we are filled with pride. Only the humble will say, "I am wrong; I have sinned. Forgive me, Lord, and let me begin again."

How soon the disciples returned to pride and littleness after the high hour of the Lord's Supper! Luke 22:24–27 relates the strife that arose because these grown men, like little children, were arguing over "which of them should be accounted the greatest" (Luke 22:24). This would be unbelievable if it were not such a common occurrence with the church today.

Christ reminded his disciples that the lost world, "the Gentiles," were filled with such pride, but that as believers they were to emulate his humility of self-giving, which had just been dramatized through the Last Supper.

Conclusion

Would you like to stop right where you are and start all over again? If so, you have come to the right place at the right time, for the observance of the Lord's Supper is a time for a fresh dedication, self-examination, meditation on the death of Christ, and humility. If you would begin again, simply bow your head and tell the Lord that this is what you want to do.

Title: The Call of the Cross

Text: "He went a little farther, and fell on his face, and prayed, saying, O my Father, if it be possible, let this cup pass from me: nevertheless not as I will, but as thou wilt" **(Matt. 26:39).**

Scripture Reading: Matthew 26:36–41

Introduction

All through our Lord's ministry he heard the call of the cross. There is really no point in time when it is apparent that he became aware that the cross lay ahead. It seems that he had always known.

But as Jesus neared the sunset of his earthly ministry, he seemed to hear more loudly and clearly the call of the cross. As we gather around the Lord's Table, we too can hear the call of the cross. The call of the cross is:

I. A call to compassionate prayer.

"Then Jesus went with his disciples to a place called Gethsemane, and he said to them, 'Sit here while I go over there and pray'" (Matt. 26:36 NIV). The nearer Christ came to the cross the more he felt the need for prayer. He prayed for himself, for God's will to be done, and for the salvation of humankind. Knowing what would accompany the cross and what rested beyond it, he encouraged Peter to pray (Matt. 26:41). But Peter did not heed the call to prayer, and his humiliating denial of Christ followed.

We can never face the pressures of life and the temptations it holds apart from a daily pattern of compassionate prayer.

II. A call to go a little farther.

"And he went a little farther" (Matt. 26:39). The cross always calls us to go a little farther than the rank-and-file Christian will go. It calls us to go a little farther with the Lord than we have ever gone before. As we look at the cross and see Christ's dying for us, how can we be content to stay where we are?

III. A call to go it alone.

"Then saith he unto them. . .tarry ye here, and watch with me. And he went a little farther" (Matt. 26:38–39). The disciples went with Christ to the garden. Peter, James, and John went still a little farther with him. But those last lonely steps he made all alone!

There will be some who will go with you part of the way. Others will go with you most of the way. But if you are going all of the way into the will of God, you had better be prepared to make those last steps all alone.

IV. A call for a total surrender to God's will.

"O my father, if it be possible, let this cup pass from me: nevertheless not as I will, but as thou wilt" (Matt. 26:39). Christ is saying, "If there is any other way for people to be saved than by my death on the cross, save them that other way. Nevertheless, if not, your will be done." He is saying, "More than I want to live, I want your will done."

The call of the cross is a call for total surrender to God's will. If you hear that call and respond as Christ would have you to, you will also say, "God, more than I want to live, I want your will to be done." That is real surrender!

V. A call to an untiring persistency.

"He cometh unto the disciples, and findeth them asleep, and saith unto Peter, What, could ye not watch with me one hour? Watch and pray, that ye enter not into temptation: the spirit indeed is willing, but the flesh is weak" (Matt. 26:40–41).

The cross calls us to experience victory in our lives through persistent vigilance and prayer. Unlike the disciples who did not persist and failed Christ in his greatest hour of need, we are beckoned to "watch and pray," knowing all the while that although "the spirit indeed is willing, the flesh is weak."

Conclusion

As we have heard the call of the cross, our response will surely be:

My life, my love I give to Thee,
Thou Lamb of God who died for me;
O may I ever faithful be,
My Saviour and my God!

MESSAGES FOR CHILDREN AND YOUNG PEOPLE

Title: Youth Speaks to the Church

Text: "Don't let anyone think little of you because you are young. Be their ideal; let them follow the way you teach and live; be a pattern for them in your love, your faith, and your clean thoughts. Until I get there, read and explain the Scriptures to the church; preach God's Word" (**1 Tim. 4:12–13 TLB**).

Scripture Reading: 1 Timothy 4:12–13

Introduction

Young people have something to say to the church, and we should listen. Surprisingly, little of what young people have to say is negative. And this is normal, for unless young people have been prejudiced by unhappy adults, they think positively about their church, its program, and its leadership.

Much of the criticism of the church allegedly leveled by youth is nothing more than an adult's efforts to be a religious ventriloquist by putting words in their mouths. Therefore, today our interest is not what adults say youth are saying, but rather what youth themselves are saying to the church. I need to hear it as a pastor, you need to hear it as an adult member, and youth need to know that they have been heard by us. Then, where we can improve our ministries in response to what youth say, let us have the grace to improve them.

Young people are as interested in this church as any adult because this is as much their church as it is yours or mine. So since youth sit and listen to us week after week, let us pay them the courtesy of listening as they speak to the church.

I. "Teach me the Bible. I can learn other things somewhere else."

One hundred fifty teenagers were asked to make some definite suggestions for the church and its youth leaders. "Teach us the Bible" appeared on most lists. Christian youth are demanding a Christian faith that is for real. "Wherewithal shall a young man cleanse his way? by taking heed thereto according to thy word" (Ps. 119:9).

II. "Lead me to Jesus. This is your primary task."

Young people are saying to the church today what the Greeks said to Philip: "Sir, we would see Jesus" (John 12:21). "Lead us to him, we need and want to know him personally." In a church that averages 920 in Bible study, 78 young people in junior high and high school enrolled in Sunday school have not made a public profession of faith and been baptized. This raises the question of whether or not the youth workers realize what is the church's primary task.

III. "Give me some answers. . .even though I may not agree."

"Always be prepared to give an answer to everyone who asks you to give the reason for the hope that you have" (1 Peter 3:15 NIV). There is an abundance of ill-equipped people who are more than willing to venture an answer to youth questions, and therefore the church must not fail to deal openly and honestly with the questions youth face.

IV. "Include me in your program and decision making."

Paul reminds us that "we [all Christians of all ages] are labourers together with God" (1 Cor. 3:9). Too often we forget this. We treat our youth as though they are not capable of joining us in deciding what their program should be. Young people are not demanding an abdication of adult leadership. They are simply saying, "I would like to be heard and be a part of the decision-making process."

V. "Show an interest in my world; it is where I happen to live."

Paul must have had some of us in mind when he wrote, "Don't think about your own affairs, but be interested in others, too, and what they are doing" (Phil. 2:4 TLB). For instance, be interested in school. Know something about what is going on. Get to know youth personally in their own environment, learn to listen, and develop a genuine interest in people not just their presence.

VI. "Let me be me. After all, that's how God made me."

In our adult effort to press young people into our molds we need to ask ourselves, "Are all apostles? are all prophets? are all teachers? are all workers of miracles?" (1 Cor. 12:29). One pressure youth say they feel at church is the pressure to live up to a certain image because they don't feel they are accepted for who they are. Young people should be changed by the presence of Christ in their lives. But even then, God does not negate their individuality. Just as adults, young people are different and should be accepted as such.

Conclusion

Young people are saying to the church:

I'd rather see a sermon than hear one any day,
I'd rather one would walk with me than merely tell the way.
The eye's a better pupil and more willing than the ear,
Fine counsel is confusing, but example's always clear.
The best of all the preachers are the men who live their creeds,
For to see good put in action is what everybody needs.
I soon can learn to do it, if you'll let me see it done,
I can watch your hands in action, your tongue too fast may run.
The lectures you deliver may be very wise and true,
But I'd rather get my lessons by observing what you do.
I may not understand the high advice you give,
But there's no misunderstanding how you act and how you live.

—Author Unknown

Now that's a challenge to each of us!

Title: Peer Pressure

Text: "Don't let the world around you squeeze you into its own mould, but let God remake you so that your whole attitude of mind is changed. Thus you will prove in practice that the will of God is good, acceptable to him and perfect" (**Rom. 12:2** PHILLIPS).

Scripture Reading: Romans 12:2

Introduction

"Pressure—a constraining force of influence, a squeezing." That's how Webster defines it. Youth face all kinds of pressure. But peer pressure—the force exerted by others their own age—is the greatest pressure they face.

The desire to belong, to be a part of the group, to be accepted, is probably the strongest motivating force in the life of a youth. To youth, being alone, isolated from the group, is a fate worse than death itself! The Christian young person has an uphill battle all the way because most of his or her peers are either not Christians or do not take their relationship with Christ seriously.

So that parents may better understand youth, and so that youth may discover a force within that is greater than the pressure without, let us look at three points of peer pressure to which the Christian young person often is subjected.

I. The pressure of drugs.

Paul reminds us as we face the pressures of life that our body is the "temple of the Holy Ghost which is in you" (1 Cor. 6:19).

A. *The pressure of drugs is of epidemic proportions.* The week that four students died in the Kent State University shootings, seventeen young people died in the city of New York from drug overdoses. During the time that 58,000 young men died in the Vietnam War, 140,000 died in the United States as a result of drug overdoses.

B. *The pressure of drugs becomes greater in a vacuum.* Just as a balloon becomes larger in a room where a vacuum is created, so the pressure to use drugs becomes greater in a spiritual vacuum. Young people need a Christian community that provides a spiritual environment where they can find support in resisting this pressure.

II. The pressure of alcohol.

"Wine is a mocker, strong drink is raging; and whosoever is deceived thereby is not wise" (Prov. 20:1).

A. *The reality of the pressure.* Alcohol was once primarily an adult problem. Now it is also a teen problem. It used to be just for parties; now it is also for school. Some carry alcohol in pop bottles in their lunch.

A recent survey shows that 75 percent of all high school students drink. One out of seven gets drunk at least once a week.

B. *The reason for the pressure.* Alcohol is readily available. Teens can obtain alcohol without much trouble. It is much more acceptable than drugs, especially among parents. Many parents are glad to see young people turning to alcohol rather than drugs. But is one really any better than the other?

C. *The remedy for the pressure.*
  1. Be alert to the trend. Why does one out of every seven of your class-mates get drunk once a week? Is he or she lonely, insecure, bored, dissatisfied? If you understand the need your classmates feel for alcohol, you will be better able to help them.

     You also need to be able to discriminate between what your peers and advertisers say about alcohol and what you know to be the facts. Understanding will keep you from making an emotional decision when you are cornered by your peers.
  2. Build your own convictions. The Bible gives us guidelines for form-ing our convictions. God trusts you, under the direction of the Holy Spirit, to form your own conclusions based on his principles that will enable you to withstand the pressure. God created you to be unique and special. Individualism is the mark of strong character.

     Learn to like yourself and to give your real self to others. Be gen-uine. Others respect truth. If you like yourself, you will not need arti-ficial alterations. Use your senses to their fullest. Don't dull them.

     You only go around once in life, so reach for all of life that God has designed for you to experience. Don't let artificial devices keep you from God's best.

III. The pressure of sexual experimentation.

"Avoid sexual looseness like the plague! Every other sin that a man commits is done outside his own body, but this is an offence against his own body. Have you forgotten that your body is the temple of the Holy Spirit, who lives in you and is God's gift to you, and that you are not the owner of your own body? You have been bought, and at a price! Therefore bring glory to God in your body" (1 Cor. 6:18–20 PHILLIPS).

A. *Sexual experimentation reveals chronic immaturity.* Insecurity prompts a girl to land a boy, at whatever cost, and a boy to make a conquest to report back to his peer group.

B. *Sexual experimentation results in the loss of self-respect.*
  1. Because of guilt. There is no such thing as "getting by." You may not get pregnant, but you will not get by. There is no pill made that can take away a conscience that is guilty for breaking God's laws. When you step out of the boundaries of morality, you get hurt. It may seem that nothing happens at first, but there will be a payday someday. The Bible says, "Be not deceived; God is not mocked: for whatsoever a man soweth, that shall he also reap" (Gal. 6:7).
  2. Because of becoming "used merchandise." Studies reveal that most men who have premarital sexual relations expect the women they marry to be virgins.

C. *Sexual experimentation lessens your chances of a happy and secure marriage.*

D. *Sexual experimentation damages all concerned.* Anything that damages everyone concerned can never lead to happiness. In the matter of sexual experimentation, everybody loses. There can be no happy ending to an affair, either premarital or extramarital.

IV. The power to resist the pressure.

"Don't let the world around you squeeze you into its own mould, but let God remake you so that your whole attitude of mind is changed. Thus you will prove in practice that the plan of God is good, acceptable to him and perfect" (Rom. 12:2 PHILLIPS).

The power to resist pressure from *without* comes from *within* by the grace of God. As you allow God to remold your minds you will find yourself asking three questions.

A. *"Why do others do this?"* All peer pressure reveals a feeling of wanting to be accepted, needing to be loved, to be understood, and to be one of the crowd. Economic or social advantages do not lessen this desire. Christian young people need to realize that they are marching to a different tune and may never be accepted by the majority of their peers.

B. *"What happens to them?"* Some develop sexual hang-ups to the point that they cannot function in a normal manner after marriage. Some become neurotic. Some become suspicious marriage partners. Some have affairs.

C. *"Do I want to become that kind of person?"* "As a Christian I may do anything, but that does not mean that everything is good for me. I may do everything, but I must not be the slave of anything" (1 Cor. 6:12 PHILLIPS).

Conclusion

When the pressures of your peers would squeeze you into their mold, "let God remake you." If you have already been squeezed into the wrong mold, God can remold and reshape your life. Now is the time to start over.

Title: Now, Make Something of Yourself!

Text: "Don't let anyone look down on you because you are young, but set an example for the believers in speech, in life, in love, in faith and in purity" (**1 Tim. 4:12** NIV).

Scripture Reading: 1 Timothy 4:12

Introduction

In a day when society is so complex that young people are likely to feel buried in the crowd, they must redouble their efforts to make something worthwhile of themselves. It is all too easy to assume that we simply drift into certain predetermined levels of success in life. But nothing could be further from the truth!

We cannot excuse ourselves from the personal moral responsibility of making something worthwhile of our lives. To assume that it is of no importance what you make of yourself is a false assumption and is the prelude to a life lived on a level far lower than God ever intended.

God has given your generation the rare combination of education, intelligence, and opportunities that few, if any, generations before have ever known. To squander these ingredients results in an unnecessary tragedy.

Make something of yourself! It is just as easy twenty years from now to look back and say, "I made something worthwhile of myself," as it is to look back and say, "What a shame that in those formative and critically important years I squandered it all, and for the rest of my life I must reap the years of folly I have sown."

If you would make something of yourself, there are *gods* to be avoided, *goals* to be attained, and *guides* to be followed.

I. Gods to be avoided.

Our world is filled with gods. To allow ourselves to be sidetracked into worshiping at their shrine is to curtail our life and its potential from the outset. The Lord realizes this, and thus his first commandment is, "Thou shalt have no other gods before me" (Ex. 20:3).

When students leave high school and enter life on a college campus, they experience the cultural and spiritual shock of being away from home and from parental guidance. They also confront a nearly overwhelming array of campus gods.

A. *The god of social service.* This rather current god appeals to students who are sensitive and concerned about human needs. This god says, "Working for an improved society, alleviating suffering and hunger, is all that really counts. Faith, the church, and the Bible are outdated and are of no real value today."

  I would remind the worshipers of the god of social service that no one has done more than Jesus Christ did to feed the hungry, heal the sick, alleviate suffering, elevate womanhood, and free the enslaved. Yet it was Jesus who said that many would come on the day of judgment (having made a god of social service), saying, "Lord, Lord, did we not prophesy in your name, and in your name drive out demons and perform many miracles?" Then Jesus will tell them plainly, "I never knew you. Away from me, you evildoers!" (Matt. 7:22–23).

  Jesus is not downgrading social concern, but he is saying it is a very inadequate god in that it meets only social needs and neglects spiritual needs.

B. *The god of subjectivism.* Perhaps you know this god under the name "situation ethics" or "moral relativity." Worshipers of this god say, "It all depends on how you look at it, and how you look at it depends on your cultural and social background. Right and wrong are relative. If you think something is right, it's right. If you think it's wrong, it's wrong."

The Bible says, "There is a way which seemeth right unto a man, but the end thereof are the ways of death" (Prov. 14:12). This god actually robs people of individuality and makes them slaves to the current subjective morals of the crowd. Subjectivism must be replaced by an objective, infallible standard of morality.

C. *The god of sex.* To let sex become a god is to curtail your life. Paul said to Timothy, "Flee also youthful lusts" (2 Tim. 2:22). And to the church at Rome, "Make not provision for the flesh, to fulfil the lusts thereof" (Rom. 13:14). The Christian faith does not say that sex is dirty. It says that it is good when it is an expression of love within marriage. When sex is not an expression of authentic Christian love, it becomes little more than an instrument of exploitation.

II. Goals to be obtained.

You never become anything that you don't intend to become unless it is a failure. In Philippians 3:14 Paul writes, "I am pressing onward toward the goal, to win the prize to which God through Jesus Christ is calling us upward" (WILLIAMS). I think the reason the apostle Paul was a great success was that he intended to be a great success. To be a success some goals must be attained.

A. *The first goal is self-respect.* No matter how others may respect you, if you cannot respect yourself, life is not really a success.

B. *Another goal to be attained is academic preparation.* Paul told Timothy when he was a young man, "Study to shew thyself approved unto God, a workman that needeth not to be ashamed" (2 Tim. 2:15). There is no reason in the world that any one of you twenty years from now ought to be ashamed of your educational preparation. It is inexcusable for young people not to get as much education as they need today. One way or another, education is obtainable. The Bible reminds us, "Wisdom is the principal thing. . .with all thy getting get understanding" (Prov. 4:7).

C. *A third goal is a goal of marital happiness.* The Bible says, "A man shall leave his father and his mother, and shall cleave unto his wife: and they shall be one flesh" (Gen. 2:24). This means legally as well as becoming one in harmony and happiness.

Do not date anyone you would not marry. You see, falling in love is like slipping on ice—you never know when it is going to happen, but you know when it has happened. Marry someone of your own faith. It is a strange kind of love that says, "We love each other and we want to be married; we want to share everything in life, except the most important relationship—our relationship with God." Religion ought to be the most shared thing in all of your relationships.

D. *A fourth goal is professional success.* Former Green Bay Packer coach Vince Lombardi once said, "Winning is not a sometime thing; it's an all-the-time thing. You don't win once in a while, you don't do things right once in a while, you do them right all the time. Winning is a habit. Unfortunately so is losing."

III. Guides to be followed.

At least four tests can be used to determine if something is right or wrong.

A. *First, ask yourself what about the test of affect.* "How will doing this affect myself, my body, my mind, my relation to God? How will it affect others? And how will it affect the cause of Christ?" The Bible says, "When you sin against your brothers...and wound their weak conscience, you sin against Christ" (1 Cor. 8:12 NIV).

B. *Second, apply the test of secrecy.* Ask, "Would it be all right if everyone knew about this? Would it bring shame or pride to me if my mother, my father, my pastor, or my teacher knew about it? Would it change anyone's opinion of me if they knew the real me?"

C. *Third, there is the test of universality.* Ask, "Would it be acceptable if my Sunday school teacher did it? What kind of church would my church be if everyone were just like me?"

D. *Finally, the most difficult—the test of prayer.* "Can I pray about it? Can I ask God to bless me in it? Can I ask him to help me? If needs be, can I even pray while I am doing it? Can I ask Christ to go with me in this matter?"

Conclusion

Make something worthwhile of yourself. Your whole life is ahead. No matter how humble your life is, you will influence others. Your life can help build or tear down a church. It can dignify or degrade your profession. It can bless or curse your home. The question is, "What are you going to do with your life?"

I urge you to make something worthwhile of yourself—something you can be proud of, something that will have a tremendous testimony for Christ in the years to come.

FUNERAL MEDITATIONS

Title: The Meaning of Death

Text: "Let not your heart be troubled: ye believe in God, believe also in me. In my Father's house are many mansions: if it were not so, I would have told you. I go to prepare a place for you. And if I go and prepare a place for you,

I will come again and receive you unto myself; that where I am, there ye may be also" **(John 14:1–3)**.

Scripture Reading: 1 Thessalonians 4:13–17; 2 Corinthians 5:6–8

Introduction

> *We can see only a little of the ocean as we*
> *stand on the rocky shore,*
> *But out there beyond the eyes' horizon*
> *there's more.*
> *We can see only a little of God's loving kindness,*
> *A few rich treasures from his mighty store,*
> *But out there beyond the eyes' horizon*
> *there's more, there's more.*

As we face death we are compelled to believe that there is more involved than the physical. Unlike the brute beast of the field, we cannot pass by the remains of one of our own without learning something from death.

Death has something to say to each of us. We will leave this place better and wiser people than when we came if we grasp the meaning of death.

I. To deceased Christians.

A. *Death means that their life's work has been done.* Paul believed this, for he said, "I am now ready to be offered, and the time of my departure is at hand. I have fought a good fight, I have finished my course, I have kept the faith" (2 Tim. 4:6–7). When the apostle said, "I have finished my course," he was not saying, "I have done all that I want to do" or even "I have done all that I ought to do." Rather he was saying, "The fact that I shall soon die means that the mission on which Christ sent me has been completed."

B. *Death means that their reward is ready.* "Henceforth there is laid up for me a crown of righteousness, which the Lord, the righteous judge, shall give me at that day: and not to me only, but unto all them also that love his appearing" (2 Tim. 4:8). No one knows what the reward is. Nevertheless, death means that their reward is ready.

C. *Death means that their heavenly abode is prepared.* Jesus promised, "In my father's house are many mansions: if it were not so, I would have told you. I go to prepare a place for you" (John 14:2).

D. *Death means that they shall renew old acquaintances.* A parent, child, or sibling may have preceded them in death, and years have passed since they last saw their loved one. But death is a homecoming for Christians, a time for renewing old acquaintances.

E. *Death means that they are free from life's hurts.* "God shall wipe away all tears from their eyes; and there shall be no more death, neither sorrow, nor crying, neither shall there be any more pain: for the former things are passed away" (Rev. 21:4).

A young deacon lay dying after a prolonged illness. His aging and beloved pastor sat by his side. The deacon began to recall the many blessings God had given him in life. Tears streamed down his face. The tender old man of God took out his soft, white handkerchief and wiped away the tears. Then the young deacon said, "Pastor, that is the last time any man will wipe away my tears, because the Bible promises that in heaven God will wipe away all tears from my eyes."

F. *Death means that they shall see Jesus.* This must be the greatest meaning of death for deceased Christians! They have experienced the presence of Christ, who has wonderfully changed their lives and ours. He is here today, but none of us has ever seen him. Death means that at last we shall see Jesus face to face.

II. To living Christians.

A. *Death means that our loved one has experienced a great gain.* "For to me to live is Christ, and to die is gain" (Phil. 1:21). Paul is saying, "For me to live is for Christ to have my hands through which to serve, my mouth through which to speak, and my heart through which to love. But to die is far better, for this is gain!"

B. *The death of our loved one means that God still has some use for us on this earth.* God is no God of chance. If there were no need for you to continue to live, this would be your service and not that of our loved one. But the fact that you are still alive means that God has some noble purpose in mind for you. There are burdens to be shared, hearts to be mended, lives to be touched.

What a tragedy it would be if we failed to fulfill the purpose for which God has left us on this earth. Paul said that he would prefer to die and go on and meet his Lord. But he realized that since God left him here there was some need for him yet to meet. "Nevertheless to abide in the flesh is more needful for you" (Phil. 1:24).

C. *Death means that "we should live soberly, righteously, and godly in this present world" (Titus 2:12).* It means that we should live each day to be unashamed to meet Christ whether it be through death or through his return.

Conclusion

> There is no death.
> The stars go down
> To rise upon another shore
> And bright in heaven's jeweled crown
> They shine for evermore!

Title: Sources of Strength to See Us Through

Text: "Be ready always to give an answer to every man that asketh you a reason of the hope that is in you with meekness and fear" **(1 Peter 3:15).**

Scripture Reading: 1 Peter 3:15

Introduction

Passing Through

When thou passeth thro' the waters,
Deep the waves may be, and cold,
But Jehovah is our refuge
And His promise is our hold;
For the Lord Himself hath said it,
He the faithful God and true:
When thou comest to the waters
Thou shalt not go down, but thro'.

Threatening breakers of destruction,
Doubt's insidious undertow,
Shall not sink us, shall not drag us
Out to ocean depths of woe;
For His promise shall sustain us,
Praise the Lord, whose word is true!
We shall not go down nor under,
He hath said, "Thou passeth thro'."

—Annie Johnson Flint

What is the "reason for the hope that is in us" as we face this hour? Though we weep, it is not as those who have no hope. We have sources of strength to see us through that others do not have. Consider these:

I. The Lord our loved one trusted.

A great source of strength for this hour is found in the Lord he trusted.* He trusted the Lord as his Savior, and that makes all the difference in this world and in the world to come! Like the apostle, he could say, "I know whom I have believed, and am persuaded that he is able to keep that which I have committed unto him against that day" (2 Tim. 1:12). Notice that the apostle said, "I know whom I have believed" and not, "I know what I have believed." It is not a system of theology that saves, but a person, and his name is Jesus. So long as one has trusted in Christ he is safe, and we have a real source of strength that will see us through.

---

*Masculine pronouns are used in this sermon for ease of reading.

Years ago our deceased friend acted on Christ's promise and forever placed his trust in him. Jesus said, "Whosoever therefore shall confess me before men, him will I confess also before my Father which is in heaven" (Matt. 10:32).

He trusted the Lord as his strength. There is no other explanation of the manner in which he was able to face the difficulties of life. "I can do all things through Christ which strengtheneth me" (Phil. 4:13) could well have been spoken by our friend.

II. The life our loved one lived.

Beyond the Lord he trusted we find a real source of strength in the life he lived. It was a life of unselfish service reflecting Philippians 1:21: "For to me, living means opportunities for Christ, and dying—well, that's better yet" (TLB).

He discovered early in life that one cannot have happiness until he first gives himself away. This our Lord said many years ago: "Whosoever shall seek to save his life shall lose it; and whosoever shall lose his life shall preserve it" (Luke 17:33).

His life was a life of quiet confidence and optimism. He lived in the reality that "God hath not given us the spirit of fear; but of power, and of love, and of a sound mind" (2 Tim. 1:7).

III. The love our loved one shared.

He felt constrained to share the love he had come to know in Christ with others. Like Paul, he would say, "The love of Christ constraineth us..." (2 Cor. 5:14).

He shared the love of Christ with fellow Christians. And "we know that we have passed from death unto life, because we love the brethren" (1 John 3:14).

He shared Christ's love with those in need. Jesus describes this spirit of self-giving love when he says, "I was an hungered, and ye gave me meat; I was thirsty, and ye gave me drink; I was a stranger, and ye took me in: Naked, and ye clothed me: I was sick, and ye visited me: I was in prison, and ye came unto me. Then shall the righteous answer him, saying, Lord, when saw we thee an hungered, and fed thee? or thirsty, and gave thee drink? When saw we thee a stranger, and took thee in? or naked, and clothed thee? or when saw we thee sick, or in prison, and came unto thee? And the King shall answer and say unto them, Verily I say unto you, Inasmuch as ye have done it unto one of the least of these my brethren, ye have done it unto me" (Matt. 25:35–40).

IV. The loyalties our loved one had.

A man who has strong loyalties has strong character. And our friend was a man with intense loyalties. He was loyal to his family, friends, church, pastor, and most of all to his Lord. I am confident that his loyalties were met by these words of Christ: "Well done, thou good and faithful servant: thou hast been faithful over a few things, I will make thee ruler over many things: enter thou into the joy of thy Lord" (Matt. 25:21).

Conclusion

Christians face death in a way unlike the way of the world. The secret is found in these sources of strength that see us through—the Lord our friend trusted, the life he lived, the love he shared, and the loyalties he had.

Title: How a Man Ought to Die

Text: "For me to live is Christ, and to die is gain" **(Phil. 1:21).**

Scripture Reading: Philippians 1:21

Introduction

Once in a while someone comes into our lives who enriches us and leaves us better than we were before. By the way they live, they teach us how to live. And by the way they die, they teach us how to die.

In the life and death of this loved one, we learn how a Christian ought to die. A Christian ought to die:

I. With his faith in God.*

It is always a tragedy when a person allows hardships and reversals, heartaches and disappointments to smother his faith in God. When one's faith dies within, he is a walking corpse; he experiences living death.

But this friend permitted no such tragedy to invade his life. He died with his faith still strong! This he did, not because he had no problems, disappointments, or hurts, for like the rest of us, he too has had his fair share. Rather, he died with his faith in God because, like Job, he had an unflinching confidence in God regardless of his adversities. Job said, "Though he slay me, yet will I trust in him" (Job 13:15).

II. With an undimmed vision.

To be pitied is that man whose life extends beyond his vision—who lives past any purposeful meaning in life—who does not see some challenge in each new day!

Caleb was a man with an undimmed vision. After he and others went to search out the Promised Land, the majority reported all the problems they faced and stated why they could not conquer the land. But "Caleb stilled the people before Moses, and said, Let us go up at once, and possess it; for we are well able to overcome it" (Num. 13:30). Still the people would not believe, for theirs was a dim and limited vision.

---

*Masculine pronouns are used in this sermon for ease of reading.

Years passed, and when God determined to allow Israel to conquer the land, the aged Caleb became a key leader in the invasions. The Bible tells us why: "My servant Caleb, because he had another spirit with him, hath followed me fully; him will I bring into the land whereinto he went" (Num. 14:24). Caleb was a man whose vision could not be dimmed by the passing of years or the disappointments of life.

Our deceased friend, like Caleb, had a vision that was undimmed by the events of his life.

III. In the pitch of battle.

For a man to die while still involved to the fullest of his ability in the service of God is both a comfort and an inspiration!

Jesus promises, "He that endureth to the end shall be saved" (Matt. 10:22). To die as a faithful and active soldier of Christ whether in some place of leadership in the church or as a prayer warrior on a bed is to die in the pitch of battle. This is how a man ought to die!

IV. Leaving behind a testimony that will live on.

We do not bury the testimony and influence of our brother when we lay his body to rest, for his testimony shall live on. This is one reason the judgment does not come until the end of time.

Every good deed and every kind word continues to live on. His influence is like a pebble thrown into the center of a calm pond that puts into motion waves that reach out until at last the final wave reaches the shore. So this man's life has touched another, and that life yet another, and that one still another. And the full impact of his testimony will not be known until his final wave of influence reaches the shore at the end of time.

The apostle John writes in Revelation, "I heard a voice from heaven saying unto me, Write, Blessed are the dead which die in the Lord from henceforth: Yea, saith the Spirit, that they may rest from their labours; and their works do follow them" (Rev. 14:13).

V. With great expectation.

Paul faced death with a spirit of great expectation, for he said, "To die is gain" (Phil. 1:21).

Conclusion

Tennyson expresses poetically how a man ought to die in the closing lines of *Crossing the Bar:*

> *For tho' from out our borne of Time and Place*
> *The flood may bear me far,*
> *I hope to see my Pilot face to face*
> *When I have crossed the bar.*

WEDDINGS

Title: A Wedding Ceremony

Order of the Service

Organ Prelude

"Arioso"
"Chaconne"
"We Pray Now to the Holy Spirit"
"Andante in D Minor"
"Pastorale"
"My Soul Ever Rejoicing"
"Beautiful Saviour"
"Antiphon III"

Chiming of the Hour
   "Meditation" from *Thais* . . . . .Violin and Piano

Lighting of the Altar Candles
   "The Wedding Song" . . . . Soloist

Processional
   "Trumpet Voluntary in D"

Meaning of Marriage . . . . Minister

Ceremony
   Exchanging of Vows
   Exchanging of Rings

Meditation
   "Eternal Life" . . . . .Soloist

Lighting of the Unity Candle

Benediction
   "The Lord's Prayer" . . . . Minister and People

Recessional
   "Fanfare"

The Ceremony

   The minister: At the dawn of human history, God recognized the need of a man for a woman and a woman for a man. As early as the second chapter of Genesis, God said, "It is not good for the man to be alone. I will make a helper suitable for him" [v. 18 NIV]. Verse 22 of the same chapter says, "Then the LORD God made a woman from the rib he had taken out of the man, and he brought her to the man" [NIV].

And Adam said, "This is now bone of my bones, and flesh of my flesh: she shall be called Woman, because she was taken out of Man. Therefore shall a man leave his father and his mother, and shall cleave unto his wife; and they shall be one flesh" [Gen. 2:22–24].

Exchange of vows

The minister's questions to the groom. Will you, _____ , take _____ to be your wife, to live as God has ordained, in the fullness of Christian marriage? Will you love her, honor her, cherish her, and keep her? Will you, forsaking the priority of all other human devotions, give yourself in faith to her as long as the two of you shall live?

[Following the affirmative response, the minister will say:] Husbands, love your wives, even as Christ also loved the church, and gave himself for it. . . .So ought men to love their wives as their own bodies. He that loveth his wife loveth himself. For no man ever yet hated his own flesh; but nourisheth and cherisheth it, even as the Lord the church. . .For this cause shall a man leave his father and mother, and shall be joined unto his wife, and they two shall be one flesh. Nevertheless, let every one of you in particular so love his wife even as himself; and the wife see that she reverence her husband.

The minister's questions to the bride. Will you, _____ , take _____ to be your husband, to live as God has ordained, in the fullness of Christian marriage? Will you love him, honor him, cherish him, and keep him? Will you, by forsaking the priority of all other human devotions, give yourself in faith to him as long as the two of you shall live?

[Following the affirmative response, the minister will say:] Wives, submit yourselves unto your own husbands, as unto the Lord, for the husband is the head of the wife, even as Christ is the head of the church: and he is the Savior of the body. Therefore as the church is subject unto Christ, so let the wives be to their own husbands in every thing.

First Corinthians 13:4–7 presents a clear definition of the Christian love necessary for a happy marriage. "Love suffereth long, and is kind; love envieth not; love vaunteth not itself, is not puffed up; doth not behave itself unseemly, seeketh not her own, is not easily provoked, thinketh no evil; rejoiceth not in iniquity, but rejoiceth in the truth; beareth all things, believeth all things, hopeth all things, endureth all things."

The minister: Who gives _____ to be married to _____ ?

The father: Her mother and I.

The minister: Do you, _____ , take _____ to be your wife?

The groom: I do. I now take you to be my wife, to love, to honor, and to cherish, in sickness and health, whether in poverty or in wealth, and I give myself to you until death separates us.

The minister: Do you, _____ , take _____ to be your husband?

The bride: I do. I now take you to be my husband, to love, to honor, and to cherish, in sickness and in health, whether in poverty or wealth, and I give myself to you until death separates us.

Exchange of rings

The minister: What do you present as a pledge of your vows to _____ ?

The groom: A ring.

The minister: The ring has long been a fitting symbol of the kind of love and faith that you have pledged to each other. As the ring is an unbroken circle, so it is God's will that your union be unbroken except by death. And it is my prayer that as these rings sparkle in their brilliance, your love will ever continue to be as radiant and pure as it is now. Place this ring on her finger and repeat after me.

The groom: [Repeating after minister] With this ring I take you to be my wife. You have my all, and this I do because I love you.

The minister: What do you present as a pledge of your vows to _____ ?

The bride: A ring. [Repeating after minister] With this ring I take you to be my husband. You have my all, and this I do because I love you.

The minister: Because you have pledged your love and lives to each other, in the holy presence of God and before these, your friends and families, who are witnesses to your vows, I joyfully pronounce that you are husband and wife in the name of Jesus Christ our Lord.

"Beloved, let us love one another; for love is of God; and every one that loveth is born of God, and knoweth God. And we have known and believed the love; and he that dwelleth in love dwelleth in God, and God in him. Herein is our love made perfect, that we may have boldness in the day of judgment."

The minister and the people: "Our Father which art in heaven, Hallowed be thy name. Thy kingdom come. Thy will be done in earth, as it is in heaven. Give us this day our daily bread. And forgive us our debts, as we forgive our debtors, And lead us not into temptation, but deliver us from evil: for thine is the kingdom, and the power, and the glory, for ever. Amen."

Embrace

Recessional

Title: A Marriage Ceremony

Prelude (fifteen minutes before service)

Seating of parents

   Groom's first
   Bride's second

Candles lighted

Song

Minister enters

Groom and best man enter

Groomsmen enter

Bridesmaids enter

Maid of honor enters

Ring bearer and flower girl enter

Bride and father enter (Mother of bride may lead congregation to stand by standing and facing bride)

Ceremony

Song (Bride and groom may kneel)

Embrace

Recessional

Usher out parents

The Ceremony

The minister: That you have chosen to be with us this evening, to witness this public declaration of the love of this young couple, adds to the joy and beauty of the occasion. _____ and _____ come this evening to be joined in holy matrimony. Who gives this woman to be wed?

The father: Her mother and I.

The minister: This marriage is but a symbol of a love that already exists, and which, in its persistence and patience, will keep the marriage flourishing in times of adversity.

Marriage is a state that embodies all the warm and precious values that grow from human companionship. It is, therefore, not to be entered into unadvisedly or lightly, but reverently, soberly, and with high purpose in the knowledge that enduring love is both humankind's greatest accomplishment and God's most precious gift.

Paul speaks of love in the thirteenth chapter of 1 Corinthians: "Love is patient and kind; love is not jealous or conceited or proud; love is not ill-mannered or selfish or irritable. Love does not keep a record of wrongs; love finds no pleasure in injustice done to others, but joyfully sides with the truth. Love knows how to be silent. Love never gives up; its trust, hope, and patience never fail."

This marriage is a union created by your loving purpose and kept by your abiding will and enduring trust in one another. There must be a giving of one to the other in the spirit of generosity, of selflessness, and steadfast devotion to the highest ideals of human relationship. It is with this in mind that _____ and _____ come to join their lives.

Exchange of Vows

The minister's questions to the groom. Will you, _____ , take _____ as your wife, loving what you know of her and trusting the unknown? Will you share with her the joys and sorrows of life and bring her into the very depths of your being? Will you honor her, trust her, respect her individuality and integrity, and love her uniquely in all the world as long as you both shall live?

The minister's questions to the bride. Will you, _____ , take _____ as your husband, loving what you know of him and trusting the unknown? Will you share with him the joys and sorrows of life and bring him into the very depths of your being? Will you honor him, trust him, respect his individuality and integrity, and love him uniquely in all the world as long as you both shall live?

Exchange of Vows

The minister: And what token do you share to represent your love and commitment to each other? [Holding up the ring] The ring is the symbol of wholeness and perfection. It is made of gold, which is a precious and durable metal. What better representation of your feelings for each other!

The groom's vows: With this ring I thee wed. I choose you this day to love and confide in, to honor, take pride in, to believe in and share with, to go everywhere with. I choose you this day to give you my heart.

The bride's vows: With this ring I thee wed. "Intreat me not to leave thee, or to return from following after thee: for whither thou goest, I will go; and where thou lodgest, I will lodge: thy people shall be my people, and thy God my God."

The minister: Let us pray.

The soloist: "The Lord's Prayer"

The minister: It gives me great pleasure to pronounce you, _____ and _____ , man and wife. May God bless you richly.

You may kiss the bride. [Embrace]

Friends, allow me to introduce to you Mr. and Mrs. _____ .

Recessional

SENTENCE SERMONETTES

The years teach much that the days never know.
The advantages of wealth are greatly exaggerated.
Great happenings turn on hinges of little things.
Faith without action is as dead as a body without a soul.
Opportunity looks bigger going than coming.
Little is much if God is in it.
Grace is getting freedom when you deserve a flogging.
God did not come to take sides—he came to take over.

No man is free who cannot command himself.

Think all you speak, but speak not all you think.

God will supply, but we must apply.

A small leak will sink a great ship.

The prayer of the humble pierces the clouds.

Habits are at first cobwebs, then cables.

No door is too difficult for the key of love to open.

Faith is God's gift to you.

Every request given to God should be placed in the envelope of faith.

Jesus Christ is the mind of God fully revealed to men.

Your attitude determines your altitude.

The latch to the door of willingness is on the inside.

Memory is the mother of Thanksgiving.

The world crowns success, but God crowns faithfulness.

How you feel tomorrow depends on what you do today.

To every child of God, the best is yet to come.

Grace is amazing because it stoops so low and it lifts so high.

He who is born once, dies twice. He who is born twice, dies once.

He is no fool who gives away what he cannot keep in order to gain what he cannot lose.

The perfume of kindness travels even against the wind.

Anger rests in the bosom of fools.

The Bible informs us, reforms us, and transforms us.

The best book of success principles ever printed is the Bible.

There is no time when we cannot go to God.

If a thing is big enough to worry about, it is big enough to pray about.

It is never too late to learn.

Who gossips to you will gossip about you.

Flying into a rage assures a bad landing.

You cannot put things across by getting cross.

Friendship is like a flower—it flourishes with nurture and it wilts with neglect.

Hope is faith written in the future tense.

The resurrection of Jesus Christ means that death is not the last word in our vocabulary.

Keep your fears to yourself, but share your courage with others.

God is looking for channels through which he can pour his blessings to a needy world.

He who cannot forgive breaks the bridge over which he himself must pass.

Character is what you are in the dark.

To break God's law is to spit in your own face.

INDEX OF SCRIPTURE TEXTS

SUBJECT INDEX

Obedience, 70
One way of salvation, 315, 323
Opportunities, seizing, 395

Paralytic healed, 78
Parenting, 148, 154
Parting words of Jesus, 385
Paul as example, 102
Peace of God, 117
Peer pressure, 409
People of God, the, 18, 39
Peter, 277
Philip, disciple, 284
Plan of God, 367
Prayer, 24, 132, 173
Prejudice, 309
Problems, handling, 117
Profit and loss, 89
Promises of God, 146
Prophecy, 397
Purity in the church, 136

Reality, search for, 382
Red Sea, crossing the, 195
Redemption, 210, 226
Relationships in family, 161
Renewal of the church, 143
Repentance, 243
Responsibility, 70, 180
Resurrection, the, 80, 97
Revelation of God, 163

Sacrifice, 391
Saints, Christians as, 16
Salvation, 182, 307, 315
Scripture, 163
Second chance, 166

Second Coming, the, 93
Servanthood, 382
Service, Christian, 76, 182, 252, 335, 395, 397
Sickness, 348
Significance, 327
Simon, disciple, 352
Sinfulness, 78, 187, 210, 246, 321
Solitude, 339
Soul, the, 48
Stewardship, 192, 260, 350, 357
Stilling the storm, 84
Strength of character, 277
Suffering, 348
Sufficiency of Jesus, 84
Surrender to God, 313

Teachings of Jesus, 68
Temptation, 28
Thaddaeus, 345
Thomas, 318
Time, the, 214
Transformation of character, 302
True believers, 82

Unity of the church, 57

Virgin birth, the, 14

Water into wine, 65
Welcoming Christ, 126
Witness of the church, 52
Witnessing, 237, 254, 287, 305
Word of God, the, 163
Worship, 272

Youth ministry, 407, 409, 412

Zeal, Christian, 293, 352